Roads Not Taken

Roads Not Taken

The Struggle of Opposition Parties in Twentieth-Century China

EDITED BY

Roger B. Jeans

Routledge
Taylor & Francis Group
LONDON AND NEW YORK

First published 1992 by Westview Press

Published 2019 by Routledge
52 Vanderbilt Avenue, New York, NY 10017
2 Park Square, Milton Park, Abingdon, Oxon OX14 4RN

Routledge is an imprint of the Taylor & Francis Group, an informa business

Library of Congress Cataloging-in-Publication Data
Roads not taken : the struggle of opposition parties in twentieth-century China / [edited] by Roger B. Jeans.
p. cm.
Includes index.
ISBN 0-8133-8619-5
1. China,—Politics and government—20th century. 2. Political parties—China—History. I. Jeans, Roger B.
DS775.7.R64 1992
320.951—dc20 **92-21651**
CIP

ISBN 13: 978-0-367-28616-3 (hbk)

ISBN 13: 978-0-367-30162-0 (pbk)

For my late friend and colleague
Minor Lee Rogers

Contents

Acknowledgments

The idea for this collection of articles grew out of the work a number of historians are doing on an assortment of minor political parties, groups, and their leaders. These opposition parties have not received sufficient attention from specialists on twentieth-century China. Moreover, writings on these groups and figures are scattered (mostly journal articles and dissertations). Hence, the time has come to collect and publish such writings in a single volume.

These essays focus on either a single figure, a party or parties, or a movement. Most deal with political opposition in the Republican period (1912-1949). In addition, four contributors have written about the fate of opposition organizations from the pivotal year of 1949, when the Chinese Communists took the Mainland and drove the Guomindang into exile on Taiwan, through the Communists' crushing of the popular demonstrations in Beijing in June 1989. The final essayist has transcended the case studies to present an overview of oppositional politics in twentieth-century China.

The editor has incurred many debts while preparing this book. Its publication would not have been possible without the generous support of the Andrew W. Mellon Foundation and Washington and Lee University. I am grateful to Don C. Price, Stephen R. MacKinnon, Bradley K. Geisert, William C. Kirby, Thomas A. Metzger, James P. Harrison, Shao-chuan Leng, and Frederic Wakeman, Jr., for many insights, which they will readily recognize in the introduction.

Publication of this volume would not have been possible without the excellent work of Mrs. Karen Lyle, who rendered valuable assistance with the editing of the essays, as well as preparation of the final manuscript. I am indebted also to Mrs. Adrienne Bodie for her superb editorial assistance.

Many other people at Washington and Lee helped with this work. Two in particular should be singled out. My late friend and colleague, Minor Lee Rogers, provided irreplaceable moral support over the years that have gone into this work, and I shall miss his counsel very much in the years to come. The idea for the book owes much to Dean John W. Elrod, and his support has never wavered during the years of preparation.

My wife, Sylvia, has listened patiently far too long to my mutterings about this work. I am deeply grateful to her for being such a good friend and source of support, as well as for shouldering the onerous task of the final proofreading of the volume.

Last, but certainly not least, I am indebted to the contributors. They cheerfully responded to repeated deadlines and requests for corrections and clarifications. I hope the appearance of our book has made all their hard work worthwhile.

Roger B. Jeans

A Note on Romanization

Since almost all the essays in this volume, when originally submitted, used the pinyin system of romanization, the decision was made to adopt it for the entire work. Introduced by the Chinese in the 1950s, it is the official romanization system in the People's Republic of China. In this country, it has been the standard in the press for some dozen years or so, and many recent works of scholarship have adopted it, rather than the older Wade-Giles system. Students of modern Chinese history, of course, need to be familiar with both systems.

Exceptions to the use of pinyin in this volume have been made for names and terms that are more familiar in earlier spellings, such as Chiang Kai-shek, rather than Jiang Jieshi, and the Whampoa, instead of the Huangpu, Military Academy. A table of conversions between pinyin and Wade-Giles may be found in a number of general works on modern China (e.g., Jonathan Spence's *The Search for Modern China*).

Introduction

Roger B. Jeans

The contributors to this volume have believed for some time that the history of Republican China, as written by both Chinese and American scholars, has been skewed toward a two-dimensional study of the major combatants, the Guomindang (GMD) and the Chinese Communist Party (CCP). That struggle, which lasted throughout the 1920s, 1930s, and 1940s--now hot, now cold--was undeniably the main historical story. However, it was not the *only* nor the *complete* story. Many educated Chinese rejected both of the one-party dictatorships, and some chose to found or support alternative parties or movements.[1] Without an examination of these "other roads," the history of these decades takes on a teleological air, that the CCP was *destined* to triumph over the GMD, and the historian's sole task is to go back and identify the reasons for that victory.[2] Or, as Soviet scholar Peter Ivanov's essay puts it, without consideration of the potential political alternatives of the time, "history is incomplete, simplified, and too burdened with the triumphs of the 'great forces', leaving no room for the natural pluralism of thought, romanticism, and intrigue." A concentration on the two major parties denies the various choices that were made and the roads that were still open during these years, until closed by the march of events. In short, history, as always, is more complex than hindsight would seem to indicate.

This volume of essays on opposition figures, parties, and movements attempts to flesh out the incomplete history of this period.[3] It is the first extensive collection of case studies on these men and groups to appear in the English language and includes essays by Australian, Canadian, Chinese, and Soviet, as well as American, scholars. Despite their different nationalities most of the contributors, it is safe to say, shared a single bias, that is, a desire to see China move in the direction of democratization. In a number of cases, the articles are based on full-length studies that have been in progress for some time. Hence, there is ample evidence here of what these men thought, what they did, and what their fates were.

These essays focus on some--but by no means all--of these parties and movements, which are sometimes labelled "third forces" (TF) or "third parties," since they (including the anarchists) opposed both the GMD and the CCP and attempted to offer political alternatives to them. In doing so, they assumed the roles of opposition parties, partly because of their own ambitions and China's circumstances but also because the two major parties viewed them that way. In addition, they have been labelled "middle parties," for they were often trapped in the cross fire between the two dictatorships.

While these figures and parties did not have sufficient influence to alter the course of Chinese history (leading one essayist to label them "marginal men," like today's exiled democratic activists), they do offer opportunities to raise the issue, very much in the headlines today, of why democracy has not succeeded in China. Beyond that, they are inherently fascinating characters, and through their eyes one has the opportunity of seeing much of twentieth-century Chinese history unfold as they experienced it.

This volume might not have been possible ten years ago. In the United States, scholars were gazing into the mirror of American liberalism, where we saw and studied such failed liberals as the American-trained Hu Shi.[4] On the other hand, during the Cold War, U.S. diplomats and soldiers sought "third forces" that could be harnessed to American strategic goals,[5] a phenomenon that Yang Tianshi's essay reminds us of in taking up the Fighting League for Chinese Freedom and Democracy (FL).

On the Chinese side, the study of these parties, groups, and figures was officially discouraged. This began to change in Taiwan after the lifting of martial law in 1987 and the subsequent steady trend in the direction of liberalization. During the 1980s, scholars in the People's Republic of China (PRC) also began to investigate these organizations, which they labelled the "*minzhu dangpai*," or "democratic parties and groups" (DPGs).[6]

The essays in this volume have eschewed old approaches. Moreover, they have benefited from the new materials from the PRC and Taiwan, which were not available a few years ago. The crackdown of June 1989 has lent a sense of urgency to the studies, as hopes for a "thaw" in China, like those occurring in Eastern Europe and the Soviet Union, were cruelly dashed. The struggles of the Chinese opposition parties during the three decades preceding the Communist victory in 1949 (which occupy the bulk of this volume) offer historical perspectives on the battles being waged by the Chinese democratic activists in exile in the U.S. and elsewhere today.

The results of all these changes in Taiwan and the PRC are careful, detailed, and critical studies that view these opposition movements through their participants' eyes, in their settings, and in their times. The authors of these essays have sought to understand the rationales of their subjects' thought and how their political activism made sense to them. In short, these are essays that take seriously what these figures proposed and how their plans fared.

The Historical Setting

It is impossible to understand these opposition movements without a sense of the historical environment in which they operated. It was the march of events that brought them into existence. For example, the Manchurian Incident in 1931 led to the formation of opposition parties such as the National Socialist Party of China (NSP). As will become clear, they faced distinctly inhospitable conditions.

The 1911 Revolution had overthrown the Qing, the last of China's dynasties, and striven to replace it with a republic and a constitutional regime. Following the revolution, political parties sprang up like mushrooms, only to be cut down by the repressions of Yuan Shikai. Following his death in 1916, China was fragmented into a land dominated by militarists, large and small. This warlord period lasted until 1928, when the GMD National Revolutionary Army (NRA) unified enough of China so that a centralized regime could be established in Nanjing.

The lack of a centralized government during the warlord period made it easier, in some ways, to launch political movements. On the other hand, the warlords recognized no laws or rights beyond their own arbitrariness, and hence life could be dangerous (as the 1927 execution by a warlord of Li Dazhao, one of the founders of the CCP, showed). The GMD's centralization made it more difficult to mount a political opposition, as a number of the articles in this work make clear.

It was not long after Yuan Shikai's death that the Bolshevik Revolution presented the Chinese with what appeared to be a successful revolutionary model and ideology. The CCP was established in 1921, while the GMD was reorganized in accordance with the Soviet model in 1923-1924. Hence, the stage was set for a decades-long rivalry between the two Leninist parties, which culminated with the CCP victory in 1949. This was the background for the struggles of the oppositionists taken up in this volume.

The GMD dominated the Nanjing Decade (1928-1937), during which the Japanese invaded China, triggering the war that lasted until 1945. Beset by warlords, Communists, and the steady Japanese encroachments on Chinese territory, the Nanjing regime stressed national unity above all. There was to be one state ideology--the Three People's Principles of the regime's patron saint, Sun Yat-sen--and one party, the GMD. All opposition was to be treated as treasonous and suppressed. And yet, despite this repressive climate, the Japanese threat produced an explosion of small parties and groups worried about the possible extinction of the Chinese nation.

The need for support from all quarters during the life-and-death struggle in WWII forced the GMD to liberalize its dictatorship, to a certain extent, and tolerate the opposition parties. A quasi-parliament, the People's Political Council (PPC), was set up, with minority party representation. Even the CCP was tolerated, and a United Front (UF) joined the two erstwhile enemies in the common struggle against Japan.

Victory brought a renewal of the civil war of the 1920s and 1930s, however. The two heavily armed protagonists, pursuing a "*dada tantan*" (fight, fight; talk, talk) strategy, struggled for victory. Part of the all-out competition, in which each had to seize any advantage possible to tip the balance, were efforts by both sides to win over the minor parties and groups. As the competition turned into full-fledged civil war in 1947, these "TFs" found it impossible to remain "middle parties" any longer, and were forced to "lean to one side." Some viewed the GMD as the lesser of the two evils, and others, the CCP. In the face of the suffering of the Chinese people from hyperinflation and civil war, some liberals (e.g., many of those associated with the journal *Guancha*) began to emphasize the economic side of life and conclude that economic equality was the most important goal, which naturally brought them closer to the CCP.

Following the victory of the CCP in 1949, many of the third parties and their leaders chose to take their chances with the newly established PRC. Others, often from the more conservative Chinese Youth (CYP) and Democratic Socialist (DSP) parties, followed the GMD into exile on Taiwan. On both Taiwan and the Mainland, the minor parties--which had attained the zenith of their influence during the war and civil war days when they were needed and hence courted by the two major parties--were relegated to the status of "window dressing" or "flower vases." Some of the oppositionists elected to maintain their integrity as a "TF," and chose the diaspora, moving to Hong Kong, Japan, the United States, or elsewhere, where they lived out their days (for example, the former leader of the DSP, Zhang Junmai, who sided with the GMD following the war only to reject it, along with the CCP, in 1949).

In both Taiwan and the PRC, the 1980s brought exciting political change. In Taiwan, martial law was lifted, leading to an explosion in the number of political parties. On the Mainland, the Deng Xiaoping era saw an improvement in the status of the DPGs, with key roles played by Hu Yaobang and Zhao Ziyang. During the mid-1980s, according to James Seymour, these groups hoped that multiparty government might one day come to China. These hopes were shattered by the crackdown that ended the democracy movement of 1986, and even more decisively by the aftermath of the 1989 June Fourth Massacre. Another wave of Chinese political exiles ended up abroad, just as had happened periodically ever since the failure of the "Hundred Days' Reforms" in 1898, and they have formed the present-day Overseas Democracy Movement (ODM).

Despite being the political and intellectual heirs of the Republican-era figures examined in this volume, few of these new political exiles, as Andrew Nathan notes, have studied the lives and works of their predecessors in the opposition parties of the 1920s, 1930s, and 1940s. Instead, they have looked abroad for their answers, just as did the oppositionists in the Republican period.

Characteristics of the Opposition Parties, Groups, and Figures

The contributors to this volume faced a number of questions when preparing their essays. Who were these men (and they were all men)? What did they advocate? What did they think it would take to "save China"? How did these views differ from those of the GMD and the CCP, with which these leaders took issue? What were their relationships with the two major parties? By what means--through the educational world, the press, mobilization of the rural populace, recourse to armed force--did they propose to succeed in the harsh political and military environment of Republican China? From which classes did they draw their membership? What were the markets for their ideas? What were their motives in electing to become oppositionists, a stance they must have known was very dangerous in the climate of the times? Did they always know that their actions would be perceived as "opposition" by those in power? Why did they fail--for they did fail, if we judge them by their inability to take over the government of China or even to exert a significant influence on events.

The case studies included in this volume present the programs and motives of a number of these characters. They were not cut from the same cloth; there was a great range of views, including those of the military oppositionist, Deng Yanda; the anarchists, who defined politics in terms of cultural reforms; the National Salvation Association (NSA), whose leaders steered mass demonstrations against Chiang Kai-shek's policies in the mid-1930s; and the individual minor-party leaders. In fact, not all of these movements were led by one outstanding figure; in the case of the NSA, the group took precedence over a single, charismatic figure, and it is significant that the heroes were the "*seven* gentlemen" [emphasis mine].

The following represents an attempt to identify some commonalities, as well as differences, in these disparate figures and groups.

The Influence of the West and the Persistence of Chinese Tradition

Clearly, the role of the West was a seminal one. Many of the oppositionists studied in these essays were returned students from the U.S. or England, (Luo Longji), France (Chinese anarchists, Zeng Qi, Li Huang), and Germany (Zhang Junmai and Deng Yanda). Moreover, those who studied in Japan before the 1911 Revolution often learned about the West secondhand (Huang Yanpei, Zeng Qi, Zhang Junmai, Chinese anarchists).

The West offered the oppositionists such beliefs as constitutionalism, parliamentary government, individual freedoms, the concept of political parties as "loyal oppositions," and much more. Moreover, some Western thinkers, such as Harold J. Laski, show up again and again as influences on these Chinese oppositionists.[7] In many cases, however, these doctrines did not replace the earlier Chinese outlooks, based upon such *Weltanschauungs* as Confucianism, but were combined with them in syncretic ideologies.[8] In her essay on the CYP, for example, Marilyn Levine argues that its members were caught between modern politics and Chinese tradition, or "frozen in time"; hence, while heading a modern political party, Zeng Qi avidly propagated the idea of cultural revival. Zhang Junmai and the CYP leaders also tried to reconcile the Chinese political approach, which stressed "government by men" (*renzhi*) and the Western emphasis on "rule of law" (*fazhi*), and CYP leader Chen Qitian wanted to combine the two approaches in constitutional government. In short, some of these oppositionists wanted to combine Western thought with the best of Chinese culture. Thus, to view them as replacing traditional Chinese political beliefs with modern Western views would be as simplistic as seeing them as "Confucian scholars in modern dress." The point--and this makes their stories more interesting--was the creative tension between the two influences, in particular between the Western democracy that Thomas Metzger has described as "competition between selfishly inclined people, regulated by some sort of morally neutral constitutional procedures," and the Chinese notion that "the lynchpin [of government] is the idea that morally enlightened people ... is how you keep the whole thing together."[9] In Nathan's view, this led to an unsophisticated view of democracy on the part of these oppositionists, one that failed to acknowledge that democracy involves conflict and vested interests.

The West also clearly offered different messages to different people. For example, the Communist leaders Zhou Enlai, Zhu De, and Deng Xiaoping also studied in Europe, yet they did not return to China imbued with the same values as most of the oppositionists taken up in this volume.

Emigre Politics

Many of these movements were also examples of emigre politics, i.e., the party state occupied the core and the oppositionists were forced to work from the periphery. The essays in this work provide a number of examples of this type of politics: Zhang Junmai in exile in Germany from 1929-31, the leaders of the CYP in Europe in the early 1920s (along with some of the future leaders of the CCP), Deng Yanda in Germany, the anarchists in France, the FL in Hong Kong, Japan, and the U.S. in the early 1950s, and the refugee democratic activists in the U.S. and Europe today.

Liberalism and Illiberalism

A number of these oppositionists were liberals. However, not all oppositionists were liberals and not all liberals were oppositionists. In the interwar period, democracy was not the dominant intellectual vogue in China or the world. Hence, even minor parties in China emulated the Leninist pattern of organization (for example, the NSP [10]), with central committees, party congresses, and the like. Moreover, some liberals complained (like Sun Yat-sen at an earlier time) that there was too much, rather than too little, democracy. They argued, in the debate over democracy versus dictatorship in the mid-1930s, that an authoritarian government would be best for a China faced with tremendous military and economic challenges. As a result, some liberals worked for the GMD government. This problem has continued up to the present ODM members. Like their predecessors, they face the problem of whether to try to influence the course of events by joining the Communist regime or opposing it. Hence, in twentieth-century China, there has been some ambiguity in oppositionists' feelings about the party state, which may be glimpsed in the essays in this volume. J. Kenneth Olenik, for example, has pointed out that Deng Yanda despised Western-style liberals. Instead, he was influenced by both Marxism and the Three People's Principles.

Some of the party leaders were pragmatists, and hoped for the reform of the GMD (e.g., Huang Yanpei and Luo Longji), until events in the late 1940s convinced them to give up those dreams. A number of them (such as Huang Yanpei, Luo Longji) stayed on after 1949, and tried to come to terms with the new party state (Luo was eventually attacked by the new regime). As noted in Nathan's essay, some of the democratic activists, in exile following June 1989, argue that China will need the leadership of a reformist CCP, as the country democratizes, and favor reform from the top (reminding one of the abortive Kang Youwei effort in the 1890s).

The attempt to measure a party leader's "liberalism" is not always easy. As Frederic Wakeman has pointed out, it is difficult to always draw the line between opposition politics as a liberal-democratic position and as a tool of bureaucratic maneuvering--as a lever used by the "outs" against the "ins" (as in the rise of political parties in Meiji Japan). In short, opposition politics often involved more than a concern for democracy. Hence, it is more accurate to refer to these figures as "oppositionists." (However, the essays in this collection do not deal with opposition *within* the two major parties, i.e., with factionalism within the GMD and the CCP.)

Similarities of the Oppositionists

If there were differences in these leaders' thought and actions, there were also similarities. All were drawn from the educated elite and were professionals of one sort or another, with some (e.g., Luo Longji, Zhang Junmai, and others) serving as college professors.[11] Many of them (e.g., Zhang Junmai, Luo Longji, and Huang Yanpei) showed a common faith (perhaps derived from the Confucian legacy) in the transformative power of education, although they also recognized that the latter would be futile without political reforms to create a climate in which education could succeed. Some (Luo Longji and Huang Yanpei) supported student activism, while others were uneasy about it (Zhang Junmai). Almost all, however, strove to promote student nationalism in the face of the Japanese invasion during the 1930s. In fact, the Japanese impact was a critical event in the political lives of many of these oppositionists, prodding them into intensified action. As a result, almost all (the anarchists rejected nationalism) were strong nationalists, especially the members of the CYP (such as Zeng Qi), but also men such as Zhang Junmai. In fact, the CYP members thought they were better than the GMD (whose name, after all, means "Nationalist Party") when it came to support for nationalism. Some--perhaps again revealing a lingering traditional prejudice against *dangs* as "cliques," rather than "political parties" and pillars of parliamentary governments--either refused or were reluctant participants in political party politics (e.g., Zeng Qi, Huang Yanpei, and Deng Yanda[12]), while others (e.g., Luo Longji and Zhang Junmai) had no aversion to politics. At least one group--the anarchists--explicitly denied any intention to form a political party and preferred to remain a "movement."[13] None of these men, however, could escape politics. Some sought a philosophical foundation for their political and military actions (Deng Yanda and Zhang Junmai). Several had access to Chiang Kai-shek and the GMD prior to the Nanjing Decade (Deng Yanda); others, during the 1930s (Huang Yanpei); and some, not until WWII (Zhang Junmai).

A few were similar in the sense that they were initially optimistic about the GMD's ability to reform (for example, Huang Yanpei). Huang even accepted the necessity of the GMD's political tutelage, while Luo Longji and

Zhang Junmai abhored that policy. A number of the oppositionists began to lose hope in the GMD by 1943, 1944, or during the Civil War. This would seem to suggest that the GMD blew their chances by not reforming; however, as pointed out below, the whole outlook of the GMD--as molded by Sun Yat-sen, Chiang Kai-shek, and other GMD theoreticians--militated against the GMD tolerating any opposition to its dictatorial rule.

Almost to a man, they were either suspicious of the CCP or ardently opposed it (Zeng Qi, Zhang Junmai, the anarchists, and others), although in the end several cast their lot with it when the time came to choose sides or leave China (Huang Yanpei and Luo Longji). Although Deng Yanda leaned toward the GMD (while opposing the Nanjing regime and Chiang Kai-shek), he was capable of flirting with the CCP (efforts were made to include it in the planned uprising against Chiang). Most opposed the idea of the class struggle (e.g., the members of the CYP and Zhang Junmai), which gave them something in common with Sun Yat-sen and the GMD. On the other hand, most were also opposed to capitalism, with the most common policy the advocacy of a mixture of socialism and capitalism (the CYP and Zhang Junmai). Finally--and grimly--all of them were repressed by either the GMD, the CCP, or both.

Publications

Another similarity had to do with the written word. One way, in lieu of better organizations (partly precluded by the repressive environment), in which the oppositionists kept in touch and disseminated their programs was through their publications, on which there was a tremendous emphasis and reliance. This was perhaps a way of continuing to carry out the traditional duty of intellectuals to remonstrate with the regime, as well as indicating the persistence of the traditional sacredness of the written word.

It was *de rigueur* for these opposition groups to have a journal. In this way, they also could cultivate public opinion. For example, Zhang Junmai and Li Huang published *Xin lu* (The New Way); Deng Yanda and his colleagues published *Dengda* (Lighthouse); and Luo Longji built his fame as a liberal intellectual through his editorials in the newspaper *Yishi bao* (The Social Welfare Daily). In fact, journals were akin to political parties, with their own constituencies and influence. It was amazing how much they were able to express through this medium (in sharp contrast to the PRC's muzzling of the oppositionist press after 1949), despite persistent, although perhaps fitful, GMD censorship. In Taiwan today, the Democratic Progressive Party (DPP) complains about lack of access to the media, but in fact it has its own journals. It is now television that the GMD controls in Taiwan, not the press.

Reasons for Failure

It is essential, in this introduction, to address the major question: Why did these forces fail? On the surface, it seems simple: they failed because of their own weaknesses. However, such a conclusion would ignore the complexity of the issue. It would be more accurate to argue that the oppositionists failed because of a combination of their own weaknesses and repression by the GMD and the CCP. Hence, one may question Edmund Fung's greater emphasis on the GMD failure to introduce democratic reforms when they had the chance in the 1930s than on the weaknesses of the minor parties, in accounting for the failure of democracy before 1949.

In addition, these parties should not be judged failures by implicit comparison with the GMD and CCP. In light of Republican and PRC history, the term "failure" should not be reserved for these oppositionists, who at least are, on the whole, sympathetic figures. One might easily argue that the two major parties, which do not elicit the same kind of sympathy from the historical observer, have not governed well, if the misery of the Chinese people under the GMD during the Republican period and under the CCP since 1949 is taken as the measure.

But why did the oppositionists fail to successfully challenge the GMD and the CCP?

Inhospitable Environment

Perhaps the clearest explanation was the harsh setting in which they were forced to operate. In addition to a tradition of autocracy, as well as political and intellectual orthodoxy, an important element in that environment was the repression by both the GMD and the CCP one-party dictatorships (this will be explored in greater detail below).

In addition, the period since the 1920s has been one of revolution, war, and the supremacy of militarism. In the 1920s, there was the Northern Expedition and the split between the GMD and the CCP; in the 1930s, the Japanese invasion and the clashes between the warlords and the new GMD government; in the 1940s, the war with Japan and the subsequent Civil War between the CCP and the GMD; and finally, since 1949 there was political repression in Taiwan until 1987, while in the PRC millions have suffered from the political campaigns of the Communist regime, with the Cultural Revolution the worst. In short, this has been an age in which violence has reigned supreme in China, and clearly this made it nearly impossible for these oppositionists to accomplish much.

In writing of the inhospitable environment, one also has to ask whether a democracy based on individual rights was even possible in a China that stressed the prerogatives of the group and the family over the individual.

Democracy is the most selfish of all systems, based as it is upon individualism. The situation is made worse, perhaps, when one recalls that individualism has always been thought of in a pejorative sense by the Chinese. Yet, one can be optimistic that someday they will come to understand the relationship between constitutional freedoms and the interests of the group and the family.

Failure to Take Up Arms

These oppositionists were not pacifists, for they supported military resistance to the Japanese (state violence) and some of them supported one or another of the parties in the GMD-CCP Civil War. Moreover, they were not averse to allying with warlords who used military force. However, these essays make it abundantly clear that most were unwilling or unable to meet violence with violence in their own struggles with the two major parties (the anarchists also rejected armed struggle).

Partly, this may have been because to establish one's own army was expensive. Moreover, to do so would call down upon their heads even more severe repression, as Chiang Kai-shek's execution of Deng Yanda showed. Chiang tolerated his *shudaizi* (bookworms) but executed his military opposition (Deng and members of the CCP). Hence, lack of funds and fear may have stood in the way of a military response to the repression they suffered.

However, there were other reasons for their failure to fight. Temperamentally, these men were college professors, journalists, and professionals--hardly military men--who preferred to struggle with the pen and the use of personal networks. Moreover, as proponents of constitutionalism and democracy, they mostly refused to accept a key dictum of twentieth-century China (as coined by Mao Zedong): "Political power grows out of the barrel of a gun."

In democracies, of course, this outlook is repugnant, and the idea of civilian control of the military dominates. When the cause is judged right, however, a democratic state such as the U.S. is quite capable of resorting to force, both at home (George Washington and the Revolution, the Civil War) and abroad (the World Wars, the Korean War, Vietnam, etc.). Hence, liberalism does not automatically mean a rejection of force.

Both the GMD and the CCP (with the latter learning its lesson in 1927, which is one reason Mao Zedong was reluctant to abide by the military agreements of the 1946 Political Consultative Conference) swore by the gun. Chiang Kai-shek was, first and foremost, a military man and, as one scholar has put it, "No Chinese Communist leader has so strongly and so categorically stressed military power as Mao...."[14] Hence, the oppositionists had to function in an environment dominated by militarism. This may well have made the idea of democracy, with its emphasis on peaceful competition, even more attractive.

Discussion of this issue drives one to ask: if everyone else took up arms, but most of these oppositionists refused (e.g., Zhang Junmai), can one say they really participated in twentieth-century politics? At least one of the oppositionists (Huang Yanpei) was cognizant that his inability to take up arms--or don the cloak of a powerful politician--doomed his efforts at political reform in an environment dominated by the two armed parties.

In addition, the refusal to fight had to be based either on the Western ideal of civilian control of the military or personal pacifism (or both), rather than Confucianism, for Confucian scholars such as Zeng Guofan had been willing to raise armies and fight for the preservation of the Confucian order against the Taipings and other rebels in nineteenth-century China, i.e., they had been willing to serve as scholar-generals. In short, if liberalism elsewhere, as well as China's Confucian tradition, could countenance the use of violence under the right circumstances, why did these Chinese oppositionists reject it? Perhaps the answer lay in their personalities and the overwhelmingly hostile environment, rather than their ideological beliefs.

However, not all of the oppositionists turned their backs on the use of military force. Deng Yanda was a military man and recognized that the environment of Republican China demanded a military response. Hence, he and his colleagues planned an armed uprising against Chiang Kai-shek, in line with his group's dictum of "Military affairs as the first priority." Although Edmund Fung points out in his essay that the CYP had few military men in their ranks and opposed armed struggle, the Party did have military connections with the Manchurian warlord, Zhang Xueliang, and the Sichuan militarists.[15] Moreover, Levine reports that in the early 1920s Zeng Qi called for the adoption of assassination as a political tactic, which placed the CYP in the same category as the GMD, the CCP, and the anarchists, as far as the resort to terror went (it is not clear whether the CYP actually responded to Zeng's call). The remainder of these figures, however--although not averse to accepting protection and financial support from warlords when necessary--embodied the civilian over the military spirit (in traditional Chinese terms, *wen* over *wu*).

Limited Membership and Audience

For the most part, these opposition parties were small groups, counting their memberships in the thousands, rather than, as in the cases of the GMD and the CCP, the millions.[16] One also has to ask about the targets--or "markets"--of the oppositionists' programs. Who was interested and who supported them?

In most cases, the targets seemed limited to the thin stratum of elite at the top of Chinese society. Luo Longji, for example, aimed his editorials at the student audience in the Tianjin-Beijing area. Zhang Junmai's journal and recruitment efforts also targeted the students, as well as his fellow intellectuals, for the most part. Some oppositionists reached a larger audience than others. Today in Taiwan, the minor parties are attempting to reach the workers and farmers, an effort that would set off alarms in the heads of Beijing's leaders (as did attempts of the students to link up with the workers during the demonstrations in the spring of 1989).

However, despite these efforts, the oppositionists, for the most part, were unable to develop popular bases. The CYP, for example, was aware of the need to pay attention to mass mobilization and socioeconomic reforms, but their membership--like most of the opposition parties and groups--was drawn almost entirely from the educated classes. Part of the answer to that failure of these leaders to go beyond their backgrounds may have been a traditional Confucian belief in their duty to lead the masses, not consult with them (an outlook that made the Communist idea of the "vanguard" very appealing to people like Chen Duxiu). Even a liberal like Luo Longji, who was one of the few to argue for democracy and human rights for their own sakes, rather than as means to the end of strengthening the nation, believed that reform would come from above. Perhaps their lack of interest in cultivating a broad base was related to the intellectuals' self-perception of their role as the ultimate arbiters of China's fate.[17]

They were isolated from the rural people, who then as now constitute over 80 percent of China's population. Mao and the CCP mobilized these people, whom Chiang Kai-shek largely ignored. In this sense, the oppositionists resembled the latter. Deng Yanda and the leaders of the Third Party (TP) did argue that the "common people" (*pingmin*) would play an important role in the future society, that the elites alone could not succeed in building the future. Yet even they could not escape an elitist approach to Chinese politics, for they went on to argue that it was the duty of youth and the intellectuals to provide leadership for the masses. However, unlike his fellow oppositionists, who concentrated their educative efforts on the university and the training of an elite, Huang Yanpei focused on vocational training to prepare the millions for the demands of the modern age. Moreover, some of the tiny parties active during the civil war period of the late 1940s attempted to reach a broader audience of peasants, workers, and even secret societies, but they were doomed to true marginality by their sizes, as well as repression by the two major parties.

Part of the reason for the oppositionists' failure to build popular bases was due to their identities. For the most part, they behaved like the members of higher culture they were--urban intellectuals, educated abroad, graduates of and professors at the leading universities in the land, publishers of the most important newspapers and journals--unlike someone like Mao, a member of the medium culture, who was from a rural family and attended a normal university. The oppositionists took their roles as an elite seriously. Perhaps they were, by their nature and training, characterized by "intellectual irresolution," a weakness that Mao and his colleagues seem to have avoided. Yet, the oppositionists deserve to be viewed with sympathy.

If they were largely isolated from the rural population, were they also out of touch with the urban dwellers? Here the evidence is thinner, with Parks Coble's essay on the NSA suggesting that an oppositionist movement could mobilize broad support in the cities if the cause was as explosive as perceived appeasement of the Japanese. The NSA brought together under one umbrella workers, educators, college students, women, writers, professionals, journalists, bankers, lawyers, banks clerks, and shopkeepers, with thousands taking to the streets in sometimes violent demonstrations.

Lack of Adequate Funds

These opposition movements also suffered from financial debility. It took money to found parties, establish schools to train members of their organizations (as the CYP, and in a sense, Zhang Junmai did), and publish newspapers and journals. Lack of funds sabotaged their autonomy, and hence their movements, by forcing them into dependence upon the wrong people, especially the two major parties and the warlords.[18]

Hence, the NSP and the CYP were subsidized by the GMD government during WWII, while the CCP gave money to the Democratic League (DL). In addition, both Zhang Junmai and the CYP accepted financial support (and protection) from warlords at times, just as at an earlier time a man much admired by them, Liang Qichao, had depended on Yuan Shikai for financial support of his Progressive Party.[19] During the early 1950s, the FL failed in part due to an inadequate financial base. Finally, as Nathan's analysis makes clear, today's ODM suffers from the same weakness.

Inadequate Organizational Structures

The opposition parties also suffered from the lack of tight organizations. Many of them were parties in name only, with very small memberships. They were groups of figures enmeshed in a complex web based on personal relationships (or what the Chinese refer to as *guanxi* or "connections"), rather than modern political parties. Hence, Deng Yanda was clearly connected by the old school tie to a number of other military men with whom he plotted against Chiang Kai-shek. As former commandant of the Whampoa Military Academy (WMA), Chiang himself profited from the strength of the teacher-student bond in China and attracted the loyalty of many of his former students. The CYP was never able to build a tight organization, and its formal party structure was secondary, as one analyst put it, to the "informal, personal relationships among members of its small leadership core." [20] The defection of one of Zeng Qi's most promising proteges to Zhou Enlai and the CCP in Europe--a "betrayal" punctuated with weeping--lent drama to these personal ties, which were broken only at great emotional cost to both leader and follower. During the Cultural Revolution, Zhou Enlai is said to have protected many of those with whom he had connections, including liberals.

Perhaps the sole exception to this stress on personal connections over political platforms was the NSA studied by Coble. It was perhaps very unChinese (and unJapanese, too) in that it was the political program (resistance to appeasement of the Japanese), rather than its leaders, that lay at the heart of the movement.

In short, the personal network among the educated elite was a densely woven one; enemies or not, many of them travelled in the same elite circles and knew each other. Hence, Zhang Junmai was Chiang Kai-shek's guest at lunch at the same time he was confined to Chungking and his school precipitously closed by the Generalissimo. In January 1949, he could meet with Chiang and tell him face to face to resign as president of the Republic, without being shot for his temerity.

Factionalism

In addition to the lack of strong organizations, factionalism weakened the opposition parties. Zhang Junmai's DSP was largely destroyed by a split in the late 1940s over the issue of whether or not to participate in the various GMD-sponsored assemblies and enter the GMD-dominated government. Fredric Spar's Luo Longji was an example also, for he quit the NSP (the DSP's predecessor), thus depriving it of his very real (if acerbic) talents. The DL also split, with the more conservative CYP and then the DSP pulling out, which considerably weakened what had once been China's hope for a viable and strong TF. Squabbling and divisions were also obvious in Ivanov's "tiniest of the tiny" parties during the Civil War. Even after all realistic chances for turning back the tide of history seemed to be gone, factionalism destroyed the FL.[21] During its short life (1952-1954), it assembled a disparate group of men--generals, scholars, bureaucrats--and it was conflict among them that at least partly accounted for the failure of the organization.

Factionalism is still very much a part of the Chinese political world today. It is to be found among the democratic activists in exile in the U.S., as Nathan's essay makes clear. Moreover, it is strong in Taiwan, according to John Copper, who believes that Taiwan will follow the Japanese model, rather than the two-party example, in the future. In his view, the GMD will remain the dominant party as a grouping of factions, like the Liberal Democratic Party in Japan, and in elections members of the GMD will compete primarily against each other, rather than other parties. This will have a fragmenting effect on the GMD, with factionalism the result. The Liberal Democratic Party in Japan is really several parties rolled into one, and the same thing will happen in Taiwan, argues Copper, unless the multi-district, single-vote system is altered.

Failure to Unite with Other Opposition Parties

The number of minor parties has varied, with more in the late 1940s and today on Taiwan than at other times since the 1920s. With so many groups in existence, it was natural that some would be similar in membership and beliefs (e.g., the NSP and the CYP were not far apart[22]). Hence, the question arises: why did they not unite and increase their strength and ability to survive in the repressive climate of Republican China (it is doubtful they would have been allowed to form coalitions in the PRC and in Taiwan before the lifting of martial law)?

This is largely an unstudied question. Jeans' essay on Zhang Junmai suggests that the failure to unite may have stemmed from the clash of personalities and egos, rather than incompatible ideologies--a conclusion that makes sense considering the predominance of personal networks and relationships over organization and ideology in these opposition movements.

Single-Issue Movements

Another result of the lack of strong organizational structures was that much of the successful political activity of the oppositionists was based upon single-issue movements. Coble's depiction of the tremendous appeal of the opposition to appeasement of Japan in the 1930s is an excellent example of this phenomenon. Unlike the other oppositionists studied here, the NSA's resistance to the GMD's appeasement was the movement's sole *raison d'etre*. The appeal of the "peace" slogan--in a China that had been at war, more or less continuously, since the fall of the Qing in 1911-1912--during the Civil War of the late 1940s is another example of the power of a single issue.

Lack of a Supportive Civic Society?

A more tenuous argument is that these oppositionists failed due to the lack of a supportive civic society, a weakness that has plagued them from their beginnings up to the present ODM. Many of these figures were college professors offering their largely Western-derived programs to a population overwhelmingly comprised of peasants. Hence, these oppositionists were islands of--in most cases but not all--liberalism in an illiberal society. This line of thought is supported by the problems besetting Chinese society during the 1920s, 1930s, 1940s, and afterwards. There was poverty, starvation, war, illiteracy, ignorance, and revolution. Perhaps the GMD and CCP had a right to ask how the oppositionists proposed to solve the immediate, practical problems of China.

There may be hope for the future, however. Nathan has suggested that the DPGs in the PRC represent progress toward, if not democracy, at least the civic society.

Moderate Personalities in an Extremist Environment

At the heart of the oppositionists' failures was a contradiction: most of these men who had chosen the path of opposition, with all of its attendant risks, emphasized moderation, peaceful consensus, compromise, reason, and tolerance, and opposed coercion. They abhored social science quackery and advocated rational solutions (reminding one of Hu Shi's argument in the 1920s in favor of a gradual, piecemeal solution of "problems," rather than the advocacy of abstract "isms").

Men like Zhang Junmai admired nothing more than reason and the "golden mean" approach of Confucianism. Yet, the blunt truth was that it would have taken extremism to dislodge the GMD or the CCP. These dissidents were no more prepared (with the exception of men such as Deng Yanda) to "go to extremes" (as Mao Zedong once put it) than to take up arms. Hence, it could be argued that some of the oppositionists overemphasized tolerance at the expense of rights.[23]

"Sins" of the Oppositionists

The above weaknesses were not so much sins of commission as omission for the oppositionists. They were not saints, however, and it is important not to idealize them.[24] It is true, though, that the influence of Confucian ethics on many of them was still strong, a scant two or three decades after the abolition of the Confucian examinations and the fall of the Confucian monarchy. Moreover, it is probably true that they competed with the CCP, prior to 1949, for the "moral charisma."

Corruption

Yet, in his essay on minor parties during the Civil War, Ivanov points out that "narrow personal ambitions" moved these figures, as well as more lofty considerations. Lloyd Eastman's essay on two of the leading minor parties in the late 1940s is even more damning, when he argues that the members of these parties could be as corrupt (seeking to *shengguan facai* or "become officials and grow wealthy") as those in the GMD, the CCP (especially after 1949), or many other societies and times, and were more interested in fame and fortune than in democracy. However, the essay also notes that it was the rank and file that lusted after office and wealth; the leaders of those parties--the older men who, for the most part, had been steeped in the Confucian classics (such as Zhang Junmai, Li Huang, Zeng Qi, Zuo Shunsheng, and Chen Qitian)--were above that scramble for office, which was traditionally seen as the key to wealth in China.[25] In fact, one is reminded that Chiang Kai-shek was said to be personally incorruptible, while presiding over a rotten government and party.

While admitting that what happened in China was a manifestation of a universal "frailty of human ideals," Eastman criticizes China's political culture, which caused many Chinese to be "easily corrupted by the temptations of political power." "In all probability," he writes, "China would not have known democracy, or good government, even if these minor parties had somehow, against all odds, become a major force in Chinese politics." China must, he concluded, devise institutions to contain the *shengguan facai* phenomenon, or it may never experience "good government."[26]

In his essay in this volume, Nathan adds that participants in the current democracy movement also suffer from this tendency to lose sight of the long-term goal of democracy in favor of a short-term desire for money and power.

Eastman's thesis is not unchallengable. One may argue that political perfection in the opposition was too much to ask for. It was only natural for members of the CYP and the DSP to desire to hold office, and there was nothing "bad" about it. One also could take issue with Eastman's implication that there would be progress in China only when their political culture was reformed. Democracy always possesses its "pork barrel" or spoils aspect; in fact, this led to broad political participation in the past in the U.S. Hence, greed for office in the late 1940s in China was not necessarily bad. In Eastman's defense, one could argue that he was merely pointing out that the oppositionists, despite their claims to higher moral authority, were no better than the GMD and the CCP when it came to coveting office and wealth. Moreover, it was easy for the leaders of the minor parties to remain pure, while the rank and file scrambled for gain, for the former had non-monetary rewards, such as prestige, forums in which to express their views (such as ready access to the press, as leaders of their parties), and were generally well known. Finally, one should not forget the times; there was great pressure to be corrupt in order to survive in the midst of the hyperinflation of the late 1940s, which saw those on fixed salaries worse off with each passing day.

Brutality

Although it would seem rare, oppositionists could also be brutal. In April 1927, eight veteran union organizers, who opposed the CCP's domination of the Hubei unions, were arrested in Wuhan by Deng Yanda's NRA Political Department, and executed a few days later.[27]

Proto-Fascists?

Were some of these figures and groups "proto-fascist," in their fervent nationalism, calls for cultural revival, and emphasis on youth? Levine argued, in her paper on Zeng Qi and the CYP, that their thought was quite similar to that of the French radical right in the 1920s. Like the right (and the May Fourth Movement), they placed their hopes in youth. They did not, however, abandon their emphasis on democracy nor advocate racism, as Fung's essay on the same party in the 1930s and 1940s points out. Hence, they differed from the fascists. Whether or not the CYP actually helped prepare the way in the 1920s for the fascism that Chiang Kai-shek flirted with in the 1930s, as one scholar has suggested, is difficult to prove, barring the establishment of a direct causal link.

Did They Practice What They Preached?

There were sometimes contradictions between the oppositionists' professed ideals and their activities. Zhang Junmai could write reams on democracy, human rights, and constitutionalism, but also disregard the wishes of many of his party members, as well as refuse to accept the idea that illiterates could have the franchise. The minor parties examined in Ivanov's essay spoke of the Political Consultative Conference's (PCC) ideals but operated like secret societies; spoke of democracy but protected their special interests. Finally, although one can sympathize with the tremendous pressures placed on the DPGs, following the Tiananmen massacres, the overnight change from supporting the student demonstrators, before June Fourth, to praising the People's Liberation Army for putting down the counterrevolutionary turmoil, following June Fourth, is not a pretty picture. This is not to judge them, but merely to note the pressures--even greater than those brought to bear by the former GMD government of Mainland China--associated with political opposition in the PRC.

Manipulation by the GMD, CCP, and the Japanese

Another question that has to be asked about these oppositionists is the extent to which they might have been manipulated by the GMD and the

CCP. Certainly, Chiang Kai-shek and the GMD believed the oppositionists were the cat's paws of the CCP. Moreover, both the GMD and the CCP saw the oppositionists as targets for recruitment. Coble rejects the charge that the NSA was a front for the CCP. Although it was true that many involved in the CCP underground in Shanghai joined the salvationist movement, that was due, he argues, to the popular appeal of the NSA's platform, rather than CCP orders. One could also make the case that Zhang Junmai was conned into supporting the GMD at a crucial moment in modern China's history (the fall of 1946) by Chiang Kai-shek's promise to ensure the passage of the constitutional draft Zhang had played a large role in writing. That constitution, of course, was stillborn in GMD China, with conditions immediately added to it that rendered it a dead letter for the duration of the CCP "rebellion." One also wonders whether liberals such as Huang Yanpei were "snowed" by their trip to Yanan in 1945, much as Western journalists and diplomats are said to have been impressed with the contrast between Yanan and Chongqing during WWII. Finally, some of the leadership of the DPGs in the PRC have held dual memberships, belonging to the CCP at the same time they are members of one of the eight minor parties (e.g., *Jiusan* Society member, Zhou Peiyuan).[28] Hence, one presumes that they are manipulated by the CCP at will.

In concluding, it is impossible to speak of manipulation of the oppositionists without recalling that during the war the Japanese also attempted to win them over and, in fact, had some success. Some members of the NSP, as well as of the CYP (mentioned in Ivanov's paper), defected to the Japanese. Hence, there was the spectacle of figures opposed to the GMD dictatorship joining the Japanese, whose record in Asia during WWII was a particularly brutal one.

Reasons for the Repression by the GMD and the CCP

Lack of the Concept of "Loyal Opposition"

To attribute the failure of these men solely to their own weaknessses would be an oversimplification. Their defeat was due in no small measure to the repressions of the GMD and the CCP, which did not differentiate "loyal opposition" from other kinds. Their control systems have been so repressive it is no wonder these men did not get anywhere with their proposals for reform.

Moreover, persecuting the oppositionists was not good for China in other ways. Under the GMD, there was a diversion of resources from maintaining public order to political persecution of the oppositionists, which led to an increase in criminality and public and social violence. Hence, the oppositional politics of the time resulted in a criminalization and delegitimization of GMD power. In short, state violence ended up as a weapon against the state.

In addition, traditional China lacked the concept of a loyal opposition. As John Israel puts it in his essay, "legitimate opposition [had been] inconceivable" in China. In his article on the CYP, Fung argues that it hoped to work with the GMD, as a loyal opposition, to institute change.[29] There was simply no room for that concept, however, in either GMD China or the PRC. In Chinese history, opposition was opposition, and it was dealt with harshly. During the GMD period, the dominant outlook was clearly "If you are not with us, you are against us." The price for dissidence was arrest (Luo Longji), kidnapping (Zhang Junmai), execution (Deng Yanda), or stigmatization as a "war criminal" (Zeng Qi, Zhang Junmai, and others). The leaders of the DL who elected to remain in China soon discovered that the Communists would reject the idea of "loyal opposition" just as decisively as the GMD had. As one of the democratic activists who fled China following the June Fourth crackdown put it: if we win, we become the rulers; if we lose, we die (an outlook which parallels the traditional view that winners become emperors while losers are labelled bandits).

The One-Party Dictatorship

The rise of the modern one-party dictatorships was a new phenomenon in Chinese history. These dictatorships were only made more severe by the fact that men such as Chiang Kai-shek and Mao Zedong had little tolerance for opposition and viewed alternate visions of China's future as personal affronts, rather than "politics as usual" in the Western sense. Some of the forms repression took have been mentioned above. The regimes also censored the publications of the oppositionists. They did not have to close them down; they attempted to bring them to heel by denying them newsprint, refusing to accept them at the post office, raising postal rates to prohibitive levels (a result sometimes achieved by simply failing to control inflation), confiscating issues, and threatening those inclined to purchase them.

The "Metzgerian Thesis"

It is easy to identify the forms repression took. The more difficult question is why? In a recent paper, Thomas Metzger suggested that Chinese thinkers strove to find a *tixi* or "deductive, comprehensive, correct system of political principles." This concept constituted one of the premises, he argued, that have served as the foundations of China's political discourse since the turn of the century.

At the risk of oversimplifying and distorting his thesis, it is easy to see that both the GMD and CCP claimed to possess such a "perfect" political ideology. It is also clear that neither of these parties took kindly to the oppositionists' rejection of their *tixi* or claims (explicitly or implicitly) that the oppositionists' *tixis* were superior and should replace those of the ruling parties.[30] The liberals' *tixis* stressed democratic government, scientific progress, Western influences, etc. In fact, this rhetoric of democracy could be viewed as one of the few useful weapons the oppositionists had, in dealing with the GMD and the CCP.

The GMD and CCP *tixis* were "a bit vague around the edges," and hence it was not always easy for the oppositionists to know whether their actions would be labelled "opposition." What is clear is that the regime defined "opposition," rather than the oppositionists themselves. Moreover, terror during the GMD period (as in the PRC, e.g., during the Cultural Revolution) was sometimes random and arbitrary. This must have added immeasurably to the sense of uncertainty and fear with which the oppositionists went about their tasks of formulating programs, recruiting members, and pressuring the regimes to reform. One has to wonder how many potential members of these oppositionist movements were deterred from joining by simple fear of the force wielded by the GMD and the CCP.

The Political Doctrines of Sun Yat-sen

The repression of the oppositionists also may be traced to the three-stage revolution concept of Sun Yat-sen, which asserted that the revolution would consist of a military period, an era characterized by a provisional constitution, and a final stage of constitutional government. In his later years, Sun increasingly downplayed the idea of the provisional constitution in the second stage and placed more emphasis on the political tutelage he viewed as necessary during that transitional stage. The Chinese did not understand democracy, he argued; hence, it was the task of the GMD to train them during that phase. In 1923-1924, he strengthened the GMD for that all-important task by adopting the Soviet model of one-party rule and placing the Party in a supreme position above the state. The success of the Russian Revolution, he argued, was "due to the fact that the party has been placed above the state."

There would be only one ideology--or *tixi*--in the new system, his own Three People's Principles of nationalism, people's rule, and people's livelihood. When Zhang Junmai refused to adopt that ideology into the curriculum at his Shanghai school, the GMD considered this a slap in the face for their *tixi*--a case of *lese majeste*--and closed his institute and issued a warrant for his arrest.

This is not the place for a full-scale exposition of Sun's thought.[31] Suffice it to say that Sun was opposed to individualism and natural rights. Only those who were loyal to the Republic deserved political rights, while they would be denied to those who opposed it. The Chinese, he argued, were a "loose sheet of sand"; rather than lacking individual liberty, as many of the oppositionists during the Republican period argued, they actually had too much of it, which undermined the unity of the nation. It was the duty of the members of the revolutionary parties to sacrifice individual liberty for the freedom of the nation.[32]

This was, of course, the opposite of what most of the oppositionists treated here argued. Luo Longji, for example, asserted that individual freedom would lead to the *strengthening* of the nation, an argument that both earlier Chinese figures, such as Yan Fu and Liang Qichao, and the British thinker Harold Laski preached. Moreover, influenced by Confucianism, the liberals tended to stress the worth of the individual.

The Oppositionists' Links to Power

The *tixi* concept is important, but there were other answers as to why the parties in power repressed the oppositionists. In some cases, the party in power viewed the oppositionists as having real or potential links to sources of power, and hence as being true threats to the regime. In this sense, the oppositionists may have courted repression.

In GMD China, this can be clearly seen in several of the cases outlined in these essays. When Deng Yanda began to try to win over the thousands of graduates of the Whampoa Military Academy (WMA), he was striking at the very underpinnings of Chiang Kai-shek's power. It is no wonder that, despite the fact that they were blood brothers, Chiang threatened to kill him (and did).

The NSA had tremendous success mobilizing urban dwellers against Chiang's policy of appeasing the Japanese, while devoting his military resources to defeating the CCP ("first internal pacification, then external resistance"). This mobilization threatened Chiang's power, for he feared the movement would spread from the intellectuals, students, and clerks to government employees, GMD members, Blue Shirt cadre, and even his own army officers. He also worried that the movement would force him into war with Japan before he had defeated the Communist threat. Finally, he feared that it was cooperating with his archenemies, the Communists, and hence would strengthen them. Hence, his reponse was to order the arrest and trial of the top leaders of the NSA. Although the beginning of war with Japan brought their release, one wonders--in light of Deng Yanda's fate--what would have happened to them if war had not broken out at that juncture.[33]

The GMD was especially sensitive to links between these dissenters and the military men who opposed the GMD, between the traditional leaders of China, the intellectuals, and the gun. The intellectuals needed protection and financial assistance and the warlords needed administrators and advisors. These alliances placed the intellectuals at the center of events and made them much less "marginal" than they might have been otherwise. Hence, during the Republican period, Zhang Junmai was associated with one warlord after another (Sun Chuanfang, Zhang Xueliang, Chen Jitang, the Guangxi Clique, and Long Yun), while the CYP also looked to the military men for funds and protection (Zhang Xueliang and the Sichuan militarists). Chiang Kai-shek was quick to arrest Zhang Junmai's old friend, Jiang Baili, for the latter's connections with the warlords Sun Chuanfang and Wu Peifu. During the 1930s, any call for a united front against Japanese aggression could be interpreted as pro-Communism, as in the late 1940s an appeal for a coalition government could mean incurring the wrath of the GMD. All of this yielded an ironic result: the more the GMD repressed the oppositionists, the more they were driven to seek protection from the military men.

In the case of the PRC, the ideas of such figures as Hu Shi and Liang Shuming were thought so potent and dangerous (as alternative *tixis*?) that nation-wide campaigns were launched against them in the 1950s. In the case of Liang, he challenged one of the cherished tenets of the Communist revolution and one of the sources of their victory and power when he criticized the poverty of the peasantry under Communist rule.[34]

The Oppositionists as Threats to Unity and Order

The parties in power also repressed these dissenters because they threatened national unity and order. The leaders of modern China (perhaps barring Mao Zedong) have greatly feared disorder (*luan*), which is understandable in light of the historical record of twentieth-century China. Chiang Kai-shek feared it during the Republican period; in fact, during the late 1920s and early 1930s, the CCP thought disunity in the ruling group of the GMD would help the revolution.[35] Finally, some analysts argue that Deng Xiaoping was driven to action in 1989 by his fear that China was threatened with yet another outbreak of the disorder China had suffered during most of his lifetime.

Chiang Kai-shek's Reaction to Opposition

During the Republican period, China was beset with foreign aggression (Japan) and internal rebellions (the warlords and the CCP). As a result, many Chinese put a powerful state at the core of their definition of Good.

It is not surprising, then, that Chiang Kai-shek saw his task as saving the nation and, in order to do this, felt that a unified country with a strong central government was the *sine qua non*. He viewed the state as more important than the individual; the latter should be totally loyal to the state and be willing to make the supreme sacrifice for it. As Eastman wrote in an earlier work: "There was no room in Chiang's world for a loyal opposition; if they [the opposition] opposed him they were, ipso facto, disloyal to the nation."[36]

Like Sun Yat-sen, Chiang took the subordination of the individual even further by identifying the GMD with the state, which meant the individual was inferior to both state and Party. In fact, he identified the GMD with China itself: "So long as the Kuomintang [GMD] remains in existence, so long will China continue to exist. If China today did not have the Kuomintang, there would be no China."[37] In view of this approach, there was obviously no room in Chiang's thinking for opposition parties. It was the duty of all citizens, he believed, to join the GMD.

As for the democracy propounded by many of the oppositionists, there was also no room in Chiang's thought for natural rights. Individual rights, he believed, along with many modern Chinese thinkers and the drafters of the Meiji Constitution in Japan, were created by law and should be delineated by law. The Chinese did not need more freedom, he argued, but more discipline, in order to cope with foreign aggression (and the CCP uprisings). Hence, he called for unanimity of thought as a prerequisite of national unification. A central idea would create a central will, and then China's problems could be overcome.[38]

In this environment, opposition (which Chiang saw as divisive) was treated harshly. In the eyes of the GMD, the Party, state, and nation took precedence over individual rights, which was an alien concept, imported from the West by Western-trained intellectuals. In the 1930s, another GMD leader, Wang Jingwei, argued in an attempt to reconcile liberty and party rule that while the people should enjoy freedom of speech and assembly, too much emphasis on different ideas could only lead to national disunity. The Three People's Principles, he argued, were all China needed, and any attempt to replace them with another ideology would only result in political chaos.[39]

In sum, the roots of the repression of the oppositionists were clear: Chiang Kai-shek and the GMD were trying to unify and recentralize China, in order to deal with the two most serious threats to their power and China's survival--the Japanese and the CCP--and were quite willing--nay, thought it mandatory--to crush any individuals or groups that got in the way.

Democracy in WWII China

Life was very difficult for the oppositionists during the Nanjing Decade. This was a period of alternatives to democracy, ranging from fascism in Germany and Italy to the "militarism" of imperial Japan to the Communism of the Soviet Union. Hence, the leader of the NSP, for example, later recalled that he had been forced to live an underground existence throughout this period.

The beginning of the Sino-Japanese War brought relief, for China was on the side of the democracies. Moreover, the GMD government needed all the support it could get during those years, while the CCP adroitly practiced its united-front policy in an effort to win over the oppositionists and hence shift the balance of power between themselves and the GMD. There seemed to be no major or minor political actor who was not ostensibly for democracy during the war. Thus, the GMD was forced to tolerate--although not legalize--the small parties, for the sake of the UF against the Japanese.

This ensured that these years were, as Lawrence Shyu argues in his essay, fruitful ones for the oppositionists, who worked mostly through China's "wartime parliament," the PPC. The opposition parties joined together to form larger organizations (such as the 1944 DL), rallied support behind the wartime government, opposed the various defectors such as Wang Jingwei (although this was sticky, since some members of the NSP and CYP went over to the Japanese), asserted themselves in demanding civil liberties and pushing for constitutionalism, and played important roles in mediating between the GMD and the CCP as a self-constituted TF and thus helped to maintain the UF. When one looks back on these years from the perspective of the PRC, it is clear that this was a time of remarkable political activity, which would never have been tolerated by the CCP in power after 1949 (as was shown by what happened to these minor parties after the Communist takeover).

And yet even with those more favorable conditions, progress toward democracy was limited. The need for national unity in the face of "total war" and the struggle between the two militarized parties limited the real possibilities for oppositional politics. Wartime mobilization tended to override the possibilities for democracy. In 1942, while the CCP continued to try to use the TF, the GMD began to crack down again, by limiting the number of minor party delegates in the PPC. The GMD shelved plans for a new constitution and tightened the screws on civil liberties. Ultimately also, the TF's attempts to fend off a civil war between the two major parties failed. In the end, these opposition parties and their various leagues and associations suffered from most of the problems common to oppositionists at different times in the Republican period: they lacked military backing, territorial bases, and the support of the common people.[40]

Oppositionists Caught in the Middle

In the end, then, these parties and groups existed at the sufferance of the GMD and the CCP. During WWII, circumstances forced the former to tolerate the minor parties. During its climb to power, the CCP pursued a UF policy with these parties, only to crack down on them, after the founding of the PRC, in the Anti-Rightist movement in the late 1950s.

At the end of the Republican period, these men were forced to choose between following the GMD to Taiwan, staying with the CCP on the Mainland, or joining the Chinese diaspora. Those who stuck to the middle way courted the hostility of both sides. In short, there was a polarization of politics, which fostered not only the repression of those who disagreed with one but of those who failed to attack the enemy. In both Taiwan (until recently) and the PRC, as before 1949, the minor parties lived on at the sufferance of the rulers and were financially dependent on them. Hence, in his essay, Seymour concludes that the DPGs' future really depends on how useful the CCP finds them to be.

Conclusion: Prospects for Chinese Democracy

Power in twentieth-century China lay in taking up the gun and mobilizing the peasants. The oppositionists studied here, like many others who could have been included, were manifest failures at both these tasks.

In the end, however, these historical essays wrestle with another question that disturbs some, especially in light of the stunning liberalization in Eastern Europe and the Soviet Union in recent years. As an article in the press put it following the Tiananmen shootings, "deep self-doubt exists in the [Chinese] intellectual psyche about whether Chinese culture is . . . capable of sustaining a democratic society."[41] How can you argue for absolute rights in a repressive China? How can you be a liberal in China? Was treating constitutionalism as something sacred a "Utopian" ideal in China? Did not the very minor nature of the little parties demonstrate clearly for all to see the futility of opposition in twentieth-century China?

At the moment, prospects for the DPGs in the PRC do not seem promising. As Seymour has noted, none of the names of the DPGs--such as "democratic," "peasants and workers," and the like--mean anything. During the 1980s, some thought they were being offered "genuine liberalization," whereas they were really being offered "enhanced window-dressing status." Moreover, there is a gap between the "authentic" rank and file and the "non-authentic" leaders, who often concurrently belong to the CCP. There also are restrictions on who can join the DPGs; they are allowed to function only in large cities; and there is a special branch of the Public Security Bureau in

Beijing charged with responsibility for them (some members were arrested after the June Fourth massacre).[42] Yet, Seymour is reluctant to dismiss these groups out of hand, for, as he argues, they do represent constituencies in China and there are many "enlightened" people in their ranks, as well as in exile.

Meanwhile, as Nathan notes, many of the best democratic activists are in exile in the U.S. or elsewhere, and hence, to some, are "out of the game," even though they may possess the "moral charisma." The dynamic for change in the future may well come from China itself, rather than from those in exile, for this was the pattern in the political liberalization of Taiwan. Yet, Nathan argues that the ODM is still significant, for it lobbies for U.S. support and keeps the spotlight on China's human-rights abuses. Moreover, its members now have the chance to wrestle with the questions of how to implement democracy in China and what kind of democracy it will be. In doing so, he adds, they have a chance to go beyond their predecessors and "do good intellectual work during the time history allots them."

On the Mainland, the regime has continued the policies traced in these essays of repressing the opposition and refusing to countenance democracy. In June 1991, Premier Li Peng stated that China would not follow in the footsteps of the Eastern European Communist parties and adopt a multiparty government. Instead, it would continue with its multiparty "cooperation," in which the eight non-Communist parties are allowed to exist under the leadership of the CCP, without any decision-making power. Appealing once again to the ancient Chinese fear of *luan* (turmoil or disorder), Li predicted a doleful scenario if multiparty government was permitted: "Should China adopt a multiparty system, the country would be thrown into chaos, its economy would decline and its people would once again be thrown into an abyss of misery."[43]

In light of this, Seymour's suggestion that the DPGs may someday serve as "bridges" between a crumbling CCP and the rise of a new order seems problematical; yet who would have predicted the collapse of the Communist regimes in Eastern Europe? Seymour thinks it more likely that new parties will form in response to new situations in China, as has happened with the eclipse by the DPP of the old-line minor parties in Taiwan (the CYP and the DSP) and the failure of the minor parties in elections in Eastern Europe, once their function as bridges had been served. Moreover, today's China is obviously different from that under Mao Zedong. Because of economic pressures and the need for technology, China is much more open. CNN, the BBC, the Voice of America, and the "fax" machine have made it impossible for the PRC to keep its people totally in the dark, as during the Mao Zedong era.

The dismal record of failures during the Republican period and in the PRC is brightened by the advances toward democracy in Taiwan since the lifting of martial law and the ban on other parties over five years ago, as Copper's essay makes clear. The greatest differences with the Mainland are that in Taiwan there are elections, in which parties other than the GMD can participate, and a vibrant opposition press. The appearance of fifty-two minor parties (as of July 1990) is reminiscent of the late 1940s, when nearly one hundred parties and groups were active in China and when the tiny parties described in Ivanov's essay "bloomed and contended" (a period which resembled Hu Shi's concept of a "political kindergarten" at work). The only nagging question concerning Taiwan, in light of China's modern history, is: How far will this process go; what are the limits? Will Taiwan become a model for the democratic evolution of Chinese society?

Some scholars think the answer is yes, while others--dwelling on the GMD record of political intolerance on the Mainland and in Taiwan before the mid-1980s--are not so sanguine.[44] Copper argues in his essay that if conditions are right--i.e., the GMD suffers from factionalism, several of the small parties form a coalition, or the DPP splits, thus benefitting the smaller parties (i.e., the GMD and the DPP weaken or the small parties find a way to strengthen themselves)--the minor parties may do better in the future. He concludes on an ambiguous note: "Thus, the possibilities for the minor parties, while not good, are not bad either. The minor parties seem destined to be around for the time being. However, conditions must change for them to play a significant political role in Taiwan."

According to Zhang Junmai's daughter, in the past the DSP did strive for a broader base in Taiwan, with one member running for mayor of Taibei. However, when they began to run for election in the counties, they were threatened by the GMD. "So, under the circumstances," she concluded in 1990, "I do not see how any opposition party leader could go very far."

Recently, Chinese elsewhere have proved themselves quite capable of selecting democracy, when the choice is theirs to make, supporting the notion of some Republican oppositionists (e.g., the leaders of the CYP and Zhang Junmai) that the way to implement democracy was to simply begin practicing it. In elections in Hong Kong in September 1991, pro-democracy candidates swept to victory over CCP-backed candidates (pro-Beijing candidates lost nearly every race) in that colony's first direct elections for the legislature in 150 years of British colonial rule. "It's been pretty close to a tidal wave for democracy," noted an American historian studying Hong Kong.[45] However, in 1997, Hong Kong--democratic elections or not--will be taken over by the PRC.

In the final analysis, historians are not prophets and only time will tell how democracy will fare in the future China. Despite their failures in this century, perhaps in the long run the democratic faith expressed by many of the TF figures studied in this volume--beliefs which Nathan has termed a "useable past"--will emerge victorious over the dictatorships that have ill served the Chinese people for so long. As Nathan has put it: "Maybe this notion of failure is not so important. I think we are still under the Sinological shadow [see n. 2]. We are still talking too much about the 'bottom line', and maybe it is the discourse that is more important."

Hence, perhaps liberalism is not a failure, and twenty years from now these oppositionists will be remembered in a more positive light than the GMD and the CCP.[46] We hope these essays help to fill the historical vacuum, revive the memory of these figures, and acquaint the present-day democratic activists with their oppositionist forebears. In the final analysis, these figures did not lack courage, to have braved the perils of "being in the middle," and may represent a positive legacy of variety and dynamism. Even though they are not remembered today by the current generation of democratic activists, someday they will receive their due as champions of the same democracy these activists so fervently advocate.

Notes

1. For a selected list of these parties and their romanizations, see the list at the end of this volume. In cases where there is more than one English translation of the party name, I have tried to be as faithful to the original Chinese as possible, while also taking into account the translations accepted by most scholars over the years. For example, *Zhongguo guojia shehui dang* is usually translated as the National Socialist Party of China, and this volume follows this precedent. However, it could also be translated as the "State Socialist Party of China," which at least has the advantage of avoiding that confusion with the National Socialist Party of Germany that plagued the Chinese party for a good part of its lifetime.

2. The dangers of this approach to twentieth-century Chinese history were incisively pointed out in Ramon H. Myers and Thomas A. Metzger, "Sinological Shadows: The State of Modern China Studies in the United States," *The Washington Quarterly*, Spring 1980, 87-114.

3. Most of the articles focus on political parties or individual leaders. However, two deal with "movements": Krebs' study of the anarchists and Coble's essay on the National Salvation Association (which, despite its name, was more of a movement than an organization).

4. See, e.g., Jerome B. Grieder, *Hu Shih and the Chinese Renaissance: Liberalism in the Chinese Revolution, 1917-1937* (Cambridge: Harvard University Press, 1970).

5. The classic study in literature of this phenomenon is Graham Greene's novel, *The Quiet American*.

6. Whether these studies are frank ones is another question. Writing of the recent Chinese translation of Rhoads Murphey's *Shanghai: Key to Modern China* (Cambridge: Harvard University Press, 1953), a Chinese scholar who has spent time in prison noted: "Rarely in China does one read anything so untainted by ideology. We know nothing about our own contemporary history, really, because everything that has happened since the Chinese Communist Party entered the picture has been mythologised. What

passes for history here is not fact, but fiction." "1990 on the Shelf: A Sampler of Asian Booklists for the Past Year," *Far Eastern Economic Review*, 3 January 1991, 26.

7. Laski influenced Luo Longji, Chen Qitian, and Zhang Junmai, for example. Laski is also an example of the dangers of generalizing about Western influences on these Chinese, however. Although a prominent spokesman for individual freedom, he was also an apologist for the Soviet Union in the 1930s. See Paul Hollander, *Political Pilgrims: Travels of Western Intellectuals to the Soviet Union, China, and Cuba, 1928-1978* (New York: Oxford University Press, 1981), 144, 147-49, 342, and 561-62 (n 185).

8. Deng Yanda may have been the exception. In his essay, Olenik argues that Deng rejected traditional Chinese culture. Whether he could free himself totally from its influence (e.g., his continued reliance upon an elite to direct the masses) is another question.

9. Thomas A. Metzger, "Oppositional Politics and the Problem of Secularization in Modern China," Paper presented at the Conference on "Oppositional Politics in Twentieth-Century China," Washington and Lee University, Lexington, Virginia, 20-22 September 1990.

10. Roger B. Jeans, "Chinese Democratic Socialist Party," in *Political Parties of Asia and the Pacific: Afghanistan-Korea (ROK)*, eds. Haruhiro Fukui et al. (Westport, CT.: Greenwood Press, 1985): 213.

11. This should not be taken as a dismissal of their capacity for action, for two of the leaders of the CCP in the 1920s--Chen Duxiu and Qu Qiubai--were also college professors.

12. Olenik argues that Deng would have preferred the world of the intellect in normal times, but the 1920s and 1930s were abnormal; hence, he took the military path. Deng was not the only military man who bridged the worlds of the soldier and scholar in Republican China. Jiang Baili (Chiang Pai-li, Chiang Fang-chen) was another important example. Howard L. Boorman and Richard C. Howard, eds., *Biographical Dictionary of Republican China* (New York: Columbia University Press, 1967): 1:314 (hereafter, *BDRC*).

13. As Krebs points out in his essay, the anarchists resorted on occasion to the terms *dang* (political party) and *pai* (faction or group), but preferred the suffix *zhe* ("one," as in *wuzhengfuzhuyizhe* or "anarchist").

14. Chester C. Tan, *Chinese Political Thought in the Twentieth Century* (Garden City, New York: Anchor Books, 1971), 350.

15. See the biographical sketch of Li Huang in *BDRC*, 2:303, as well as the memoirs of Li and Zuo Shunsheng [Tso Shun-sheng] collected by the Chinese Oral History Project at Columbia University.

16. The CYP may have been the largest party. By the end of 1948, it claimed a membership of 300,000. Chen Qitian, *Jiyuan huiyilu* (The Memoirs of Chen Qitian), enl. 2nd ed. (Taibei: Shangwu yinshuguan, 1972), 306 (cited in n. 1 in Fung's essay in this volume). The China Democratic League had perhaps 100,000 members during its heyday from 1944-1947. Roger B. Jeans, "China Democratic League," in *Political Parties of Asia*, 169.

17. For the prevalence of that attitude in the political approach of another important intellectual of the Republican period, see Charlotte Furth, *Ting Wen-chiang: Science and China's New Culture* (Cambridge: Harvard University Press, 1970).

18. When urged to form a party in the early 1920s, Ding Wenjiang replied that it would be simply too expensive. Financial weakness, he added, had forced parties under the republic to depend upon the government in power for subsidies, and that had weakened them. Ibid., 149-50.

19. Tan, 34.

20. J. Kenneth Olenik, "Young China Party [Chinese Youth Party]," in *Political Parties of Asia*, 263.

21. Leng Shao-chuan has recalled that he saw no evidence in the early 1950s of any influence of the League on Chinese students and teachers in the U.S. According to Leng, he asked Hu Shi then if the League was a viable alternative. Hu replied that Leng was naive, and should just do his teaching and research and not worry about the TF. In the early 1950s, Wellington Koo, the Republic of China's ambassador to the U.S., was advised to report one of the FL leaders, Zhang Junmai, to Taiwan as a "dangerous" figure. If the FL was so harmless, one wonders, why was Zhang considered dangerous?

22. See the sketches of the two parties by Olenik and Jeans in *Political Parties of Asia* (cited above).

23. In arriving at that viewpoint, perhaps some of these figures were influenced by the Confucian virtue of *shu* (reciprocity).

24. For example, Spar points out in his essay on Luo Longji that Luo had character and personality flaws that made him unpopular in some circles.

25. Ironically, the GMD used the same appeals to fame and fortune to split, and thus render harmless, both the DSP and the CYP in the 1950s in Taiwan.

26. Here one recalls Hu Shi and his colleagues' call for "good government," expressed in the pages of *Nuli zhoubao* (The Endeavor) in 1922. Little seemed to have changed in a quarter of a century. "What we call 'good government'," they wrote in a manifesto entitled "Our Political Proposals," "is, in its negative aspect, the existence of proper organs to oversee and protect against all illegal, self-seeking, and madly corrupt officials." Grieder, 191.

27. C. Martin Wilbur, *The Nationalist Revolution in China, 1923-1928* (Cambridge: Cambridge University Press, 1984), 112.

28. Stefan B. Polter, "Jiusan Society," in *Political Parties in Asia*, 240.

29. Fung argues that, lacking access to the country's military, economic, or financial resources, the CYP had to make use of the "loyal opposition" approach.

30. Metzger, "Oppositional Politics and the Problem of Secularization in Modern China."

31. For a concise analysis of Sun's ideas, see Tan, chap. 5.

32. Ibid., 126-27. Sun's right-hand man, the abrasive GMD theoretician Hu Hanmin, made it clear that there was no place for individualism nor natural rights in a China governed by the Three People's Principles. Individuals were granted rights by society, he argued, and hence only those rights supporting the welfare of society and the existence of the nation should be recognized by law. Ibid., 202.

33. The NSA was a true TF, for in addition to being persecuted by the GMD, the organization was dissolved by order of the CCP in December 1949. Lyman P. Van Slyke, *Enemies and Friends: The United Front in Chinese Communist History* (Stanford: Stanford University Press, 1967), 211-12.

34. Tan, 246-248, 273.

35. Ibid., 349.

36. Lloyd E. Eastman, *China Under Nationalist Rule: Two Essays*, Illinois Papers in Asian Studies No. 1 (Urbana: Center for Asian Studies, University of Illinois, 1980), 27.

37. Tan., 163.

38. Ibid., 163-64.

39. Ibid, 214-15.

40. Moreover, living in landlocked Sichuan, they were even denied the traditional sanctuaries for those pursued by Chinese governments, the foreign concessions in the treaty ports (although the war eventually brought an end to these).

41. *The New York Times*, 7 May 1989, 3.

42. Leng Shao-chuan has expressed more optimism than Seymour concerning the prospects of the DPGs. Leng has urged that people pay attention to the "Young Turks" in the DL, who made some progress in obtaining better treatment from the CCP when Hu Yaobang and Zhao Ziyang were in charge. If the minor parties have good leadership, he has argued, they could have an impact. If the Chinese regime follows the path of change the Soviet Union has taken, then these parties will have "an important role to play in the future." If China, on the contrary, follows the East European path and overthrows the Communist regime, then the minor parties, due to their association with the regime, will not play much of a role. The danger, one might add, is that the closer the minor parties get to the CCP, the harder it may be to sell their case to the public.

43. "Chinese Premier Rejects Multiparty System," *Roanoke Times and World News*, 15 June 1991, A9.

44. It was more than twenty years, for example, before Zhang Junmai's writings were published in Taiwan, and then only in censored form. Leng Shao-chuan has suggested that a third party (in addition to the GMD and the DPP) might arise in Taiwan from a non-mainstream faction of the GMD. Many Taiwan press people, he noted, favored such a party, and some supported the notion that a dissatisfied group in the GMD might split off to establish such an organization.

45. "Communists Lose in Hong Kong," *The Seattle Times*, 15 September 1991, A2. The drawback in the elections, according to this article and television reports, was that less than 40 percent of the eligible voters cast ballots.

46. One scholar has asserted that in five hundred years the Chinese will have their own version of democracy, i.e., there would be a "Sinification of democracy" (an argument which echoes Communist claims that Mao Zedong and the CCP "Sinified" Marxism).

PART ONE

Opposition Party Intellectuals in the 1920s and 1930s

1

The Trials of a Third-Force Intellectual: Zhang Junmai (Carsun Chang) During the Early Nanjing Decade, 1927-1931

Roger B. Jeans

Introduction

In March 1927, the National Revolutionary Army (NRA) entered Shanghai. Less than a month later, the Guomindang (GMD) carried out the bloody purge of the Chinese Communists in that port city. The fate of the Communists is well known to Western historians. Less frequently mentioned (except in the memoirs of the victims) are the concurrent purges of other opponents of the new GMD regime.

One of those foes was Zhang Junmai (1887-1969), better known to Western historians as Carsun Chang, a professor, university president, journalist, and long-time follower of Liang Qichao. Although rarely mentioned in Western histories of twentieth-century China, he was a well-known figure in Chinese political and intellectual circles from the 1920s through the 1940s.

This essay is a study of the fate of this liberal intellectual during the early Nanking Decade (1927-1931). His story was not unique; a number of liberal intellectuals had experiences similar to his at the beginning of the Nanjing period. Moreover, like him, some of them later became leaders of minor parties, as the Nanjing era wore on. Yet, during this era for the first time a modern one-party dictatorship claimed to rule China. Hence, the question arises: how did the modern educated elite fare? Many, of course, made their peace with the new regime and served it (including Zhang's own brother, Zhang Jiaao, better known as Chang Kia-ngau). Others, frequently influenced by their admiration for Western democracy and constitutionalism, opposed it, which almost invariably brought them hardships. It was to this latter group that Zhang belonged.

In this article, I have attempted to portray his "third force" (TF) position by describing his clash with the Reorganized GMD in 1927, as well as his strong opposition to both Chinese and Soviet Communism. I then examine his struggle for survival from 1927-1929, which partly took the form of cooperation with another persecuted group, the Chinese Youth Party (CYP).[1] The essay ends with his mysterious kidnapping, which convinced him that Shanghai was too dangerous, and his second period of exile in Germany during the period 1929-1931.

This study is an attempt to restore to the pages of history the story of one politically active scholar during the early Nanjing Decade, in hopes that it will give flesh and bones to abstractions about "persecuted intellectuals" under GMD rule. Since Zhang's fate was all too common among his generation of scholars, his story serves as a case study of the fate of these men at this pivotal moment in China's modern history.

First Clash with Chiang Kai-shek and the Reorganized GMD, 1926-1927

By 1927, Zhang had a long history of opposition to the GMD. A disciple of Liang Qichao since 1906, he maintained a healthy suspicion of the GMD through the quarter of a century that followed.[2] This historic, mutual hostility between the Liang group and the GMD finally exploded in the spring of 1927, when the Northern Expedition's NRA reached Shanghai.[3]

Believing, like a good Confucianist, that education was a (if not *the*) fundamental approach to saving the nation, Zhang founded a school in Shanghai in the fall of 1923. Dubbed the National Institute of Self-Government (*Guoli Zizhi Xueyuan*), it was founded with the approval of the civil governor of Jiangsu, Han Guojun, who may also have contributed to its funding.[4] Initial support also was provided by Shi Liangcai, the publisher of *Shen bao* ("The Shun Pao") and a native of Jiangsu.[5]

The school itself was a result of Zhang's involvement in the federalist movement in the early 1920s. When the movement evaporated, he retreated to his native province to pursue self-government on a smaller and more manageable scale.[6] Initially set up in the French Concession, in 1925 the school changed its name to the National Institute of Political Science (*Guoli*

Zhengzhi Daxue) and moved to a new site in Wusong, thanks in part to financial support from the new ruler of Shanghai, the warlord Sun Chuanfang.[7] A number of the school's professors and students were to join the National Socialist Party of China (NSP) during the early 1930s.[8]

When the NRA reached Shanghai in the spring of 1927, it cracked down on Zhang and his school. Not only had he been a thorn in the side of the GMD for years, in November 1926, only four months prior to the arrival of the GMD, he published views in the press (based on a clandestine visit to GMD-occupied Wuhan) critical of the GMD and the Northern Expedition.[9] His report also revealed some ambiguity about that party, which may have been responsible for tensions between him and his lifelong mentor, Liang Qichao. He clearly approved, for example, of the GMD's successes against the Beiyang warlords (even though one of his sponsors, Sun Chuanfang, was a Beiyang warlord!). He also expressed admiration for the GMD's clear and pervasive ideology, politicized and well-behaved army, and skill at obtaining the support of the populace. "The Guomindang's strong points are courage and boldness in action," he wrote, "and it is especially good at arousing the masses." Moreover, he confessed, "Our admiration for the party-army (*dang jun*) may be called extreme."

There was nothing about these views to arouse the enmity of the GMD. However, he went on to criticize his old rivals for their intolerance of different views and doctrines, reliance upon force and one-party dictatorship, "partyization" (*danghua*) of education, and incorporation into their ranks of the former warlords. Fearing that the old-style dictatorship would be replaced by a new-style one, he expressed his belief in natural rights (making him a rare bird indeed in twentieth-century China, according to Andrew Nathan [10]) and issued an impassioned appeal for "true freedom" and "true democracy." Wuhan's leaders, he lamented, considered important only the "propagandizing of party principles" and "rallies." They had "no idea how to open up and channel the underground springs of democracy."

As a result of his observations in Wuhan, he knew what to expect if the NRA took Shanghai. He cited various GMD regulations which called for the banning of private schools and the "partyization" of education. It was quite clear, he wrote, that education under the GMD would be "subordinate to the politics of political parties and groups." At the least, private schools would be required to register with the government, and the party would have the final say in the curricula.[11] He was right, for later on the teaching of GMD principles was made a part of university curricula.[12]

During the winter of 1926-27, he sat in Shanghai and awaited the outcome of the struggle between the revolutionaries and Sun Chuanfang. As it became clear that the former were winning, his mood turned desperate. Writing (in German) on 1 March 1927 to his old friend, the German Sinologist Richard Wilhelm, he reported that all of South China was then under the control of the Nationalist Regime, with "Party rule ... the first principle of all administration." Fearing for the future of his school, upon which he had lavished so much attention since 1923, he complained that the Nationalists wanted to "convert all institutes of learning to party purposes. Academic freedom no longer exists." Expressing sentiments quite similar to those he voiced on the eve of the Communist take-over of China more than twenty years later, he continued:

> Under these conditions, I cannot cooperate. I am thinking of emigrating.... I shall be bringing my wife and baby along and, if possible, staying outside China forever. You can imagine how the situation is in China. Dear Friend, I am being serious about everything I am telling you.[13]

Three weeks later (22 March), the NRA entered Shanghai. As a member of the Progressive Party and the Research Clique, which had opposed the GMD in the past, and an associate of Liang Qichao, a leading opponent of the revolutionaries, there was no way Zhang could avoid being labelled a "reactionary." Moreover, as a leader of the CYP later recalled, to be "non-revolutionary (*bugeming*)," during the first GMD-CCP United Front (UF) (1923-27), was to be "counterevolutionary (*fangeming*)."[14]

According to a former student at Zhang's institute, at first the GMD gave him a chance to come around to its point of view. A party official was sent to his school to order him to incorporate the Three People's Principles into the curriculum as a required subject. Perhaps predictably, he refused, and the school was closed.[15] The GMD Municipal Party Headquarters placed its seal on the gate,[16] and the institute's funds and library were confiscated.[17]

Things became worse for him when the Shanghai Municipal Government issued a warrant for his arrest as a "dissident (*yiji*)."[18] In addition to his connections with Liang and his refusal to accept Sun Yat-sen's teachings as Holy Writ, his relationship with the enemy of the revolution, Beiyang warlord Sun Chuanfang, did not endear him to the GMD. According to a leader of the CYP, Chiang Kai-shek "refused to tolerate anyone having connections with militarists," and later had Zhang's old friend, Jiang Baili, arrested for his connections with Sun Chuanfang and Wu Peifu.[19]

With his livelihood gone, a family to support,[20] and facing arrest, Zhang retreated into the world of scholarship. Settling down in his home on Seymour Road in the International Settlement, he devoted himself to translation and writing. His major project was a translation of Harold Laski's *A Grammar of Politics*, for which he received two hundred *yuan* a month from the Commercial Press. Even scholarship carried out in the relative safety of the International Settlement was not free from the long reach of the GMD, however. He related what happened after he agreed to write an ABC of political science for the World Bookstore's ABC Collected Works:

> Unexpectedly, after the publication of the advertisement, the bookstore received notification from the Shanghai Municipal Party Headquarters of the Guomindang order to burn the plates. The bookstore, assuming that the [foreign] concessions still existed, ignored it [the order] and did not reply. Several months later, the Chief Justice of the Shanghai Provisional Court, Wu Jingxiong, received an order from Party Headquarters commanding him to close the World Bookstore. Wu was my friend and immediately came to see me and report what had happened. I said: "The book has not yet been written. How [can the bookstore] obey and destroy the plates?" Later, the bookstore came to an agreement with the Party Headquarters, and the affair then ended.[21]

The ramifications of the incident did not stop there, however. Like others who had displeased the GMD, he was forced to shield himself against persecution by adopting a pseudonym:

> The Commercial Press heard of the affair and then asked Mr. Yu Songhua to inform me: you cannot use your real name for the [Laski] book you are translating. At the time, I depended on this [work] for [my] livelihood. [Hence,] I did not even dare to insist on the freedom to use my own name. Therefore, I changed [it] to "Zhang Shilin." I selected the *shi* from the top of *jia* and the *lin* from the foot of *sen*, i.e., from my name, Jia-sen. This was the pain I suffered because there was no freedom of the press.[22]

Opposition to Communism

Like many of his fellow intellectuals in China, during the May Fourth period Zhang became a socialist largely in hopes of avoiding a feared social revolution.[23] As a result of his sojourn in Europe, 1919-1921, he became an admirer of German Social Democracy as the preferred model for China.[24] At the same time, he became a lifelong anti-communist. This was partly a result of his contact with German Social Democrats, from whom he heard about the activities of the Communist Party.[25] It also was due to his studies of Soviet Communism during his stay in Europe.[26] More dramatically, in 1921 he witnessed an abortive Communist uprising in Germany.[27] Hence, on the eve of his return to China, he declared that "the system of proletarian dictatorship is emphatically not suitable for our country."[28]

Following his arrival in China in 1922, he clashed with the Chinese Communists.[29] He was alarmed by the Sun-Joffe Agreement of January

1923 and opposed the Soviet-GMD-CCP UF that ensued.[30] In particular, he blamed Sun Yat-sen for the "worship" of the Soviet Union and for the GMD-CCP alliance, and ridiculed him as "just like a boy playing with fire."[31] He later claimed he met the Soviet Ambassador, Lev M. Karakhan, but was "unable to detect any sincerity, on the part of the Soviet Union, regarding China."[32]

When he returned from Europe, he recalled, Chen Duxiu's group had become very powerful. He wanted nothing to do with it, however, and "determined to oppose Marxism my entire life."[33] He derided Chen, the general secretary of the CCP, terming his claim to be a member of the working class "really childish and ridiculous."[34]

His criticism of the Communists was amply reciprocated by the CCP. Chen Duxiu "cursed" him, in the pages of the CCP journal, *Xiangdao zhoubao* (The Guide Weekly), as "Master Zhang" (*Zhang laoyeh*)."[35] In late 1923, during the course of the "Debate over Science and a Philosophy of Life," Chen used a Marxist point of view to attack Zhang's contributions to the polemic.[36] In reply, Zhang questioned how those "such as Chen..., who still observe Marx's theories as if [they were] classics...," could be seeking truth. "I say that it is [merely] a political scheme and Moscow's orders!" Chen's motive in participating in the debate, he declared, was not to establish a new kind of theory but only to "promote social revolution."[37]

In view of this vehement opposition to Communism, it was not surprising that when he founded his school in Shanghai, he warned his students about the dangers of that modern "ism." Each week, he later recalled, he taught a class in which he criticized Marxism.[38] At the end of each year, those lectures were compiled into a volume.[39]

In 1924, when the UF between the GMD and the CCP was just beginning, he pleaded for democracy and the rule of law in China, in opposition to "those who support communism in China," as well as those who regarded "dictatorship ... as a kind of ideal and prayed for its realization." In a slap at the CCP, which argued for "liberation" during the May Fourth era, he wrote: "How can those who are described as loving freedom not raise the masses and enable them to progress together, but, on the contrary, pray for the appearance of a government by heroes?" In his view, the Communists' practice was just the opposite of what they preached.[40]

By the time of his clash with the GMD in 1927, then, he was bitterly opposed to the Communists, as well as the GMD. In view of his opposition to the GMD-CCP UF, it is doubtful he shed any tears over the rupturing of that alliance when, on 12 April, Chiang Kai-shek and the GMD launched a purge of the Communists in Shanghai. Zhang later recalled that Chiang "won the cooperation of the Chief of the Blue [Green] Gang, Tu Yueh-sen [Du Yuesheng], in his project of disarming the Communists in Shanghai where they were just then making preparations to attack the Shanghai Settlement.... after the Shanghai massacre of April, 1927 ... the Kuomintang [GMD] and the Communists definitely broke with each other."[41] It is unlikely that Zhang's constantly reiterated beliefs in natural rights, freedom, and democracy extended to the CCP.

In fact, at the time of the break between the GMD and the CCP, he seemed to see the anti-Communist GMD and the CCP as equally bad. "Although the Nanking Regime declares itself anti-communist," he wrote to Wilhelm, "it nevertheless intends to subject China to a party dictatorship." Hence, instead of cheering the GMD for attacking the Communists, he saw nothing but continued warfare in China. In July, he complained: "The war between Nanking and Hankow has begun, and Chiang Kai-shek has ceased marching north. One no longer hears anything about political reconstruction."[42]

Despite the fact that the CCP had been routed by the end of 1927, he kept up his criticism of Communism. In December, while still a refugee--ironically, like his foes, the Chinese Communists--in the International Settlement, he published a sustained attack on the Soviet Union entitled *SuE pinglun* (A Critique of Soviet Russia).[43] As in the case of his translation of Laski's work, he had to resort to a pseudonym in order to avoid the GMD censors. This time, however, he used "Master of the World Chamber" (*Shijie shi zhuren*). Although, unlike his careful explication of his other pseudonym (Zhang Shilin), he never explained his choice, it seems evident that it was a reference to his interest in foreign affairs. This work was published before his translation of the Laski volume. Zhang later stated that it was actually drafted during 1926.[44] Hence, it is possible that it was derived from his anti-Marxist lectures at the Institute of Political Science.

It also is possible that the immediate background for the work was a debate that erupted in Beijing academic circles in October 1925. Focused on the question of whether Russia was China's friend, it attracted the participation of such luminaries as Zhang's mentor, Liang Qichao; his archopponent in the "Science and Metaphysics" polemic, Ding Wenjiang; Hu Shiqing, who later became one of the founding members of the NSP; and Li Huang, a leader of the CYP who became one of Zhang's closest friends in adversity during 1927-28. Although Zhang was then in Shanghai, the articles generated by the debate were published in at least three newspapers.[45] Given the participants and his lifelong inability to avoid a good intellectual fray, this debate may have stimulated the drafting of *SuE pinglun*.

In any event, he made clear his intentions in writing the work:

> Since 1918, those sojourning in Europe all have realized that the Soviet Russian system is absolutely not worthy of emulation. Unexpectedly, the Communist movement has been able to gain influence in our country. This

> book has been written to demonstrate that the actual situation in Russia is the complete opposite of [that portrayed] in its overseas propaganda.... The Russians' willingness to sacrifice for the peoples of the world is admirable. However, the price they have paid is too great. Therefore, the author does not dare to treat Russia with the appreciative attitude of the artist, and also expects that [his] countrymen will not regard weighty national affairs as experimental objects in Russia's political laboratory. In sum, every day more people are studying foreign affairs; hence, every day there is less uncritical copying of others.[46]

As one might expect from this preface, as well as the previous views he had expressed regarding Communism, his analysis of the Soviets was not favorable. In describing the adoption of the New Economic Policy, he was struck by the fact that, after all the slaughter of the years of revolution, they had ended up right back where they had began, in economic terms. Moreover, the constitution was a joke. The terror and intraparty struggles were repulsive. Running through his entire analysis was the fear that his countrymen did not comprehend Soviet Russia. He clearly hoped that, as a result of his study, "those who sing the praises of Communism may see the light."[47]

Flirtation with the Chinese Youth Party, 1928-1929

Throughout his life, Zhang was never content to be an "armchair scholar." Hence, he was ready, when the opportunity presented itself in the fall and winter of 1927-1928, to plunge back into the world of political activism. It was Li Huang who helped to give him new hope in the efficacy of political action, and the close relationship between Zhang and the CYP that began at this time lasted until the end of his days.

Li arrived in Shanghai in October 1927. Earlier that year, he lost his professorship at the National Sichuan University. Moreover, the GMD had issued a warrant for the arrest of his "counterrevolutionary nationalist group." Hence, he feared for his safety and, like Zhang, ended up in the International Settlement, where he took charge of the CYP as acting chairman. Again, as in Zhang's case, living in the foreign concessions did not guarantee safety. Hence, Li recalled, "I was forced to hide in the daytime and work at night." Thus, he felt "quite isolated and lonely." It is not surprising that when the two dejected scholars met, they took comfort in each other's company.

Zhang had already read some of Li's writings and knew Zeng Qi, the chairman of the CYP. Moreover, Zhang's and Li's situations and outlooks were similar: both were under heavy pressure from the GMD and both were anti-communist. In addition, the CYP's headquarters was near Zhang's home, making it easy for the two to get together "repeatedly."[48] He also met Zuo Shunsheng, another leader of the CYP, at this time,[49] and it was proposed that a new party be formed with Zeng as chairman and Zhang, vice-chairman. However, due to Zeng's "stubborn personal opinions," the project fell through.[50]

Xin Lu Magazine

Zhang and Li successfully cooperated, however, in establishing a new journal, *Xin lu*, which attacked both the GMD and the CCP, and thus adopted a TF position. In fact, Zhang's work with the journal may be viewed as a "way station" between his earlier involvement in Liang Qichao's groups and the formation of the NSP in the early 1930s. Some of the proposals in the twelve-point program which appeared in the first issue of the journal, published on 1 February 1928, also had been broached in his work, *Guo xian yi* (Suggestions on the National Constitution), published in the early 1920s, and some would continue to appear in his writings and political party programs throughout the remainder of the Republican period.

On the positive side, the journal advocated democracy, civil rights, independence and equality of the nation, unification in accordance with the spirit of self-government, development of production and improvement of the lives of the peasants and workers, advancement of China's national culture and development of the scientific spirit, implementation of a budget and financial unification, education of sound citizens, establishment of a system for the protection of civil servants, complete independence of the judiciary, use of the army for national defense, and an emphasis on peaceful reconstruction in national progress. On the negative side, it declared its opposition to monarchy and one-class and one-party dictatorships; foreign aggression and all actions that sold out and wronged the nation; deprivation of human rights in the name of political party or military rule; unification through military subjugation; class struggle and other movements that hindered economic development; completely indiscriminate conservatism, as well as uncritical pursuit of the new; the lack of a budget and the imposition on the people of illegal taxes; church and "partyized" education; the arbitrary appointment and removal of government personnel; the "partyization" of the judiciary and excessive use of military law in trying people; the use of the army in private or political party disputes; and destructive revolution.[51]

According to Li, he and Zhang were the main contributors to the journal. Zhang undertook to raise funds for it, while Li took responsibility for its publication. Zhang concentrated on attacking the GMD's political tutelage, while Li focused his fire on the CCP. The magazine seems to have been quite successful; according to Li, circulation rose to three thousand copies, with some read in the concessions while others were smuggled out by "covert dispatches." Just as in the case of his books, though, Zhang was forced to resort to a pseudonym in order to avoid immediate banning of the journal. Hence, he used "Li Zhai," while Li used "Chun Mu." However, people eventually identified them. Hence, after *Xin lu* had published ten issues, the GMD banned it. The GMD had all the cards, according to Li: "Since it was not easy to mail and the print shop did not dare print it any longer, it was then forced to cease publication."[52]

The CYP's Zhixing Institute

Again confronted with the problem of livelihood (ironically, the third of Sun Yat-sen's Three People's Principles) after the publication of the last issue of *Xin lu* on 1 December 1928, Zhang once again became an editor of the Shanghai paper, *Shishi xinbao* (The China Times).[53]

As an indication of his continuing interest in political involvement, in the spring of 1929 he volunteered to teach without pay at the Zhixing Institute, a school affiliated with the CYP and located in the International Settlement. Founded by Li Huang, it was designed as a training institution for CYP cadre. The students were drawn from the CYP's national membership, and the curriculum included party-training courses.

Significantly, according to Li, the name meant "to know is to be able to act."[54] Hence, it echoed the famous Ming Dynasty philosopher, Wang Yangming, who argued that "knowledge is the beginning of action, and action is the completion of knowledge."[55] It also was reminiscent of Sun Yat-sen's attempted rebuttal of Wang. Sun blamed Wang's concept for China's failure to implement Sun's program. According to Sun, Wang's doctrine had fostered the idea that "to know is easy and to act is difficult." Sun argued for a reversal of the concept--declaring that "it is easy to act but difficult to know"--in hopes that the Chinese would then act, rather than conclude that "there is nothing that can be done in this world...."[56] Hence, at one and the same time, the name of the school carried overtones of traditionalism, as well as flaunting Sun Yat-sen's attacks on it.

More important for Zhang, Li also saw the school as a place for his friends, who were being suppressed by the GMD, to teach. The teaching load was only two hours a week, and they would have more freedom of speech than if they taught in the public or private universities.[57] On one occasion, Zhang recalled that he taught political thought and, on another, that he gave classes in political science;[58] according to Li Huang, Zhang taught the history of European political thought.[59]

Like *Xin lu*, this school embodied cooperation between the CYP and some of the intellectuals who founded the NSP in the early 1930s. Six of the fourteen professors who took up posts at the institute--Zhang Junmai, Zhang Dongsun, Zhu Qinglai, Pan Guangdan, Liang Shiqiu, and Luo Longji--later participated in the establishment of the NSP.[60] Most of the other faculty members seem to have been members of the CYP.

The Kidnapping, June 1929

Zhang was not present when, due to changed circumstances, the institute closed in the summer of 1930.[61] By that time, he was in exile in Germany, and his path there reveals much about the uncertainties of life in Shanghai in the late 1920s. One of those uncertainties was the threat of kidnapping. In mid-June 1929, he was seized and held for three weeks, before being ransomed.[62] He later recalled the circumstances:

> One afternoon at five o'clock, I gave a lecture [at the Zhixing Institute]. At 7:00 P.M., I [set out] on foot to return home. When I got to the intersection of *Jingan Si* Road, two gangsters suddenly forced me into an automobile. They stepped on my back with both feet and prevented me from making a sound. After travelling for twenty to thirty minutes, [I] was imprisoned in a room. Everyday the so-called chief of staff (*canmouzhangzhe*) came at 10:00 P.M. and made me kneel on a chain of iron rings. Furthermore, he asked: what is your purpose in running a school in Shanghai in opposition to the Guomindang? I replied that I considered this a political problem. I was unable to explain it there. It would be better to escort me to Nanjing, and I myself could explain the reasons. Everyday four men guarded me in the room, without resting day and night. [They] blindfolded me, [but] every morning I heard the sound of a bugle and realized that the place in which I was staying was in the vicinity of the Wusong-Shanghai Garrison Command. At that time, Zhang Taiyan [Binglin], Du Yuesheng, and others came to my rescue. My eighth brother [Jiazhu] negotiated with the kidnappers, only then learning that the Shanghai Garrison Command had conspired with the kidnappers to embarass me. The two sides published an advertisement in *Shen bao* offering an antique vase for sale as a way of negotiating a ransom. After negotiations, the ransom was set at three thousand, and I gained my release. When I emerged, first I was driven by car in several circles and then abandoned by the roadside. I returned home by rickshaw. I asked the puller what place this was, and he replied: Longhua. [That] was the location of the Garrison Command. Several days later, a fortune-teller told me: you have escaped with your life from the bottom of a coffin.[63]

Throughout his days, he clung to the belief that it was the Shanghai Garrison Command that kidnapped him.[64] Zuo Shunsheng agreed that the

GMD was responsible, adding that Zhang was "not the Kuomintang's only victim.... Our [CYP] comrades were kidnapped too."[65]

In an interview a half-century later, however, Jiazhu, the younger brother who handled the negotiations for Zhang's release, rejected his brother's belief that the culprit was the GMD. It had been, he asserted, simply a kidnapping for ransom. The kidnappers demanded money; yet, when he repeatedly sent payments, they claimed he had not and threatened to cut off Zhang's ears. Finally, Jiazhu got in touch with some gangsters and paid them, with opium purchased from a hotel, to act as middlemen. Ten days later, Zhang was released, although with a leg injury that left him limping for the remainder of his life.[66]

The exact truth of this tragic episode in Zhang's life may never be known. It is possible, however, that both Zhang and Jiazhu were correct, i.e., Zhang was kidnapped by gangsters working for the GMD. It is well documented that Chiang Kai-shek and his party resorted to kidnapping for ransom in order to raise funds for the regime.[67] Kidnapping of wealthy Chinese, sanctioned by the authorities, was a common occurrence in Shanghai in the late 1920s.[68] The gangsters may have been used because it was difficult for the GMD to operate freely in the International Settlement.[69]

The specific setting for Zhang's kidnapping may have been the clash between GMD headquarters and the business community in Shanghai during the spring of 1929. The target of the GMD attack was the Shanghai General Chamber of Commerce.[70] In May 1929, Zhang's brother, Jiaao, then head of the Bank of China and thus an important member of the Shanghai business community, left China for nearly a year.[71] He may have done so in order to escape being kidnapped; a number of wealthy Shanghai citizens fled the city in 1928 when the renewed Northern Expedition led to another wave of kidnappings for ransom.[72] The GMD, foiled by Jiaao's departure, may have seized Junmai as a way of tapping the resources his brother commanded as head of the Bank of China.

The final mystery concerns the role of Du Yuesheng, the Green Gang (*Qing Bang*) leader whom Chang credited (along with Zhang Taiyan) with his release. The Green Gang was known for its involvement in kidnapping and opium-dealing.[73] After money failed to win his brother's release, Jiazhu used opium to purchase the assistance of some gangsters. Since opium was the latter's main source of income, the cash may have gone to the GMD and the opium to the Green Gang, thus satisfying Zhang's kidnappers.

Finally, the kidnapping of Zhang may have had its political edge. It finally allowed the GMD to strike at a man whom they had wanted to arrest for the past two years. Moreover, this was someone who had compounded his earlier sins by becoming a mainstay of the anti-GMD journal, *Xin lu*.

Their views on such "counterrevolutionaries" certainly had not changed. In late March 1929, the director of the special GMD headquarters in Shanghai issued an official warning against "counterevolutionary" activities, defining "counterrevolutionaries" as "all those who oppose the Three Principles of the People."[74]

The Second Exile in Europe, 1929-1931

Escape to Manchuria

Regardless of the truth of his kidnapping, it was clear that even the International Settlement could not protect Zhang while he lived in Shanghai. Years later he wrote that it was "too difficult to live in safety in Shanghai...."[75] Hence, in the fall of 1929, after his leg wound healed, he travelled to Shenyang, where he stayed with the family of Luo Wengan,[76] a well-known figure who served both the Beijing and Nanjing governments before retiring from government service in 1935.[77] Zhang and Luo had first become acquainted while the latter was in jail in Beijing, 1922-1924,[78] and remained friends until Luo's death in 1941 during the War of Resistance. During the 1930s, Luo became a member of the NSP.[79]

At the time of Zhang's visit to Shenyang, Luo was a councillor in the headquarters of the Northeast Peace Preservation Forces, serving under the Young Marshall, Zhang Xueliang.[80] The famous diplomat, Wellington V.K. Koo, recalled that Luo was one of the "highest advisers to the Young Marshall...."[81] Another of Zhang Xueliang's advisers, the Australian, William Henry Donald, remembered Luo as "a personal friend of the Young Marshall's...."[82] This close relationship, along with the NSP's call for resistance to Japan following the Mukden Incident, may explain why the Young Marshall later became one of the financial supporters of the NSP.[83]

Zhang may have had another motive for travelling to Manchuria at that time. He had been interested in Russian policy toward China since 1912, when he protested its actions concerning Outer Mongolia.[84] The latest manifestation of that concern had been the publication of *SuE pinglun* less than two years earlier. Hence, while in Manchuria, he took the opportunity to observe the Sino-Soviet War, which had broken out over the issue of control of the Chinese Eastern Railway (CER). On 10 July, the Chinese authorities in Heilongjiang had seized the CER from the Soviets. When a Soviet ultimatum demanding a return to the *status quo ante* went unsatisfied, war erupted between the Soviets and Zhang Xueliang's troops in August. The fighting lasted until late December, when Chinese and Soviet representatives concluded the Khabarovsk Protocol, restoring the pre-July 10 status of the CER. The Soviets then withdrew their troops from Manchuria.[85] During his stay in Manchuria, Zhang travelled to the Suifen River in Manzhouli to observe the course of the war. He must have wondered if he was any safer there than in Shanghai, for on the day following his visit, the Soviets bombed the Suifen Railway Station.[86]

In addition to the need to flee the dangerous situation in Shanghai, the presence of his friend Luo Wengan, and the opportunity to observe the clash between China and the Soviet Union, his friendship with leaders of the CYP may have played a role in his decision to visit Manchuria. The CYP had a connection with Zhang Xueliang, and in September 1929 held their Fourth Congress in Shenyang, where the group formally adopted the name "Chinese Youth Party."[87] In addition, the party had a sizeable following in the Northeast Army (*Dongbei Jun*), as Zhang's army was called. It was even said that "the Northeast Army is not the army of the northeast but of the Chinese Youth Party." In 1933, however, Zhang purged his army of members of the CYP and, as a result, more than six hundred middle and low grade officers were expelled.[88]

Exile in Germany

Whatever Zhang's reasons for going to Manchuria, he did not linger. For over two years, he had been deeply interested in going to Germany, where he had lived on two previous occasions. It was apparently his old friend Wilhelm who finally made it possible. In 1925, Wilhelm founded the China-Institut in Frankfurt as a center for academic and cultural exchange. During the Nanjing Decade, it served as one of the vehicles for a close Sino-German relationship.[89]

Anxious about the approach of the Northern Expedition, in March 1927 Zhang wrote to Wilhelm that he was thinking of emigrating. "I shall be happy to do research in Germany," he declared. "Would it be possible for me to make my knowledge of China in general and Chinese philosophy in particular useful at any German university?... I hope you will be of assistance to me on this question."[90] Evidently, Wilhelm was encouraging, for in July Zhang declared his willingness to "temporarily give up all hopes of becoming politically active in China" if his plan to go to Germany succeeded.[91] After some further exchange of correspondence, in 1929 the trip finally became a reality.

As he later recalled, he was "compelled" to leave China.[92] Perhaps as a way of getting out, he told Wilhelm that he would be glad to serve as China's representative at the "Conference of the Peace Society."[93] As for funds, Zhang's banker brother, Jiaao, was abroad at the time. Hence, Zhang recalled, "Through Luo Wengan, I borrowed seven hundred *yuan* from Zhang Xueliang and purchased a steamer ticket to Germany."[94] There also may have been aid from the China-Institut, for in an earlier letter to Wilhelm, Zhang begged his friend to tell him if "his connection with your institute is a financial burden," adding that he was awaiting Wilhelm's "frank answer."[95]

Although he began his stay at the China-Institut,[96] and also may have lectured on Chinese philosophy in Berlin,[97] he later recalled that he went to Germany to "earn my living as a [visiting] Professor of Philosophy at the University of Jena,"[98] where he had spent some time during 1920-1921 studying with the philosopher, Rudolf Eucken.[99] Although he and his family were apparently not well off during their stay in Germany, this period has been termed the happiest and most peaceful part of his life since childhood.[100]

While in Germany, he devoted himself to philosophical studies. From China, he had written Wilhelm of his desire to publish books on Chinese philosophy and the history of Buddhism.[101] He also expressed interest in German Sinology, as well as his old love, European philosophy.[102] Although he did not publish any monographs, he did find time, during his two years in Germany, to write several lengthy articles on the history of Chinese philosophy, in which he praised such Neo-Confucianists as Zhu Xi, Lu Xiangshan, and Wang Yangming, as well as such European thinkers as Immanuel Kant.[103] He also wrote on the fate of Chinese tradition in the modern world, approaching the question through a consideration of the current standing of the Classics.[104]

He was in a reflective mood, after his trials of the past few years. "Does China," he asked, "still have faith in tradition?" The country had gone through a lot during the past three decades, he mused: the 1898 Reform Movement, the 1911 Revolution, and the "1927 Communist danger." Now it had begun to turn back to "self-reflection." The fate of tradition was directly related to politics. Following constitutional reform in Japan, he noted, Confucianism was studied and highly esteemed. Since the Japanese were content with the political situation, they respected the bearers of their own culture. From this he drew the logical conclusion: "Someday, when China becomes a stable Republic, the attack on Confucianism will ... cease."[105]

Despite his desire to take refuge in quiet academic study, he could not get politics nor the desire to run his own school again out of his mind. According to Li Huang, Zhang often wrote to him from Germany. "[He] said," reported Li, "that regardless of whether [we] operated a political party, it was our duty to train youth with genuine knowledge so they would have the ability to work for the future of the nation."[106] He also retained interest in another of his lifelong pursuits, constitutionalism. During the same year that he was worrying about the state of tradition in China, he also was expressing anxiety about what he called "The Constitutional Crisis in the Republic of China."[107]

It was a combination of his interest in education and philosophy that brought him back into the political strife of China after an absence of two years. In 1931, John Leighton Stuart, the president of Yenching University, cabled and invited him to teach the philosophy of Hegel.[108] As a private university, Yenching had been spared the degree of political control the GMD had established over the national universities, like Qinghua and Beijing. During the 1920s, it had engaged in a drive to add more Chinese professors to the faculty. Moreover, it had a reputation for excellence.[109]

These reasons, as well as the presence of his old friend, Zhang Dongsun, in the Philosophy Department, may have led to his decision to accept the post.[110] Hence, in August 1931, he and his family began the long trek home via the Soviet Union and the Trans-Siberian Railroad.[111] Although he had no way of knowing it, the years ahead were to be every bit as taxing as those just past.

Conclusion

At first glance, Zhang's story appears a straightforward one. He stood for the right--democracy--and was suppressed by the GMD for daring to oppose its political tutelage. This view, of course, is true. Upon closer examination, though, things were not quite that simple.

The twin goals of the Northern Expedition were to overthrow the warlords and expell the foreign "imperialists." In light of the former objective, the GMD had grounds for its hostility to Zhang. He had a long record of cooperation with China's warlords, in which Sun Chuanfang's financial support of his Institute of Political Science was only the most recent example. In fact, following his visit to Wuhan in October 1926, he stopped in Jiujiang to call on the beleaguered General Sun,[112] a gesture that, if the GMD leadership knew of it, could not help but further doom him once the NRA took Shanghai, for Sun was one of the main targets of the Northern Expedition and had been responsible for the deaths of many revolutionaries.[113]

In other ways, too, the GMD's enmity was understandable (from its point of view). Zhang was thoroughly identified as a follower of Liang Qichao, with whom the GMD had fought bitterly since its days of exile in Japan prior to the 1911 Revolution. Although one does not have to admire vindictiveness when it surfaces, as it did in 1927, one can understand (again, from its viewpoint) the GMD's thirst for revenge against its long-time opponent. Hence, while pursuing the Party Purification Movement against the CCP during 1927-1928, it made time to suppress Liang's followers as well.

Even Zhang's views of the GMD, at least in October 1926, were more complicated than one might have anticipated from an old rival of the Nationalists. There were things Zhang admired about the Reorganized GMD, as we have seen above. On the other hand, they were outweighed by those aspects of GMD rule that troubled him.

In the final analysis, one cannot help but admire him. In a China dominated by militarists, he had no choice but to solicit aid from the wealthy generals if he wanted to establish a school. Moreover, the contrast between such aid and GMD repression was all too clear in the fate of his Institute of Political Science. During the 1930s, his quest for a sanctuary from GMD persecution, as well as for some way to construct a modern China, led him into the arms of warlord after warlord. Like Sun Yat-sen, he never gave up searching for a "good" warlord.

Moreover, in Zhang's case, there was no question of remaining out of politics, as did some of his fellow liberal intellectuals. As a descendant of the scholar-gentry class of imperial China--nay, a member of that class, since he earned the *shengyuan* degree in 1902, the *jinshi* in 1910, and the "Hanlin bachelor" (*shujishi*) in 1911--[114] he took the idea of political activism very seriously. When his demand for democracy clashed with the GMD's program of political tutelage, something had to give, and that something was Zhang, since the GMD had all the instruments of force on its side (police and army). The GMD, in the final analysis, had no more use for liberalism than the governments that preceded and followed it.

Hence, following the arrival of the GMD in Shanghai (Zhang's home town), it suppressed him and other opponents of its rule. Schools and journals were closed, arrest warrants issued, and there is even some evidence, in Zhang's case, to suggest kidnapping for ransom. Such repression drove others into the embrace of the Chinese Communists. Yet, throughout his ordeal, Zhang maintained his opposition to the CCP, the only alternative to the GMD besides the warlords.

In the end, however, the harsh political climate proved too much for him, and he fled to Germany, as he had done when he escaped Yuan Shikai's wrath sixteen years earlier.[115] When he returned in the fall of 1931, the Manchurian Incident was to offer him and his colleagues a renewed chance for political action, an opportunity which they grasped with the formation of the NSP.

Notes

1. Although the group was known as the "Nationalist Clique" (*Guojiazhuyi Pai*) until 1929, when it adopted the name, Chinese Youth Party, the latter name will be used in this essay for the sake of clarity. See Chan Lau Kit-ching, *The Chinese Youth Party, 1923-1945* (Hong Kong: Centre for Asian Studies, University of Hong Kong, 1972), 22-23.

2. For details of his relationship with the GMD from 1906 through 1923, see Roger B. Jeans, "Syncretism in Defense of Confucianism: An Intellectual and Political Biography of the Early Years of Chang Chun-mai [Zhang Junmai], 1887-1923" (Ph.D. diss., George Washington University, 1974).

3. For an account of the progress of the Northern Expedition, as well as the taking of Shanghai, see Donald A. Jordan, *The Northern Expedition: China's National Revolution of 1926-1928* (Honolulu: The University Press of Hawaii, 1976).

4. Han Guojun, *Zhisou nianpu* (My Chronological Biography Upon Arrival at Old Age) (Taibei: Wenhai chubanshe, 1966), 49-50; Cheng Wenxi, "Junmai xiansheng zhi yanxing" (The Words and Deeds of Mr. [Zhang] Junmai), 19-20, in *Zhang Junmai xiansheng qishi shouqing jinian lunwen ji* (A Collection of Essays Commemorating Mr. Zhang Junmai's Seventieth Birthday) (Taibei: Editorial Committee for the above work, 1956) (hereafter, *YX*).

5. Ibid., 19.

6. Jeans, 352-63.

7. *YX*, 19; Howard L. Boorman and Richard C. Howard, eds., *Biographical Dictionary of Republican China* (New York: Columbia University Press, 1967), 1: 131 (hereafter, *BDRC*).

8. Five members of the faculty--Zhang Dongsun, Luo Wengan, Qu Shiying, Lu Dingkui, and Pan Guangdan--later joined one of the parties (the NSP or the Chinese Democratic Socialist Party) Zhang headed from 1932 until his formal resignation as party leader in May 1950. Four members of the student body--Cheng Wenxi, Jiang Yuntian, Yang Yuzi, and Feng Jinbai--also participated in his parties. Jeans, 369, 373.

9. Unless otherwise noted, the following discussion is summarized from Zhang Jiasen [Junmai], *Wuhan jianwen* (Observations in Wuhan) (Wusong: National Institute of Political Science, 1926).

10. Andrew J. Nathan, *Chinese Democracy* (New York: Alfred A. Knopf, 1985), chap. 5.

11. Great Britain, Foreign Office (hereafter, GBFO) 371/12499 [F3210/3210/10], dispatch, Acting Consul General Brenan, Canton, 25 February 1927, to Foreign Office, "Control of Private Schools."

12. Franklin L. Ho, "The Reminiscences of Ho Lien (Franklin Ho)," as told to Crystal Lorch, unpub. ms., postscript dated July 1966 (Special Collections Library, Butler Library, Columbia University), 287.

13. Carsun Chang to Richard Wilhelm, 1 March 1927, Richard Wilhelm Papers, privately held by Hellmut Wilhelm, Seattle, Washington (hereafter, *RWP*).

14. Li Huang, "Jing dao Zhang Junmai xiansheng" (Solemnly Mourn for Mr. Zhang Junmai), *Minzhu shehui* 5, no. 2 (1969): 18.

15. Cheng Wenxi, interview by author, Taibei, Taiwan, 24 June 1976.

16. Hu Ziping, ed., *Zhongguo zhengzhi renwu* (Chinese Political Personalities) (Fuzhou: Dada tushu gongsi, 1948), 186.

17. Zhang Junmai, *Bianzheng weiwuzhuyi bolun* (A Refutation of Dialectical Materialism) (Hong Kong: Youlian chubanshe, 1958), 191; Zhang Junmai, *Zhonghua minguo duli zizhu yu Yazhou qiantu* (The Republic of China's Independence and the Future of Asia) (Hong Kong: Ziyou chubanshe, 1955), 46.

18. Shi Yi, "Wo suo zhidao Zhang Junmai xiansheng shengping" (What I Know about Mr. Zhang Junmai's Life), *Zaisheng* (The National Renaissance), no. 345 (1953): 13. In a letter dated 1 April 1927, Zhang's former brother-in-law, Xu Zhimo, noted that Zhang was "under order of arrest...." Xu Zhimo, *Xu Zhimo Yingwen shuxin ji* (The Collected English-Language Letters of Xu Zhimo), ed. Liang Xihua (Taibei, 1979), 62.

19. Tso Shun-sheng [Zuo Shunsheng], *The Reminiscences of Tso Shun-sheng*, as told to Julie Lien-ying How (Glen Rock, N.J.: Microfilming Corp. of America, 1977), 108, 132.

20. In 1929, Xu Zhimo described Zhang as a "penniless, almost mendicant scholar," adding that he had to "part with all his books, his only property[,] last year in order to keep his family fed at all...." Xu, 100.

21. Zhang Junmai, "Nianyu nian lai shijie zhengchao jitang zhong women de lichang" (Our Position Amidst the Turmoil of the World's Political Trends Over the Past Twenty-odd Years), *Zaisheng*, no. 108 (1946): 5.

22. Ibid. His translation of Laski's work was not published until October 1930, while he was in Germany. Harold Laski, *Zhengzhi dianfan* (A Grammar of Politics), trans. Zhang Shilin [Zhang Junmai] (Shanghai: Shangwu yinshuguan, 1930). There must have been a steady demand, for it was reprinted in 1934, 1939, 1965, and 1970.

23. For a discussion of the desire of many Chinese to avoid social revolution by adopting socialism, see Arif Dirlik, *The Origins of Chinese Communism* (Oxford: Oxford University Press, 1989).

24. Jeans, chap. 8.

25. Carsun Chang [Zhang Junmai], *The Third Force in China* (New York: Bookman Associates, 1952), 184-85.

26. For example, he translated the new Soviet constitution and reviewed Arthur Ransome's *Six Weeks in Russia*. Zhang Junmai, "Eluosi suweiai lianbang gongheguo xianfa quanwen" (The Complete Text of the Constitution of the Russian [Socialist] Federated Soviet Republic), *Jiefang yu gaizao* (Liberation and Reconstruction) 1, no. 6 (1919): 25-39; Zhang Junmai, "Du *Liu xingqi zhi Eguo*" (On *Six Weeks in Russia*), *Gaizao* (Reconstruction) 3, no. 1 (1920): 61-71; no. 2 (1920): 51-63.

27. Zhang Junmai, "Yijiuyijiu zhi yijiueryi nian lu Ou zhong zhi zhengzhi yinxiang ji woren suo de zhi jiaoxun" (My Political Impressions and the Lessons I learned While Living in Europe, 1919-1921)," *Xin lu* 1, no. 5 (1928): 24; Chang, *Third Force*, 184-85. The attempted uprising made a deep impression on him, as evidenced by his frequent retelling of his experiences in the years that followed.

28. Zhang Junmai, "Xuanni zhi Shehui Gaizao Tongzhi Hui yijianshu" (Presentation of a Proposal by the Association of Comrades for Social Reform), *Gaizao* 4, no. 3 (1921): 7.

29. He was attacked, for example, in the pages of the CCP organ, *Xiangdao zhoubao*. Zhang Junmai, *Shehuizhuyi sixiang yundong gaiguan* (A General View of Socialist Thought and Movements) (Taibei, 1978), 3.

30. Zhang, *Zhonghua minguo*, 46; Zhang, *Shehuizhuyi*, 3.

31. Zhang Junmai, "Wu guo zhengdang fazhan zhi huigu yu wu dang zhi jianglai" (Retrospect on the Development of Our Nation's Political Parties, and the Future of Our Party), *Zaisheng*, no. 109 (1946): 3.

32. Zhang, *Shehuizhuyi*, 3.

33. Zhang Junmai, "Zhang Junmai xiansheng fang Ri jiangyan jiyao" (Extracts from Mr. Zhang Junmai's Lectures While Visiting Japan), *Minzhu Zhongguo* (Democratic China) 2, no. 5 (1959): 8.

34. Zhang, *Shehuizhuyi*, 3.

35. Ibid.

36. Ssu-yu Teng and John K. Fairbank, *China's Response to the West: A Documentary Survey, 1839-1923* (New York: Atheneum, 1963), 249-51.

37. Zhang Junmai, "*Renshengguan zhi lunzhan* xu" (Introduction to *The Polemic over a Philosophy of Life*), in *Renshengguan zhi lunzhan*, 3rd ed. (Shanghai: Taidong tushuju, 1928), 1: 6, 9.

38. Zhang, *Zhonghua minguo*, 46.

39. Zhang Junmai, "Tan zuijin zhengzhu" (On the Recent Political Situation), *Zaisheng*, no. 244 (1948): 2.

40. Zhang Junmai, "Zhengzhixue zhi gaizao" (The Transformation of Political Science), *Dongfang zazhi* (The Eastern Miscellany) 21, no. 1 (1924): 5-6.

41. Chang, *Third Force*, 73, 75-76.

42. Chang to Wilhelm, 14 July 1927, *RWP*.

43. Shijie shi zhuren [Zhang Junmai], *SuE pinglun* (A Critique of Soviet Russia) (Shanghai: Xinyue shudian, 1927). A second edition was published in April 1929.

44. Zhang, "Nianyu nian lai," 4.

45. Wu Xiangxiang, *Jindai shishi luncong* (Collected Essays on Events in Modern History) (Taibei: Wenxing shudian, 1964), 2: 303-312.

46. Zhang Junmai, "Fanli" (Foreword), 1-2, in *SuE pinglun*.

47. Ibid., 97.

48. Li Huang, "Zhang Junmai," 17-18; Li Huang, *The Reminiscences of Li Huang* (Glen Rock, N.J.: Microfilming Corporation of America, 1975), 326-27; *BDRC*, 2: 303.

49. Zuo Shunsheng, "Zhuidaohui zhici" (Speech at the Memorial Service), *Ziyou Zhong* (Liberty Bell) (H.K. ed.) 1, no. 1 (1970): 30-31.

50. Li Dasheng, "Guoshi: Zhang Junmai xiansheng" (National Scholar: Mr. Zhang Junmai), *Ming bao* 4, no. 5 (1969): 72.

51. "Fakanci" (Foreword), *Xin lu* 1, no. 1 (1928): 3-4.

52. Li Huang, "Reminiscences," 328; Li Huang, "Zhang Junmai," 18.

53. Cheng Cangpo, "Zhuiyi Zhang Junmai xiansheng" (Recollections of Mr. Zhang Junmai), *Zhuanji wenxue* (Biographical Literature) 48, no. 1 (1986): 27-28. Following his return from Germany in 1916, Zhang served as editor-in-chief of the then Progressive Party organ from November 1916-March 1917. Jeans, 134, 151-52, 157.

54. Li Huang, "Reminiscences," 331-32; Li Huang, "Zhang Junmai," 18.

55. William T. De Bary et. al., comps., *Sources of Chinese Tradition* (New York: Columbia University Press, 1960), 579.

56. Ibid., 783-86.

57. Li Huang, "Reminiscences," 331; Li Huang, "Zhang Junmai," 18.

58. Zhang Junmai, "Zhuiyi [Zeng] Muhan" (Recollections of Zeng Qi), *Minzhu chao* (Current Democracy) 2, no. 18 (1961): 3; Zhang, *Bianzheng*, 191.

59. Li Huang, "Reminiscences," 332.

60. Ibid., 332-33; Li Huang, "Zhang Junmai," 18. Although Li does not mention him, another future member of the NSP, Lu Dingkui, also is reported to have taught at the school. Li Dasheng, 72.

61. Li Huang, "Reminiscences," 334-35.

62. Xu Zhimo, 100. Xu wrote that Zhang was kidnapped around June 13-15 and held three weeks. Zhang himself later recalled that he was held "about a month,..." Chang, *Third Force*, 24.

63. Zhang, *Bianzheng*, 191-92.

64. See, for example, the account in his *Third Force*, 24.

65. Tso Shun-sheng, "Reminiscences," 76.

66. Zhang Jiazhu, interview by author, San Francisco, California, 28 July 1976.

67. Parks M. Coble, Jr. *The Shanghai Capitalists and the Nationalist Government, 1927-1937* (Cambridge: Harvard University Press, 1980), chaps. 2, 3.

68. Ibid., 32, 34-36, 45. A British report stated that for some time there had been a "wave of the abduction of prominent Chinese and their children for ransom ...." GBFO 371/12446 [F9193/143/10], Clearing Office (Enemy Debts), [Shanghai?], to The Controller, The Clearing House (Enemy Debts), [London?], "Situation in China (Monthly Report for October 1927)," 9 December 1927.

69. Police of the three sections of Shanghai were not allowed to enter each other's territory. Hence, it was easier for the GMD to rely on the Green Gang, rather than extradiction. Coble, 37.

70. Ibid., 60-65.

71. Jiaao spent ten and one-half months visiting eighteen countries, before returning to China in March 1930. Chang Kia-ngau [Jiaao], "Chang Kia-ngau Autobiography," Chinese Oral History Project, (Special Collections Library, Butler Library, Columbia University), 66 (English version).

72. Coble, 45. According to Xu Zhimo, due to the "alarming news of Carsun Chang's ill-fortune," Xu's "terror stricken" father considered moving the entire family to "some safer places than Shanghai, such as Tsingtao." Xu, 102.

73. Kidnapping was said to be one of the Green Gang's "trades." Harold R. Isaacs, *The Tragedy of the Chinese Revolution*, 2nd rev. ed. (New York: Atheneum, 1966), 142. Opium-dealing, however, was their main source of income. Coble, 37.

74. Cited in Jerome B. Grieder, *Hu Shih and the Chinese Renaissance: Liberalism in the Chinese Revolution, 1917-1937* (Cambridge: Harvard University Press, 1970), 240-41.

75. Zhang, *Bianzheng*, 192.

76. Li Dasheng, 71; Wu Xiangxiang, "Zhang Junmai laohe wanlixin" (Zhang Junmai: Old Crane with the Ten-Thousand-*li* Heart), in *Minguo bai ren zhuan* (Biographies of One Hundred Men of the Republic) (Taibei: Zhuanji wenxue chubanshe, 1971), 3: 18.

77. *BDRC*, 2: 438-41.

78. On Luo's jailing, see ibid., 2: 439-40. On Zhang's visit to Luo, see Luo Wengan, *Yuzhongren yu* (Words from a Prisoner) (Taibei: Wenhai chubanshe, 1971), preface.

79. According to an official party history, Luo joined the NSP in 1933, as a result of a trip south by Zhang Junmai. "Zhongguo Minzhu Shehui Dang jianyao shigao" (A Brief Draft History of the Chinese Democratic Socialist Party), *Minzhu Zhongguo* 1, no. 10 (1951): 19.

80. *BDRC*, 2: 440.

81. Wellington V.K. Koo, *The Wellington Koo Memoir* (Glen Rock, N.J.: Microfilming Corp. of America, 1977), 3: 292-302.

82. Earl Albert Selle, *Donald of China* (New York: Harper & Brothers Publishers, 1948), 256.

83. According to an October 1941 interview with Xu Fulin, one of the leaders of the NSP in Hong Kong, the party was originally supported by the Young Marshall. Support from that source, Xu added, had been cut off some years before (following the 1936 Xi'an Incident and Zhang Xueliang's arrest?). National Archives, Military Archives Division, Military Reference Branch, RG 226, Records of the Office of Strategic Services, no. 7724, Addison E. Southard, Consul General, H.K. to SecState, dispatch no. 1035, "Transmitting a Memorandum of a conversation with the representative in Hong Kong of the 'Chinese National Socialist Party' on the subject of that party and of the 'Federation of Democratic Parties in China'," 23 Oct. 1941, p. 4 of the memorandum.

84. Jeans, 103-05.

85. Colin MacKerras, *Modern China: A Chronology from 1842 to the Present* (London: Thames and Hudson, 1982), 326, 328.

86. *YX*, 22; Li Dasheng, 71.

87. *BDRC*, 2: 303; P.K. Yu, *Research Materials on Twentieth-Century China: An Annotated List of CCRM [Center for Chinese Research Materials] Publications* (Washington, D.C.: CCRM, Association of Research Libraries, 1975), 111.

88. Chan, 31.

89. William C. Kirby, *Germany and Republican China* (Stanford: Stanford University Press, 1984), 70.

90. Chang to Wilhelm, 1 March 1927, *RWP*.

91. Chang to Wilhelm, 14 July 1927, ibid.

92. Chang, *Third Force*, 24.

93. Chang to Wilhelm, 30 August 1928, *RWP*.

94. Zhang, *Bianzheng*, 192. The Young Marshall seems to have had a weak spot for Luo and his friends. In addition to bankrolling the NSP and lending Zhang Junmai money, he once paid off Luo's debts, amounting to $100,000 (Chinese, no doubt). DepState, R.G. 84, China Diplomatic Post Records (Peiping), 1934, Vol. 40, 800

decimal series, Willys R. Peck, Counselor of Legation, to Johnson, American Minister, Peiping, 30 July 1934, on the general political situation in Nanking.

95. Chang to Wilhelm, 14 July 1927, *RWP*.

96. Zhang later implied that he heard a pair of Wilhelm's lectures at the China-Institut in late 1929. Carsun Chang, "Richard Wilhelm, Weltburger," *Sinica* 5, no. 2 (1930): 73.

97. *BDRC*, 1: 32.

98. Chang, *Third Force*, 24-25.

99. Jeans, chap. 7.

100. Cheng Cangpo, 28; Li Dasheng, 71-72.

101. Chang to Wilhelm, 14 July 1927, *RWP*.

102. Chang to Wilhelm, 30 August 1928, ibid.

103. Carsun Chang, "Der Idealismus in der chinesischen Philosophie zur Zeit der Sung-Dynastie," *Forschungen und Fortschritte* 6, no. 17 (1930): 224-25; Carsun Chang, "Philosophisches Ringen im heutigen China," *Die Tatwelt* 6, no. 1 (1930): 25-33; Carsun Chang, "Die Hauptfragen in der Konfuzianischen Philosophie," *Sinica* 5, nos. 5/6 (1930): 213-26.

104. Carsun Chang, "Die Stellung der Kanonischen Literatur im modernen Geistesleben Chinas," *Sinica* 6, no. 1 (1931): 13-26; no. 3 (1931): 97-108.

105. Ibid., 103, 107-08.

106. Li Huang, "Zhang Junmai," 18.

107. Carsun Chang, "Die staatsrechtliche Krisis der chinesischen Republik," *Jahrbuch des offentlichen Rechte der Gegenwart* 19 (1931): 316-55.

108. Zhang, *Bianzheng*, 192.

109. Philip West, *Yenching University and Sino-Western Relations, 1916-1952* (Cambridge: Harvard University Press, 1976), 116-21.

110. In the fall of 1930, Dongsun moved from Shanghai to Beiping to take up an appointment in the Department of Philosophy at Yenching University. He was serving as department chairman (1931-33) when Zhang was offered the appointment. *BDRC*, 1:131.

111. Zhang, *Bianzheng*, 192; *YX*, 22.

112. Chang, *Third Force*, 91.

113. In Jiangxi, Sun executed hundreds of students, teachers, and GMD members suspected of cooperation with the NRA. Jordan, 85.

114. Jeans, 31, 84-86.

115. Ibid., 105-07.

2

Human Rights and Political Engagement: Luo Longji in the 1930s

Fredric J. Spar

In the decade from the late 1920s to the start of full-scale war with Japan and the formation of the Second United Front (UF) in 1937, Luo Longji emerged as a preeminent advocate of a liberal political alternative in China. His advocacy, expressed through an outpouring of essays and editorials, is distinguished from that of other Chinese articulators of the liberal outlook with respect to both theory and practice. Altogether, his experience suggests certain exceptions to generally held conclusions about the course of liberalism in modern China.

First, it has been noted that Western liberal principles were typically inverted in the process of translation and dissemination by Chinese thinkers. Thus, the progress, growth, and development that buoyant nineteenth-century English liberals saw only as corollaries to the central principle of the liberal creed--the intrinsic worth of the free individual--became the primary objectives of Chinese whose paramount concern was the survival of a weak state. When freedom is viewed chiefly as a means to such an end, its value was inevitably diluted. However, in contrast to the earliest transmitters of the Western liberal vocabulary into China--Yan Fu and Liang Qichao--as well as later architects of political orders of both the Left and Right who incorporated at least a veneer of democratic values into their constitutional frameworks, Luo unwaveringly placed the individual, not the state, at the center of his deliberations.[1]

Second, it has been observed, especially in the case of Hu Shi, the foremost Chinese disciple of John Dewey and the most renowned upholder of the liberal standard in the May Fourth era, that China's Western-trained intellectuals exhibited a distaste for politics narrowly understood, preferring to find in professional careers a public relevance. Despite a deep appreciation for freedom, intellectual pluralism, and their accompanying political frameworks, they remained skeptical, if not disdainful, of the rough and tumble of political activism.[2] This general observation does not apply to Luo. An intensely political person from his days as a student leader at Qinghua College in the May Fourth era through his attempt to question the Communist Party (CCP) monopoly four decades later in the Hundred Flowers period, Luo never withdrew from the public arena to pursue a private calling. On the contrary, a principal message he sought to bring to his audience among students and intellectuals was the urgency of political engagement.

A third assessment of the fate of liberalism in China is that in the post-May Fourth era its appeal withered under the challenge of advocates of "fundamental solutions" on the scale of the Bolshevik Revolution. In the face of the overwhelming social crisis and the threat of foreign aggression, the liberal outlook, favoring gradualism and pragmatism, became largely irrelevant; the political stage was essentially cleared of all actors except those adherents of the Leninist parties of the Left and Right.[3] Further evidence of the disappearance of the center is found in the disillusionment with liberal democracy expressed in the mid-1930s by a number of prominent Western-educated intellectuals, who pointed to emerging fascist and Stalinist models as surer means of furthering national aspirations.[4]

At least through the early stages of the Second UF, however, the dismissal of a liberal alternative may be premature. This is suggested, in a limited way, by Luo's ability to build an audience among students and intellectuals for the Tianjin daily *Yishi bao* (hereafter, YSB), while serving as chief editorial writer in the 1930s, and in a more significant way by the fact that with the First People's Political Council (PPC) in 1938, China had the most broadly representative political assembly ever convened in the Republican period.[5] Not democratically chosen, and with only sharply limited powers to question and criticize the government--not legislate--the PPC was hardly a parliament. Yet, at least in concept, it was a forum for a diversity of opinion, a liberal, if not a democratic, institution. Such an assembly was greeted by Luo and like thinkers as a step toward meeting one of their principal demands--the recognition that talent and ability in China were not limited to one political party and that national salvation required an end to monopoly politics and the acceptance of pluralism.

It was anguish over the specter of the imminent devouring of China by the powerful states of the West that had led, around the turn of this century, to a search for the sources of Western wealth and power and the first systematic study in China of Western liberal values. This paramount concern for the strength and well-being of the nation colored Chinese interpretations of liberal precepts from the beginning. The "actualization of man's potentialities," the release of individual creative energies through the construction of liberal political institutions, and the stimulation of free thought and expression were seen by both Yan Fu and Liang Qichao as means to national well-being, not as ends in themselves. Approached from the perspective of a weak state, the question of individual freedom was ultimately subordinated to the task of national survival. Thus, Yan and Liang both ranged themselves in opposition to Sun Yat-sen's Revolutionary Alliance, regarding revolution as giving free rein to the retrograde tendencies of an ignorant people. Instead, a slow process of orderly reform and education under the guidance of an enlightened authoritarian regime to create a "new citizen" (*xin min*), in Liang Qichao's terms, was needed before freedom and republicanism could flourish on Chinese soil.

Sun, although both more sanguine about the political maturity of the Chinese and more insistent on the need for a quick and fundamental reordering of the political system than either of his more scholarly opponents, nevertheless saw the need for a period of "political tutelage" before constitutional government could be consummated. Moreover, as he pointed out in his Second Lecture on Democracy, he saw China's predicament as resulting not from a lack of liberty but from an excess of it. China had become a "sheet of loose sand," invaded by foreign imperialism and oppressed by the economic control and trade wars of the powers because of excessive individual liberty. "The individual," he proposed, "should not have too much liberty, but the nation should have complete liberty. When the nation can act freely, then China may be called strong."[6]

Sun's views provided doctrinal sanction for the Guomindang's (GMD) efforts to squash political opposition and to achieve, as a prior condition for national political unity, a unification of thought. This effort--manifested especially in the Nanjing government's press censorship regulations, the consecration of Sun's Testament (*yijiao*) in school curricula and civil service exams, and the drafting of the Provisional Constitution for the Period of Political Tutelage (*Yuefa*) adopted by the GMD government in 1931--provided the context for a series of political essays by Luo in the periodical *Xinyue* (The Crescent). Principally a literary monthly concentrating on short fiction, poetry, translation, and criticism, it was founded in 1928 by Xu Zhimo, Hu Shi, Wen Yiduo, and other graduates of Qinghua and returned students from America and British universities. Although the school tie was what joined Luo, a Qinghua scholar and recipient of a Ph.D. in political science from

Columbia University, with the "Crescentists," his political outlook was consistent with that of this literary group, which stressed its fundamental commitment to freedom of thought and expression.[7] Defense of this position in the face of GMD crackdowns, moreover, prompted Luo's colleagues, Hu Shi and Liang Shiqiu, to join with him in producing a set of political commentaries, published first in the journal and then as *Collected Essays on Human Rights* (*Renquan lunji*). In the ensuing decades, in scores of essays, editorials, and speeches at political rallies, Luo would consistently adhere to the basic tenets he first sketched in *Xinyue*.

The irreducible core of Luo's political outlook was the concept of man as a thinking being: "Where there is man, there is thought. Where there is thought, there is the desire to express the thought. If there is the desire to speak one's mind, it cannot be denied. A man wants to say what is on his mind, not what others want him to say."[8]

Man, wrote Luo, following the utilitarian argument, seeks happiness, and this can be obtained only when his individual personality and character can grow. "If freedom of speech is proscribed, not just speech but thought is proscribed; and not just thought but the [development of] personality and character as well. To proscribe the [development of] personality and character is to terminate life for the individual man and to destroy life for the mass of men."[9]

For man to be man, he must have freedom and freedom must be absolute:

> The scope of free speech is such that there is nothing in the world that cannot be uttered, nothing in the world that cannot be discussed.... In mathematics, one can propose a theory that three plus two equals four or that four minus two equals three. In political matters, it is entirely possible to carry on propaganda for monarchism or to promote communism.... Freedom is absolute; it is whole. Freedom cannot be a matter of degree or quantity. If we say that free speech should be limited in degree or quantity, then if we say A's opinions cannot be discussed and B is a follower of A, inevitably B's opinions cannot be discussed either. If C is a friend of a follower of B, then inevitably C's opinions cannot be discussed either, and if D is a friend of a friend of a follower of C, then inevitably C's opinions cannot be discussed.... Such a limitation . . . will inevitably reach a point where there is nothing that can be discussed, nothing that can be criticized. As a result, if there is not absolute freedom, there is absolutely no freedom.[10]

That absolute freedom could be abused--e.g., through the spreading of lies, baseless rumors, and premeditated slander--Luo conceded, but control of such abuses was a delicate matter to be defined by carefully crafted legal codes and not subject to the arbitrary power of government.

Charges must be filed and an open trial before judge and jury must be held before the individual's right to free speech could be curtailed. Freedom of speech, Luo emphatically argued, is a right which is prior to law.[11]

This was a fundamental departure from the drafters of the Provisional Constitution, as well as other constitutional frameworks later developed by the GMD and CCP regimes. Rights, according to the Provisional Constitution, were derived from citizenship in the state; they could be limited or withdrawn by the state because the state had granted them. If freedom is only conferred by law, Luo observed, it can be abrogated by law, and indeed the Provisional Constitution made this explicit by including in each right the phrase "according to the law." To suggest that "outside the law there is no freedom," that freedom is derived from man's social institutions and can be extended or limited by law, is to make freedom relative and tenuous. Even in those societies where legal institutions are in the hands of representative bodies, if freedom of speech is not made absolute, what is at one moment bestowed may be at another moment withdrawn.[12]

Luo distinguished the domain of "human rights" (*renquan*) from that of "citizen's rights" (*minquan*)--rights that were derived from the state. Citizen's rights are created by man through social institutions; they do not exist prior to the state and cannot be conceived of in any transcendent sense. The Manifesto of the First National Party Congress of the GMD in 1924 pointed out that the "citzen's rights" of the GMD differed from the so-called "natural rights" (*tianfu renquan*) in that they embraced only that which was appropriate to the present needs of the Chinese revolution. "Rights of citizenship in the Republic can only be enjoyed by those loyal to the Republic; they must not be carelessly bestowed upon those who oppose the Republic lest they use these rights as a means to destroy it."[13] Under the GMD dictatorship in the period of political tutelage, the logical conclusion to be drawn from such a premise was that loyalty to the Republic meant loyalty to the GMD. GMD theorists argued that the rejection of the theory of "natural rights" by scholars in the West, beginning in the nineteenth century, and the failure to incorporate the term "human rights" in constitutions promulgated in Europe after the World War signaled a rejection of the rampant individualism which had proven harmful to the public welfare. Luo responded by pointing out that, although Rousseau's theory of natural rights may have been rejected by the nineteenth-century utilitarians, the notion of rights which transcended the political state remained, and were in fact validated in the German Constitution of 1919 and the Czechoslovakian Constitution of 1920:

> In my view, "human rights" mean the right to be man; the rights of a citizen are the rights of a citizen in a political state. The political state is one of many kinds of human organization. It is possible for a man not to be a citizen, but it is not possible for a citizen not to be a man. Thus, we can easily see that the scope of human rights is even greater, even more basic than the rights of a citizen. We can state quite simply that the rights of the citizen are only one part of human rights--the part that emphasizes the political.[14]

The failure of the Nanjing regime to understand the basis of human rights was paralleled, in Luo's view, by its failure to define the nature and purpose of the state. He pointed out that in the entire corpus of Sun Yat-sen's works there is no mention of the nature and purpose of the state. Instead, what concerned Sun was the strategy for "national salvation" and "national reconstruction," and because he was so preoccupied with these goals, he failed properly to evaluate the means. The means chosen were to place the party above the state (*dang gao yu guo*) and to use the party to build the state (*yi dang jian guo*).

The consequence of the failure to understand properly the nature and purpose of the state, and the imposition of a party dictatorship on the state, Luo argued, was that politics in China had not changed much from imperial times. Pointing out that the GMD was organized on the Bolshevik model, he proposed:

> If the Guomindang can copy the Communist strategy of putting the party above the state, other parties can copy the doctrines of the Guomindang and place themselves above the state. Qin Shi Huangdi conquered the country and made himself emperor. Cao Cao and Sima Yi conquered the country and naturally made themselves emperors. This was the story of the empire of the family (*jia tianxia*). If after the success of their revolution the Guomindang can say "the party above the state," other parties after the success of their revolution can also say "the party above the state." This naturally will become a continuous empire of the party.[15]

The result of both the "empire of the family" and the "empire of the party" is dictatorship, and dictatorships cannot fulfill what Luo described as the threefold function of the state: protecting the rights of the people, nurturing and developing the people, and furnishing the people with an environment of peace, tranquility, order, and justice. Dictatorships, he pointed out, recognize the rights of the ruled so long as they are not in conflict with the rights of dictatorial power. Such a phenomenon is regarded by the dictatorial power as an act of benevolence, not a responsibility. Dictatorships, by denying freedom, thwart the nurturing and development of personality and character, fostering instead the development of passive, dependent personalities--what Luo deplored as "unthinking mechanical devices." In a dictatorship, whether of an individual, a party, or a class, the dictator always occupies a special position in the affairs of the state. "This is a fundamental denial of equality and justice. The special position of the dictator inevitably arouses the indignation and hatred of the ruled for the ruler, and indignation and hatred are the source of all revolutions. In a society of recurrent revolution, peace, tranquility, and order naturally are not to be found."[16]

The greatest enemy of a dictatorship, no matter how enlightened, he argued, is freedom of thought, and thus the first order of business of a dictatorship is to cast the people's minds in a mold and gag discordant elements. But the consequence of such a unification of thought, Luo warned, is not harmony but an obsequious silence, and imposing such a limitation was to perpetuate the very condition Chinese concerned about the fate of their nation most feared: a stationary society. Luo was no less motivated by a sense of urgency "to save China" than the likes of Yan Fu, Liang Qichao, or Luo's contemporaries across the political spectrum. But the growth and development sought by all would not, in Luo's mind, take place at the expense of freedom; they were freedom's consequences. His affirmation of the social desirability of freedom is perhaps best expressed in his translation of Harold Laski's "The Dangers of Obedience": "Stationary societies . . . are distinguished by the degree to which they are bound by traditional codes of behavior.... The preservation of avenues through which originality may flow is the condition upon which our well-being depends."[17]

Laski was a seminal influence on Luo's intellectual development; a year studying British politics with him at the London School of Economics helped provide the basis for Luo's confidence in the efficacy of the gradualist reform approach of the English Fabians. The spread of education, the reform of municipal administration, and the extension of social welfare policies in England, all promoted by the Fabians in the half-century since 1880, contrasted with the lack of material change in Russia after the Bolshevik Revolution and confirmed that progress comes incrementally (*yidian yidi*)--violent revolution could not achieve it. Still, Luo understood the psychological appeal of a violent overthrow of the old order and fully appreciated the allure of communism in China. The idea that China's problem was poverty, not the unequal distribution of wealth, a notion cited by Sun Yat-sen and Liang Qichao to disclaim any relevance for Marxism in China, was rejected by Luo: it was precisely because of poverty that it could succeed. Although China was poor, private ownership of the means of production still existed and could be collectivized. Poverty forces people to take desperate action to survive, and the seizure of privately owned means of production was one response. Luo correctly read the trend towards fascination with communism in industrially less-developed countries--the tendency which would stand Marxism on its head and make it less relevant in lands where the bourgeoisie was most powerful. He argued that in America, where the standard of living was high, there was little chance of communism developing. "The real problem in economics is not whether the people have more or less, but whether they have anything. The poorer the country, the greater the hope for the success of communism."[18]

Although the overthrow of the property owners by the propertyless was the final goal of the revolution, he wrote, the starting point was the overthrow of the powerful by the powerless. Inequality of political power, not economic inequality, was the wellspring for revolution. "In poverty-stricken China, there is perhaps no property to collectivize (*wu chan ke gong*), but in one-party-dictatorship China, there is power that can be divided (*you quan ke fen*)." This, he stressed, had a mass psychological appeal which the CCP could utilize in its revolutionary strategy, and this was the reason the CCP could succeed. It was "*wu chan ke gong*" and "*you quan ke fen*" that created a revolutionary situation in China. Whatever signboard was hung up, or whatever banner was unfurled, was totally irrelevant. Red imperialism, the assistance of the Third International, and the plots of the Russians were supplementary factors--they were not the reasons the CCP could succeed in China.

In the early 1930s, Luo perceived a China trapped in a perpetual cycle of military confrontration, chaos, and economic decay in which neither the GMD nor the CCP could achieve complete victory. The reliance on military solutions to solve political problems and the advocacy of "party rule" by both sides resulted, as Luo described it, in local government in which those elements who had some knowledge, prestige, and leadership qualifications, but whose political views were at odds with those of the GMD and the CCP, were killed or forced to flee. What was left, especially in war-riven areas of Hunan, Hubei, and Jiangxi, was either a bunch of wily merchants or ruffians into whose hands local control had fallen. The two parties, because of their mutual advocacy of "the party above the state" and their reliance on some of the worst elements in society to sustain power were thus described as "beasts of the same stripe" (*yi qiu zhi he*).[19]

It was as an impassioned publicist, seeking to mould support for a political arrangement that would break the cycle of fratricidal war between these "beasts of the same stripe," bring the most capable leadership into office, and promote effective resistance to Japanese aggression that Luo found his métier. In 1931, he was engaged as chief editorial writer (*zhubi*) for YSB, which had been founded in 1915 by the Belgian Vincentian, Father Vincent Lebbe. Earning a reputation for objective reporting of domestic politics and foreign affairs (with offices in the Italian Concession in Tianjin, it was relatively free from press control), the paper attracted readers from among students and intellectuals in Tianjin and Beijing and Catholics in the Hebei countryside.[20] In the late 1920s, however, declining readership and competitive pressure from its rival, *Dagong bao* (L'Impartial) (reorganized and under new ownership), forced adjustments at YSB, including the expansion of editorial comment, the initiation of a social-service section devoted to the problems of women and youth, and the publication of several scholarly weekly supplements with articles on history, literature, religion, education, and international affairs by professors from Beijing and Tianjin universities. It was as part of this effort to compete with *Dagong bao*, particularly for student readers, that the position of chief editorial writer was specially created for Luo. Luo's reputation among students and young intellectuals had been established with his essays in *Xinyue*, and as a lecturer at Nankai University in Tianjin he was able to comment on student trends from personal knowledge. The editorials (*shelun*), as in all Chinese newspapers, were unsigned, but Luo was widely known as their author.[21] Typically featured on the front page, without any other news or editorial content, these 1500-character opinion pieces contributed to a competitive turnabout at *YSB*. Daily circulation, which had dwindled to only 7,000 in 1927, reached a peak of 50,000 copies, surpassing *Dagong bao* during the time of the Mukden Incident, and remained at around 30,000 throughout the mid-1930s. The newspaper staff also expanded from thirty or forty persons to more than three hundred.[22]

Usually focused on a specific political, economic, social, or military event, Luo's editorials invariably reiterated a fundamental prescription for China's ills: democracy in domestic affairs and resistance in foreign affairs, or, more specifically, the use of "military force to resist Japan, and politics to purge the Communists" (*wuli kangRi, zhengzhi qing gong*).[23]

The formula was in direct response to the policy which guided Chiang Kai-shek's actions following the Mukden Incident, and which he affirmed in the midst of the encirclement drives to destroy the "Soviet Republic" in Jiangxi: "Until the bandits have been purged, [there should be] absolutely no talk of fighting the Japanese." The GMD, Luo proposed, should take the initiative by recognizing the CCP as a legitimate political party, and then if the Communists continued to use military efforts to seize power while the nation was fighting Japan, they would in the end only defeat themselves (much as the GMD was presently doing) by losing the support of the patriotic movement. There was an underlying premise to this proposal: that the political system had room for rival ideologies and political organizations to contend peacefully in an atmosphere of mutual toleration--a perspective Luo was all too aware was held by neither of the two principal parties. It was, however, a view he considered appealing to the majority of Chinese students and intellectuals at a time when the shadow of Japan had fallen over most of North China. Nationalism and mobilization of the nation's energies for military resistance to a foreign foe were not inimical to liberal politics. On the contrary, the threat posed to all Chinese by the Japanese afforded a special opportunity for diverse elements in the Chinese polity to develop that spiritual prerequisite for liberal politics--tolerance for diversity:

> What we advocate is that the present government stop using the terms "red bandits" and "communist bandits" and, to the fullest extent possible, openly and courageously establish conditions for a political compromise with the responsible leaders of the Communist Party.... Those who today in China enter the Communist Party for ideological reasons are actually quite few. If the government were to make a sincere compromise with the Communists for the sake of devoting full strength to resistance against Japan, this would rouse the nationalism of youth and reduce the Communist Party's inner unity and strength.[24]

The compromise with the CCP would set the stage for the convening of a national salvation assembly with non-GMD representation. "What we are asking the present authorities to do is open their eyes and recognize clearly that talent is not limited to one party.... What we hope for is the formation of a government of talent that will be representative of all the political views of the nation. Only this kind of government can bring about the spiritual unity of the citizens and cope with the present situation."[25] He first called for the convening of a national assembly giving representation to all parties and groups--including the CCP--and for coordinated resistance to Japan immediately after the Mukden Incident.[26] He was thus among the earliest advocates of the type of UF which the CCP would not begin to promote until 1936. Though promoting a "UF from below," the CCP and the Comintern, until after the beginning of the December Ninth movement in 1935, maintained that resistance to Japan was impossible as long as the "fascist regime" of Chiang Kai-shek still functioned as "the agent of domestic feudalism and foreign aggression."[27]

How was such a broadly representative political assembly, which would promulgate and observe constitutional strictures, to be formed? In spite of his familiarity with the mechanics of an electoral system, obtained during research in Britain for his doctoral dissertation, "The Conduct of

Parliamentary Elections in England,"[28] Luo was short on the specifics of popular participation in the political process. In theory, the system is embraced. "In democratic countries," he wrote, "the people enjoy the right of franchise. The nation's men of talent, virtue, distinction, and mark can be chosen collectively by all the people of the nation.... If we want a 'capable government', it is first necessary for the people to have rights. The people of England have rights and so a MacDonald or a Lloyd George can become prime minister. The American people have rights and so a Hoover or a Roosevelt can become president."[29]

In the *Xinyue* essays, Luo firmly challenged the GMD concept of political tutelage, questioning how people could be taught the meaning of political rights in a political system apart from the power to exercise them. If one is to learn how to swim, one has to go into the water, he suggested. The GMD's method of instruction in political rights made no more sense than training someone to swim on dry land.[30] In reply to those such as Jiang Tingfu, Ding Wenjiang, and Qian Duansheng, erstwhile liberals who in the mid-1930s wrote favorably of fascist and Stalinist regimes, Luo emphasized that notwithstanding current theorizing about an "ideal dictatorship," dictatorship ultimately meant "rule of man" (*renzhi*), as opposed to "rule of law" (*fazhi*). Rule of man for a time could prove effective, but it depended on the fortuitous rise on the political scene of an individual of exceptional political talent. "What sort of magic do the defenders of dictatorship have that they can invent a person with the talent to be a dictator?"[31]

Nevertheless, to create a broadly representative government under the rule of law, a government which would protect rights (*quan*) and allow those with ability (*neng*) to assume office, Luo looked for decisive reform from above, not for a massive outpouring of popular yearning for democracy. His editorials proposed that the political leaders of the country, Chiang Kai-shek or anybody else, heed the righteous remonstrances of the intellectual community and establish a government based on virtue and talent and disregard party loyalties and ideology. On the twentieth anniversary of the formal opening of the first parliament of the Republic of China, Luo wrote:

> The failure of constitutional government during the past twenty years in China resulted from the governing authorities lacking knowledge of and a sincere attitude toward constitutional government. One should not look to the people for progress toward constitutional government, but rather to those leaders who hold dictatorial power. What we should be asking today is not whether the people have reached the level of constitutional government, but whether the persons holding dictatorial power have or have not a knowledge of constitutional government; not

> whether the people have or have not had the necessary training, but whether the dictatorial governing authorities have a sincere attitude toward constitutional government.... If the mental outlooks, ambitions, minds, and thoughts of the present governing authorities have progressed from those of Yuan Shikai and Duan Qirui, and if the governing authorities have not only the knowledge of how to utilize constitutional government, but a sincere attitude toward carrying it out, then there is no doubt that constitutional government can be realized.[32]

In importuning political authorities to embrace "correct thought," to maintain a sincere attitude, and to undertake reform from above, Luo resembles a righteous memorialist of old more than a modern politician organizing a constituency into a powerful pressure group. His optimism about reform from above is much more redolent of Kang Youwei's approaches to the Guangxu Emperor than Sun Yat-sen's efforts to form a revolutionary alliance. Implicit in Luo's formula for reform, however, were certain assumptions about the intellectual community in China. Most fundamental was that in a China "poor in knowledge," intellectuals had a critical role to play in the nation's destiny, and their voices would have to be heeded by the authorities. "In today's semi-developed China," he wrote, "where is the talent? The total of our returned students from abroad is not equal to the graduates of a top-ranked American university. In a China with this dearth of talent, to further limit matters by declaring 'party members first hired, non-party members first fired' is certainly national political suicide."[33]

The use and misuse of talent had always been a popular theme in Chinese writings on politics, and in writing about bringing all the talent of the realm together to save the nation, Luo broke no new ground. But in his vision, that intellectual community would endorse a political system that institutionalized freedom of expression and protected the individual from the whims of a government possessing arbitrary power--a radical alternative to the traditional and prevailing mode of politics in China. Furthermore, that intellectual community would maintain a high level of political engagement. Its members would embrace the Liberal Way and, moreover, though that way did not currently prevail, they would not forsake politics. In a society which for over two millennia had instructed its educated elite to "hide" when the way did not prevail (*Analects* VIII.13) and to be concerned not about whether one was in office but about whether one had the qualities that entitled one to office (*Analects* IV.14), this too represents a radical departure. Taken as a whole, Luo's editorials in the 1930s can be seen as an effort both to educate the intellectuals (literally, the "elements with knowledge"; *zhishi fenzi*) on the content of the Liberal Way and to appeal to their sense of patriotism and public duty, so they would remain politically engaged and pressure the regime to reform.

In the face of a government crackdown on "leftist" students and professors, and in order to achieve consensus and unity (*yizhi tuanjie*) before facing the Japanese, Luo did not defend the leftist position. Rather, he insisted, again and again, on informing his audience of the validity of the liberal position, that bludgeoning the opposition to conform was futile, and that consensus and unity could be built only on mutual respect for differences. The "correct," the "orthodox," and the "legitimate" inevitably correspond, he wrote, to the "contrary," the "heretical," and the "illegitimate":

> Where there is "*zhengdong*" (orthodoxy), there is "*fandong*" (reaction). It is useless to try to purge one; there is no way it can be done. As far as a strategy for purging "*fandong*" is concerned, the more one adopts an attitude of tolerance and forgiveness, then although there will be opposition (*fan*), there will not be a movement (*dong*). The more one adopts stern and severe methods, then the more "*fandong*" will become a big opposition (*da fan*) and a big movement (*da dong*).... We should think for a minute--if soldiers and police could thoroughly purge "*fandong*," then how would we have recorded in history the story of France in 1789, or Russia in 1917, or China in 1911? The precedents are all there, but mankind is forever unwilling to accept the lessons of history. How this is to be regretted.[34]

At the same time, in the face of Japanese advances, he repeatedly admonished his student readers to maintain their patriotic resolve, along with a sincere attitude toward academic responsibilities. For example, in early 1936, as the Japanese Kwantung Army stepped up military operations and attacked passes along the Great Wall, he chastised students for their weakness of resolve and for allowing the patriotic movement, so fervid after the Mukden Incident a little more than a year earlier, to abate.

> Young students: do you have the right to become frightened, panic, flee, and hide from danger in the face of the current Japanese advance? What is your intention when now in schools you ask that final examinations be held ahead of schedule and that the vacation be moved forward? If you do this in order to join the struggle to defend the nation, to prepare for resistance, to fulfill your responsibilities as citizens, to fulfill your leadership responsibilities, then we certainly will not reproach you, we will praise you. But if because the enemy approaches rapidly you panic, become frightened, seek means to withdraw, and hide

from danger, then this is cowardice; these are the actions of the people of a conquered nation.[35]

.Three years later, in the wake of the "December Ninth" outpouring of patriotic energies in opposition to Japanese attempts to create an autonomous region in North China, Luo again challenged the students to combine their love of country with a conscientious attitude to study. When students at Qinghua opposed taking special make-up exams in February 1936, after voting to return to classes, he reminded his readers that the value of the young patriotic movement came "entirely from 'sincerity and purity'. Only by acting in this manner can the strength of virtue for national salvation be produced." The extra hardship of preparing for exams was insignificant.[36]

Luo himself had earned his stripes as a student activist at Qinghua two decades earlier. As president of the student union and editor of the *Qinghua zhoukan*, the student weekly, he played a leading role in the May Fourth demonstrations and the student strikes that followed. Of these experiences, he boasted in later years: "Nine years at Qinghua, three school presidents dismissed."[37] Although in the 1930s, he beseeched the new generation of students to fulfill their academic responsibilities, he never questioned the value of student activism, a significant point of departure from the position of Hu Shi, with whom he had collaborated in articulating and defending human rights in the pages of *Xinyue*. As Dean at Beijing University (*Beida*) in the mid-1930s, Hu urged students to recognize that, at a time of national crisis, their foremost responsibility was to develop their knowledge and abilities. He cautioned against mass demonstrations and actions which violated the spirit of the law, warning students to be wary of minority manipulation.[38]

The difference is critical. Luo and Hu held common views on the relationship between the individual and the state, on intellectual pluralism, on the preparedness of the Chinese people for democracy, and on the shape of the political institutions China required.[39] But Luo understood the impetuous temperament of students, which led them to lie across railroad tracks, boycott classes, and deliver massive petitions to leaders in Nanjing. He understood, too, how these passions were leading them to find in the CCP a more promising vehicle for saving the nation. As a publicist, he attempted to infuse the liberal political alternative with an emotional charge that would elicit a broad response from students and intellectuals. Private pursuit of academic achievement, of economic, social, or philanthropic endeavors, which many of his fellow Western-trained intellectuals turned to, certainly had public relevance for China. China needed these talents for national development. But in his view, more was required. Building a political system that would allow Chinese to live as men, not "unthinking mechanical devices," a system which would allow talent to flourish, foster national construction, and marshal resistance to the foreign aggressor, required political assertiveness on the part of the intellectual elite.

Luo would become increasingly assertive in Chinese politics in the years following the outbreak of full-scale war with Japan, in the summer of 1937, and through the formation of the People's Republic. As a member of the First PPC, a leader of the Democratic League (DL), and a would-be architect of a GMD-CCP compromise through the agency of General George C. Marshall in 1946, his rhetoric would become increasingly strident, and his optimism that the GMD was capable of enlightened reform would vanish. At the same time, he would become increasingly isolated from other proponents of a democratic alternative to the two principal parties. In the process, he would be tagged with the opprobrious label of "politician."

His character, ambitions, and personal life would be called into question, even by his associates among the parties seeking to fashion a political rapproachement. Thus, in the late 1940s, Liang Shiqiu, his close friend and colleague for over thirty years, characterized him as a man who was too often "the lonesome warrior" (*pima danqiang*). Liang described him as impetuous, incautious, too quick to reveal himself. He did not "nourish and cherish" others, and therefore compared unfavorably to the likes of Zhang Junmai and Liang Shuming, whom Liang respected as "upright, honest and magnanimous, sincere and resolute."[40] In a similar vein, Chu Anping, an associate of Luo's since the early 1930s and, in the late 1940s, editor of the liberal periodical, *Guancha* (The Observer), described him as one whose "virtue failed to equal his talent." Yet, Chu recognized that Luo had the knowledge and instinct for politics. Moreover, he conceded that among the leaders of the DL in the late 1940s, Luo was the only one really qualified for hard-nosed practical politics.[41]

Disdain for politics and politicians is not unique to China; the distinction between the statesman and the politician is probably understood everywhere. Some Americans in China in the late 1940s also found Luo discomforting. One member of the Marshall team went so far as to say that he found him "instantly disagreeable," and compared him unfavorably to Carsun Chang (Zhang Junmai), who "seemed a reasonable, intelligent liberal," and to Huang Yanpei, who was "the most delightfully Chinese of the three, expressing his opinions with gestures that made me think of him as a character in the Chinese opera."[42]

Luo may have had an abrasive personality. He was hot-tempered, and his relationships with members of his family were known to be fractious.[43] Character and behavior flaws may indeed have compromised his ability to have a greater impact on Chinese politics. But more than personal failings are needed to explain why he was a "lonesome warrior" within the liberal camp. A far more significant factor would appear to be the lack of a deeper appreciation, on the part of China's liberal intellectuals, for the value of the kind of political engagement he espoused. It is one thing intellectually to endorse challenging authority, criticizing policy, and questioning officials. It is another actually to do so. In the end, not enough did.

It is difficult to measure the persuasiveness of Luo's efforts as a publicist in the 1930s. On the one hand, the failure of more liberals to enter politics suggests a lack of response to his message. Yet, on the other hand, substantial acceptance of a major component of the liberal "platform" Luo promoted is suggested by the formation of the PPC in 1938. A manifestation of the UF forced upon Chiang Kai-shek after the Xi'an Incident, the PPC was neither an elected assembly nor a parliament to which the government could be held responsible. Nevertheless, the stated purpose of the institution, expressed in the Program of Armed Resistance and National Reconstruction, "to unify the national strength, to utilize the best minds of the nation, and to facilitate the formulation and execution of national policies," was a considerable step toward the type of national salvation assembly Luo and many other liberals had called for.[44] And, with independents and representatives of opposition parties holding more than half of the two hundred seats in the body, it was the most diversified group of prominent political leaders ever convened in Republican China, even though all members were ultimately picked by the GMD Central Executive Committee (CEC).[45]

Luo was named to the PPC as a member of the National Socialist Party (NSP), a small "party" of prominent individuals led by Zhang Junmai, which championed an end to one-party dictatorship and the importance of popular participation in politics for fostering a spirit of national unity--themes reiterated countless times by Luo.[46]

The PPC was a welcome development to him. He saw it as a contemporary manifestation of what he described as "the politics of public opinion" (*minyi zhengzhi*), a system of government with an ancient heritage in China. In antiquity, the politics of public opinion was reflected in the collection of songs and poems by sage emperors. "Duke Shao remonstrated King Li: 'Gagging the people's mouths is more dangerous than blocking the flow of the rivers'." Luo compared the Chinese notion that popular opinion represented "the will of heaven" favorably with the European divine right of kings. But he went on to distinguish between the politics of public opinion, a system in which the ruler was morally enjoined to be responsive to the ruled, and democratic politics (*minzhu zhengzhi*), in which the leaders were legally responsible to the people.

The politics of public opinion depended on the wisdom and virtue of the ruler, and Chinese history was replete with examples of violent upheavals that occurred when such wisdom and virtue did not prevail. Democratic politics, by institutionalizing responsibility, provided greater certainty that the "flow of the rivers" would not be blocked.[47]

In the PPC, Luo sought to advance Chinese politics along the path toward democratic politics, first as a leader of an effort to have H. H. Kung removed as Minister of Finance, and then in an attempt to alter the provision in the GMD's Draft Constitution (the 5 May 1936 draft) allowing virtually unchecked executive power.[48] He was outspoken in his efforts to advance this agenda, and his reproaches were sufficiently vexing to Chiang Kai-shek that he was dismissed from the PPC after the Second Council (1941). Furthermore, on Chiang's order, he was forbidden to teach at Southwest Associated University in Kunming or to publish.[49] The order did not silence him, but it did essentially complete his estrangement from the GMD regime. In the relative sanctuary of Kunming, he would become more of an agitator and organizer than simply a publicist. But in the final analysis, in the absence of a leader "wise and virtuous" enough to heed his entreaties, or of a constituency both sufficiently powerful and determined enough to force the type of change he advocated, he could only be an irritant in Chinese politics. The simple conclusion one comes to after a review of his work, however, is that he regarded such behavior as a virtue. He did not desist from such a course: he proceeded on the conviction that China needed not more obedience but more democracy, no matter how irritating.

Notes

1. On Yan Fu, see Benjamin I. Schwartz, *In Search of Wealth and Power* (Cambridge: Harvard University Press, 1964). On Liang Qichao, see Hao Chang, *Liang Ch'i-ch'ao and Intellectual Transition in China, 1890-1907* (Cambridge: Harvard University Press, 1971); Philip C. Huang, *Liang Ch'i-ch'ao and Modern Chinese Liberalism* (Seattle: University of Washington Press, 1972); Joseph R. Levenson, *Liang Ch'i-Ch'ao and the Mind of Modern China* (Cambridge: Harvard University Press, 1959). On Republican and Communist constitutions, see Andrew J. Nathan, "Political Rights in Chinese Constitutions" and "Sources of Chinese Thinking," in R. Randle Edwards, Louis Henkin, and Andrew J. Nathan, *Human Rights In Contemporary China* (New York: Columbia University Press, 1986).

2. On Hu Shi's aversion to politics, see Jerome B. Grieder, *Hu Shih and the Chinese Renaissance: Liberalism in the Chinese Revolution, 1917-1937* (Cambridge: Harvard University Press, 1970), chap. 10 passim.

3. This conclusion is widely shared. See, for example, Maurice Meisner, *Li Ta-chao and the Origins of Chinese Marxism* (New York: Atheneum, 1973), 107-108; Y.C. Wang, *Chinese Intellectuals and the West* (Chapel Hill: University of North Carolina Press, 1966), 498; Lucien Bianco, *The Origins of the Chinese Revolution* (Stanford: Stanford University Press, 1971), 49-50.

4. Lloyd E. Eastman, *The Abortive Revolution: China under Nationalist Rule, 1927-37* (Cambridge: Harvard University Press, 1974), 140-180.

5. Lawrence N. Shyu, "The People's Political Council and China's Wartime Problems, 1937-1945" (Ph.D. diss., Columbia University, 1972).

6. Sun Yat-sen, *San Min Chu-i: The Three Principles of the People*, trans. Frank W. Price (Shanghai: Commercial Press, 1929), 213.

7. The prologue for the first issue of *Xinyue* (hereafter, *XY*), "*Xinyue* de taidu" (The Attitude of *Xinyue*) 1, no. 1 (1928), proclaimed the group's commitment to freedom of thought. The prologue was unsigned, but Liang Shiqiu identified Xu Zhimo as the author. See "Yi *Xinyue*" (Recalling *Xinyue*), in *Qiushi zayi* (Miscellaneous Recollections from the Autumn Chamber) (Taibei: Zhuanji wenxue chuban she, 1970), 65-67.

8. Luo Longji, "Lun renquan" (On Human Rights), in Hu Shi, ed., *Renquan lunji* (Essays on Human Rights) (Shanghai: Xinyue shudian, 1930), 39.

9. Ibid., 43.

10. Luo Longji, "Gao yapo yanlun ziyou zhe" (A Word to Those Who Oppress Freedom of Speech), in ibid., 99-105.

11. Ibid.

12. Luo Longji, "Dui xunzheng shiqi yuefa de piping" (Criticism of the Provisional Constitution for the Period of Political Tutelage), *XY* 3, no. 8 (n.d.).

13. "Zhongguo Guomindang diyici quanguo daibiao dahui xuanyan" (Manifesto of the First National Congress of the Guomindang), in *Zhongkuo guomindang diyi, er, san, si ci quanguo daibiao dahui huikan* (Proceedings of the First, Second, Third, and Fourth National Congresses of the Guomindang) (Taibei: Wenhai chubanshe, 1966), 55.

14. Luo Nusheng [Luo Longji], "Renquan buneng liu zai yuefa li?" (Can Human Rights Not Be Incorporated into the Provisional Constitution?), *XY* 3, no. 7 (n.d.).

15. Luo Longji, "Women yao shenmeyang de zhengzhi zhidu?" (What Kind of Political System Do We Want?), *XY* 2, no. 12 (1930): 9.

16. Ibid., 11-12.

17. Luo Longji, "Fucong de weixian" (The Dangers of Obedience), trans. of Harold Laski's essay, *XY* 3, nos. 5-6 (n.d.). See Harold Laski, *The Dangers of Obedience and Other Essays* (New York: Harper and Brothers, 1930).

18. Luo Longji, "Wei gongchan wenti zhonggao Guomindang (A Sincere Word of Advice to the Nationalist Party on the Issue of Communism), *XY* 3, no. 10 (n.d.): 2.

19. Ibid., 3-7.

20. Rudolf Lowenthal, *The Religious Periodical Press in China* (Peiping: The Synodal Commission in China, 1940), 51-53.

YSB, produced by the Center for Chinese Research Materials (Washington, D.C.), covers the period from 26 February 1936 through 18 July 1937, with a few lapses. Although unsigned, the authorship of the editorials referred to in this essay can be attributed to Luo in several ways. He always wrote lucid vernacular prose, and rarely resorted to ornate phraseology and classical references. Among the writings of his associates, the simple fluid sentence essay of Hu Shi were perhaps most similar, but the tone of Luo's essays and editorials was always more incisive. Liang Shiqiu, who occasionally wrote signed "*shilun* (Essays on Current Topics)" in *YSB*, was by contrast consistently more literary, even when discussing political matters. Content further helps to identify authorship. The advocacy of free speech, constitutionalism, a "government of capable men," toleration of diverse intellectual and political views, cessation of military measures against the CCP, and united resistance against the Japanese were constant themes in Luo's writings. Events in Western political history, especially English history, are set up as mirrors for Chinese to examine their own politics. Further assurance on authorship has been provided by Ji Wenxun, who served as international news editor (and for a time as national affairs editor) of *YSB* from 1932 until the paper moved from Kunming to Chongqing in early 1939. Ji reviewed all the editorials cited in this paper and was "extremely doubtful" anyone else associated with *YSB* could have written them. Ji Wenxun, interview by author, 3 May 1979.

22. Lowenthal, 51-53.

23. *YSB* editorial, 12 April 1933; reprinted in *Guowen zhoubao* 10, no. 15.

24. Ibid.

25. Luo Longji, "Gao Riben guomin he Zhongguo de dangju" (A word to the Japanese People and the Chinese Authorities), *XY* 3, no. 12 (n.d.). Similar views, combined with a fervid appeal to patriotic sentiment, were expressed by Luo in *Shenyang shijian* (The Shenyang [Mukden] Incident), a tract published by Luo in 1931 (Shanghai: Lianyou tushu yinshua gongsi).

26. Ibid.

27. Lyman P. Van Slyke, *Enemies and Friends: The United Front in Chinese Communist History* (Stanford: Stanford University Press, 1967), 42-43.

28. His dissertation was published as *The Conduct of Parliamentary Elections in England* (New York: Julius Lewin and Son, 1928).

29. *YSB* editorial, 15 February 1933; reprinted in *Guowen zhoubao* 10, no. 7.

30. Luo Longji, "Zhuanjia zhengzhi" (Experts and Politics), in *Renquan lunji*, 183.

31. Luo Longji, "Wo dui Zhongguo ducai zhengzhi de yijian" (My Views on Dictatorship in China), *Yuzhou xunkan* (The Universe), no. 5 (1935): 9.

32. *YSB* editorial, 8 April 1932; reprinted in *Guowen zhoubao* 9, no. 15.

33. Luo Longji, "Wo dui dangwu shang de 'jinqing piping'" (My 'Sincere Criticism' of Party Affairs), *XY* 2, no. 8 (1929): 13.

34. *YSB* editorial, 3 March 1936; Center for Chinese Research Materials, microfilm reprint.

35. *YSB* editorial, 9 January 1933; reprinted in *Guowen zhoubao* 10, no. 3.

36. *YSB* editorial, 22 February 1936; Center for Chinese Research Materials, microfilm reprint.

37. Liang Shiqiu, "Qinghua ba nien" (Eight Years at Qinghua [University]), in Liang Shiqiu, *Qiushi zayi*, 13-48.

38. John Israel, *Student Nationalism in China, 1927-1937* (Stanford: Stanford University Press, 1966), 133-134.

39. See Hu Shi, "Renquan yu yuefa" (Human Rights and the Provisional Constitution), *XY* 2, no. 2 (1929); "Women zou neitiao lu" (Which Road Shall We Take?), *XY* 2, no. 10 (1929).

40. Liang Shiqiu, "Luo Longji lun" (On Luo Longji), *Shiji pinglun* (Century Critic) 2, no. 15 (1947).

41. Chu Anping, "Zhongguo de zhengju" (The Political Situation in China), *Guancha* 2, no. 2 (1947): 7.

42. John Robinson Beal, *Marshall in China* (Toronto: Doubleday, 1970), 76.

43. Ji Wenxun, interview by author, 3 May 1979.

44. Lawrence K. Rosinger, *China's Wartime Politics, 1937-1944* (Princeton: Princeton University Press, 1944), 101.

45. Membership in the PPC is described in Shyu, 35-49.

46. Luo was apparently present at the founding of the *Zaisheng She* (Renaissance Society), established in Beijing shortly after the Mukden Incident. The group, which had fewer than one thousand members on the eve of the First PPC, adopted the name NSP in 1934. Luo never contributed any articles to the group's monthly, *Zaisheng* (The National Renaissance), and although he was a member of its CEC, his involvement and influence are uncertain. See *Zhongguo gexiao dangpai xiankuang* (The Present State of Affairs of Minority Parties in China) (n.p., 1946; reprinted by the Center for Chinese Research Materials, Washington, D.C., 1969), 65-66; "Democracy vs. One-Party Rule in Kuomintang China," *Amerasia*, 25 April 1943. The latter suggests Luo favored expansion of the Party's membership base, a position not supported by Zhang Junmai.

47. Luo Longji, "Zhongquo yu minyi zhengzhi" (China and the Politics of Public Opinion), *Jinri pinglun* (Today's Commentaries) 4, no. 21 (1940); Luo Longji, "Ba nian lai de Zhongguo minzhu de dongxiang" (The Course of Chinese Politics in the Past Eight Years), *Minzhu zhoukan* (Democratic Weekly) 2, no. 9 (1945): 6-9.

48. On the efforts to oust H. H. Kung, see *Guomin canzhenghui shiliao* (Historical Materials on the PPC) (Taibei, 1962), 29; Ward to State, 22 July 1944, State Dept. 893.000/7-2244, p. 4. On the effort to revise the May Fifth Draft, see ibid.; Luo Longji, "Wuwu xiancao de quanli yiwu zhang" (The Rights and Duties Section of the May Fifth Draft Constitution), *Jinri pinglun* 3, no. 10 (1940).

49. Ringwalt to Charles E. Gauss, 29 January 1944, State Dept. 893.00/15292, p. 4.

PART TWO

Opposition Parties and Groups During the 1930s and 1940s

3

From Educator to Politician: Huang Yanpei and the Third Force

Thomas D. Curran

Introduction

Huang Yanpei (1878-1965) was a professional educator who spent the first twenty years of the Republican Period working hard to promote vocationalism within China's modern school system. A modest man with a peaceful disposition and a passion for classical poetry (he composed nearly two thousand poems of his own), he had little tolerance for the underside of Chinese political life, and tried with mixed success to avoid personal involvement in it. By the late 1920s, however, he was drawn by his reform activities into the orbit of a group of progressive, but non-Communist, opponents of the Guomindang (GMD) regime, whose publishing activities eventually made them and Huang targets of Nationalist repression. A patriot with intense pride in China's heritage, he then moved further into politics and the ranks of Chiang Kai-shek's potential enemies, as he became active in the movement for national salvation. Finally, by the outbreak of the Sino-Japanese War in 1937, he had become thoroughly engaged in defense-related activities, and was soon to become a committed member of the Third Force (TF), a loose coalition of intellectuals, educators, businessmen, and professional politicians dedicated to the introduction of

The author wishes to acknowledge the support of the Sacred Heart University Research and Creativity Grants Program.

democratic reforms and the maintenance of national unity, in the interest of fighting the Japanese.

As a member of the TF, he was active indeed. He was a major force behind the organization of the League of Chinese Democratic Political Groups (LCDPG), and served as a member of the central executive committee (CEC) of its successor, the Democratic League (DL). As a leading figure in that group, his activities touched many different areas, but his major preoccupations became the fostering of democratic institutions and, most important, mediation of the conflict between the GMD and the Communist Party (CCP). He never became a member of the GMD and, as shall be shown, his early support for the Nationalist Government (NG) gradually withered away as his faith in the Party's commitment to democracy was repeatedly shaken by Chiang Kai-shek's reluctance to initiate genuine reforms and the Party's repression of organized opposition. On the other hand, he was not a Communist. His peaceful nature would not permit him to condone class struggle in any form, and he believed that, given the country's low level of industrial development, China must allow its capitalists sufficient freedom to develop its economic resources in the most effective manner possible.[1] Therefore, unable to support either the Nationalists or the Communists, he opted for a middle course, attempting to bridge the gap between the two parties in order to facilitate their cooperation in the construction of a unified and democratic nation.

Interestingly, he never seems to have contemplated building a force that could compete on equal terms, politically or militarily, with either the GMD or the CCP. He chose instead to play the role of mediator, struggling to help the two parties find common ground. When that task proved impossible, he envisioned no alternative other than withdrawal from politics, and attempted to fade into his more comfortable role as a senior fellow in the educational establishment, to await the inevitable resolution of the GMD-CCP conflict by military means.

The pattern that he established in his political career was quite similar to that of the TF as a whole. Neither could accept the leadership of either the CCP or the GMD, and both tried hard to play a mediative role. As one of his friends and allies in the TF movement explained: while the GMD had no political program, basing its claim to legitimacy solely upon the exercise of force, the CCP advocated a radical social and economic program that alienated the intellectuals and struck terror into the hearts of China's businessmen.[2] The only hope, therefore, was to chart a middle course, weaving a path between the Scylla of the GMD and the Charybdis of the CCP.

The hopes of Huang and the TF were ultimately dashed by the inability of the two major parties to work together. By late 1946, it had become clear to him and many others that the effort to reconcile the GMD and the CCP was doomed. At that point, he decided to abandon politics and return to his studio, hoping to write for a living and renew his associations in the Shanghai educational world (which had never been severed, since many of his friends also had been drawn to the TF).

His resolution to avoid further political attachments was not to be fulfilled. He, like others, was eventually compelled to choose between the GMD and the CCP, and, when forced to decide, went to Beijing to welcome Mao Zedong to the capital. That he chose the Communist side is interesting, for it is an indication of how alienated he had become from the party which had at first attracted his greatest sympathy. What is more important, however, is that in the end he did choose. Rather than continue trying to sustain an autonomous existence on the fringes of the mainstream of Chinese politics, he felt he had only two options: (1) remove himself entirely from political life, as he was always strongly tempted to do; or (2) ally himself with the side that seemed destined to win the Civil War and, in the long run, unify China and lead it into the modern world. For him, there really was no third alternative in the form of a loyal opposition.

The reasons for this are both simple and complex: simple because the preponderance of military force lay clearly in the hands of the two major parties and at least one side, the GMD, was not prepared to allow a third alternative to exist; complex because Huang and others like him never really conceived of a third party that could stand as an equal to the Nationalists and Communists. He was a leading member of the TF and, if his career in politics may be considered a reflection of the life of the TF movement as a whole, one might suggest that the movement was doomed from the start, because its leaders lacked the vision even to try to create a sustainable base of power.

This essay has been written in the hope that a study of his political career will shed light on the fate of the TF. He was an educator and a patriot who was drawn into politics by the unprecedented nature of the crises facing China during his time. Like him, the TF sprang from a crisis environment, which mobilized into political activity many who might under normal circumstances have lived out their lives peacefully as teachers, journalists, and businessmen. That they lacked the skills to build real political power at a time when, to paraphrase Mao, power grew out of the barrel of a gun, is no surprise. Their behavior was also, however, conditioned by the political culture into which they had been born, and the pattern of political action that people like Huang exhibited can reveal much about both their political world and their attitudes regarding the political roles that people such as themselves should play.

Early Political Career

Throughout most of his early career, he sought to avoid political involvement of any kind. His early activities as an educator drew him by accident into the late Qing revolutionary movement, and he later served as Commissioner of Education for Jiangsu Province and as a member of the Jiangsu Provincial Assembly. By 1917, however, his interest in government had waned, and he decided to withdraw from politics entirely, devoting himself instead to the cause which became his professional passion, vocational education.[3]

He believed that the greatest problem facing China was its economic backwardness, and he felt that the only way to save the country was to reform its education system, creating within it a commitment to the cultivation of skills that would prepare students more concretely for the realities of China's workplace and contribute to the nation's economic development. He claimed in his autobiography (1965) that he never accepted the view of pragmatists such as Hu Shi that students should avoid politics and devote themselves solely to study,[4] and he did in fact offer verbal support for the student activism of the May Fourth era, striving as well to promote among students a heightened sense of patriotism. He still argued, however, that China's most urgent problems were economic, and that a fundamental solution could come only through education. As a result, the bulk of his activities during the 1920s were directed toward the promotion of educational reform in general and the vocational-education movement in particular.[5]

Despite his lack of interest in a political career, events conspired to draw him ineluctably into the vortex of Chinese politics. First, the logic of his reform proposals led him to form associations that would inevitably make him politically suspect, from the point of view of the GMD. The vocational-education movement, for example, advocated curriculum reforms aimed at obliterating the prejudice against manual labor that was borne by China's intellectuals, and students in the schools that were founded by his organization, the Vocational Education Society (VES), were expected to work in school-affiliated factories, as well as study. These ideas attracted the attention of early Communists, who then appeared to have considered him a potential ally.[6]

By 1926, he had also come to sense that educational reform could not succeed without political struggle, and he resolved that, while he personally held no political ambition, educators in general must begin to play a more active role on the political scene. Indeed, he had come to believe that his own movement for vocational education was threatened by China's political difficulties, and he urged the VES to become more directly involved in political affairs.[7] Using an address before the VES to test his new vision (to which he attached the term "greater vocational education"), he declared that if China's modern schools were to thrive, the leaders of the educational establishment must participate more purposefully in the nation's political life, "since in order to manage education we must first exert ourselves to put society in order." His Chinese biographer believes that this speech, made in April 1926, marked his "awakening from his infatuation with the notion that 'education can save the country'"; i.e., it represented his final acknowledgement that educational reform alone could not solve China's problems.[8]

The VES responded aggressively to his call for greater social and political activism, and founded a number of progressive bookstores and journals (e.g., *Jiaoyu yu zhiye* [Education and Vocation] and *Shenghuo zhoukan* [Life Weekly]), as well as a movement for village reform.[9] These and other activities of the Society earned it and its founder the enmity of right-wing elements within the GMD and, in 1927 when Chiang Kai-shek occupied Shanghai and began his suppression of dissidents, Huang was labeled a "scholar-tyrant (*xuefa*)" and a warrant was issued for his arrest. Upon hearing that he was marked for assassination, he escaped to Dalian, where he spent the next half-year reading in a railroad library maintained by the Japanese Kwantung Army.[10]

By the spring of 1928, he felt it safe to travel, and formally withdrew from his position as head administrator of the VES and began a tour of Korea and Japan. This trip brought him into contact with the other force that was to propel him back into politics: Japanese aggression. While in Japan, he took note of the rising tide of militarism, especially among youth groups and rural militia, and he resolved to alert the authorities at home to the danger posed by the threat of Japanese invasion.

It took a long time for his opportunity to arrive, but by the spring of 1931, the order for his arrest had been rescinded, and he anxiously returned to China. He arrived in Shanghai on 24 April 1931, in possession of three books he had purchased in Japan that appeared to him to reveal the plans of the Japanese government to invade China, and he was determined to sound the call for national defense. He went directly to Nanjing and obtained an audience with Chiang Kai-shek, during which he gave the Generalissimo the books. According to Huang, Chiang's response was to make no comment other than suggest that he report to Foreign Minister Wang Zhengting. When he did, this skeptical official suggested that no invasion was imminent, for if the Japanese were actually planning to attack Chinese territory, they most certainly would have kept their plans secret from Huang.[11]

He was disappointed by the GMD's reluctance to adopt a more aggressive posture with respect to the Japanese, and upon his return to Shanghai, he began working to mobilize the public to plan the nation's defense. Soon, he counted among his close associates a number of individuals, such as Shi Liangcai, Zhang Naiqi, Zhang Yilin, Zou Taofen, and Shen Junru, who were to become staunch critics of the NG during the 1930s, either independently or as leaders of the National Salvation Association (NSA), a group that was highly critical of the government's reluctance to resist Japanese encroachment upon Chinese sovereignty.[12]

Thus, by the early 1930s, his concerns over educational reform and national defense had thrust him into the murky world of Chinese politics and involved him with a number of individuals who harbored distinctly anti-GMD political preferences. Indeed, his activities in Shanghai and his association with critics of the NG earned him once again the resentment of GMD officials, and he was forced off the staff of the Shanghai newspaper, *Shen bao*, where he had served as co-director of the Planning Department since 1929.[13]

Political Activities During Wartime

Upon the outbreak of the Sino-Japanese War in July 1937, Huang became fully engaged in the effort to mobilize the population of Shanghai on behalf of the city's defense. Serving as vice-chairman and secretary of the Shanghai Municipal Council, he had made important contacts within the Shanghai business community, and they, together with his allies in the Shanghai educational establishment, played an important role in directing the local campaign to supply the front, rescue wounded soldiers, and provide relief for civilians affected by the fighting.

The attempt to defend the East Coast was, of course, unsuccessful, and by the end of 1938, he had moved to Chongqing with the NG. Thanks in large part to his experience as a defense leader, he was appointed to both the National Defense Advisory Council and the Standing Committee of the People's Political Council (PPC). Though the VES continued its educational activities, with Huang maintaining a watchful eye over the enterprise, he in fact devoted most of his attention during the war to the resistance effort, spending much of the next several years traveling abroad to raise money, as an officer of the War Bond Sales Commission.

Early in the war, he had already struck upon the theme that was to dominate his political activities for the rest of the conflict and for several years prior to the Communist victory in 1949, i.e., reconciliation of the CCP and GMD, first in the interest of defending China from the Japanese and later in order to facilitate national reunification and reconstruction. By 1940, he had already made a number of attempts to mediate between the two sides and had earned a reputation as a peacemaker.[14]

Having chosen for himself the role of mediator, he was uncomfortable with criticism of the GMD that might impair his efforts to settle the dispute between it and the Communists. He became one of the principal organizers of the Association of Comrades for Unity and National Reconstruction (ACUNR), the forerunner of the LCDPG, which itself subsequently gave birth to the DL.[15] Formed in late 1939, largely in response to the GMD stepped-up program of intimidation directed at critics of the government, the essence of the ACUNR's program was contained in three demands it made upon the Nationalist authorities: continue unequivocally the war against Japan; combine and nationalize China's armed forces; and institute genuine democracy. Regarding the first two, he had no reservations at all. He campaigned vigorously on their behalf throughout the war, and continued to press for the integration and depoliticization of China's armed forces during the postwar period. Although he felt the implementation of democratic government to be an essential long-term goal, he was not yet prepared to concede that China was ready for democracy in the short term and was content to let the GMD carry out its promise to implement constitutional reform in due time. Adopting, more or less without challenge, Sun Yat-sen's view of the need for political tutelage, he wrote in his diary that while China undeniably needed more democracy, it could only come through a process that involved training. What he envisioned was a "nursery-style democratic government," within which the people could learn the habits of democracy while practicing it on a limited scale.[16] He was thus prepared to accept the GMD's promises that it would launch a constitutional democracy after war's end, and was careful to avoid pushing that party too fast in the direction of political change.

Perhaps more important in view of his major objective of promoting CCP-GMD cooperation in the war effort, by 1941 he had cultivated a relatively secure relationship with Chiang Kai-shek and the GMD, which he hoped might aid him in his efforts to bring the two sides together. He was not prepared to jeopardize that relationship by adhering to a rigid set of demands regarding political reform. Although he did remain actively engaged in the ACUNR's activities (he also contributed one thousand *yuan* and was especially helpful in launching the LCDPG's mouthpiece, *Guangming bao* [Light]), when he became concerned that too much criticism could derail the process of mediation and play into the hands of the Japanese, he succumbed to GMD efforts to censure the ACUNR, resigned his post as its provisional chairman, and urged its members to be more tactful in voicing their dissent.[17]

His determination to defend the GMD's leadership would eventually weaken, as he found his position shaken by actions taken by that party which either threatened to destroy his hope of a peaceful settlement of the GMD-CCP struggle or were aimed at his friends in the reform community. He was particularly disturbed by the government's January 1941 attack upon the Communists' New Fourth Army and by its repeated suppression of left-wing publications. After the New Fourth Army Incident prompted the withdrawal of the CCP's delegates from the PPC, he met several times with Chiang Kai-shek, attempting unsuccessfully to heal the rift.[18] When in February 1941 the government closed all of the *Shenghuo* Bookstore's fifty-odd branches, prompting Huang's friend, Zou Taofen, to flee to Hong Kong, Huang arranged for the VES to take over *Shenghuo*'s facilities and open a new establishment, the *Guoxun* Bookstore, engaging many of the personnel formerly in the employ of *Shenghuo*.[19]

By the fall of 1941, his concerns over the government's autocratic methods had inspired him to call upon it to introduce democratic reforms more rapidly, in order to install restraints upon the regime's excesses and to pacify its critics. On 25 November, he signed a petition with twenty-three other people challenging the government to speed up the process of political tutelage, while terminating secret-police activity and reinforcing the state's guarantees regarding personal freedom.[20] Thus far, despite those signs of his growing disenchantment with the Nationalist regime, his faith in Chiang Kai-shek and the GMD remained largely intact. He continued to believe that Chiang and the GMD could be relied upon to implement their promises regarding political reform, and met frequently with the Generalissimo himself to discuss the Party's plans for constitutional change.[21] Indeed, his hopes for democratic political reform were boosted decisively by Chiang's announcement, in September 1943, that the GMD was prepared to speed up the implementation of the new constitution.[22] Following that announcement, the Party's CEC authorized the formation of an organization to prepare for constitutional government, and on 12 November 1943, the Association to Assist in the Inauguration of Constitutionalism (*Xianzheng Shishi Xiejin Hui*; hereafter, AAIC) formally convened in an atmosphere made bright by Chiang's promise to "implement constitutional government and return government to the people."[23]

Tapped to serve on the AAIC Standing Committee, Huang was more than happy to join the movement for constitutionalism, and plunged into the project with considerable enthusiasm. With the help of activists from the VES, he immediately organized a series of monthly seminars on constitutional government and published a journal, *Xianzheng yuekan* (Constitutional Government Monthly; hereafter, *XZYK*), to disseminate speeches and articles generated by the movement. He succeeded in enlisting the support of notable individuals with a wide range of backgrounds. Among the journal's sponsors were many influential members of China's commercial and banking communities,[24] as well as a number of the country's leading intellectuals.[25] Most had at one time or another been staunch supporters of the GMD, and there was little in either the tone or the content of the first issue of the journal that would lead one to conclude that its editors intended for it to fun afoul of the authorities. Huang himself prepared an essay for the second issue, in which he defended the GMD's record of promoting constitutional government and expressed his confidence that the government had the capacity to take the steps necessary to prepare for true democracy. In that piece, he argued that the GMD was the legitimate heir to Sun Yat-sen's legacy, and that had it not been for the outbreak of war, the Party would already have carried out Sun's plans for constitutional rule. He maintained, in fact, that while the entire nation was preoccupied with war, it was the GMD that kept alive China's hopes for democratic government, and he welcomed the government's "heroic decision" to reopen the process of constitution-building, with the admonition that even with government leadership, the process would take several years and be completed only after the war had ended.[26]

He devoted much of his time during the next year to his activities on behalf of the movement for constitutional government. He spent a great deal of energy lecturing and writing pieces for *XZYK* and *Guoxun* (National News), and he managed for the first six months of 1944 to sustain a relatively optimistic attitude. While acknowledging abuses among government officials, he seemed confident that given the support and encouragement of China's intellectual and business communities, the government would develop the means to police itself. Facing repeated questions concerning the GMD's sincerity with respect to the constitution, he consistently asserted that the government's enthusiasm for the movement was genuine and urged others to cooperate with it in its effort to promote government by law.[27]

While he continued during 1944 to profess support for the government's reform efforts, the abuses of its officials, especially the violations of civil rights by security organs, made his position increasingly difficult. In a speech he gave at Fudan University in July, he revealed his growing frustration, making a point of distancing himself from the GMD by referring to himself explicitly as an independent and a liberal (*ziyouzhuyizhe*).[28] Then, in the 1 September issue of *XZYK*, he joined others in launching a direct attack upon the government for its corruption and violations of human rights.[29] That piece was followed by an article of his own in which he registered his anger over a case of false arrest (based upon mistaken identity), called upon the government to enforce its own guarantees of personal freedom, and urged it to make public the names of official organs with the authority to make arrests and severely punish security officers who abused their power.[30]

By the spring of 1945, he was sufficiently concerned about the government's continuing corruption to want to clarify his relationship with the GMD and elaborate upon the bases of his support for its leadership. "I am not," he wrote, "a member of the Guomindang, but I was a member of the Revolutionary Alliance, the forerunner of the Guomindang, and I am familiar with virtually all of the Party's leaders. Indeed, most of my friends are Guomindang members, and I have observed from the sidelines the Party's entire history." Such a close association with the Party's leadership and history gave him, he believed, the authority to criticize the behavior of GMD personnel and comment upon the legitimacy of its claim to leadership.

He began his critique with the charge that within the GMD there were many individuals who were using it as a vehicle for the self-interested pursuit of personal wealth and power, and a warning that such behavior, should it continue, could lead to the collapse of the Party's claim to legitimacy:

> There are some in the Guomindang who possess a high spirit but little knowledge and who feel that China belongs to the Party, i.e., that China is the private possession of the Party and that the Party members are its only rulers.... If this attitude is not expunged, the future both for the Party and for China is not bright, [for] if the Party considers the leadership of China to be its right [rather than its responsibility], the people of the entire nation will look upon it with contempt.[31]

Despite the harsh tone of his warning, he had not yet abandoned his faith in Chiang Kai-shek and was still prepared to grant the GMD the leading role in guiding China through the difficult times ahead. In recognition of the Party's accomplishments, while leading China's struggle against the warlords and Japan, and its continued strong position, he argued that the GMD had earned the right to a preeminent position in China's political life. It was, he reasoned, analogous to the construction of a chair. The chair will require four legs, but one must have the first leg in order to begin work. As for the question of whether the GMD would be content to accept the participation of the other parties (in his words, "join the others in holding up the chair"), he referred to a statement made by Chiang on 4 February 1945 before a meeting of the Standing Committee of the AAIC to the effect that there must be more than one political party to prevent the inevitable slide of the ruling party into corruption.[32] He hoped that Chiang was sincere, and took comfort in the fact that Chiang's point was reinforced in a speech by Wu Tiecheng, co-chairman of the Party's Central Secretariat. His optimism was not without reservations, however, his chief concern being that there be established within the GMD, and in Chinese society in general, a tradition of respect for the rule of law, without which he believed any movement toward a multiparty system would be meaningless. Nevertheless, despite his developing awareness of the GMD's tendency to employ dictatorial methods, he clung tenaciously to his argument that the Party offered the best hope for a peaceful and democratic future. As he put it, "We must still yield to those with merit, and currently it is the Guomindang that is in control of the country's affairs."[33]

Meanwhile, the seminars that he had helped to organize in association with the founding of *XZYK* had, by the middle of 1944, become fora for the expression of wide-ranging views on a variety of social, economic, and political issues. Many speakers, some from the CCP,[34] expressed opinions distinctly hostile to the NG, and the seminars attracted the increasing attention of GMD authorities, culminating in a government attempt to close them down by force.[35]

While suppression of the *XZYK* seminars placed Huang in a most difficult position with respect to the NG, an additional set of circumstances pressed him even further in the direction of a break with the GMD, i.e., the approaching end of the war and the issue of GMD-CCP relations in the postwar era. In early 1945, while the GMD was planning the introduction of a constitution, the leadership of the CCP began to reconsider the possibility of reopening the talks that had been terminated abruptly following the New Fourth Army Incident. In late January, Huang attended an informal meeting at the home of Sun Fo, during which Zhou Enlai raised the possibility of resurrecting the GMD-CCP relationship and proposed the formation of a coalition government by the GMD, the CCP, and various parties representing the TF. The formation of a coalition government, which in turn would manage the formulation and introduction of a constitution, had become mainstream CCP policy by early 1945, and was enshrined as such in a speech by Mao Zedong during the Party's Seventh National Congress in late April.[36] Chiang Kai-shek, however, absolutely refused to consider it, arguing that such a proposal was merely an attempt to overthrow the GMD's leadership, and vowed instead that the issue of the new constitution would be placed in the hands of the National Assembly (NA) that the government planned to convene following the end of the war.[37] Nevertheless, Huang saw the Communists' offer as an opportunity to develop a relationship between the two parties that might forestall the re-emergence of civil war, and he was disappointed by Chiang's apparently intransigent position. Hoping to resurrect the spirit of cooperation between the two parties, he and his ally, Chu Fucheng, convened a group of TF activists and sympathetic GMD leaders to formulate a response to the Communists' proposal.[38] The group agreed that the time was right to reopen the CCP-GMD talks, and after informing Chiang of their intentions (and receiving what was in Huang's eyes an evasive reply), they decided to act as the catalyst to initiate negotiations. By 2 June, the group had wired Yanan their hope that the CCP and the GMD would reopen communications in the interest of finishing the war and beginning the reconstruction of China on the basis of national unity.[39] The Communist leaders responded cautiously that they would neither re-enter the PPC nor support the government's plans to convene a NA for the purpose of ratifying the draft constitution.[40] They did offer, however, to discuss, in the context of a conference of all China's political parties, the formation of a coalition government, and they invited the seven signatories of the 2 June telegram to visit Yanan to review the matter.[41]

These seven individuals (Zhang Bojun, Chu Fucheng, Fu Sinian, Huang Yanpei, Leng Yu, Zuo Shunsheng, and Wang Yunwu) met on 26 June to respond to Mao's note. They formulated a proposal of their own, calling on the government to immediately organize a conference of representatives of all interested parties (including the CCP) to resolve the constitutional question, and asking the government to begin implementing political reforms of its own. After presenting their ideas to both the American Ambassador, Patrick J. Hurley, and Chiang (and apparently receiving no significant reply from either party), the group made plans to go to Yanan.

On 1 July, the group (less Wang Yunwu, due to illness) departed for Yanan for a five-day visit that was to have a decisive impact upon Huang's political future, marking a turning point in both his relations with the GMD and his attitude toward the CCP. Upon his return, he wrote a short book, recording both his impressions of life in the Communist capital and the significant details of the group's discussions with the CCP leadership. The book, *Yanan guilai* (Return from Yanan), became an important impediment to his maintenance of good relations with the Nationalists. With his permission, the book's publishers decided to release the work without following the government's regulations regarding prior censorship, hoping to generate a movement against the government's censorship laws.[42] That he was willing to allow his manuscript to be used for such a purpose is not surprising, since he had been working within the PPC for years to try to have the government's censorship laws removed. It does, however, reflect his growing disenchantment with the GMD and his willingness to put his still-comfortable relationship with the Party at risk.

The book is also important as a summary of his views regarding the political situation in the Communist border region, as the war in the Pacific was about to end. He was quite favorably impressed by what he saw in Yanan, and was especially interested in the apparent flexibility of the CCP's leadership as it dealt with the problems of rural Shaanxi Province. "They often," he noted, "clutch fast to an individual or a local success which they then develop into a broad movement."[43] He recalled a conversation with Mao in which the Chairman expressed his commitment to finding practical solutions to concrete problems and his opposition to "subjectivism," i.e., the tendency to follow Marxist ideology blindly. Indeed, he quoted Mao as having told him that "one cannot always follow [Marx] in studying the realities of Chinese history. One must, rather, create one's own theory in accordance with China's actual needs. Many Chinese Communist Party members cannot see China but only see the revolutionary writings on their bookshelves. The fewer such Marxist theorists the better."[44] This apparent lack of dogmatism among the CCP leadership made a distinctly favorable impression upon him, presenting him with welcome evidence that the Party had changed direction and adopted methods that entitled it to play a legitimate role in the coming rearrangement of political forces in China.

Not being a Marxist and never having had much confidence in collectivist solutions to China's economic and social problems, he was also pleased by the Party's abandonment of radical social and economic policies. Rather than implementing a massive campaign of land redistribution, the Communists had created a flexible program of rent, rent security, and interest-rate reductions, and he was both surprised and delighted to discover that they had managed to resolve the basic issues of equity in the countryside without challenging the principle of private ownership of productive property.

He was so impressed with the overall standard of living in Yanan and the Communists' approach to education and rural development that he noted in his diary that what he saw there was actually quite close to what he had been advocating as an ideal for years.[45] As an educator, he had long promoted a pragmatic approach to education, designed to match the training received by China's youth to the real needs of China's economy. His hope was that the gap that had customarily existed between China's educated elite and the common people would disappear as China's education system was reoriented toward providing skills that could find ready application in the world beyond China's classrooms and government offices. He was clearly impressed by Mao's personal disregard for intellectualism and his effort to prompt his own educated cadres to turn away from book learning and devote themselves to practical work.[46] Moreover, rather than merely preaching the virtues of pragmatism, he believed the CCP was actually carrying out its program, i.e., "looking for the suffering of the masses" and attempting to find practical solutions. This, he claimed, was precisely what he himself had been advocating for years. At times perhaps prone to hyperbole in his writings, he referred to the Communists in terms that reflected his obvious delight at what he found in Yanan, but which could not help but arouse the ire of the GMD leaders:

> I feel it is not surprising that the Communist Party manifests itself this way. Having gathered together such a group of talented scholars and soldiers to put this ... place in order, naturally they have made a good contribution.
>
> I believe that the most precious spirit of these Communist Party friends is that they unceasingly seek the good and strive for progress. If this kind of spirit is completely developed, my hopes for the future are limitless.

> Some may suspect that the Communist Party is moving backward. I agree with them that perhaps [by adhering to Marxist-Leninist doctrine] they have swallowed the poison of a foreign eight-legged essay [a foreign dogma], as Mao himself suggests. But I believe that it would be a good thing for such people to study the Party's rectification documents and reconsider.
>
> I also feel that a man should stand on his own two feet rather than let others make decisions for him. One must serve the truth. After all, perhaps there is some good even in that which is bad. One must be open-minded and try sincerely to understand reality. One must look at what [the Communists] do rather than merely listen to what they say.[47]

Considering his preoccupation with political matters, the CCP's new political line ("new democracy") may have appealed to him even more than its social and economic programs, offering him hope that the CCP could become an ally in the area of constitutional reform. In one of his conversations with Mao, the Communist leader told him that the ultimate solution to China's problems was democracy. In that conversation, Mao struck upon a theme that had long troubled Huang himself, as he pondered the question of how to moderate the behavior of the GMD and the officials of the NG. Mao made the point that the only real check upon tyrannical rule was public oversight through democratic means. Indeed, Mao asserted, "only by allowing the people to oversee the government will the government not dare to be careless or idle on the job. Only if the people take responsibility will the government be prevented from standing by at rest while the people perish." In *Yanan guilai*, Huang expressed his profound agreement with Mao's assertion, pointing out (with the expectation, one senses, that both TF activists and the GMD would be listening) that "only by having the people determine the direction of the government will we be able to avoid the tendency for government officials to use their offices to pursue their private interests."[48] As for his impression of the attitude of the CCP toward the visitors' primary mission of facilitating the reopening of negotiations between the CCP and the GMD, he recorded hopefully that Mao had agreed with the group that the "door to negotiations between the two sides really is not closed."[49]

His visit to Yanan seems to have been the catalyst that drove him toward assuming a more active oppositional role. While prior to the summer of 1945 he had been more or less content to let the GMD direct the postwar reconstruction, he now doubted the Party's ability to do so, and was prepared to make demands upon the government that indicated that he was ready to go further than before in the direction of organized opposition. Indeed, shortly after his return from Yanan, he not only elevated the level of his criticism of the GMD, he also began to toy with the idea of forming a political party of his own.

Huang's Role in the Civil War

In mid-August, Chiang Kai-shek invited the Communist leadership to Chongqing to begin talks, and in preparation for the anticipated discussions with Mao, he asked Huang for his opinion regarding the Communist problem. Both the tone and substance of his response indicate that he was no longer willing to confer upon the GMD, simply by virtue of its history and powerful position, the mantle of leadership. For the Party to retain its legitimacy and the talks to succeed, he insisted that the GMD must initiate reforms of its own immediately to create an environment conducive to free political competition. "Even though Chairman Chiang appears to be sincere," he told Chiang's negotiator, Zhang Qun, "to merely invite Mao Zedong to come to Chongqing is not enough. He must also do a number of things after Japan's surrender. He must permit personal freedom and freedom of expression, dismantle the special forces, release political prisoners, accept the legality of all the other parties, and immediately summon a political conference [including the CCP and the third parties]." Venting his frustration at the government's reluctance to act, he demanded to know why Chiang was not implementing these measures on his own. "If he waits another week or another month," he warned, "we may lose a tremendous opportunity!"[50]

The same day he delivered this stern admonition, he met with two of his friends from the VES, Yang Weiyu and Hu Juewen, to plan the organization of a new political association. This group spent the next four months gathering support from businessmen, educators, and intellectuals with close connections to the business community, and, on 16 December 1945, they held in Chongqing the first congress of their new enterprise, the Democratic National Construction Association (NCA).

The NCA's political platform called for the peaceful reunification of China with democratic means, nationalization of China's armed forces (i.e., removal from the control of political parties and reorganization into a national force under the control of a democratically elected government), and recognition of basic political freedoms and human rights.[51] Embodying the essential goals of the TF movement, these specific points were neither remarkable nor unique. What marked the NCA as an innovative organization and a creation of Huang's was its aspiration to rise above the selfishness of the political parties and pursue the interests of the common people, using methods untainted by partisan politics. He boasted that this association was composed of producers and educators, i.e., persons with "legitimate social positions," rather than politicians with a professional interest in politics. The NCA admitted neither political officials nor military personnel on active duty. It was thus free from the compulsion to become engaged in partisan wrangling, and as representatives of the common people its members could, he argued, act objectively in the best interests of the people.[52] As the organization's manifesto stated: "All of us in the Association have our own positions in life and do not need to resort to political power to pursue our own ambitions.... We wish instead to use only the common efforts of the people and, leaning neither to the right nor the left, build for China a model of peaceful political struggle."[53]

With respect to the CCP-GMD split, the NCA adhered to a policy of strict neutrality. Several of the main speakers at the congress emphatically endorsed the "middle road," and expressed their view that the goal of the NCA should be to create a truly popular force, which could pursue the national interest in an atmosphere free of petty partisanship. Posing an interesting commentary upon their view of public sentiment, several speakers expressed concern that to appear aligned with either the CCP or the GMD could cost them valuable public support. As Huang himself stated, "this association must with all its energy grasp the middle ground and not lean to either side. This may make it hard for us to recruit the most dedicated activists, but it will still place us in the position of being closest to the mainstream of public opinion."[54]

One senses in the writings and speeches of the NCA's organizers a lack of clarity about precisely how they expected to accomplish their objectives. They seem to have consciously avoided hardball politics, hoping to generate a ground swell of public support for their cause but failing to formulate a concrete strategy for translating that support into political action. Indeed, most of their activity was focused upon mobilizing public opinion on behalf of a negotiated settlement between the GMD and the CCP. Thus, while they approved of neither, ultimately they relied upon the cooperation of both parties to accomplish their objectives.

By the end of August 1945, the CCP and the GMD had agreed to reopen direct talks, and by 10 October, the two sides had reached an agreement (the Double Tenth Agreement) calling for a conference of political-party representatives and nonparty leaders to discuss the national situation. The product of that decision, the Political Consultative Conference (PCC), met from 11-31 January 1946 in Chongqing to reorganize the NG and the armed forces, and in general to prepare the way for a peaceful transition to democratic government.[55]

Given the high stakes and the antagonism that existed between the CCP and the GMD, it is remarkable that such a conference could be held at all. It was even more remarkable that, by the end of January, it had produced agreement on each of the major topics under consideration. On 31 January, the conference adjourned amidst an atmosphere of jubilation, as many Chinese caught a glimpse of "the first distinct rays of hope for peace since the civil war had threatened in the fall of 1945."[56] This is not to suggest, however, that the meeting had proceeded entirely without incident. From beginning to end, it was plagued by maneuvering and bickering over the membership and the proposals placed on the table by the various participants.

The GMD, for its part, assumed that it could count upon the support of the great majority of third-party delegates. When this turned out to be a miscalculation, the Party launched a campaign to split the DL, one of the major representatives of the TF. While GMD leaders went out of their way to entertain and cajole DL delegates whom they considered potential allies, Party activists who were dismayed by the direction in which the conference appeared to be headed attempted to subdue their opposition by other means.

Huang, who attended the conference as a representative of the DL, was hopeful that it would succeed. He was aware, however, of the issues under consideration, and was skeptical of the ability of the conference delegates to muster the political will to ensure a result favorable to the cause of democracy. Therefore, he encouraged the NCA to mobilize public opinion in support of the conference. Functioning within a consortium composed of a number of like-minded groups, the NCA inaugurated a series of open meetings, to which PCC delegates were invited to report on conference activities and hear the people's response. Altogether, from 12 January until the end of the conference on 31 January, there were eleven such meetings, which attracted as many as two thousand observers each.[57]

These efforts of TF leaders to mobilize public support for the PCC did not escape the attention of right-wing elements within the GMD who were hostile to the talks, and they quickly became the object of "special forces'" harassment. On 16 January, at the fourth open meeting, a gang of approximately one hundred thugs infiltrated and disrupted the session. The organizers immediately made a detailed report of the event to the conference, and demanded that the GMD delegates urge their party to guarantee its commitment to freedom of speech and assembly.[58] Their efforts proved futile, and "special forces'" activity increased, becoming more and more violent, as chairs were smashed, observers beaten, and rocks thrown at speakers.[59]

Despite repeated attempts of right-wing forces to intimidate their opposition,[60] the PCC successfully concluded its business on 31 January, with a set of agreements ordering the creation of a democratic, constitutional government and a united national army isolated from party influence.[61] While the results of the conference were welcomed by many Chinese as a sign that a peaceful solution to the country's problems might be found, they represented, on the whole, a clear defeat for the GMD's political program and prompted a crisis within that Party's leadership. Although Chiang Kai-shek's personal intentions remained unclear, he publicly supported the PCC resolutions and urged their ratification by the

GMD's CEC. He was, however, strongly opposed by elements within his own party who were violently opposed to any kind of political arrangement that would allow the CCP a share in the new government. Although the CEC did ratify the PCC agreements, it simultaneously recommended a number of revisions that were interpreted by the Communists as an attempt to derail the entire negotiating process.[62] As a result, the CCP abandoned the effort to find a political solution, and, by mid-April, the civil war, which had been declared in abeyance since 13 January, was resumed.

Huang's reaction to these events was to return with his family to Shanghai in a state of depression. Although at that point it was not absolutely clear that the PCC agreements would fail to achieve ratification, he was profoundly disturbed by the GMD right-wing's efforts to disrupt the conference, and he was concerned that the deteriorating military situation in the Northeast might make further progress impossible. Nervously anticipating CCP and GMD action on the conference recommendations, he and several of his friends issued a statement on 23 April calling for a new round of discussions to solve the Northeastern problem and insisting plaintively that civil war must be avoided at all costs.[63] While he must have sensed the futility of further talks, as long as there was even a glimmer of hope he was prepared to do whatever was within his power to keep the process of negotiation alive.

The next few months saw repeated assaults upon his hopes for a peaceful settlement. By and large, these came in the form of an escalation of right-wing attacks upon TF leaders and their publications. On 23 June, secret police attacked a group of Shanghai leaders (including Ma Xulun) as they left a train in Nanjing on their way to reopen two-party talks. During the month of July, the DL leaders, Li Gongpu and Wen Yiduo, were assassinated under circumstances which implicated right-wing GMD leaders. Meanwhile, throughout the summer of 1946, there were a number of assaults upon DL publications and many local branches of the League were closed. All of these events had a profound effect upon Huang. Scolding the GMD bitterly for its violence, he prepared a letter of resignation from the PPC. Meanwhile, he expanded his contacts with CCP leaders (including Zhou Enlai) and began to express privately his deepening regret that he had been drawn into politics in the first place. Finding himself in straitened financial circumstances, he sold off some of his collection of historical works and decided to write for a living, noting that to do so would be an effective way to support his family, as well as enable him to avoid further involvement in politics.[64]

Despite his resolution to devote the remainder of his life to more sedentary pursuits, events would not let him rest. In the middle of October, Chiang Kai-shek invited members of the TF to Nanjing, stating that the GMD still wanted to discuss peace and that he was prepared to order a cease-fire. After consulting both CCP and GMD representatives and deliberating for several days with other members of the proposed TF delegation, Huang prepared a summary of their position and set out for Nanjing on 21 October.

Since this took place merely one month prior to the government's planned opening of the NA, it is likely that the purpose of Chiang's move was to lure TF leaders to Nanjing and induce them to support it. In any case, while in Nanjing Huang was visited by a number of GMD activists, who pressed him to leave the DL and enter the NA. His answer was to state publicly and unequivocally that he had no intention of supporting the GMD's effort to launch a constitutional government outside the purview of the PCC, since for him to do so would be an act of self-betrayal. He then drafted a statement on behalf of the DL, pledging the League to refrain from participating in the NA until the provisions of the PCC agreements had been carried out. Finally, on 17 November 1946, he returned alone to Shanghai, convinced that the GMD could not be trusted, the civil war would be carried out to the bitter end, and his involvement in politics had been a mistake. It was now his intention, once and for all, to leave the world of politics and return to the realm of education and scholarship where, he had always felt, lay his true vocation. In despair, he composed a poem, reflecting his frustration at having become so fruitlessly engaged in political life and his sense of foreboding over the prospect that China was about to embark upon a protracted and destructive civil conflict:

"Dark Frost"

It is already twilight and yet the morning frost has not lifted;
I have waited all day hoping to see the sunlight return.
Behind my closed door, I ignore the cries of the people;
With my hands in my sleeves, I ponder why I have been so
    concerned about mere dust.
Perversely, I cast in my whip to make still the dark waters;
I should only have concerned myself with carrying my melons to
    the yellow terrace.
The old fellow next door has gone to warn the others about the
    impending draft;
The village head will conduct a midnight search.[65]

He did, in fact, re-enter the world of politics shortly after writing this poem. By the spring of 1947, the GMD had launched a campaign of vilification against the NCA and the DL, and before long goon squads were once again harassing their meetings. By late October, the government had declared the DL to be an illegal organization and ordered local police to ban its activities. Huang could hardly remain aloof while the GMD attempted to destroy the organizations that he had worked so hard to help construct. It is ironic, however, that the last service he was to perform for the TF was to negotiate an agreement with the government by which the DL was allowed to continue in existence only under condition that its leaders resign their positions and the League cease its political activities.[66]

Conclusion

Under the circumstances, Huang's decision to leave politics, temporary though it may have been, was as rational as it was sincere. There was little he could do, either to induce the CCP and GMD to work together toward democratic reforms or to stem the rising tide of civil war. The option of honorable withdrawal was, moreover, one that had always been available to him, educated as he was in the classical tradition in which the ideal of withdrawal from politics in the face of political impotence had a long and venerable history. In writing "Dark Frost," he was responding as much as anything else to the same impulse that produced an entire genre of eremitic literature, dating as far back as Qu Yuan (340?-278 B.C.).[67]

He was also responding, however, to the constraints he had voluntarily imposed upon himself from the very beginning of his political career. He seems never to have had serious political ambitions of his own, and, on more than one occasion, rejected offers of positions that might have led to the exercise of real power. In fact, he quite openly acknowledged that his choice of a nonpolitical approach to the performance of his political obligations was a self-conscious act.

That he was unable to conceive of an alternative to working either with the GMD or the CCP was no accident, for he sincerely believed that he could make the greatest contribution to Chinese society as an educator and social reformer, rather than as a politician. As an intellectual and educational leader, he reasoned, he could have an important impact upon the direction of long-term evolutionary change. As a politician during a time of revolutionary crisis, he felt he lacked the cleverness and daring to make a major contribution, or, as he put it, "overthrow the evil forces."[68] Thus, despite his understanding of the critical nature of the issues he faced and the causes of his political impotence, he was never able to move beyond his self-imposed limitations to formulate a plan of action that might lead to real political influence. While he comprehended the nature of his weakness, he could never bring himself to compete on the same ground as either the CCP or the GMD, i.e., by organizing a political party dedicated to building military power of its own. For all his campaigning on behalf of democracy and national unity, politics and the exercise of power were for him nothing more than a necessary evil.

It would probably be wrong to state unequivocally that he was wedded to the traditional model of literati political behavior, which tended to legitimate literati politics in proportion to the extent to which they served the crown. For him, as for others of his generation, the image of an intellectual was changing, and a new conception of the role that intellectuals ought to play in the political process had yet to be formed. One thing that was certain, though, was that for him the image of an intellectual and educator was not to be transformed into that of a politician leading an autonomous political apparatus.[69] Despite his multifarious activities on the fringes of the power structure, it was difficult for him to conceive of himself in a truly oppositional role. Indeed, in their search for a new role, many of his contemporaries preferred, as did he himself, to pursue social or cultural reform, rather than politics.[70] Whatever their private convictions, they did not, in the final analysis, cross the boundaries of a political culture that denied for them a legitimate role as loyal opponents.

He could, of course, admire those who were capable of forging the military and political tools to implement their own versions of change. While in Yanan, he noted that much of what the Communists had already accomplished in the border area was what he himself had advocated and tested for years. In *Yanan guilai*, he remarked self-consciously that his own efforts rarely proceeded beyond the stage of experimentation, and he was clearly awed by the contrast between his own failure and the Communists' success. His language, as he reflected upon that difference, reveals his awareness that without the means to control the instruments of power his efforts to promote peaceful change could have only modest success at best. "Because I have had no political or military power," he mused, "my efforts are hardly worth mentioning."[71]

This statement, made as he pondered his dilemma, might be considered a fitting epitaph for the entire movement for a democratic alternative in the 1940s. His recognition of his own political impotence was meaningful for him personally, but it was also symbolic of the futility of the TF movement in general. Without military power of its own, the movement was dependent upon the good will of its enemies and utterly incapable of inducing them to act in ways that they perceived to be contrary to their interests. Led as it was by intellectuals like Huang, who consciously avoided direct political action, the movement was inspired by a vision of political participation that precluded the accumulation of real power. As a result, it remained locked into its role of mediator, and it was bound to fail as the process of mediation reached its inevitable conclusion. Proving itself either unable or unwilling to build instruments of military force, the TF was wedged firmly between the CCP and the GMD. Those parties, by contrast, were organized and guided (for better or for worse) by military men and professional revolutionaries, who not only understood, but were prepared to respond positively to, the realities of Chinese political life. Ultimately, they were the only forces willing to compete on terms that were meaningful in China during the 1940s.

Notes

1. He believed that the state should intervene to moderate the relationship between capital and labor, but he also was a strong advocate of free enterprise. He also was convinced that in China's state of underdevelopment, there could be no class struggle because there was no significant bourgeoisie. The only serious polarity that he perceived in Chinese society was that which existed not between economic classes but between the educated and the uneducated. Huang Yanpei, *Zhonghua fuxing shi jiang* (Ten Lectures on the Revival of China) (Chongqing: Guoxun shudian, 1944), 24.

2. Shi Fuliang, "Zhongjian pai de zhengzhi luxian" (The Political Line of the Middle Groups); "Zhongjian pai zai zhengzhi shang de diwei he zuoyong" (The Political Position and Function of the Middle Groups), in Wei Hongyu, ed., *Zhongguo xiandai shi ziliao xuanbian* (Collected Materials on Contemporary Chinese History) (Harbin: Heilongjiang renmin chubanshe, 1981), 5:156-74.

3. Howard L. Boorman and Richard C. Howard, eds., *Biographical Dictionary of Republican China*, 4 vols. (New York: Columbia University Press, 1968), 2: 210-213 (hereafter, BDRC).

4. Huang Yanpei, *Bashi nian lai* (A Memoir at Eighty) (Beijing: Quanguo renmin zhengzhi xieshang hui, 1964), 117-118.

5. Shang Ding, *Huang Yanpei* (Beijing: Renmin chubanshe, 1986), 51-53.

6. In 1921, Li Dazhao and Chen Duxiu each approached Huang with proposals to have the VES and the CCP collaborate secretly with one another. Huang, *Bashi nian lai*, 118-119.

7. Shang, 59-60.

8. Ibid., 61.

9. The VES founded a Village Education Study Group (under the management of Guo Bingwen), instituted special courses to train "village service personnel," opened a village education laboratory (experimenting with a program to send teachers and doctors out to the countryside to work in the villages), offered interest-free loans and medical services to villagers, founded a "farm implements extension bureau" to purchase new tools for farmers, and encouraged its branches to intervene, during hard times, to induce landlords to reduce rents and creditors to permit debtors to delay payments. Ibid., 62.

10. Huang, *Bashi nian lai*, 125.

11. Ibid., 127.

12. When hostilities did occur in September 1931, Huang was already in a good position to play a leading role in the effort to mobilize resistance. He responded with enthusiasm, helping, among other things, to organize an Anti-Japanese National

Salvation Study Group. In addition, he made the VES' weekly magazine, *Shenghuo zhoukan*, available to the resistance movement, and began publication of a new magazine, *Jiuguo tongxun* (National Salvation News; later renamed *Guoxun*), aimed at stimulating the resistance effort. Following the Japanese attack upon Shanghai on 28 January 1932, Huang and a number of associates from the Shanghai business, education, and publishing communities organized the Shanghai Citizens' Local Defense Association to provide support for the front-line troops, maintain local order, and support the local currency. Throughout the crisis, personnel working for the VES and teachers and students of the Zhonghua Vocational School were mobilized to transport wounded soldiers and deliver munitions and supplies to the front lines. Shang, 68-69.

13. Ibid., 69; Huang, *Bashi nian lai*, 130.

14. Ibid., 75-80.

15. The Association was composed of a diverse body of individuals representing the Chinese Youth Party, the National Socialist Party, the Third Party, the Rural Reconstruction Group, and the VES, in addition to a number of nonparty people. Li Qimin, *Zhonguo minzhu dangpai shi gao* (Draft History of China's Democratic Parties and Groups) (Chengdu: Sichuan renmin chubanshe, 1987), 65-66.

16. Shang, 88.

17. Xu Hansan, *Huang Yanpei nianpu* (A Chronological Biography of Huang Yanpei) (Beijing: Wenshi ziliao chubanshe, 1985), 141.

18. He did secure from Chiang a private commitment to organize a special commission within the PPC to close the fissure. Ibid., 138.

19. *Guoxun* Bookstore continued to operate until March 1948, when it and *Guoxun* magazine were closed by the government, following the bookstore's publication of the CCP's land-reform program. Shang, 82.

20. Xu, 143.

21. In July 1943, for example, he attended a dinner with Chiang and thirteen members of the PPC, during which he raised the issue of official corruption and suggested that the solution would be to enforce the government's commitment to popularly elected assemblies at each administrative level, in order to institutionalize public oversight of official behavior. Ibid., 151. In 1938, the government enacted legislation requiring local units of administration to establish such assemblies, and on paper there was much progress toward fulfillment of that objective. In practice, however, the assemblies were chosen and controlled by local government and party authorities, and often served to reinforce, rather than check, the abuses of local officials. Ch'ien Tuan-sheng [Qian Duansheng], *The Government and Politics of China, 1912-1949* (Stanford: Stanford University Press, 1950), 306-307.

22. Xu, 152. The NG had adopted a draft constitution in May 1936, but had not had time to call the NA to ratify it prior to the outbreak of war. Progress toward constitutional government was interrupted by the conflict and, although a subcommittee of the PPC worked from September 1939 to March 1940 to revise the draft constitution, a decision (18 September 1940) of the Standing Committee of the GMD CEC postponed indefinitely the convening of the NA, placing the entire issue in limbo. Ch'ien, 303-308. Chiang Kai-shek's announcement came at the Eleventh Session of the Fifth CEC.

23. Shang, 90.

24. E.g., Du Yuesheng, Qian Xinzhi, and Lu Zuofu.

25. E.g., Fu Sinian (editorial board) and Wang Yunwu (sponsor and contributor).

26. He cautioned that the constitution would be meaningless unless it was accompanied by a well-developed habit of respect for law, both among the people and on the part of government officials. His advice to the government was to do all that it could to implement the political tutelage laws, so that citizens would "understand that the laws are the standard of loyal behavior and ... the basis for personal security." Only with such an understanding, he argued, would the people learn to respect laws and seek to pursue their private interests only through legal means. As a first step, he urged, the government must put its own house in order by attacking corruption and abuse of the laws by its own officials. The greatest enemies of constitutional government, he wrote, were the "unlawful officials and gentry hegemons," who by applying the laws selectively in accordance with their own self-interest destroyed the public's confidence in the principle of rule of law. Huang, "Yuan quanguo shangxia jinli fengxing yuefa lai lianxi fengxing xianfa" (Let Everyone Wholeheartedly Carry Out the Tutelage Laws as Training for Implementing the Constitution), *XZYK*, no. 2 (1944): 1-2.

27. See, for example, his contribution to the 1 June issue of *XZYK*. He reported a rising current of concern, expressed in Sichuan newspapers, over the government's commitment to constitutional rule, and he took special note of the strident tone taken by Kunming's Society for the Study of Constitutional Government. Rather than accept the government's leadership in the movement toward constitutionalism, the Society suggested that the government itself was an obstacle to democratic rule, and demanded that the regime demonstrate its commitment to reform by obeying its own regulations limiting the terms of political office and enforcing the provisions of the political tutelage laws that guaranteed the personal freedom of Chinese citizens. The government must, the Society demanded, "refrain from indiscriminately arresting, detaining, beating, tying up, or executing people. Moreover, it must immediately implement the judicial codes present in the [political] tutelage laws and cease subjecting civilians to military law." In response, Huang testified to the government's sincerity and enthusiasm regarding the movement toward government by law, and urged critics to cooperate with the government in its effort to cultivate among the citizens and officialdom alike a habit of obedience to law as an essential foundation for constitutional rule. Huang, "Women gongtong xiezhu zhengfu cucheng quanguo shangxia chinli fengxing yuefa" (Let Us Together Assist the Government in Helping the Entire Country to Diligently Carry Out the Tutelage Laws), *XZYK*, no. 6 (1944): 1-2. In another case, during a lecture he gave at Fudan University, he took note of student suspicions regarding the government's sincerity on the constitutional issue, and urged them not to doubt the government's intentions. Huang, "Cong xianzheng yundong kan Zhongguo qiantu" (Looking at China's Future from the Perspective of the Movement for Constitutional Government), *XZYK*, nos. 7/8 (1944): 40.

28. Ibid., 43.

29. Huang et. al., "Minzhu he shengli xianyan" (On Democracy and Victory), *XZYK*, no. 9 (1944): 1-2.

30. Huang, "Yin bashi lushi fabiao guanyu baozhang renquan yijian wei jin yibu zhi jianyi" (Some Proposals Advanced in Response to the Views on Guaranteeing Human Rights Expressed by Eighty Lawyers), *XZYK*, no. 9 (1944): 28.

31. Huang, "Zhi Guomindang youhao gongkai xin" (An Open Letter to My Good Friends in the Nationalist Party)," *XZYK*, nos. 14/15 (1945): 64-65.

32. Huang provided the following quote from the Generalissimo's statement: "If a country has only one party, then that party will inevitably become corrupt and cannot last long. It is not only bad for the party, it is also bad for the country. Therefore, a country must have two or more parties that will reason with each other and guide each other and progress together." Ibid., 65.

33. Ibid., 66.

34. Dong Biwu was a frequent speaker.

35. On 10 May 1945, the thirteenth session was raided and broken up by the secret police. Shang, 92-93; Xu, 168.

36. Tang Peiji, Wang Guangxing, and Zuo Rongkang, *Liangci guogong hezuo shi gao* (A Draft History of the Two Attempts at GMD-CCP Cooperation) (Hangzhou: Zhejiang renmin chubanshe, 1989), 372; Xu, 164; Shang, 96.

37. Xu, 165.

38. Shang, 97.

39. Xu, 168-169; Shang, 97-98. The telegram was endorsed by Chu Fucheng, Huang Yanpei, Leng Yu, Wang Yunwu, Fu Sinian, Zuo Shunsheng, and Zhang Bojun.

40. The convening of the NA had become an important political issue, because many within the CCP and the TF feared that, as it was planned by the government, it would be dominated by GMD members and their allies. Ch'ien, 313-316.

41. Xu, 169; Shang, 98.

42. This episode did, in fact, lead to a broadly based challenge to the government's censorship policies. Shang, 113-117.

43. Huang, *Yanan guilai* (Dairen: Dachung shudian, 1946), 7.

44. Ibid., 7-8.

45. Ibid., 44.

46. Ibid., 8.

47. Ibid., 44.

48. Ibid., 43.

49. Ibid., 8.

50. Shang, 119; Xu, 171-172.

51. "Minzhu jianguo hui chengli xuanyan" (Inaugural Manifesto of the Democratic National Construction Association), in Wei Hongyu, 5: 52 (hereafter, cited as "Manifesto".)

52. Li Qimin, 101.

53. "Manifesto," 53-54.

54. Shang, 135. Much later in his autobiography (a somewhat self-interested account that perhaps exaggerates the extent of his affiliation with the CCP in the immediate postwar period), Huang stated that, from a political perspective, the most important thing about the NCA was its gradual slide away from the middle toward the Communist side. Huang, *Bashi nian lai*, 139.

55. Ch'ien, 377.

56. Lloyd E. Eastman, *Seeds of Destruction: Nationalist China in War and Revolution, 1937-1949* (Stanford: Stanford University Press, 1984), 114.

57. Li Qimin, 125-126.

58. Ibid., 126; Shang, 142. Chiang Kai-shek, in his opening statement as chairman of the PCC, had pledged the GMD to uphold the basic freedoms of assembly, speech, and publication. Li Youren and Guo Quanhai, *Zhongguo Guomindang qian shi* (A Short History of the Chinese Nationalist Party) (Beijing: Dangan chubanshe, 1988), 369.

59. Shang, 141-143. As founder of the NCA and organizer of the public meetings, as well as a PCC delegate who appeared to be leaning increasingly toward the Communist side, Huang himself became a target of gang violence. His residence was ransacked by "special forces" in broad daylight on 26 January. Shang, 144; Xu, 178.

60. Perhaps the most memorable example was the Jiaochangkou Incident of 10 February, in which a gang of some 300-600 thugs raided a pro-PCC rally attended by some ten thousand people. Wielding benches and iron rods, they attacked and bloodied some sixty people, including such leading liberals as Guo Moruo, Li Gongpu, Zhang Naiqi, Shi Fuliang, and Ma Yinchu. Eastman, 114; Shang, 149.

61. Tang et. al., 398-400; Li Qimin, 127-133.

62. Tang et. al., 401-403. For a sample of CCP opinion regarding the GMD CEC's actions, see "Ping Guomindang er zhongquanhui" (Criticize the Guomindang CEC's Second Plenum), *Jiefang ribao* (Liberation Daily), 19 March 1946; reprinted in Wei Hongyu, 98-103.

63. Shang, 149.

64. Ibid., 152-154.

65. Composed on 16 November 1946; in ibid., 160.

66. Ibid., 169-171. Following that episode, Huang returned once again to a relatively sedentary life in Shanghai, writing and receiving information from the Communist underground regarding the military situation in the North, but under constant police surveillance. After the Communist victory, he re-entered public life and served the new regime in a number of capacities, including that of Minister of Light Industries from 1949 to 1954. *BDRC*, 2: 213.

67. Liu Wuji, *An Introduction to Chinese Literature* (Bloomington: Indiana University Press, 1966), 25, 31.

68. Shang, 136.

69. He shied away from power even when it came from within an established political organism. When, for example, he was offered an official position in what was to have become a coalition government (1946), he declared that he would accept only if his educational interests were secured first. Ibid., 144-145.

70. Barry Keenan, *The Dewey Experiment in China: Educational Reform and Political Power in the Early Republic* (Cambridge: Harvard University Press, 1977), passim.

71. Huang, *Yanan guilai*, 44.

4

Deng Yanda and the Third Party

J. Kenneth Olenik

The following essay focuses on the program of the Provisional Action Committee of the Guomindang (PAC) during the years, 1930-1931. The PAC, since it embraced the democratic, populist revolutionary style of the 1924-1927 period, was the radical left wing of the Guomindang (GMD). The central concern of the PAC, during this period, was organizing a military coalition capable of dislodging from power Chiang Kai-shek and the Nanjing government. What distinguished the PAC challenge to Nanjing from others was a distinct ideology and the fact that, for a brief moment, it stood a very good chance of succeeding. Since the ideological component was significant, discussion of the action program will be preceded by a brief analysis of the ideology and history of the PAC.

The Ideology of Mass Revolution

In his explanation of the failure of the GMD, Zhang Junmai included a critique of Sun Yat-sen's final efforts to synthesize his ideas on revolution. Zhang argued that Sun's inability to resolve the contradiction between his courtship of Marxist materialism and the fundamental metaphysical orientation of his ideas created an atmosphere of confusion and ambiguity within the revolutionary movement. His descendants were left to find their own way out of this contradiction and, while doing so, they contributed to the introduction of Marxist patterns of thought into the Chinese intellectual and political universe.[1] In other words, while Sun remained loyal to Confucian metaphysics, he legitimized Marxist thought and action programs, opening the door to experimentation by a new generation of Chinese revolutionaries. Hence, even as Sun was reformulating his ideas during 1923-1924, his organization began to factionalize along ideological lines. Shortly after his death in 1925, the extent of ideolgical bifurcation became evident.

Among the earliest and most important exponents of a Chinese, metaphysical interpretation of Sun's revolutionary ideas was Dai Jitao. Dai, who had flirted with Marxism during the storm of Western-inspired rationalism which accompanied the May Fourth era, had grown disillusioned with the foreign origins and orthodox iconoclasm of the Russian-inspired communist movement developing in China. He was among the first GMD ideologists to publish the idea that Sunism and Marxism rested on mutually contradictory and exclusive primal intuitions, materialism and traditional Confucian principles.[2] He defined the legitimacy of GMD ideology in historical and moral terms, providing a metaphysical foundation for the party's belief system. His interpretation of Sunism, which became the foundation for an orthodoxy promulgated in Nanjing, rejected Marxism and the materialist trends within the GMD.

Dai's return to metaphysics was powerfully attacked by both the CCP and independent GMD ideologists like Hu Hanmin. Within the party, there was also a small but very influential group of eclectic thinkers and activists. This group, which drew inspiration from Zhu Zhixin and Liao Zhongkai, included Song Qingling, Peng Zemin, Deng Yanda, Ji Fang, Zhang Bozhun, Chen Yuren, Qiu Ting, Guo Guanjie, Luo Renyi, and Huang Qixiang, as well as numerous less-well-known individuals. Intensely nationalistic, but cultural iconoclasts, this group placed Sun's principles at the center of its ideology. At the same time, they took a historical-materialist standpoint, preferring to supplement their interpretations of Sun's ideas with science rather than metaphysics. This small, but very influential group, constituted the true left wing of the GMD and included members who accepted historical materialism. A narrow definition of the left wing of the party excludes large factions that have traditionally been included, such as Wang Jingwei and his followers. People like Wang, who were willing to enter into pragmatic alliances with Marxists, rejected a materialist standpoint.[3]

The PAC was organized in 1927 by GMD members who accepted historical materialism and others who had recently been expelled by the CCP. Between 1927 and 1930, this organization underwent a fermentation period, during which two factions appeared. One, associated with Tan Pingshan, emphasized the need for an autonomous organization distinct from the GMD and closely associated with the CCP. A second faction, attached to Song Qingling and Deng Yanda, insisted that, for practical and ideological reasons, the PAC retain its identity with the GMD. This latter faction was highly critical of the CCP's blind adherence to Third International directives, and rejected the idea of a leadership role for the Communists during the current revolutionary stage.[4] By the summer of 1930, Deng had returned from Germany. Tan and the pro-Communist faction left the PAC, which then reorganized itself around the personal leadership of Deng. His presence at the epicenter of the PAC influenced both its ideology and practice.

In the iconography of the People's Republic of China, he is a revolutionary martyr who fearlessly sacrificed himself for his principles.[5] He is also a bourgeois revolutionary who, in spite of his flirtation with Marxism and cooperation with the CCP, could not accept the leadership of the Communists or their ideology. Indeed, his independence and critical spirit infused the personality of the PAC during its early years. His personal style of study, amassing large amounts of information, commissioning his colleagues to do research, and picking the brains of the most talented and knowledgable people he could find, constituted the practical and scientific orientation which attracted philosophers and scholars into his circle.[6] He had spent more than three years in Germany, was fluent in German, and was strongly influenced by Immanuel Kant and Georg Wilhelm Friedrich Hegel, as well as Karl Marx. While he accepted historical materialism, he rejected its claims to absolute truth and admitted only to a complex ontology beyond the ability of the human mind to grasp in its entirety. For him, human knowledge was limited and thus relative. One could know the universe, but not its entirety.[7] A theory of limited knowledge did not prevent action, but it could result in indecision and a tendency toward caution in action.

The same scientific orientation that attracted Deng to Marxism and materialism caused him to reject both traditional Chinese culture and the dogmatic posturing of the CCP. He was convinced, however, that China and all of humankind were headed toward a socialist future and that the common people (*pingmin*) would assume leadership in the newly reconstituting human order. At the core of PAC ideology was the belief that the good society of the future would be built on the active participation of the masses of common people. Classes would disappear. "Elite" and "common" would cease to be distinctions. The basic program needed to work toward the ideal future in the least traumatic way was to educate the youth and intellectuals, so they could serve as a leavening and organizational force which could help the common people play their historical role. The PAC had to include totally dedicated and altruistic youth, who would go to the masses and organize and energize them so they could participate in revolutionary struggle.

Apropos of the emphasis on mass action and the essential role of the selfless revolutionary in the PAC program were articles in *Dengta* (Lighthouse), an early PAC journal. One, entitled "Revolution and the Masses," echoed a theme Deng first proclaimed in 1926 and later, in 1927, made the rallying cry for the organization of a group to challenge Chiang Kai-shek. The author argued that modern revolution meant the integration of an enlightened, selfless leadership with the common people who shared the historical responsibility to build a better, more humane, and egalitarian world. The future could not be made by an alliance of elites separated from the people. The new government forming in Nanjing, and its opponents in the Reorganization Clique, had to be opposed, since they were combinations of old elites which worked under the illusion that the new society could be built without the active participation of the common people.[8] Finally, the writer claimed that only loyalty to the masses insured ultimate victory.

A second essay was entitled "An Invitation to Revolutionary Youth to Shatter the Dream of Romantic Love." Its author argued that true love was not possible in a class society built on greed and selfishness:

> Real love cannot happen in this kind of world. It can happen only after the revolution, in a world of Grand Harmony (*datong shijie*). When that time comes, there will be no distinction between rich and poor, no separation between beautiful and ugly, female and male. There will be common production, common benefits, equal knowledge, and education will be the same. Beauty will also be equal, and people will all come together on the basis of love. Never again will there be a need for ulterior motives or some sort of calculated material motivation. This kind of love is what can be called true love.
>
> At present, revolutionary and counterrevolutionary struggles are still going on. The garden of freedom has not yet opened its gates. The victories of the future await our resolve. Thus, in this period, all one can do is to ask the youth to go and make revolution first and talk about love later. Once the revolution has succeeded, then love will have succeeded. If the revolution fails, love, too, will have failed. So it is that we must loudly proclaim: revolutionary youths, the revolution has not yet succeeded. Resolutely smash the dreams of impossible love.[9]

The Practice of Revolution

No sooner had the PAC been formally constituted in the summer of 1930 then a Japanese-language newspaper in Shanghai dubbed it "the Third Party." It was viewed as an organization somewhere between the GMD and the CCP. Deng had always argued that communism was untimely in semicolonial, semifeudal China, a nation with a miniscule proletariat and underdeveloped industrial base. He felt that whatever power the CCP did acquire derived from its ability to exploit the grinding poverty and misery of the people. The suffering of the Chinese masses was caused by a combination of foreign exploitation (imperialism) and the concentration of domestic feudal forces in the new Nanjing Government. Communism was taken to be a political problem which would fade into insignificance with the appearance of a popular government which addressed the actual needs of the common people. Thus, the immediate concern of the PAC was the Nanjing Government, which not only foolishly tried to oppose the Communists by destroying the mass movements, but also relentlessly pursued all political opposition, including the PAC. PAC revolutionary policy thus had two parts: (1) a long-term program, which included organization, propaganda, recruitment, and preparation of a party capable of merging with and leading the common people; and (2) an immediate military program, which sought a massive national uprising to overthrow the Nanjing government and establish a viable revolutionary base area in which economic and political experiments could be conducted. A final option in PAC military planning was a limited guerrilla operation against Nanjing.

The immediate problem of revolutionary practice was organization. Like all other Chinese political parties, the PAC began as a complex structure of interpersonal relationships. It was a hierarchy of leaders, each with his own network of relationships, overlapping and interacting, contending and compromising. Like other Chinese political organizations, the PAC also needed a clearly visible leader. During the gestation period of the party between 1927-1930, leadership had been shared by Deng and Tan. Deng, along with Song Qingling, was in Germany during these years, and exercised considerable influence through a loyal organization of his colleagues from the General Political Department of the National Revolutionary Army (NRA). A second faction formed around Tan and included a number of his fellow CCP outcastes. In Shanghai, Tan took charge of the first efforts to organize a counterforce to the GMD and CCP. While there was a flurry of activity involving numcrous GMD leftists and ex-CCP members during 1928, by 1929 the efforts to form a distinct revolutionary party, designated "The Chinese Revolutionary Party," had foundered.[10] Some potential members drifted away in frustration to either the CCP or the GMD, but most seem to have abandoned politics for more conventional pursuits. At the center, Deng and Tan could not agree over the basic designation and orientation of the new group. The whole enterprise suffocated in an atmosphere of White Terror.

Deng returned to China in May 1930. He had intended to stay longer in Germany, but was unable to ignore the requests of his associates to take charge of a desperate situation. A short time after his arrival, he replaced Tan as head of the PAC and began rebuilding the organization.

His influence was both deep and broadly spread throughout the revolutionary movement. His personal system of relationships spanned both the military and civilian realms. In the military, he was connected to regional and national organizations, while his civilian associations extended to political and cultural circles. He was respected by both Communists and conservative figures in the GMD. He was known for his brilliant mind, photographic memory, and universal intellectual interests. His first associations with the revolution were nurtured by his father, a Hakka of lowly origins from Huiyang county in Guangdong. His father attained the *xiucai* degree under the old examination system, and went on to become a district magistrate, scholar, and teacher of local repute. The school he built in Lujing village is still impressive. For a time, it was a magnet for local talent. Through his father, Deng was sent to the local military academy, which was directed by Deng Keng. Not a relative, Deng Keng was associated with Sun Yat-sen and the complex world of Cantonese military politics. Through Deng Keng, Deng not only joined Sun's revolutionary group, he began his early contacts with Cantonese military circles. Officers associated with Deng included Chen Jiongming, Chen Mingshu, Li Jishen, Chen Cheng, Zhang Fakui, Chen Jitang, Ye Ting, Yan Zhong, Li Changda, and Chen Keyu. His attendance at the Baoding Military Academy (he graduated with the sixth class in 1919) made him classmates with Chen Cheng, Luo Zhouying, Zhou Zhirou, Bai Chongxi, Huang Shaoxiong, Huang Yuqu, Yu Zuoyao, Cai Tingkai, and Zhang Guangnai. Li Zongren, who was not a Baoding graduate, had great respect for Deng's abilities. Until 1927, Deng was also on friendly terms with Chiang Kai-shek.[11] Chiang was apparently fond of him, and through the early spring of 1927, Deng continued to hope that Chiang would return to the side of the revolution. As Vice-Director of Training and Commander of the Cadet Brigade at the Whampoa Military Academy (WMA) in 1924 and again in 1926, Deng won the lasting respect and loyalty of a large number of cadets, who would later rally to his side. Finally, his long history of military command made him well-known to all national military leaders. As we shall see, these associations provided the PAC with the potential for broad and deep military support.

His political base was equally impressive. His early and loyal association with Sun Yat-sen, and later Liao Zhongkai, provided him with a distinguished political pedigree. He was one of the earliest and most consistent advocates of Sun's policy of cooperation with the Communists. As a result, he had close working relationships with Michael Borodin, Mao Zedong, Zhou Enlai, Zhu De, Yun Daiying, Guo Moruo, Sun Bingwen, and a vast list of Communists he invited to take up positions, while he served as Director of the General Political Department of the NRA during the first stage of the Northern Expedition. In the GMD, his closest relationships were with Song Qingling, Chen Yuren, and Peng Zemin. Hu Hanmin, Sun Fo (Sun Ke), Liu Yazi, and Cai Yuanpei continued to hold Deng in high esteem. His own brilliance and inclination to associate with intellectually outstanding individuals drew him close to Zhang Bozhun, Ji Fang, Qiu Zhe, Deng Haoming (Deng Liang), and a wide circle of contacts in academic circles. Moreover, he was apparently very impressive in person. He was physically attractive and rather tall for a southerner, with the carriage of a trained military officer and the style of a scholar. His deep knowledge and quick analytical skills won many supporters.[12] Deng Haoming, for example, remembered that his large group of intellectuals in Beijing, in search of a military leader, invited Deng to visit them, and on meeting him, the group was unanimous in its praise of his genius, talent, sincerity, and warmth.

The preceding suggests the immense resources Deng brought to the task of organizing the PAC. When he first arrived in Shanghai, there was a period of intense struggle with Tan. While Tan lacked Deng's military contacts, he had his own impressive political career as a member of both the GMD and the CCP. Although an outcaste from both parties, he was unable to break his emotional ties to the CCP. One important aspect of the schism between Tan and Deng was a kind of sectarian attachment to their respective mother parties. Tan leaned toward the CCP and, in the face of rejection, continued to assume that the link between the Chinese Revolutionary Party and the CCP was critical.[13] Deng, on the other hand, insisted that as a matter of history and necessity the new organization must be taken as the legitimate leadership of the GMD.

The new organization embodied Sun Yat-sen's final and definitive articulation of his ideas and policies. These policies had informed GMD action between 1923 and 1927. In the context of these policies, Deng re-emphasized the notion of a broad united front (UF) of common people as the mode of revolutionary change suitable for China under existing domestic and international circumstances. That is to say, Deng strongly rejected the notion of Communist leadership of the Chinese revolution. Subsequent articles in the PAC journal contained scathing attacks on the Communists for blind adherence to Third International directives and cavalier sacrifice of peasants and workers in the interest of irrelevant and destructive policies. In short, while Deng was in charge of the PAC, he closed the door on any alliance with the CCP in its contemporary form. As a proud and independent nationalist, he had already been snubbed by the leaders of the Third International. Of the so-called Three Great Policies of the reorganization period--cooperation with the CCP, alliance with the Third International, and organization of a mass revolutonary base--the PAC remained committed, in practice, only to the latter. The others could be reactivated only with major changes in the CCP and the Comintern.[14]

Deng and Tan had a number of other differences. While both agreed that Chinese society was semifeudal and semicolonial and that the revolution was a capitalist-type common people's revolution, Deng emphasized the feudal character of Chinese society and consequently, as noted above, thought

Communist leadership out of the question. Tan argued that the force of revolution would be the "laboring commoner class," which he understood as an expanded proletariat. Deng agreed that this class would be the force of the revolution, but understood the concept in a much broader sense as an inclusive UF which would include all anti-feudal, anti-imperialist groups. While Tan felt that Sun's principles continued to have a place as revolutionary goals, he insisted that these principles had to be recast as "A Three People's Principles of the laboring class." Deng accepted Sun's ideas as correct objectives for the Chinese revolution and argued that the purpose of the PAC struggle would be implementation of these principles. Finally, as Yan Qi notes, while both called for a government of "the common people," Deng gave this concept a new interpretation, insisting that this government was not to be merely a tool of the proletariat. He vehemently rejected the notion that one form of dictatorship could be better than another. Rather, he believed that while the workers and peasants were to form the core of the new government, it would be a broad-based UF. The key to the formation of this new political structure was organization of the common people into occupational groups. Workers, peasants, women, soldiers, and a broad spectrum of professional organizations would elect representatives to a hierarchy of assemblies, which would exercise actual power. To insure true representation based on numerical proportions of society, peasants and workers would be insured 60 percent of the places in national-level bodies and the other occupational groups, 40 percent. A people's militia would be formed to protect the new government from its enemies.[15] His new government was both populist and democratic, and, it was hoped, could be an effective counterforce against the spectre of dictatorship. Having settled his differences with Tan, Deng called a meeting on 9 August 1930 in Shanghai. This secret meeting, the first "Congress" of the PAC, put aside the "Chinese Revolutionary Party" designation and returned to the title, PAC of the GMD, thus asserting historical legitimacy. The committee was "provisional" in that its members believed they would one day return to their rightful leadership positions over the entire GMD, and it was an "action committee" in the sense that it was dedicated to implementing the reorganization program of the GMD through a series of actions or practical policies. The Congress, presided over by Deng, had some twenty "representatives" of ten provinces. This group of twenty included Huang Qixiang, Zhang Bozhun, Ji Fang, Zhu Yunshan, Guo Guanjie, Zheng Lanpu, Yang Shuxiong, Liao Ming, Jiang Dongqin, Wang Shenxin, Luo Renyi, Zhang Ziping, Wan Can, Xie Shuying, Li Minjiu, and Yang Yitang. Most of these were intellectuals associated with Deng during various stages of his career. Many had been given work by him during his tenure as Director of the General Political Department of the NRA. Some, including Zhang Bozhun and Ji Fang, had been members of the CCP.

Like the CCP and the Nanjing GMD, the PAC adopted the Leninist model of the highly centralized vanguard party. The operational ideal was "democratic centralism." In practice, like its larger counterparts, the PAC was dominated by one person (Deng) and his circle of close associates. The operations of the party were akin to an elaborate national system of interpersonal relationships held together by the individual *guanxi* (connections) systems of leadership figures.[16] Recruitment rapidly expanded the number of activist participants, which reached perhaps several thousand by 1931, but this operation itself depended heavily on the ability of participants to use their contacts to gain access to new membership pools. This use of *guanxi* was, in fact, the modus operandi of the party in the crucial area of recruitment, especially in the academic circles on which their efforts were focused. All of the memoirs and reminiscences related to PAC operations bear out the image of elaborate systems of interpersonal relations as central. Interviews with Deng Haoming, Wan Yun, and Jin Yu all verified the primacy of *guanxi* in the actual operations of the PAC.

While the PAC, operating within the context of a traditional Chinese political style, did use the central figure and *guanxi* systems, it also made efforts to introduce a truly democratic spirit and practice. These efforts were a reflection of the uncompromising opposition of the PAC to any form of dictatorial or bureaucratic behavior. The long-term practical result of this opposition was that the PAC was an extremely loose organization. Local branches, and even individuals, were almost totally autonomous, integrated with the larger organization only by a kind of spiritual bond, a faith, an opposition to the GMD in its Nanjing manifestation, and loyalty to the populist form of Sun's Three People's Principles as articulated during the reorganization period (1923-1927). This intraparty anarchism was, to a certain extent, a function of the White Terror and illegality, but it was also a product of an abiding faith in democracy. In an interview, Wan Yun, who became a member of the PAC in 1927, described a kind of mystical body and unspoken language that enabled members of the PAC to find and recognize each other. As central offices were established, there was an attempt to reinforce democratic practice through organizational devices. The Central Executive Committee (CEC) was redesignated the "Central Cadre Conference," and Deng was given the title, "General Facilitator (*Zong ganshi*)." Other key office holders included Zheng Taipu, Director of the Central Organization Committee; Zhang Bozhun, Central Propaganda; Huang Qixiang and Ji Fang, Central Military Committee; and Li Shichang, Central People's Movement Committee. Deng also edited and did most of the writing for *Geming xingdong banyuekan* (Revolutionary Action Fortnightly), which was the official journal of the PAC.

On 10 August, the PAC officially announced its founding and principles. On 1 September, the first issue of *Geming xingdong* was published, with six more to follow under Deng's editorship. The quality of the articles--original pieces on the PAC ideology, analyses of contemporary Chinese and world affairs, translations of Japanese and Western (especially German) economic and political texts, reports on local and provincial affairs, and debates on main contemporary issues--marked the magazine as an important organ of radical GMD ideology. Deng expended immense energies on it, to the point of endangering his own health due to overwork. The journal was widely circulated, even turning up in Beiping and Guangzhou.

In April 1931, Li Shichang became editor of *Geming xingdong ribao*, an official PAC daily. The initial run was only five hundred copies, but in spite of the need to conduct a running battle against GMD interference, the paper could not fill the demand. Circulation reached over ten thousand, and its novel coverage of both domestic and international news made it popular with GMD bureaucrats, as well as curious students. Both publications stopped with Deng's arrest in August 1931.

The appearance of a PAC journal marked the public and, one might say, the official beginnings of the new organization. It is difficult to pinpoint the exact time, but there is no doubt that shortly after its formation, the PAC and Deng in particular were targeted by Nanjing for careful surveillance and finally for destruction. Chiang Kai-shek dispatched Wang Boling as a special agent to Shanghai, with his mission to arrange Deng's arrest and destroy the PAC. The PAC was also successfully infiltrated by GMD agents, who had detailed knowledge of the organization's operations.[17] An illegal organization, the PAC was continuously harassed by the Nanjing authorities. Its operations were clandestine. Key leaders, including Deng, had to move from place to place, often in disguise, and arrange meetings in "safe houses." To facilitate organization, the PAC established three semiautonomous central regions, with headquarters in Shanghai, Beiping, and Hong Kong. Central, northern, and southern cadre committees were established around the three regional centers. The central area was directly administered by the Party Central, although a Shanghai City Cadre Committee was established under Zheng Taipu and Luo Renyi. As in the other areas, most of the activities of the Shanghai committee were concentated in educational and cultural circles, although it also began work among the common people and laborers in the concessions. He Shenbai, Yang Shupu, and Jiang Wan prepared an organizational infrastructure in anticipation of the impending military struggle, but there were apparently no such activities prior to Deng's execution.

The other major areas of PAC activities in its central region included Nanjing, Jiangxi, Jiangsu, and Anhui. The Nanjing operation was directed by Wan Can and Xie Shuying, with concentration on educational and cultural work. Apparently, the Nanjing cell, in spite of operating in the dragon's jaws, was very active and bold. One of its most dramatic operations involved the distribution of copies of Deng's articles opposing the National Assembly (NA) meeting in the capital. His writings accused Chiang of packing the NA and ignoring Sun Yat-sen's demand for a truly popular representative conference. Deng's tracts were placed on the desks of the delegates, who arrived at the May 1931 conference to find a slightly different perspective on their activities. The documents sent a shock through the meeting and served as a reminder that not everyone was content with the manipulative style of Chiang. Wan Can's brother, Wan Yun, has described an unbroken line of PAC activities in Nanjing, continuing through the present. After 1949, when the small parties were shifting to accomodate the CCP victory and there was talk of disbanding, Wan Yun apparently constituted a party of one.[18] He insisted that the party must remain alive, and was later vindicated when the CCP retained the policy of the UF.

The Jiangxi operation was most active in Nanchang and Jiujiang. Again, schools and cultural organizations received the most attention, but there was also extensive work in the printing, tanning, and rattan-weaving industries. Shop clerks and workers in various businesses were organized into workers' clubs and literacy classes. In the Jiangxi-Fujian border region, PAC efforts to organize the peasants began. In villages where there were PAC members, peasant associations were formed, some of them expanding to include several thousand members. These same organizations came into direct competition with CCP cadre and GMD officials, at times with bloody results. While the PAC did tend to concentrate its efforts in educational circles, this was the result of two conditions: first, most of the leaders in the PAC were intellectuals who had good contacts in academia and, second, the PAC considered preparation of a reliable leadership corps to be among its highest priorities.[19] Once in place, the properly educated cadre were to organize the common people.

The Jiangsu leadership included Shi Fangbai, Mao Xiaojin, and Ji Fang, who prepared active cells in Zhenjiang, Wujing, Suzhou, Nantong, and numerous towns along the Ning-Hu rail line. Zhejiang leaders included Cai Yiwu and Li Shihao, who established cells in Hangzhou, Shaoxing, and Ningbo. Anhui operations were directed by He Shikun, with active cells in Hefei, Anjing, and Suxian and most work concentrated among young students. Since from its beginnings the PAC emphasized the special significance of the mass movements, there was an ongoing attempt to integrate the recruitment of leadership from students and youths with mass organizations. According to a later report:

> The PAC had always concentrated on the importance of mass movements and been critical of an exclusively military standpoint. We felt that the masses were the starting point of the revolution (*geming de chufadian*). Thus, at that time,

> work on the mass movements was totally integrated with organization and propaganda, and all aspects were mutually pushed ahead.[20]

Bearing in mind the dearth of detail on local organizational work of the early PAC, it is still possible to sketch the organization's activities in its northern and southern regional zones.[21] Zhang Hanqing and Huang Shangzhi represented the PAC central in Beiping. Party cells were established in twelve universities and middle schools, and numerous student organizations were founded. These organizations stressed the themes of opposition to Chiang Kai-shek and Japan. Student organizers were very active in the city and played a key role in rickshaw and railway workers' movements. One of the greatest successes of Deng and the early PAC was the en-masse enrollment of an activist student organization, the *Ben she* (Origin Society).[22] In October 1930, led by Deng Haoming, its four hundred members joined the PAC.[23] In an operation which relied heavily on *tongxianghui* (regional associations) and the *guanxi* of its various members, the addition of four hundred students was a major expansion of operations. Deng Yanda's appeal to the *Ben she* people rested on shared basic principles--opposition to Chiang and the Japanese pressure--and Deng's unique ability to organize a military force. As Deng Haoming noted: "We knew it would take military power to challenge Chiang. We were looking for some way to join up with such a military power. Deng Yanda had the contacts and the skills to form a viable military alliance. We wanted to talk to him...."[24] Deng Yanda considered that the Northeast would be crucial in China's destiny. During the winter of 1930-1931, he travelled incognito through the area at great personal risk. His efforts to make contacts and win support for the PAC there, however, were limited to planting a few seeds for the future.[25]

When he returned from Germany, he paid a special visit to Peng Zemin in Hong Kong.[26] Peng, a venerable GMD member who had a long association with Sun Yat-sen and the "true" left wing of the party, had also been close to Deng, Song Qingling, Liao Zhongkai, and He Xiangning.[27] Peng reaffirmed his association with Deng and the PAC, and became the nucleus of the southern regional organization with headquarters in Hong Kong. While Peng took charge of a rapidly growing organization there, Deng's regional associations with Guangdong meant there was a large number of Cantonese who felt comfortable with him and the PAC program. An especially able core included Lin Xisheng, Qiu Zhen, Xu Guangying, Zhou Lixing, and Yang Yitang. The southern organization was deeply involved in the colleges and universities of Guangdong and conducted a very effective recruitment program. The Hong Kong cell organized the core of a sailors' society, which was envisioned as the first link in a chain of such groups extending along the China coast. There was also a program of military infiltration, with party activists recruiting within the armies of Chen Jitang, the reigning Guangdong warlord. PAC publications began to appear and plans unfolded to build a mass base, both in the urban centers and the countryside. After 1931, the Cantonese organization continued, with descendants of the PAC playing important roles in the smooth progress of the Red Army as it rolled through the South.

To conclude this outline of PAC organizational work between 1930-1931, there is some indication that Deng's concern with recruiting and training students and youths, who would then go to the masses and provide them with altruistic leadership, was a priority. The objective was always the masses, but the way to them had to be through a properly prepared, idealistic, dedicated core of operatives. Thus, there was a lot of work in high schools and colleges. PAC members who were largely from the cultural elites were well placed to recruit youths for their programs. The impressive success in Beiping and other major urban centers demonstrates the potential of the PAC. Indeed, the tenacity of the organization in the face of relentless oppression was amazing. When the Communists came to power in 1949, they had to deal with more than twenty thousand activists who still claimed to adhere to the ideas of the PAC. By the time of Deng's execution in November 1931, all of the major cities and provinces, with the exception of Sichuan, had organizations. While there was little time to go deeply among the masses, the top of the PAC was taking shape.

Military Organization

Throughout Deng's brief career, there was a palpable tension between his gifted, searching intellect, which predisposed him to the world of philosophy and ideology, and his training and role as a talented military officer. One senses that he preferred the world of the intellect to that of military action, but the times demanded his talents be put to use in a profession of violence. He rationalized his military life with altruistic thoughts of the need to sacrifice the self for others. He would often say that people are all cogs in a great machine or cells in an organism much greater than any individual. Life was hardship and work, and the very meaning of it lay in toil. Work alone gave human beings a chance at dignity and honor.

Between 1927-1930, he lived and studied in Germany and travelled extensively in Europe and Asia. During these years, he indulged his fondness for study and speculation. While there was always a practical, revolutionary dimension to his efforts, it was also a time for deep thinking and searching for a philosophical foundation for his ideas. He finally came to realize that China and the Chinese people were alone in the world. His search for allies and sympathetic ears, even in the Indian subcontinent, reaffirmed that sense of isolation. The Chinese held their destiny in their own hands. China's dominant reality was violence and war; the struggle for a better world would be--had to be--a military struggle. While he preferred the struggle of ideas and even the political struggle, he felt forced by circumstances to prepare for a violent confrontation with Nanjing.

At the First Cadre Conference, held in Shanghai, he coined the phrase "Military affairs as the first priority."[28] He realized that Nanjing's power rested on a shaky alliance with regional warlords, but most importantly on Chiang Kai-shek's personal associations with young officers who made up the WMA clique. This latter group had either been cadets or teachers at the WMA. To break Chiang's control in Nanjing, it would be necessary to shatter the loose alliance of his regional props and, most importantly, to destroy his main force, the WMA cadets. To this end, a Military Affairs Committee was established in Shanghai. This key group included Deng, Ji Fang, Huang Qixiang, Deng Yuce, and Yan Lisan.[29] It spent three months preparing a strategy. Deng defined the PAC military strategy in five main points: (1) Since the political structure of China was highly militarized, it could not be overcome without a military struggle. Once the struggle started, however, it would be absolutely essential to implement a program to form the revolutionary masses into armed organizations. This would make possible force to meet counterforce and to ultimately obliterate the anti-revolutionary military. (2) During the current situation, it was necessary to seek out alliances with reactionary forces. The recent failure of new and old militarists in their attacks against Nanjing had made such alliances especially timely. Forces should be played off against each other. It was critical, however, to never become dependent on warlord forces, since they did not comprehend the purpose of revolutionary struggle. Thus, extreme caution was necessary, as they would be trying to use the PAC just as it sought to use them. Such alliances would never be stable and were only temporary. (3) The military movement had to be joined together with the mass movements. The military was important in a revolution, but the fundamental power of a revolution came from the masses. If the masses were not totally in possession of revolutionary prerequisites, then the military would eventually separate itself from the revolution. In such a case, one who tried to use weapons would be used by the weapons. The two fundamental prerequisites that would determine whether or not the Chinese revolution could be revived were (A) that the peasant, worker, and youth masses experience, on their own, an expansion and deepening of organization, and (B) that young military officers embrace the consciousness of the peasants, workers, and commoners and be willing to accept revolutionary responsibility. (4) The military must, at all times, be subservient to the political authorities. The military must obey the party and not be allowed to develop beyond its reach. (5) There were two areas for military development: the establishment of a military force of the masses and the destruction of Chiang Kai-shek's military power.[30]

Based on the above five points, the PAC drew up its military strategy. This called for concrete efforts to gain influence and control over active and inactive military people; to win over WMA students and Baoding and other provincial military-academy graduates; to approach all armies and military affairs educational programs; and even to cultivate relationships with local bandit groups (*tufei*).

Deng was ideally suited to lead a military challenge against Chiang and Nanjing. While he reserved his greatest enthusiasm for intellectual and political interests, his talent and energy were sufficient to include military responsibilities. All of his formal education had been in military academies. As a student, instructor, or administrator, he had been associated with the Guangdong Army Primary School (where he had been a protege of Deng Keng), the Guangdong Army Intensive-Course Academy, the Wuchang Infantry Second Preparatory Academy, the Baoding Military Academy, the WMA, and the Chaozhou and Wuhan branches of the WMA (on 12 January 1926 renamed the Central Military and Political Academy of the NRA [*Guomin geming jun, zhongyang junshi zhengzhi xuexiao*]). He had also been closely associated with Sun Yat-sen's military program and the building of the First Guangdong Army into a revolutionary fighting force. He was commander of Sun Yat-sen's personal bodyguard. He had close relationships with Zhu Zhixin, Liao Zhongkai, and Deng Keng. As a Cantonese, he had a long history of relationships with the Cantonese military factions led by Chen Jiongming, Chen Jitang, Li Jishen, and Chen Mingshu. He shared battle experiences and class ties with the main Guangxi militarists, Bai Chongxi and Li Zongren. His personal association with Chiang Kai-shek and the WMA were very important. At the WMA, he served as Vice-Director of Training and Commander of the Cadet Brigade, as well as Dean of Instruction during 1926 and head of the Wuhan Branch of the WMA during 1927. He also had served as Director of the General Political Department of the NRA during the first 1926-1927 phase of the Northern Expedition. During that campaign, he commanded units in key battles, including the seizure of Wuhan. In addition to his formal studies of military science in China, he had also studied in Germany, where he developed close relationships with key members of the PAC and also leaders of the communist military, including Zhu De and Zhou Enlai. In China, he had worked in a close and complementary relationship with Mao Zedong. Hence, his military credentials were impeccable.

The PAC military program was comprehensive, but Deng and others in the PAC realized that the bedrock of Chiang's personal power was the large number of junior officers who had graduated from the WMA. Building on the traditional student-teacher relationship (Chiang had directed the WMA since its beginnings in 1924), Chiang had been nurturing the personal loyalty of WMA graduates. They had been placed throughout key units of the NRA as an investment in future power. PAC strategy was to use the vast web of Deng's personal contacts, as well as those of other PAC members, to organize the WMA graduates into cells and, ultimately, a broad interconnected organization. Apparently, Deng's contacts were very substantial. His appeal met sympathetic response from thousands of WMA graduates, who were frustrated with Chiang's personal leadership and the abandonment of revolutionary populist zeal that came with Nanjing's consolidation of power. By the summer of 1931, almost six thousand WMA graduates from various classes, representing eighteen provincial organizations, had been consolidated into the WMA Revolutonary Classmates Association, which served as a cover for the PAC. This huge number represented three-quarters of all WMA graduates.

Chiang was furious with this challenge to his personal power.[31] He told an assembly of WMA students that he would kill Deng, if he did not pull back from his meddling with WMA graduates.[32] With three fourths of the WMA graduates indicating a willingness to cooperate with the PAC in the event of a military rising against Chiang, it is not too difficult to understand why He Yingqin and Dai Jitao, among other close advisers of Chiang's, were rumored to have strongly advised him to arrange Deng's execution. He was getting too close to Chiang's vitals. Chiang apparently tried all manner of inducements to get him to give up his military program.[33] He seems to have had some fondness for him to the end, but he could not tolerate a direct threat to his power.

Hence, the PAC's success would finally be the cause of its failure. The infiltration and organization of the junior-officer cadre in Chiang's personal forces left him with little choice in dealing with Deng and the PAC. In addition to the WMA Revolutionary Classmates Association, moreover, the PAC military program was expanding in other areas.

The key force in the PAC's military action, planned for the late summer of 1931, was Chen Cheng's Eighteenth Army, which was being positioned in Jiangxi Province in preparation for a military campaign against the Communists. Chen and his Vice-Commander, Zhou Zhirou, and division commander, Luo Zhouying, were all, like Deng, Baoding graduates. Although Chen was a native of Zhejiang Province, after graduating from Baoding he had served in the Third Regiment of the First Division of the Guangdong Army, along with Deng. In a battle in 1923, Chen was seriously wounded and, at great personal danger, Deng carried him from the field of battle. In 1924, Deng introduced Chen to the WMA, and it has been said that Chen had so much admiration for Deng that he even aped his dress and walking styles. It is true that ultimately Chen did become a loyal prop of his fellow provincial, Chiang Kai-shek, but in 1931 he had numerous meetings with Deng and, along with his two key division commanders, joined the PAC.[34] There were also many WMA graduates among the junior officers in the Eighteenth Army, so that PAC contacts at both the senior and junior officer levels secured the commitment of that force to support a planned late-August insurrection.

Aside from the Eighteenth Army, Deng and the PAC were close to Chen Mingshu, another Baoding graduate, and the Nineteenth Route Army. Chen, a Cantonese, had a long association with Deng. He and his top officers--Cai Tingkai, Jiang Guangnai, and Huang Qixiang--were associated with the PAC. The Nineteenth Route Army was also a fragment of the famous Fourth Army (Ironsides) of Northern Expedition fame. Many of its officers were WMA graduates, and there was a strong influence from the Left GMD and the Communists, who dominated the political departments in this force. This Army, which was stationed in Guangdong, was also being positioned for combat against the Communists in Jiangxi. The proximity of the Nineteenth Route Army provided an additional reason to focus the first stages of the anti-Chiang military campaign on Jiangxi. Indeed, the intention was to build the actual base of the campaign on the Eighteenth Army, with support from the Nineteenth Route Army; sympathetic members of the WMA Revolutionary Classmates Association would create havoc in Chiang's personal armies. If the initial uprising failed, an effort was to be made to secure a base area in Jiangxi.[35] If the base was crushed, Deng claimed he might be willing to join the Communists or, if necessary, fight an autonomous guerrilla war.

Aside from the above forces, the PAC also had a strong base in Wuhan, where Qian Dajun and Hu Boyu, who were running the Hankou Branch of the WMA, were both members of the PAC. Hu made frequent trips to Shanghai, and was especially enthusiastic about an early struggle against Chiang. Another direct associate of the PAC was Gao Ziju, a Baoding graduate and close associate of Deng's, who commanded the Second Troop Column (*zongdui*) stationed on the Henan-Anhui border. Gao had commanded the student brigade at the WMA during Deng's tenure as Vice-Director of Training. While head of the Administrative Office in Nanjing, Gao had frequent contact with Fan Shaolang, a PAC member. Gao grew increasingly hostile to Chiang and made trips to Shanghai to meet with Deng. He eventually agreed to support the PAC military program.[36]

There were other military leaders who might have supported a PAC uprising. Through Lian Ruiqi, the PAC had close relations with Yang Hucheng in Xi'an. Yang invited PAC members into his units, and several dozen moved into various positions.[37] Deng Yuce, who had been an important commander under Feng Yuxiang, promised to support the PAC's military program after holding numerous lengthy strategic discussions with Deng in Shanghai.[38] Feng sent several emissaries to meet secretly with

Deng and, as the PAC completed plans for an uprising, it sent key military leaders Zhang Bozhun and Huang Qixiang to high-level meetings with Feng.[39] There were other military contacts in Shanxi, Fujian, Henan, and Sichuan.

The above indicates the breadth and depth of the PAC military preparations prior to Deng's arrest in August 1931. While in their publications the PAC excoriated the CCP for brutality and needless violence, efforts were made to include the Communists in the planned uprising against Chiang. Many PAC members had been Communists, and contacts were made with Zhou Enlai and other CCP leaders.[40] According to Zhang Bozhun, these contacts were fruitless and, given the hostility and brutal clashes between Communist and PAC units in 1930-1931 and 1933-1934, it is hard to imagine that cooperation could have taken place. There was also little time for the grass-roots organization and preparation of the mass militias Deng had said would be necessary for a successful struggle against Nanjing. The scattered, local organizations of peasants under the leadership of isolated PAC members, especially in western Fujian Province, could, with time, have provided the popular base for a movement which remained largely directed toward cultural and military elites. The PAC understood the need for a popular base, but lacked the time and human resources to translate this understanding into a movement.

Conclusion

Numerous advisors had been telling Chiang that the only serious threat to his long-term power in the GMD was Deng. We have already noted Chiang's anger and public threat to destroy anyone who dared recruit what he perceived to be his private resource, the WMA cadets. He lived a good part of his life surrounded by enemies, yet he managed to survive in part by keeping his inner resources secure. In the early summer of 1931, he sent Wang Boling to Shanghai with unlimited funds to arrange the arrest, or "neutralization," of Deng. Just as Deng and a nucleus of his key military advisors were planning to leave for Jiangxi to begin the long-awaited military uprising, he was sold out by a traitor, apprehended, and quickly sent to Nanjing. His arrest took place on 17 August 1931, and he was secretly executed, without trial, on Chiang's personal order on 29 November 1931.

There was irony in his arrest and execution. He had been warned again and again to leave Shanghai. Everyone seemed to know he was targeted. In one instance he was, in fact, aboard ship waiting to leave for Hong Kong when he was called ashore to meet with his brother, Yancun, and Yancun's daughter, Jingyu. Deng had taken on Jingyu as a *yangnu* (adopted daughter).[41] By the time this family meeting was over, his ship was gone, and his resignation in the face of danger strengthened. Then, too, he was a proud man with a strong sense of destiny. While in prison, he likened his band of followers to the twelve apostles and himself to Christ about to be sacrificed on the cross. He was ready to be a martyr and strongly felt the need to serve as an example for others. He also was somewhat arrogant and unreserved in his criticism of others. Hence, he had his share of enemies among the great and powerful. His venemous attacks on Wang Jingwei, whom he perceived as the worst sort of opportunist, elicited Wang's hatred. When negotiations between the Canton faction and Nanjing were underway, conditions for compromise included the release of Hu Hanmin and other Cantonese held by Chiang, but Wang refused to include Deng in the discussions. When Chiang's enticements failed to sway Deng, the former had no choice but execution. Deng always seemed to limit his personal attacks on Chiang, preferring to see him as an example of a feudal mindset that was part of a transitional world. This was not to excuse Chiang, but to explain the behavior of the Nanjing GMD. It seems that Deng had his reasons for respecting Chiang, and Chiang probably found it extremely difficult to order his execution. As associates at the WMA, they had a warm relationship, though Chiang was apparently frustrated by Deng's more radical politics.

Whatever the larger picture of Deng's arrest and execution, it was a well-placed blow that crushed the immediate threat of a military challenge, for Deng had been the central figure in the PAC and clearly the key military player. Other PAC leaders were also arrested. Some fled to Hong Kong or went deeper underground. The WMA Revolutionary Classmates Association was broken by arrests and reeducation, but Chiang preferred to try to salvage the support of this important military resource rather than drive the young officers into revolt through harsh discipline; hence, other allies of Deng's were allowed to retreat into silence. While Chen Cheng made his peace with Chiang, he never forgot Deng and used his ideas on land redistribution, both in Hubei and in Taiwan. Chen Mingshu and the Nineteenth Route Army spearheaded the Fujian Rebellion during 1933-1934. Yang Hucheng made an important, though ultimately fatal, appearance during the Xi'an Uprising in 1936. Hundreds, if not thousands, of soldiers, from generals to platoon sergeants, quietly nurtured their loyalty to the principles of the PAC.[42] These men were an important resource in the War of Resistance against Japan and on the side of the Communists during the Civil War.

As early as 1935, the PAC had begun to shift from its neutral ground between the GMD and the CCP. The Communist UF policy of the mid-1930s prompted a softening toward organizations like the PAC. Remarkably, the PAC had itself retained an identity and organization. Its illegal status forced members to act autonomously, and much of its cohesion was the product of a kind of spiritual consensus, a body of shared ideas that had been expressed in the days of the GMD reorganization and later restated in the pronouncements of the PAC in 1930-1931. As noted above, in several interviews Wan Yun described a form of silent communication. Members could sense their counterparts in unspoken ways. The adherents of radical-left GMD ideology shared a pattern of behavior, which rested on an intuition that China's destiny would ultimately be determined by the common people. The traditional social structure had to change, and some kind of new order was inevitable. Members of the PAC tried to be "scientific." They frequently trumpeted their faith in historical materialism, yet they were unwilling, like Deng, to turn away from Sun Yat-sen and his Three People's Principles. They were, as their Communist critics like to say (usually it is a resigned criticism, resting on the Communist understanding that a lingering bourgeois mentality is unavoidable during a transitional phase of human development), in between realities. They were bourgeois in the sense that they were unwilling to have faith in Communist orthodoxy or blindly follow a dogmatic leadership. At the foundation of this reluctance was perhaps the immersion of key leaders in the thought of Kant and Hegel. They were, after all, intellectuals trained to doubt and question; scientists had to be skeptics. There was, then, an ever-present aura of reserve and caution, a lack of enthusiasm for blindly charging ahead. Perhaps there is some truth to the Communist assertion that the PAC, or any middle-of-the-road organization, was incapable of leading society into the future. That responsibility rested on the shoulders of those who dared to charge ahead, in their quest for a new era. Groups like the PAC were left to choose sides and follow.

In the late summer of 1931, however, there was a moment and a leader who did have the ability and will to action. Deng looked with disdain on the senseless brutality of the Communists and the failure of revolutionary vision in Nanjing. In spite of his personal weaknesses, he was an attractive leader. Seasoned revolutionaries from Cai Yuanpei to Mao Zedong and Zhou Enlai, Dai Jitao to Liu Yazi, respected his talent and feared his challenge. With his passing, what promised to become a significant part of China's revolution crumbled away, the fragments scattering throughout society to play their parts in less visible, but perhaps equally important, ways. A movement dependent on a single person is doomed to fail with his or her passing. As Deng liked to say, the revolutionary leader is nothing more than a cell, a cog in a vast process of change. In the final moment, it would be the masses of the common people who had to liberate themselves. In its program for action, the PAC wanted to help create conditions in which mass self-liberation could occur. Deng finally was consumed by the violence he disdained. His death was kept secret for several weeks, its revelation followed by tears, disbelief, and anger, but no uprising. Remnants of the PAC slipped deeper beneath the surface of Chinese politics.

Notes

1. Carsun Chang, *The Third Force in China* (New York: Bookman Associates, 1952), passim.

2. Kosugi Shufu, "Dai Jitaoshugi no hito kosatsu" (An Examination of Dai Jitaoism), *Rekishi Heiron* (Historical Criticism) 8 (1972): 62-78. Kosugi's analysis is based on Dai Jitao, *Sun Wen zhuyi de zhexue de yizhu* (The Philosophical Testament of Sun Yatsenism) (Yangmingshan: n.p., 1950).

3. See Yamada Tatsuo and Shang Mingxuan for some recent insights into the problems of factional definition. Two works by Yamada are *Chugoku kokuminto saha no kenkyu* (Research on the Chinese Guomindang Left Wing) (Tokyo: Keio Tsushin, 1980) and Yamada Tatsuo, ed., *Jindai Chugoku Jinbutsu Kenkyu* (Research on Modern Chinese Personages) (Tokyo: Keiogijuku daigaku chiki kenkyu senta, 1988). Shang's contribution is represented in *Sun Zhongshan yu Guomindang zuopai yanjiu* (Research on Sun Yatsen and the Guomindang Left Wing) (Beijing: Renmin chubanshe, 1986) and *Liao Zhongkai zhuan* (A Biography of Liao Zhongkai) (Beijing: Beijing chubanshe, 1982).

4. Ji Fang, *Zhongguo nonggong minzhu dang de qianshen: Zhongguo Guomindang linshi xingdong weiyuanhui de chansheng he douzheng* (The Predecessor of the Chinese Peasants' and Workers' Democratic Party: The Emergence and Struggle of the Provisional Action Committee of the Guomindang), draft, (n.p., n.d.); Yang Yitang, *Deng Yanda* (Guangdong: Guangdong renmin chubanshe, 1986), 85ff. Also useful are the autobiographies of Luo Renyi, *Luo Renyi tongzhi yigao* (A Preliminary Draft Regarding Comrade Luo Renyi) (n.p., 1981, handwritten draft); Lian Ruiqi, *Qinqzhu shiwu zhounian: Wo canjia minzhu geming de guocheng* (In Commemoration of the Fifteenth Anniversary: My Participation in the Democratic Revolution) (n.p., 1964, handwritten draft); Zhang Bozhun, *Zhang Bozhun zai yijiuwuyi nian tan nonggong minzhu dang de lishi* (Zhang Bozhun's Discussion of the History of the Peasants' and Workers' Party in 1951) (n.p.,n.d., draft no pagination); Wan Yun, *Jiefang qian nonggong minzhu dang zai 1927-1949 Beijingshi de dixia zuzhi huodong gaikuang* (An Outline of the Activities of the Underground Organization of the Peasants' and Workers' Democratic Party in Beijing Prior to Liberation, 1927-1949) (n.p., n.d., draft). These references are a fraction of the materials I gathered on the PAC during a recent research trip to the PRC sponsored by the Social Science Research Council.

5. Qiu Ting and Guo Xiaoqun, *Deng Yanda: shengping yu sixiang* (Deng Yanda: Life and Thought) (Lanzhou: Gansu renmin chubanshe, 1985), chap. 18.

6. The best description of his work style is found in Zhang Kesheng, "Zhang Kesheng huiyi tanhua" (Zhang Kesheng Talks About His Reminiscences) (n.p., n.d.) This is the transcript of an interview with Zhang conducted by Tu Chuande of Fudan University. Zhang was Deng's secretary during his stay in Germany following the collapse of the first UF.

7. Deng Yanda, *Women de sixiang xitong ji zhuchang genju* (The Foundation of Our System of Thought and Standpoint) (Shanghai, 1929). This source, which I have been unable to locate, is quoted in detail by Yang Yitang in an unpublished draft of his biography of Deng. Yang Yitang, "Deng Yanda," Appendix I: "The Essence of Deng Yanda's Thought" (separate pagination).

8. Shu Xin (pseud.), "Geming yu minzhong," *Dengta* 2 (May 1928): 1-2. This pseudonym means a faggot or firewood. The Communists, like Third Party members, liked to compare themselves to combustibles which would be consumed in the service of others.

9. Zhe Ren (pseud.), "Qing geming de qingnian dapo lianai meng," (An Invitation to Revolutionary Youth to Shatter the Dream of Romantic Love), *Dengta* 2 (May 1928): 10. By the above standard, the revolution has yet to succeed. One is reminded of the tragic theme of impossible love running through Cheng Naishan's recent work, for example, *The Piano Tuner* (China Books, 1988).

10. A fascinating glimpse into the organization and activities of the Revolutionary Party on the local level can be found in *Hu Langui huiyilu* (The Memoirs of Hu Langui) (Chengdu: Sichuan renmen chubanshe, 1985), 181ff.

11. According to Yang Yitang, Deng's disillusionment with Chiang began during the extensive discussions between the two at the Lushan Conference of February 1927, at which Chiang laid out his anti-communist position. For Deng, Chiang's apparent willingness to cooperate with the Western powers was even more significant than his anti-communism. Yang, 33ff., 42ff. These sections also discuss Deng's relationship with Wang Jingwei.

12. Deng Haoming, interview by author, Nanjing, 23 September 1985.

13. Just as secret societies and bandit gangs traditionally had served as surrogate extended families, the modern political party also seems to have provided many Chinese with social and emotional moorings during a period characterized by the disintegration of traditional society. Hence, attachments to a party, despite numerous examples of opportunism, could run very deep.

14. Yan Qi and Wang Youqiao, *Zhongguo nonggong minzhu dang lishi yanjiu: minzhu geming shiqi* (Studies of the History of the Chinese Peasants' and Workers' Democratic Party: The Period of the Democratic Revolution) (Beijing: Zhongguo renmin daxue chubanshe, 1984), 23ff.

15. Ibid.

16. Zhongguo nonggong minzhu dang, zhongyang dangshi ziliao weiyuanhui (Chinese Peasants' and Workers' Party, Central Party History Commission), *Zhongguo nonggong minzhu dang de douzheng licheng, 1927-1979* (The Struggle of the Chinese Peasants' and Workers' Democratic Party, 1927-1979) (Beijing: Central Party History Commission, Chinese Peasants' and Workers' Party, 1983), 9 puts the number of party members in 1930 at about two thousand.

17. Qiu and Guo, 150ff.

18. Wan Yun, interview by author, Nanjing, 9 June 1986.

19. *Zhonguo nonggong minzhu dang de douzheng*, 9ff.

20. Ibid. With regard to the PAC mass movement program, a brief note on the recent historiography of the organization is appropriate. The official CCP history of the PAC, produced at People's University, seriously distorts its early history by solely focusing on urban, elite aspects of its organization. This approach leaves the false impression that the PAC had no mass base or interests, thus suggesting that mass movements remained the exclusive reserve of the CCP. It is this kind of pseudohistory, which is being built up layer upon layer around organizations like the PAC, that makes understanding of such movements increasingly difficult. See, for example, Yan and Wang. This same editorial distortion extends to all levels of PAC activities. For example, the published, edited version of Yang Yitang's *Deng Yanda* completely excludes the author's important discussion of Deng's philosophy found in the draft version. Qiu Ting and Guo Xiaoqun include a lengthy discussion of Deng's philosophy, but focus on his use of historical materialism, while dismissing his philosophical relativism as a sad bourgeois remnant in his consciousness and a flaw which prevented him from becoming a true believer and follower of the CCP. Qiu and Guo, 212-240. Qiu concludes his discussion of Deng's philosophy by adding that "this is a case of 'minor flaws not obscuring the beauty of the jade', for the confusion in Deng's world view cannot reduce the brilliance he manifests in his philosophical historical materialism." Ibid., 239. This is a sad example of the historical determinism Deng most feared.

21. For a detailed discussion of PAC activities in Beijing, see Wan, *Jiefang qian*, no pagination. Wan's draft contains further details on PAC activities through 1928.

22. Deng Haoming, "Ben she shimo (zhaiyao): Da geming shibai hou wode yiduan geming jingli" (Extracts from the Complete Story of the Origin Society: Some Aspects of My Revolutionary Experiences Following the Failure of the Great Revolution). Unpublished draft.

23. Wan, *Jiefang qian*.

24. Deng Haoming, "Ben she"; interview with Deng Haoming.

25. Zhang Hanqing, *Daonian Deng* (Mourning Deng) (n.p., 1981). This piece, located in the private files of Wan Yun, was prepared in commemoration of the eightieth anniversary of Deng's death. Zhang Hanqing, who was very active in the Beiping branch of the PAC, accompanied Deng on his trip to the Northeast.

26. Zhou Tianxi, *Peng Zemin* (n.p., n.d.).

27. For details on the southern organization of the PAC, see Zhongguo nonggong minzhu dang, Guangdong weiyuanhui (Chinese Peasants' and Workers' Party, Guangdong Committee), *Dangshi ziliao* (Historical Materials) 1 (June 1986), passim.

28. *Zhongguo nonggong minzhu dang de douzheng*, 10

29. Zhang Bozhun, no pagination.

30. *Zhongguo nonggong minzhu dang de douzheng*, 12.

31. Yan and Wang (pp. 31-33) list the key members of the Revolutionary Classmates Association linked with the PAC. The figure of six thousand is cited in *Zhongguo nonggong minzhu dang de douzheng*, 12-13. For Chiang's declaration that he would kill Deng, see Xie Yingbai, *Guanyu Deng Yanda de yilin banzhao* (Fragments Regarding Deng Yanda) (n.p., n.d.). An old friend and Baoding classmate, Xie was from the same county as Deng. He attended the Whampoa commemorative meeting at which Chiang threatened Deng.

32. This information was supplied by several Peasants' and Workers' Party members: Deng Haoming, interview by author, 23 September 1985; Wan Yun, interview by author, 8 June 1986; and Xiao Hanxiang, interview by author, 4 December 1985. Xiao is the Party historian.

33. Qiu and Guo, 159ff.

34. Both communist scholars like Yan Qi and first-hand observers like Zhang Bozhun state flatly that Chen, Zhou, and Luo were all members of the PAC. The offical PAC history cited above makes the same assertion. Chen could not believe that Deng had been executed and wept when the news reached him. He also sent a telegram to Chiang demanding that he step down. Qiu and Guo, 166.

35. Xiao Hanxiang, interview by author, Beijing, 3 December 1985.

36. Yan and Wang, 34. A great deal of Yan and Wang's information was obtained through interviews with participants in these events. People's University sent out teams of researchers to interview numerous participants. Transcripts are not available, but some of the results are in their book.

37. Lian, no pagination. Lian, who served as Yang's emissary, provides detailed information on this contact.

38. Zhang Bozhun, no pagination.

39. *Zhongguo nonggong minzhu dang de douzheng*, 13ff.

40. Zhang Bozhun, no pagination.

41. The *yangnu* system was informal. In this case, Jingyu became part of Deng Yanda's household and was raised by his wife, so she would have someone to look after her in old age. However, Jingyu developed breast cancer and died young.

42. *Zhongguo nonggong minzhu dang de douzheng*, 15ff; *Nonggong minzhu dang dangshi weiyuanhui gongzuo huibao* (Report on the Work of the Historical Commission of the Peasants' and Workers' Democratic Party) (n.p.,n.d.), passim.

5

The National Salvation Association as a Political Party

Parks M. Coble

The National Salvation Movement of the late 1930s was among the largest and most broadly based urban political movements in the history of Republican China. Developing rapidly in the spring of 1936, it spread among professionals, students, educators, clerks, businessmen, workers, women's groups, government employees, and other urban dwellers. Although these groups were only a small minority of China's massive, mostly rural, population, their concentration and their political activism gave them a visibility and importance out of proportion to their numbers.

The phrase, "national salvation" (*jiuguo*), appeared in the names of numerous political movements in Republican China. After the Japanese seizure of Northeast China in the autumn of 1931, the phrase was frequently employed by groups favoring resistance to Japan. For the purpose of this essay, however, I shall focus on the particular *jiuguo* movement which developed in late 1935 and culminated in the formation of the All-China National Salvation Association League (NSA) on 31 May 1936. This group, organized in Shanghai, united representatives of sixty bodies from eighteen provinces and cities.[1]

The political platform of the movement was simple. It demanded resistance to Japanese aggression, a cessation of civil war in China, and a united front (UF)--including the Guomindang (GMD) and the Chinese Communist Party (CCP)--in support of national salvation. The explosive growth of this movement can be attributed to a confluence of factors: growing evidence that the Japanese military was determined to control North China; Chiang Kai-shek's continued adherence to a policy of appeasing the Japanese, while pursuing the civil war against the Communists; the willingness of Moscow and the CCP to join in a UF; and, conversely, demands by Tokyo for Nanjing to participate in an anti-Comintern alliance of Japan, China, and Manchukuo.

Japanese aggression in China did not, of course, begin in 1935. By that date, Japan had already seized the northeastern three provinces and created the puppet government in Manchukuo, later adding the province of Rehe (Jehol). In 1933, Japanese forces had fought to within a few miles of Beiping and Tianjin, during the war at the Great Wall, before imposing the humiliating Tanggu Truce on China. During this process, Chiang had followed a consistent policy of appeasement. He proclaimed that the Nanjing government must first suppress internal enemies, particularly the Communists, before it could resist external enemies, such as the Japanese.

Renewed Japanese aggression in North China in 1935 directly challenged Chiang's policy and gave rebirth to the salvation movement. Chiang's approach had been based on de facto Chinese acceptance of the loss of the Northeast, in exchange for Tokyo's recognition of the authority of the Nanjing government. During the summer of 1935, however, it became clear that extremists in the Japanese North-China Garrison (based in Tianjin) and Kwantung Army (based in Manchukuo) were demanding detachment of North China and its reorganization as an "autonomous" area (i. e., one controlled by the Japanese military).[2]

In June 1935, General He Yingqin, Nanjing's representative in Beiping, accepted an ultimatum from the Japanese military, which forced major changes in Hebei province. GMD organs were to close and Governor Yu Xuezhong was removed, as were the military forces of the central government. A similar ultimatum regarding Inner Mongolia, the Qin-Doihara Agreement, led to the removal of Nanjing organs from Chahar province. The Chinese government, bowing to pressure from Tokyo, also issued the so-called Goodwill Mandate (*dunmu bangjiao ling*), on 10 June, which effectively outlawed explicit expressions of anti-Japanese sentiment by Chinese. To the average Chinese observer, or at least the urban dweller who read newspapers and magazines, the Nanjing government appeared on the verge of abandoning North China entirely, and perhaps accepting a nation-wide arrangement subordinating China to Tokyo.

Nor were the following weeks comforting to these observers. On 2 July, Chinese authorities in Shanghai arrested the editor of the popular *Xinsheng* (New Life) journal, because he had published an article containing remarks on the Japanese Emperor which offended the Japanese. This was now considered a violation of Chinese law. In September, the commander of the Japanese North-China Garrison publicly announced that the five provinces of North China must become "autonomous" and all Nanjing's authority expelled from the region. The Japanese Foreign Minister, Hirota Koki, proposed to Nanjing the formation of a general anti-Comintern alliance, which presumably would have involved Japanese military activity in China to quell communism and defend the allied states against the Soviet Union.

In the face of this new round of demands, Chiang adhered to his policy of "first internal pacification, then external resistance" (*rangwai bixian an'nei*), and focused on the anti-Communist campaigns. In a November speech to the Fifth GMD National Party Congress, he stated that China would not give up on peace until there was no hope, until it had reached the "final point." As if acceding to Japanese demands, in December Nanjing authorized the creation of a separate political council for Hebei and Chahar, a body that might well lead to "autonomy" under the Japanese military.

The point is not to suggest that Chiang's policies were incorrect or unpatriotic. Chiang's defenders continue to argue that his task in facing the Japanese military was daunting, and that his cautious approach embodied a sound scheme to build China's strength for the ultimate clash with Japan. In their opinion, even the creation of the Hebei-Chahar Council, when viewed in retrospect, can be credited with actually preserving Chinese authority in North China. The problem is not how this appears in retrospect, however, but how it appeared to politically active Chinese at the time. We know today that Chiang did resist Japan in 1937, and that he did not sign an anti-Comintern pact with Tokyo. Based on the public record, however, this future direction was not apparent in 1935. Chiang's public speeches were few and always vague, so as to avoid offending Japan. His responses to Hirota were so ambiguous that the Japanese leader announced to the Diet, in January 1936, that Chiang would support an anti-Comintern policy. Thus, millions of Chinese, from bank clerks to shopkeepers to college students, became convinced in late 1935 that Chiang might sign away North China and join with Tokyo to defeat his bitter enemy, the CCP. The result was a massive national salvation movement, spurred by the December Ninth and December Sixteenth student demonstrations in Beiping. The salvationists were determined to force Nanjing to resist Japan, to unite with the CCP and others in common cause, and to abandon any plans for an anti-Comintern alliance.

Through a variety of journals and books, often circulated surreptitiously to avoid Nanjing censors, salvationist intellectuals blasted the policy of appeasement and demanded armed resistance by a united nation. As one salvation leader, Zhang Naiqi, wrote not long after the fourth anniversary of the Manchurian Incident:

> Four years have passed, and what have we gained? We have lost territory. The three provinces have become four and at present are becoming six! Before long, they will perhaps grow to nine! . . . In four years, we have heard the word "prepare" (*zhunbei*). And what is the result of this preparation? . . .

> Some people tell us it has all been consumed by "internal pacification." The cost of "exterminating the bandits" has been estimated to be eighty thousand yuan per person! When we hear this, we can only cry![3]

Zhang's sentiments were typical of the salvationist writers. They shared the view that the years of delay gained China little, but had merely strengthened Japan's hand. As Wang Zaoshi argued, "certain people" seemed willing to surrender the Northeast, Mongolia, and North China. They perhaps believed that "we could declare ourselves vassals and surrender or flee overseas and live comfortably in retirement as others whose nations have vanished [have done]." Wang asserted, however, that "the great majority of us compatriots are unwilling to become slaves of a foreign power."[4]

Spurred by the December Ninth movement, the salvationists began to organize. In December 1935, women leaders in Shanghai formed a Women's Salvation Association, while literary figures organized a Cultural Circles Salvation Association. In the early months of 1936, educators, professionals, students, and workers formed similar bodies in Shanghai and other key cities, a process which culminated in the formation of the NSA on 31 May.[5] Well-known intellectual and social figures provided public leadership for the movement. These included many associated with the GMD Left, such as Song Qingling (Madame Sun Yat-sen) and He Xiangning (Madame Liao Zhongkai), as well as prominent educators such as Tao Xingzhi, a student of John Dewey at Columbia, and Wang Zaoshi, who had received a Ph.D. from the University of Wisconsin in political science and served as a college dean in Shanghai. Other leaders, such as Zou Taofen (a journalist), Zhang Naiqi (a banker), and Shen Junru (a lawyer) had met through the vocational-education movement of Huang Yanpei or through their support of the League for the Protection of Civil Rights.[6]

The movement did not form a tightly organized body of the type or scope of a political party. The NSA was really an informal, umbrella-style organization made up of constituent groups. Even though the subordinate groups were often newly formed themselves, such as the Shanghai women's salvationists, student salvationists, or professional-circles salvationists, they generally were established around earlier associations of women, students, professional leaders, or others. Sometimes informal gatherings at YMCAs or chambers of commerce were converted into a formal organization. There does not seem to have been any real attempt to create the equivalent of party membership. The impact of the movement was therefore very difficult to quantify.

Certainly, much of the influence of the salvationists came through their writings, which were circulated in numerous journals. The most prominent of the journalists was Zou Taofen, who edited *Dazhong shenghuo* (Life of the Masses), which, until its suspension by Nanjing in late February 1936, averaged 200,000 copies per issue. With a readership of perhaps one million, it was one of the most widely read journals in China during its day. Other periodicals and publications of the salvationists also had large circulations.[7]

The salvationist groups promoted their cause through a variety of methods--rallies, petitions, marches, and the issuing of proclamations. On 9 February 1936, for instance, the Shanghai Professional-Circles NSA (*Shanghai zhiye jie jiuguo hui*) issued a manifesto demanding that Nanjing immediately declare war on Japan and reject Hirota Koki's proposals for peace (which included the signing of an anti-Comintern pact).[8] On 30 May, Shanghai salvationist groups held a rally at the Chamber of Commerce building to commemorate the eleventh anniversary of the May Thirtieth Incident. Later, a crowd of six thousand marched through the streets singing anti-Japanese songs.[9] On 21 June, a salvationist student group of 600-1,000 occupied the Shanghai North Railway Station, demanding to be taken to Nanjing to present petitions. They disrupted rail service for much of the day.[10] On 10 July, several salvation leaders, including Shen Junru, Zhang Naiqi, Shi Liang (a female lawyer in Shanghai), and Sha Qianli did go to Nanjing to petition the government to resist. Other actions included a 9 August rally in Shanghai opposing Japanese smuggling (then a major problem) and an 18 September gathering to commemorate the fifth anniversary of the Manchurian Incident. The latter turned violent when the demonstrators, perhaps five thousand in number, clashed with police at the old west gate of Nanshi (south city) in Shanghai.[11]

The activities of the salvationist groups also included the publication of essays and petitions. But would such a movement with no army, no formal political party, and holding modest-sized rallies really concern the GMD government, which had a large army and did not, of course, have to face a general election? In fact, it did. The NSA deeply worried Chiang, who made an immediate and sustained effort to discredit and suppress it. Pro-salvation journals such as Zou's *Dazhong shenghuo* were banned. GMD party bureaus were urged to be on guard against all salvationist literature.[12]

Shanghai mayor Wu Tiecheng, addressing an assembly of school and university directors on 5 June 1936, vigorously denounced the movement:

> At present a small group of careerists have organized a supposed National Salvation Association. Are there not only twenty to thirty in it who run the entire supposed National Salvation Association? This organization actually is counterrevolutionary. At present, with the exception of a few traitors, everyone knows that saving the nation, the real work of saving the nation, is not something that literary people writing essays can do. National salvation is a

> military activity. At present, the government is making painstaking efforts to prepare. Military and diplomatic secret difficulties cannot, of course, be made public. We ought sincerely to trust the government and obey the government.[13]

Despite Wu's curt dismissal of the NSA, Nanjing feared the movement precisely because of its political ideas, ideas which had the potential to spread and become politically potent. At a time when Chiang was trying to mount a final military campaign against the Red Army, he faced a tough sell. Japan had already seized four provinces and compromised two more. Now Tokyo appeared on the verge of gaining all of North China, and perhaps limiting Chinese sovereignty in the South as well. How could Chiang justify confining all military operations to a threat in remote Shaanxi, when the heart of the nation seemed on the verge of being swallowed up? What Chiang feared was that sympathy for the salvationist cause would infect not merely intellectuals, students, and clerks, but government employees, GMD members, Blue-Shirt activists, and even his own army officers. In this sense, Chiang considered the salvationists a threat.[14]

A second danger from the salvationists was the risk which their activities brought to the policy of appeasement. Japan required Nanjing to suppress anti-Japanese sentiment in China, in order to demonstrate its "sincerity" in pursuing peace. Japanese officials frequently complained to Nanjing that the publications and activities of the salvationists violated the "Goodwill Mandate." Japanese officials became particularly incensed over salvationist support for a wave of labor unrest and strikes which plagued Japanese-owned textile mills in China in November 1936. An estimated fifteen thousand workers participated in strikes in Shanghai alone.[15]

A final danger which Chiang felt from the NSA was his belief that it was working closely with the CCP. Four salvation leaders--Shen Junru, Zhang Naiqi, Tao Xingzhi, and Zou Taofen--had issued a manifesto on 15 July 1936, renewing their call for a UF of all patriotic Chinese to resist Japan. Less than a month later, on 10 August 1936, Mao Zedong responded favorably to their proposal, strongly increasing Chiang's suspicion of the group.

Deeply opposed to the salvationists himself and under great pressure from the Japanese, Chiang ordered the important leaders of the NSA arrested. On the night of 22 November, Chinese police, cooperating with authorities in the Shanghai International Settlement and the French Concession, arrested seven key figures: Shen Junru, Zhang Naiqi, Zou Taofen, Sha Qianli, Li Gongpu, Wang Zaoshi, and Shi Liang. Among major salvationist figures only Song Qingling, He Xiangning, and Tao Xingzhi (then in America) escaped.[16]

Far from suppressing the salvationists, however, the arrests seemed to have enhanced their prestige. The Chinese press quickly dubbed the defendants the "Seven Gentlemen" (*qi junzi*) and gave great publicity to the case. In hopes of lessening the attention, Nanjing directed that the trial be transferred to Suzhou on 4 December. Nonetheless, outpourings of support for the leaders came in from throughout China. To their admirers, the seven were patriotic leaders whose only crime was opposing Japanese imperialism and whose arrest was at the behest of the Japanese consul. Zou Taofen recalled that even their military escorts to Suzhou were sympathetic and joined in singing resistance songs. Telegrams of support came in from Chinese and foreigners; visitors included the Green Gang leader, Du Yuesheng, and many prominent capitalists; and rallies were held throughout urban China demanding their release. Their most blatant support came from Zhang Xueliang and Yang Hucheng, the military commanders at Xi'an, who included release of the seven in their demands during the Xi'an Incident of December 1936.[17]

The ground swell of support for the salvationists was so great, concluded Ch'ien Tuan-sheng, that the arrests "so boosted the number of adherents and sympathizers that they actually became the third most powerful party, next to the Kuomintang [Guomindang] and the Communist Party."[18]

On 3 April 1937, the Jiangsu Court handed down indictments charging the leaders with endangering the nation, and the case went to trial in June. Shen Junru, considered the senior leader of the seven, presented their defense. He dismissed the government's case as mere Japanese propaganda, and denied that his group sought to oppose the GMD or support the CCP. Its only goal, he maintained, was resistance to Japanese imperialism.[19]

Despite the publicity and support which the arrests gave to the salvationists, in some ways it diverted the movement from its cause. The activities of the NSA were increasingly directed at the release of the leaders and against the Nanjing government, rather than focusing on Japanese aggression and support for a UF under the leadership of the Nanjing government. On 5 July, for instance, Song Qingling led a delegation of thirty to forty people to Suzhou, and demonstrated in front of the Jiangsu Court, demanding to be arrested. Calling the movement "go to prison to save the nation," Song stated that if the seven were guilty of the "crime" of patriotism, then she and her compatriots were likewise guilty. Her strategy was to continue to pressure Nanjing to release the leaders.[20]

The Marco Polo Bridge Incident occurred only two days later. In the five weeks between that event and the outbreak of fighting at Shanghai on 13 August, the movement quickly shifted gears, as its political demands rapidly became government policy. After continued pressure, the salvationist leaders were released on bail on 31 July. Chiang opened talks with Zhou Enlai and a CCP delegation at Lushan on 17 July. A UF now seemed an imminent reality. Within a week of Marco Polo Bridge, salvationist groups began raising money for troops fighting in the North and sent telegrams of support urging total resistance. On 22 July, the Shanghai groups reorganized under the title, Association to Save the Nation From Extinction, reflecting the now military nature of the struggle with Japan. Rallies and receptions were also held for the "Seven Gentlemen," who returned to Shanghai on 1 August.[21]

When August brought the fighting directly to Shanghai, the heart of the salvationist movement, its leaders struggled to find ways of assisting the military effort. Groups, such as banking employees and department-store clerks, held fund drives to aid wounded soldiers and refugees. Some worker groups assisted in transporting wounded from the front, while student associations led a drive in late September to collect 100,000 jackets in Shanghai for soldiers at the front. In late October, efforts were undertaken to collect 200,000 gloves.[22]

The intellectual leaders of the salvationists began a campaign of wartime propaganda. On 14 August, the Cultural Circles Salvation Association in Shanghai held writing and drama workshops to both create and publish resistance literature. They also undertook a direct propaganda campaign. Teams were organized to present the salvationist message of resistance, through plays, songs, and lectures. Target audiences were active soldiers, the wounded in hospitals, and refugees.[23]

Despite this active campaign to assist the military effort, the significance of the salvationist movement clearly faded after 13 August. The center of resistance now shifted to the military. The multitudes who had sympathized with the salvationist cause either joined the military effort, retreated to the interior with GMD forces, or drifted to Communist base areas. The last major arena of salvationist activity was unoccupied Shanghai. Between the Nationalist retreat and the outbreak of the Pacific War in December 1941, the French Concession and the International Settlement (south of the Suzhou Creek) remained an unoccupied "isolated island." In the absence of effective GMD control, pro-Communist salvationists increasingly dominated the movement. They continued active publication of journals and books opposing Japan. The massive *Shanghai yiri* (One Day in Shanghai), for instance, commemorated the first year of the struggle. Fund raising and recruiting efforts were gradually focused on the New Fourth Army, and modest numbers left the "isolated island" for guerrilla camps. Salvationists also led resistance to Japan's increasing dominance over Chinese institutions in unoccupied Shanghai, such as customs and postal service.[24]

The movement gradually lost the battle with Japan in the unoccupied areas. The Japanese special services targeted salvationist leaders who were too conspicuous. On 7 April, for instance, pro-Japanese elements engineered the assassination of Liu Zhanen, an American-educated

(Columbia Ph.D.) leader of the Christian and YMCA movements. Long active in the NSA, Liu was directing the efforts of Christian churches in Shanghai to raise money locally and internationally for refugee relief. This type of intimidation increased in October 1938, when a puppet city government of occupied Shanghai was organized under Mayor Fu Xiaoen. Salvationist forces had to be increasingly circumspect, until finally suppressed when Japan seized the "isolated island" in December 1941.[25]

Such was the NSA, a political force which burst on the scene in late 1935 and, according to most observers, became a major factor in urban China over the succeeding two years. But how does the NSA fit into the schema of Chinese politics? Was it part of the "third force" (TF)? In fact, many students of the NSA would argue that it was not a TF at all, but simply a front organization of the CCP. At a time when Communist fortunes were at low ebb, the NSA, they argue, promoted the UF concept as a method of relieving pressure on the Red Army and implementing Comintern directives.

This was certainly the view of the GMD at the time. On 12 February 1936, the GMD Central Propaganda Department proclaimed that the CCP was attempting to stage a comeback by using cultural organizations and intellectuals. Under the cover of the slogan "national salvation," the Communists were opposing the central authorities and trying to topple the government.[26] GMD writers, even today, have continued to hold similar views of the salvation movement. Li Yunhan, a historian at the GMD Historical Archives Commission, wrote that the movement was a Communist front group which raised the anti-Japanese flag, but in fact parted from the path of true patriotism.[27] In this view, the NSA, far from being an independent political party and a TF, was merely an agent of the CCP.

Ironically, an almost identical viewpoint is held in the People's Republic of China (PRC), although from an opposite perspective. The salvationists are, of course, seen as great patriotic heroes, lionized as those who forced the GMD government into a course of resistance under a UF. The CCP, however, is credited with supplying the leadership and inspiration for the movement. Studies recounting activities of the salvationists routinely use the phrase "under the leadership of the CCP," or the CCP underground. Memoirs by salvationist followers published in China today invariably stress the individual's ties to the party or at least the ideals of the party.

A recent comprehensive history of Shanghai, for example, states that in regard to the salvationist movement of 1936, the CCP "led and assisted various salvationist organizations in gaining strength. . . . CCP party members were the backbone of the National Salvation Association. Under the leadership and impetus of the party, Shanghai and nation-wide salvation groups from all circles were organized and developed quickly."[28] Party leadership was exercised behind the scenes. Salvationist groups all had public administrative boards filled with well-known patriotic figures. Behind the scenes, the actual work was done by secretarial groups, which were secret and contained numerous CCP elements.[29]

Memoirs also suggest that many pronouncements of the salvationists were, in fact, of CCP origin. The July 1936 document issued by Shen, Zou, Tao, and Zhang was actually drafted by the party, one memoir states, under the leadership of Pan Hannian, who arrived from Moscow. Only after discussing it with Pan did the four leaders issue it in their names.[30]

Despite these statements, a careful reading of PRC memoirs suggests that the Communist cause may have inspired many salvationists, but that the CCP did not engineer or direct the movement. The CCP underground in Shanghai and most urban areas had been shattered by arrests and executions in late 1935 and early 1936, when the salvationist movement erupted. Only on 25 April 1936 did Feng Xuefeng arrive from Shaanxi with a radio transmitter to reestablish contacts between Shanghai and the Red Army. His assignment was to establish links with salvationist leaders, such as Shen Junru, and to convey the CCP's support for a UF policy. Feng was also to attempt to reorganize the Shanghai underground. Visiting Lu Xun, Mao Dun, and Agnes Smedley after his arrival, he located numerous party members. Pan Hannian and Hu Yuzhi arrived from Moscow (via France) in May, and Hu remained as a liaison with the salvationists. Pan returned to Shanghai from Shaanxi in late September 1936 and directed CCP activities in Shanghai; Feng served as assistant leader. By May 1937, according to the official history of the Shanghai CCP, the party organization in Shanghai had been restored.[31] What this account suggests is that there were connections between the salvationists and the CCP, but clearly not CCP control from the inception of the movement.

Memoirs by individual salvationists and Communists support this interpretation. Li Fanfu, in an interview in 1983, stated that he had lost touch with the CCP Shanghai organization in 1935, when his contacts were all arrested and killed by the GMD. He read of the Comintern's UF policy in an English newspaper, and became actively involved in the salvationist movement, contributing over one hundred anti-Japanese articles to salvationist journals. Only later did he reestablish ties to the CCP organization.[32] Wang Yaoshan shared a similar experience. He lost contact with the CCP in 1934, and learned of the August First Declaration (1935) when he obtained a copy of the Paris-based *Jiuwang ribao* (Save the Nation from Extinction Daily). He then became involved in salvationist work, participating in a rally to mark the fourth anniversary of the January Twenty-Eighth Incident. He reestablished party links when he met Feng Xuefeng through Lu Xun.[33]

A similar account emerges from the writings of Yong Wentao, who learned of the August First Declaration in the same manner as Wang. He acknowledges that underground CCP organizations were in disarray. With no contact with the party center, salvationist work was not, therefore, regular (*zhengchang*) party work, but everyone, he contends, operated within the spirit of the Declaration.[34] One active participant in the Shanghai women's salvationist group recalls:

> At that time, the dominant political situation was the nation's difficulty from the Manchurian Incident . . . to the North-China situation. Chiang Kai-shek was busy with his anti-Communist campaigns and would not resist. He talked drivel about "first internal pacification, then external resistance." This caused the people spontaneously to seek national salvation. When the CCP published the August First Declaration, we read it and felt it truly said what was in everyone's heart.[35]

The author, who was not a CCP member at the time, then became actively involved in that party.

A careful reading of these memoirs suggests that many in Shanghai who had been associated with the CCP underground (or at least wished to claim so today) became involved in the salvationist cause primarily because of their support for its political platform, not under direct orders from the party. The NSA thus had an independent existence as a group, and was not merely a front organization of the CCP, although close ties developed between the party and salvation leaders. There is still much work to be done in studying these ties (a topic being pursued by Patricia Stranahan). Such study would also shed light on the role and organization of the party underground and contribute to the debate on the manner in which the CCP adopted the UF policy.

In evaluating the significance of the salvationist movement, however, we should move away from the issue of CCP-NSA ties. To understand the movement, its origins, and impact, we must evaluate it not from the standpoint of 1949 but of 1935-1937. Because current accounts of the salvation movement focus almost entirely on the role of the CCP, it is difficult to recapture the atmosphere in which the NSA developed.

The salvationist movement was not a political party or a TF in Chinese politics. It did not have a formal party structure nor did it attempt to compete for government power as a political party. It accepted members from all political parties--the GMD, CCP, Chinese Youth Party (CYP), and others. The "Seven Gentlemen," as part of their defense at their trial, declared that the movement was not a party, and they never inquired as to the party affiliations of new members. Although many salvationist members had links or sympathies with the CCP (and with the GMD, for that matter), the driving force behind the NSA was concern over Japanese imperialism.

The salvationist movement is best understood as what we might term today a "single-issue" group. For millions of urban Chinese in 1935-1937, the prospect that Chiang Kai-shek would sign away North China and agree to an anti-Comintern pact under Japanese tutelage seemed a frightening reality. The political platform of resistance to Japan and a UF of all parties had an irresistible appeal. It was the political program of the movement, not its leaders nor surreptitious ties to the CCP, that was at the core of its power. The movement tapped the powerful force of nationalism--a force that had earlier fueled the May Fourth and May Thirtieth Movements and the growth of the GMD itself. The NSA thus represented not a TF nor political party, but the organizing potential a popular political program had in Republican China. Chiang's failure to tap this potential was symptomatic of his failure as a party political leader. As he pursued an unpopular policy, which combined appeasement of Japan with a domestic civil war, he deeply feared a movement which tapped popular sentiment for resistance.

Notes

1. Zhou Tiandu, ed., *Qi junzi zhuan* (Biographies of the Seven Gentlemen) (Beijing: Zhongguo shehui kexue chubanshe, 1989), 193; Zhonggong Shanghai shi weidang shi ziliao zhengji weiyuanhui (Commission for the Compilation of Historical Materials on the Shanghai Party Bureau of the Chinese Communist Party), ed., *Zhonggong Shanghai dangshi dashi ji, 1919.5-1949.5* (A Record of Major Events of Chinese Communist Party History in Shanghai from May 1919 to May 1949 (Shanghai: Zhishi chubanshe, 1988), 403.

2. This, and subsequent discussions of Japanese aggression, are taken from Parks M. Coble, *Facing Japan: Chinese Politics and Japanese Imperialism, 1931-1937* (Cambridge: Council on East Asian Studies, Harvard University, 1991).

3. Zhang Naiqi, "Sinian jian de qingsuan" (Settling Accounts of Four Years), in Ding Shimin, ed., *Jiuwang yanlun ji* (A Collection of Speeches on National Salvation) (n.p., 1936), 21, 24.

4. Wang Zaoshi, "Jiwang yierba" (Remembering [the Shanghai Incident of] 28 January 1932), in Ding Shimin, 9-10.

5. Zhonggong Shanghai shi weidang shi ziliao zhengji weiyuanhui, ed., *"Yierjiu" yihou Shanghai jiuguo hui shiliao xuanji* (Collected materials on the Shanghai National Salvation Association After the December Ninth Movement) (Shanghai: Shanghai shehui kexue yuan, 1987), 185.

6. Hatano Ken'ichi, *Gendai Shina no seiji to jimbutsu* (Politics and Personalities of Contemporary China) (Tokyo: Kaizosha, 1937), 388-89; Zhou, passim.

7. For additional material on Zou Taofen, see Parks M. Coble, "Chiang Kai-shek and the Anti-Japanese Movement in China: Zou Tao-fen and the National Salvation Association, 1931-1937," *Journal of Asian Studies* 44 (February 1985): 293-310.

8. *"Yierjiu,"* 99-100.

9. *Zhonggong Shanghai dangshi*, 403.

10. *"Yierjiu,"* 133-35.

11. *Zhonggong Shanghai dangshi*, 405-408.

12. "*Yierjiu*," 229-230.

13. Ibid., 95.

14. For additional discussion of this point, see Coble, *Facing Japan*, passim.

15. "*Yierjiu*," 273-75, 424-27.

16. Sha Qianli, *Qiren zhiyu* (The Jailing of Seven People) (Shanghai: Shenghuo shudian, 1938), 3-17.

17. Zou Taofen, *Taofen wenji* (Collected Works of [Zou] Taofen) (Beijing: Sanlian shudian, 1957), 3: 109, 114; *China Weekly Review*, 5 December 1936, 22.

18. Ch'ien Tuan-sheng, *The Government and Politics of China, 1912-1949* (Stanford: Stanford University Press, 1970), 357.

19. Zhou, 90-97.

20. "*Yierjiu*," 402, 464.

21. *Zhonggong Shanghai dangshi*, 426-432.

22. Ibid., 437, 443-47.

23. Ibid., 433-38.

24. Ibid., 456, 466-68, 474, 480.

25. Liu Langmo, "Aiguo jiaoyujia Liu Zhanen boshi" (The Patriotic Educator, Dr. Liu Zhanen), *Shehui kexue*, no. 8 (1987): 64-66.

26. *Zhonggong Shanghai dangshi*, 399.

27. Li Yunhan, *Kangzhan qian Zhongguo zhishifenzi de jiuguo yundong* (The National Salvation Movement of Chinese Intellectuals Before the War of Resistance) (Taibei: Jiaoyubu shehui yusi, 1977), 4.

28. Tang Zhenchang, ed. *Shanghai shi* (A History of Shanghai) (Shanghai: Renmin chubanshe, 1989), 719-20.

29. Ibid., 719-20.

30. "*Yierjiu*," 387-88, 408.

31. *Zhonggong Shanghai dangshi*, 401-04, 409.

32. "*Yierjiu*," 378-79.

33. Ibid., 379-83.

34. Ibid., 410-13.

35. Ibid., 420.

PART THREE

Opposition Parties and Their Leaders During World War II and the Civil War

6

China's Minority Parties in the People's Political Council, 1937-1945

Lawrence N. Shyu

Intellectual interest in democracy and parliamentary government had a late start in China's modern history. It was defeat by Japan in 1895 which generated interest among scholars and officials in seeking the reform of China's political institutions. This led inevitably to discussion of the parliamentary system of government and its liberal-democratic philosophical foundation. The demand for a parliament under a constitutional monarchy reached its height in the waning years of the Qing dynasty, but the effort was cut short by the 1911 Revolution. With the founding of a republican government, China had her first parliamentary experience (1912-1913) with an elected bicameral legislature and the formation of several political parties. This seemingly auspicious beginning of a parliamentary system, however, was nipped in the bud by the arbitrary and dictatorial ambitions of President Yuan Shikai and his warlord successors. By the early 1920s, the parliament in Peking was overwhelmed by factionalism and corruption, and lost even the semblance of independence. Its final dissolution in 1925 was a merciful end to what had begun as one of the more promising political movements in modern China.

The Guomindang (GMD) revolution in the 1920s brought renewed hope for a more modern and democratic government in China. In spite of its Leninist organizational model and its self-proclaimed revolutionary mission, the ideological guidance for the GMD came from Sun Yat-sen's thought. Sun's program for China's political reconstruction called for the realization of constitutional democracy, after a period of political tutelage.

The problem for democracy in China during the GMD's Nanjing decade was that, aside from the flaws and inconsistencies in Sun's theories of "political tutelage" and "direct democracy,"[1] Sun's political heirs, who gained power in the National Government (NG), paid only lip service to the ultimate objectives of constitutional government, and were interested more in the continuation of a one-party authoritarian rule as the New Order for China.

Most of China's minority parties and groups (MPGs) were born in the 1920s and 1930s, although one or two traced their origins to the early years of this century.[2] They represented a wide spectrum, in terms of their political ideologies and socioeconomic programs. However, two things that all MPGs had in common were very limited memberships and lack of grass-roots support. The activities of these groups suffered severe restrictions in the hostile political environment of China during the Warlord Period (1916-1928) and GMD rule. In fact, political repression and censorship were increasingly severe during the Nanjing decade (1928-1937), a legacy derived partly from the GMD's two-pronged war against Communism and liberalism and partly from the government's "appeasement policy" toward Japan, which entailed curbing any overt anti-Japanese expressions and banning any publications containing unfavourable references to Japan. In spite of growing popular criticism and discontent with the latter policy, the GMD leadership persisted with the aim of "internal pacification before resisting the external enemy." In 1936, this approach culminated in the arrest of the seven leaders of the National Salvation Association (NSA) in November and the kidnapping of Chiang Kai-shek in the Xi'an Incident in December. Japan's unrelenting aggression, however, soon brought about an abrupt change in the NG's policy of political repression and censorship, and offered new opportunities to China's MPGs.

This essay provides a brief account of the main political activities of China's MPGs during the Second Sino-Japanese War of 1937-45. Since the greater part of such activities, at least the overt and publicized part, took place in the People's Political Council (PPC) or used the PPC sessions as their forum, this article will focus on the MPGs in the PPC. Special attention will be paid to their leaders' efforts to uphold national unity, and their involvement in the constitutional movement and struggle for democracy in wartime. The MPG councillors were also involved in a wide range of other issues deliberated in the PPC--such as the wartime economy, military and labor conscription, educational and cultural affairs, and China's foreign policy--which will not be discussed here.

Minority Parties and the Establishment of the PPC

With the outbreak of full-scale hostilities between China and Japan in July and August 1937, the Nanjing Government urgently needed national unity and the wholehearted allegiance of the Chinese people. An anti-Japanese United Front (UF) was created, following the conclusion of a formal agreement between the GMD and the Chinese Communist Party (CCP) in August and September, and an exchange of letters between Chiang Kai-shek and the leaders of the National Socialist Party (NSP) (Zhang Junmai, or Carsun Chang) and the Chinese Youth Party (CYP) (Zuo Shunsheng) the following spring.[3] At the same time, a National Defense Advisory Council was created to advise the NG on basic policies for furthering the cause of the war.[4] Its membership of twenty-four included some leaders of the MPGs, as well as prominent public figures. During its brief existence, the Council was of considerable influence and service in promoting national unity and patriotism. However, its extremely limited membership and extralegal status could not truly represent a UF, and many public figures pressed for its expansion or reorganization to include more representatives from various walks of life. The GMD leadership agreed in principle to the request, but the reorganization of the council was delayed by the rapidly deteriorating war situation and the transfer of the nation's capital from Nanjing to Chongqing.[5]

In the early spring of 1938, when the Government found temporary respite in Wuhan, informal negotiations with leaders of the MPGs were resumed, which led to an agreement regarding the name, membership, and powers of an enlarged council. This issue was placed on the agenda of the GMD's Extraordinary National Party Congress, convened from 29 March-1 April. The Congress resolved to establish the PPC as the highest representative body of the people in wartime.[6] Article 12 of the Program of Armed Resistance and National Reconstruction adopted by the Congress reads: "An organ [the PPC] shall be set up for the people to participate in affairs of state, thereby unifying the national strength and collecting the best minds and views for facilitating the formulation and execution of national policies."[7] This resolution was confirmed by the GMD's Central Executive Committee (CEC), which also adopted an Organic Law for the PPC in April.[8]

When the first session of the PPC was convened in July 1938, it had a membership of two hundred, divided into four categories. The first category of eighty-eight delegates was "elected" from geographic regions. The second and third categories each consisted of six councillors chosen from Mongolia and Tibet (national minorities) and overseas Chinese respectively. Since the "electoral process" in the provinces, as well as the mechanism for choosing members of the second and third categories, were all controlled by the ruling party, councillors of these three categories were predominantly GMD members. The most interesting in terms of representation was the fourth category. It consisted of one hundred members chosen "from among prominent people active in political, economic, cultural, and educational affairs."[9] In practice, a quota was assigned by the GMD to each of the MPGs. During the first two councils, from July 1938 to November 1941, virtually all political parties and groups in the country had their representation in this category. The CCP was assigned seven seats; the NSP, eleven; the CYP, seven; the NSA, eight; and a few seats each were occupied by the Third Party (TP), the Vocational Education Society (VES), and the Rural Reconstruction Group (RRG).[10] However, not all MPG councillors were chosen from this category. A few were "elected" as provincial representatives in the first category.[11]

A major reapportionment of the PPC membership took place in 1942, with a drastic increase in the first category to 164 and a sharp decrease in the fourth category to sixty.[12] This was significant, because the change occurred at a time when relations between the GMD and the CCP, aggravated by the wartime competition, had deteriorated almost to the breaking point, and leaders of the MPGs had become more critical of the government's high-handed policies curtailing civil liberties. This reapportionment was, therefore, a setback for the PPC as a representative body, and reflected the decline of the UF, as well as the GMD's attempt to hold a tighter rein on future meetings of the Council.

PPC membership, at least during its first three years, came close to representing all important segments in Chinese society. It included a fair representation of prominent names from the political, educational, cultural, business, and industrial fields. In the words of a keen political observer, who was himself an active PPC councillor, PPC membership was the result of "a conscientious effort by the party [GMD] to name well-known leaders of the country, regardless of their political proclivities."[13] The PPC probably included the best group of people modern China has had, as a proto-parliamentary body. The creation and continued existence of the PPC suggested that the goals of promoting national unity and whipping up China's war effort were, to a certain degree, achieved. This might be why the GMD Government was relatively tolerant towards the PPC and the opinions expressed by its members.

In spite of the rather impressive credentials of its membership, the PPC was set up as an "advisory body" to the government, not a full-fledged legislature. The powers granted by its Organic Law were vague at best. Only those of hearing reports by government ministers, of interpellation, and of investigation carried some weight.[14] PPC members, particularly those belonging to the MPGs, not only used the Council's sessions as forums to express their concerns and criticisms, they also used the mass media to create "public opinion" to publicize their concerns. Like officials liable to impeachment by the censors in imperial China, government ministers in wartime were made more responsible by the fact that they were exposed to public opinion, as expressed by the PPC members.

Minority Parties and Wartime National Unity

During the first years of its existence, the most important issues in the PPC were how best to maintain China's national unity and continue the war effort, in the life-or-death struggle against overwhelming odds. Maintenance of internal unity after the outbreak of the war meant essentially two endeavors: first, the solicitation of support for the NG from all elements of Chinese society, in a common effort to save the country from total subjugation to Japan, and prevent defections of Chinese troops and politicians to the enemy camp and the expansion of the influence of existing puppet regimes in China; second, to continue GMD-CCP cooperation and reduce friction between the two. Members of the MPGs in the PPC were the most active in these areas, and their performance was praiseworthy.

The Japanese attempted to settle the "China Incident" by both military and political means. A military gain would be followed by political maneuvers to create dissension and nurture pro-Japanese forces in China. Puppet regimes were set up in North and Central China to create a false sense of collaboration.[15] By the time the PPC convened at Hankou in July 1938, however, the puppet regimes in China had obviously failed to stir any excitement on the Chinese political scene. The leaders of these regimes, lacking both personal prestige and independence of political action, could in no way offer the Chinese people an acceptable alternative to the NG. Japanese leaders became aware of the inadequacy of their political arrangements. To better serve their purpose, they needed someone of greater caliber and prestige to head a more unified collaborationist regime in China. After some searching and setbacks, their efforts focused on Wang Jingwei, whose pessimism concerning the prospects of the war was well known, as was his conciliatory attitude toward Japan.[16]

Wang secretly left the wartime capital, Chongqing, on 18 December. He arrived in French Indochina three days later, after a stopover in Kunming where he conferred with Long Yun, the Governor of Yunnan. He made his peace intentions known in a circular telegram to government leaders in Chongqing on 29 December.[17] His unexpected action was greeted with consternation in China and confusion among PPC members, since he had served as PPC Speaker during its first two sessions.

Nevertheless, the NG's will to resist was not seriously affected by this development. This was due partly to the vagueness of Wang's real intentions and his slow-moving negotiations with Japan, and partly to his lack of influence with China's major military commanders. His collaborationist regime was not formally established until March 1940. By then, the impact of his desertion had largely dissipated, and no major military figure defected with him.[18]

Members of the MPGs, on the whole, worked fervently for national unity and against any signs of seeking peace with Japan at the cost of China's sovereignty and independence. In the PPC, they repeatedly expressed their strong support for the government's war effort and condemned the puppet leaders as traitors to China. They accused Japan of naked aggression, and of slanders aimed at Chiang Kai-shek and the NG by spreading rumors of the imminent "sovietization" of China.[19] When Wang deserted, MPG members in the PPC were deeply disturbed. Because of his stature and prestige in the GMD, they were afraid that his action might cause a major split in the ruling party and a serious weakening of China's war effort. During the PPC's Third Session in February 1939, they initiated a proposal, unanimously passed as a Council resolution, in support of Chiang's denunciation of Japan's "peace offensive" and in strong opposition to Wang's action.[20] A year later, when the Nanjing puppet regime came into formal existence, the Fifth Session of the PPC adopted a resolution condemning Wang and his followers as traitors. It stated that the Nanjing regime was a mere puppet of Japan and in no way represented the Chinese people. It called upon the Chinese people and soldiers to overthrow the puppet regime and to resist Japanese aggression to the last. Again, members of the MPGs played an important role in the adoption of this resolution.[21]

Wang was the last important defector, but his defection was not the final major blow to China during the war nor the most serious issue that affected the country's internal unity and future development. An issue of far greater consequence after 1939 was the relationship between the GMD and the CCP.

It was Japan's aggression and the rising tide of anti-Japanese sentiment in China that finally brought peace and reconciliation to the two warring parties. Shortly after the outbreak of the war, the two sides reached a speedy agreement, which marked the beginning of the wartime UF.[22] Such an entente was to benefit the MPGs, as well as the people as a whole. The domestic policy of the NG became more tolerant and liberal: political prisoners were released; civil liberties were considerably extended to allow the publication of all patriotic works, regardless of their background; and activities of mass patriotic organizations and political parties were tolerated, if not entirely legalized.[23] Cooperation between the two major parties and the prevailing spirit of solidarity were necessitated by the onslaught of the

Japanese military machine, which was so efficient that the very survival of the Chinese nation was threatened. All political differences in the country were forced into the background by this emergency. This situation, however, could not last long. By 1939, there were ominous developments threatening the solidarity of the nation. Changing conditions were brought about by the progress of the war. Japan's impressive military gains during the first eighteen months failed to bring down the NG. In view of the immense difficulty of achieving a complete military conquest of China, Japan turned to seek a political settlement. The war gradually moved toward a stalemate, with indications that it would become a protracted struggle with no end in sight. Such a prospect boded ill for the GMD Government, which had borne the brunt of the war in this first stage and paid dearly by losing the best-equipped army units and the most advanced regions of the country to the enemy.[24] It found itself increasingly dependent upon the backward warlord and landlord-dominated interior provinces, and became even less inclined to initiate rural social reforms, lest they weaken its position.

The CCP, on the other hand, suffered more limited losses in the same period. Their ideology gave them a cohesiveness which the more diffuse GMD lacked, and this, combined with superior organization and the guerrilla warfare learned in the previous decade, made them more capable of undertaking a protracted struggle with the superior Japanese enemy. Taking advantage of the thinness of the Japanese occupation, they sent troops and cadres in small groups to infiltrate the countryside behind enemy lines, and thus succeeded in getting support from an increasingly aroused peasant population.[25] The CCP's influence expanded most rapidly in North China, where the GMD was weakest. But even in Central China, the GMD found it difficult to compete with the Communists.

Beginning in 1939, military clashes between the two sides occurred in several provinces. Chongqing countered Communist expansion by again enforcing a military blockade along the southern and western borders of the Communist-controlled Shan-Gan-Ning Border Region.[26] Efforts to end the clashes failed, and the situation deteriorated further in 1940, when the CCP made notable gains in North and Central China, mainly at the expense of GMD-controlled areas. Then came the "New Fourth Army Incident" (or Southern Anhwei Incident) in January 1941, which strained GMD-CCP relations to the brink of a complete break.[27]

Under the two-pronged pressure of Japanese occupation and CCP expansion, the GMD Government resorted to a policy of suppressing Communist or pro-Communist activities in areas controlled by itself. Political repression and the curtailment of civil liberties accompanied the increasing fury of military clashes between GMD and Communist units. The military and political situation in the country was particularly worrisome to the leaders of the MPGs in the PPC. Because of his personal interest and experience in rural education in Shandong, which led him to tour the unoccupied regions in North China during the spring and summer of 1939, Liang Shuming was the first PPC councillor to witness the tension and hostilities which existed between the Government forces and the Communist guerrillas. He became convinced that the UF was in jeopardy, and began to explore the possibility of working together with other concerned MPG members who could assist in preserving national unity. Largely through Liang's efforts, the Association of Comrades for Unity and National Reconstruction (ACUNR) was formed in November. It had over thirty members, all of them PPC councillors not affiliated with the two major parties.[28]

The first chance of mediation for the newly formed Association came in the spring of 1940, when fresh military clashes between government and Communist forces were reported. On behalf of the Association, Liang proposed to the PPC that a special committee be set up in the Council to regulate interparty relations.[29] The interparty special committee was approved by the PPC during the Fifth Session, and eleven councillors, most of them MPG leaders, were appointed by the Speaker. The committee made a number of recommendations to the government, aimed at supplementing the direct GMD-CCP negotiations then proceeding and bringing about a speedy settlement.[30] This effort was not successful, due partly to the lack of progress in the GMD-CCP negotiations and partly to the heavy Japanese bombing in 1940 that brought most political activities in the wartime capital to a standstill.

The grave situation created by the New Fourth Army Incident in early 1941 once again brought the ACUNR members in the PPC to the forefront. The ACUNR members persuaded many other councillors to join with them in the difficult task of mediation, and proceeded to inform the leaders of both the GMD and the CCP of their deep concern for the threat to national unity.[31] This mediation effort at least succeeded in cooling down the heated feelings on both sides. The CCP delegates were persuaded to end their boycott of the PPC meetings, when it reconvened in November. A conciliatory speech was delivered by Chiang Kai-shek to the PPC on 6 March, in which he conceded the importance of national unity and the role of the PPC in maintaining it: "Provided unity can be preserved and resistance carried on to the end, the Government will be ready to follow your [the PPC's] direction in the settlement of all outstanding questions."[32]

Although the mediation of MPG leaders in the PPC did not bring about a quick settlement of the rift, it made it possible for the antagonists to resume direct talks in the late spring of 1941. The talks were often bogged down on specific military issues, and little real progress was made during the next two years. The year 1943 witnessed renewed clashes between the two sides, which brought a more concerted effort at mediation by MPG leaders. To better coordinate the promotion of national unity and democratic government, leaders of the MPGs had organized the League of Chinese Democratic Political Groups (LCDPG) in 1941. It did its best to press the government for a political settlement with the CCP. It succeeded in bringing Chiang Kai-shek around to such a view, as revealed in his statement to the GMD's CEC meeting in September 1943: "I am of the opinion that first of all we should clearly recognize that the Chinese Communist problem is a purely political problem and should be solved by political means."[33]

Direct negotiations between the two sides soon entered a more serious phase. The positions taken by both sides and their bargaining were fully reported to the PPC in 1944.[34] It was a triumph of sorts for the PPC to be recognized by both parties as the proper place to present their cases. MPG leaders in the Democratic League (DL) and nonparty independents were pleased with this development.[35] Their efforts to end the GMD-CCP conflict, however, soon paralleled a major new development from an external source--the U.S. mediation effort first undertaken by special envoy Patrick J. Hurley in September 1944.[36] The presence of such a forceful personality in Chongqing, with the backing of United States prestige and a special mission to bring unity and internal peace to China, made it unnecessary for the MPG leaders in the PPC to take similar actions at the same time. However, when the Hurley Mission encountered a snag and the GMD-CCP talks reached an impasse in the spring of 1945, MPG leaders in the PPC again came to the rescue. Under the Government's urging, the PPC resolved to send a delegation of six councillors to Yanan, to resume talks with the CCP on behalf of the Government. With the assistance of Hurley, who made the arrangement for air transportation, the six flew to Yanan on 1 July, and brought back a new CCP proposal four days later, thus clearing the way for top-level talks in Chongqing between the two parties shortly after the end of the war.[37]

The delegation chosen by the PPC for this mission was noteworthy. Four of the six members--Huang Yanpei, Zuo Shunsheng, Zhang Bojun, and Leng Yu--were leaders of the MPGs belonging to the DL. The other two were Chu Fucheng, an elder statesman with a loose GMD connection, and Fu Sinian, a noted scholar and educator with no party connection. Obviously, MPG leaders were deemed the most appropriate politically to perform such a delicate task.

Events moved rapidly in the next few months. Japan surrendered on 14 August. Two weeks later, Hurley flew to Yanan and brought Mao Zedong back to Chongqing. Mao stayed in Chongqing until 11 October, and subsequent direct talks with the GMD were handled by a CCP delegation headed by Zhou Enlai. In late November, despite reported military clashes, both sides agreed to settle their outstanding problems in a Political

Consultative Conference (PCC) to be convened soon. Since the intended conference was to be attended by leaders of various parties, with the aim of settling all major political issues in the country, its convocation represented a triumph for the leaders of the MPGs, who had always promoted internal peace, and was regarded as a high-water mark of GMD-CCP relations.

Minority Parties and the Wartime Constitutional Movement

As previously mentioned, during the war China's MPGs had heterogeneous backgrounds and varied political persuasions. Yet, they shared certain broad common interests. First, they all supported the War of Resistance and were, therefore, concerned with any development which might jeopardize or obstruct the nation's war efforts. Second, they expressed a genuine devotion to a democratic, constitutional form of government, and were opposed to any arbitrary infringement on the civil liberties of the people. Furthermore, they were aware of the wretched condition of the country and desired improvement in the material lives of the people. They were not opposed to the GMD-led government. In fact, during the early years of the war, they gave all-out support to Chiang Kai-shek and the NG. Only when a military stalemate resulted and clashes between government and Communist troops became frequent and serious, resulting in an increasingly autocratic attitude on the part of the ruling party, did the leaders of the MPGs become more critical of GMD rule. Hence, in November 1939, they formed the ACUNR, which received the blessing of the government and soon found itself in a position to offer mediation in GMD-CCP relations.[38]

In March 1941, MPG leaders in the PPC decided to organize the LCDPG, in spite of Chiang Kai-shek's displeasure. What prompted them was the quick disappearance of the liberal trends, after the first years of the war, and growing repression in the country. Earlier, in 1939, the NG had proclaimed a series of new regulations to restrict publications. Most onerous were the "Measures of Wartime Censorship of Pre-published Books and Periodicals," which required all manuscripts to be checked and approved by the authorized government agencies before publication, and the "Revised Standards of Censorship of Wartime Books and Periodicals," which defined censorable material in such vaguely worded terms as "fallacious" and "reactionary" information. These regulations were aimed specifically at the suppression of criticism and dissent.[39] As PPC councillors, the MPG leaders repeatedly raised their concerns in Council meetings. They received support from the majority to pass several resolutions urging the government to repeal the new regulations and to liberalize censorship.[40] Yet, the

Government failed to heed the advice of the PPC, and the dreadful new regulations were written into law in 1940 and remained in force throughout the war.[41]

The LCDPG soon took a bold step to publicize its appeal. It adopted a ten-point program, which was made public on Double Ten Day, urging the end of one-party rule and the democratization of the NG. Some members of the LCDPG began to view themselves as part of an independent political force, standing between the GMD and the CCP.[42] To seek a more favorable environment for the free expression of opinions, the LCDPG established a propaganda center in Hong Kong, and began publishing the newspaper, *Guangming bao* (Light), in September 1941. When that colony was occupied by Japanese forces following Pearl Harbor, the LCDPG founded a journal, *Minxian* (People's Constitution), in Chongqing.[43] Yet, despite this independence of action, the LCDPG continued to function largely within the PPC.

With the worsening of economic and political conditions after 1940, the government imposed more severe restrictions on civil liberties. The National General Mobilization Act was promulgated following China's formal declaration of war on the Axis Powers, and went into effect in May 1942. Articles 22 and 23 stipulated that the government could restrict the people's freedom of speech, publications, assembly, and correspondence, when it deemed necessary.[44] This was in sharp contradiction with Article 26 of the 1938 Program of Armed Resistance and National Reconstruction, presumably in force throughout the war.[45] The government leaders, however, did not seem to care.

From 1941 on, the demand for legal protection of one's civil rights came to be particularly identified with the aspirations of MPG leaders, in and out of the PPC. This was not a surprise, in view of the political commitment and circumstances of these individuals. Having neither military backing nor territorial strongholds, lacking the support of the masses, deprived of the sanctuary of foreign concessions, still unwilling to give up their independence by going over to the Communist areas, these liberal intellectuals were at the mercy of the GMD-controlled government. They were the ones who would have benefitted the most by the extension of civil liberties and the relaxation of internal political control.

It is also interesting to note that when the government policies vis-à-vis civil liberties became more repressive after 1940, there seem to have been fewer protests and proposals from MPG leaders in the PPC. This does not mean that they lost interest in these matters. Rather, it indicated a shift of attention among MPG councillors to more fundamental political and economic issues. They realized that unless the GMD-CCP conflict was peacefully resolved, and a true constitutional government was established with the participation of all parties and groups, there could be little hope for the people to enjoy legal protection of their civil rights. Therefore, though the issue of civil liberties was never far from their thoughts, it was forced into the background in the face of the more basic immediate problem: the political future of the state itself.

The issue of constitutionalism was first raised at the PPC in 1939, during its Fourth Session. No fewer than seven proposals were made in Council meetings. Five of the seven were initiated by members of the MPGs. Their contents could be summarized by the following three demands:[46]

1. To end one-party rule by the adoption of a constitution and the establishment of a national assembly (NA).
2. To end discrimination against parties other than the GMD, and the practice of forced entry into the GMD.
3. To create a multiparty cabinet responsible to the PPC, as a transitional organ before the existence of a formal, elective NA.

These proposals drew a great deal of attention in and out of the PPC, and were heatedly debated in Council meetings. The PPC resolved to send two recommendations to the government. The first urged the government to fix a period for the convocation of a NA and the adoption of a constitution. It further suggested that a certain number of PPC councillors be appointed to an Association for the Promotion of Constitutionalism (*Xianzheng qicheng hui*; hereafter, APC), to assist the government in this regard. The second was concerned with more immediate issues, such as the equal treatment of all people through the rule of law and the improvement of the quality of government administration.[47]

Since the PPC did not have the legislative power, the implementation of its recommendations was left entirely to the discretion of the GMD government. Later events proved that the GMD leadership did not really intend to implement the PPC resolutions. The Party's CEC changed the target date for the NA several times in the following years.[48] Such frequent changes created confusion and caused the MPG leaders to seriously doubt the government's sincerity. They suspected that the government's intention was to reconvene the NA that was one-sidedly "elected" in 1936-37, not to establish a new one through an open democratic process. Therefore, by 1945, they became opposed to the idea of the hasty convening of a NA and preferred to see this issue left to the planned PCC.[49]

A closely related question was the nature and content of the constitution. The PPC Speaker appointed a twenty-five-member APC, and entrusted it with the duty of helping to draft a constitution. The majority of those appointed to the Committee were members of the MPGs or independents, including several noted jurists.[50] Yet, the APC members were not given the freedom to write a new constitution. Instead, the Draft

Constitution of May 1936 was to be used as a blueprint, from which only minor deviations would be permitted.[51] In spite of this limitation, the APC members made a conscientious effort to carefully study and evaluate the document. After a ten-day meeting just prior to the Fifth Session of the PPC in March 1940, the APC produced a revised draft constitution, and submitted it to the PPC together with a lengthy supplementary report. The revised draft differed from the original constitution in one crucial aspect: the power of the executive branch of the government was limited by the expanded powers given to the NA and its recess committee.[52] This revision obviously displeased the top GMD leaders. The result was the government's intentional postponement of the whole question for the next three years.

The year 1943 marked the revival of the constitutional movement. By that time, China had been at war for six years, and the end was not yet in sight. War weariness became quite marked, and the burden of the people was further increased by the prevailing corruption and incompetence of the government bureaucracy. The Allied Powers were also dissatisfied with China's performance in the war. Increasing criticism of the GMD leadership was voiced both in domestic and foreign quarters. To soothe the growing dissatisfaction, Chiang Kai-shek decided to revive the old issues of constitutionalism and the liberalization of the NG. In his opening address to the Second Session of the Third PPC in September 1943, he announced the Party's decision to convene the NA and promulgate the constitution within a year after the end of the war. He further promised to expedite all preparatory works, and urged the PPC councillors to assist the government in this regard.[53]

Due to earlier frustrations, his announcement was received with reserved optimism by MPG councillors. The PPC responded to Chiang's call with the establishment of the Association to Assist in the Inauguration of Constitutionalism (*Xianzheng shishi xiejin hui*). This organization differed from its predecessor of 1939-40 in two important ways: first, it had a larger membership (thirty-nine to forty-nine members), and its members were drawn from both the PPC and the government, with the Chairman of the Supreme National Defense Council--Chiang Kai-shek--serving as the President of the Association; second, it would function purely as an advisory body, and its resolutions would have no binding power on the government.[54]

During its two-year existence (November 1943-December 1945), its main task was to review the Draft Constitution of 1936. Its members, who were drawn largely from MPG leaders, as well as independents, in the PPC, were careful to recommend as little modification as possible and generally defended the Draft Constitution. It finally produced a report containing thirty-two points, which was submitted to the PPC. The gist of the report was then adopted as a Council proposal.[55] But once again the effort to promote constitutionalism fell on deaf ears. This PPC proposal, as well as the Association's report, were virtually ignored by the government.

When the war ended in August 1945, many councillors, especially those belonging to the MPGs, who had recently renamed their loosely organized League the China DL, realized that the task of constitution-making could never be achieved in the PPC. This mission would have to be carried on outside of the Council and treated as part of a general settlement between the GMD and the CCP. Consequently, the Association died a natural death, and its unfinished work was handed over to the PCC, which opened in the first month of 1946.[56]

Conclusion

The PPC was created to maintain unity in the country and increase China's resistance to Japanese aggression. Prominent people from different walks of life were appointed, including noted political activists belonging to the MPGs. During the eight-year war, national unity was threatened from three quarters. The most immediate threat was Japan's intermittent peace overtures, and the fear that many politicians and military officers might damage the nation's morale by accepting the enemy's terms. The second threat was the deep-rooted regionalism, which could split the Chinese state into a number of different governments. The third threat was the CCP challenge to the NG, for leadership and popular support.

In regard to the first, MPG members worked harmoniously with other PPC councillors to give unwavering support to the NG's decision to fight for national independence and sovereignty. They unanimously condemned those collaborators who were willing to pay any price for peace. The threat to national unity of the entrenched sentiment of regionalism in West China was not so serious a challenge to the NG as the other two. Its damage to the war cause resulted from the reluctance of some provincial authorities to obey wholeheartedly the orders of the central government, and to commit local financial and manpower resources to the war. The PPC generally supported the central government, in its demand for administrative integrity and unification of command. However, during the later years of the war, because of growing disappointment with Chongqing's leadership and policies, some councillors belonging to the LCDPG sought the protection and support of regional authorities against the NG. Some provincial militarists, for their part, were fearful of the central government's infringement on their autonomous power. They were secretly willing to establish ties with other "anti-central elements" in the country. Governor Long Yun and the Guangxi generals extended their protection and patronage to members of the MPGs. Kunming and Guilin were known as wartime havens for liberal intellectuals and students. As confided by several of its leaders, the LCDPG received substantial financial backing from Long Yun and Liu Wenhui during the period, 1941-44.[57]

With the formation of the DL, Luo Longji had the vision and ambition to create a "grand coalition" of all liberal elements and potential anti-Chiang military leaders. The coalition would be led by the DL and seek U.S. support, as well as intimate liaison with the CCP. Its ultimate goal was the establishment of a true democratic government in China.[58] Although this grand design came to naught, the League did develop close ties with some powerful provincial militarists until late 1945.[59]

The third threat, the Communist challenge, rapidly became the most serious political problem in the country, at least since 1939. Many PPC councillors soon became conscious of the situation. What worried them were the harmful effects of this internal struggle on the prospects of the war. Another concern was the authoritarian trend that accompanied the changed political situation. Councillors belonging to the MPGs formed the ACUNR, with the hope of exerting greater influence on both the government and the Communists. They succeeded in setting up an interparty committee in the PPC to deal with the problem, but before any real progress was made, the country plunged into a major crisis following the New Fourth Army Incident of January 1941.

The ACUNR members in the PPC worked hard to prevent an open split, and persuaded the two sides to resume direct negotiations. When the negotiations stopped in 1943, without an agreement, again the MPG councillors came forward to revive the talks. When the American mediation began, the PPC withdrew from active participation in the proceedings. When the American effort stalled in the spring of 1945, it was the PPC delegation of six MPG members and independents that again arranged for the exchange of views, and made possible a top-level meeting between the two sides soon after the Japanese surrender. The MPG members in the PPC did their best to bring this issue to the attention of the public and press their arguments on the leaders of both sides. They realized that the Communists were too strong to be eliminated by military force, and that a prolonged civil war could only have adverse effects on China's development into a free, democratic, and prosperous country. They, therefore, urged both sides to compromise in order to bring about a general settlement. They further warned, prophetically, that a settlement had to be reached before the end of the war, or else the country would be doomed by division and civil war.

An issue closely related to the GMD-CCP relations was that of the fate of democracy in China. The outbreak of the war created such an emergency that the NG had to make drastic changes in internal policies, which gave new hope for liberalism in the country. The establishment of the PPC was the embodiment of this new spirit. To MPG councillors and many independents, the maintenance of unity and the attainment of liberal democratic principles and institutions were two equally important tasks of the PPC. The repeated efforts made by them to promote democracy during the war, however, were largely fruitless. By 1944, most of the non-GMD councillors had come to the painful conclusion that the government leaders had no intention of voluntarily sharing their monopoly of political power with other parties and groups. They realized that only political pressure could force any concessions from the GMD leaders. The only choice left for these liberal intellectuals was whether to take the risk of joining forces with the CCP, in order to bring about a coalition government, or to give up the fight for democracy and be content with a life of limited freedom and security under continued GMD rule. Many chose the first option, and pinned their hopes upon the success of a GMD-CCP settlement which would determine the political future of the country. When the settlement failed to materialize, the peaceful struggle for democracy on the Chinese mainland under the NG was, for all practical purposes, at an end.

Notes

1. The deficiencies in Sun's political theories were discussed in detail by one of his early biographers. See Lyon Sharman, *Sun Yat-sen: His Life and Its Meaning* (New York: John Day Co., 1934; repr., Stanford: Stanford University Press, 1968), 297-298.

2. The National Socialist Party traced its political and intellectual origins to Liang Qichao and the Political Information Society (*Zhengwen she*) he led at the turn of the century. The Chinese Youth Party descended from the Young China movement of 1919-1920. The *Zhigong Dang's* (Cheekongtong) branches were established in overseas Chinese communities during the 1880s.

3. Lawrence K. Rosinger, *China's Wartime Politics, 1937-1944* (Princeton: Princeton University Press, 1944), 96-97; Lyman P. Van Slyke, *Enemies and Friends: The United Front in Chinese Communist History* (Stanford: Stanford University Press, 1967), 92-93; *China Handbook, 1937-1945* (New York: Macmillan, 1947), 73-74.

4. Ibid., 60-61, 95-96; Ch'ien Tuan-sheng, *The Government and Politics of China, 1912-1949* (Cambridge: Harvard University Press, 1950), 280-281, 422.

5. The "inside information" on the formation of the PPC was given to me by Zhang Junmai (Carsun Chang), in an interview on 7 June 1966 at his residence in Berkeley, California.

6. *The Chinese Year Book, 1938-39* (Shanghai: Shangwu yinshuguan, 1939), 336-338.

7. Ibid, 345-346.

8. *Guomin canzhenghui shiliao* (Historical Materials on the People's Political Council) (Taibei: Yutai Publishing Co., 1962), 1 (hereafter, *Shiliao*).

9. Carsun Chang, *The Third Force in China* (New York: Bookman Associates, 1952), 110-111; Wang Yunwu, *Xiulu lun guoshi* (Comments on National Affairs) (Taibei: Shangwu yinshuguan, 1967), 6.

10. Chang, 111; Li Huang, *Wode huiyi* (My Memoirs) (New York, 1968), 435.

11. For instance, Leng Yu, Jiang Hengyuan, Wang Zaoshi, Tao Xingzhi, and Hu Shiqing were all elected by their respective provinces. *Shiliao*, 9-10.

12. Ibid, 291.

13. Ch'ien, 283.

14. See *The Organic Law of the PPC*, 12 April 1938, and the later amendments of 24 December 1940 and 16 September 1944. *Shiliao*, 5, 293, 450.

15. Even before the Marco Polo Bridge Incident, the Japanese military in China had nurtured two separatist regional governments: the East Hebei Anti-Communist Autonomous Council, headed by Yin Rugeng in November 1935, and the Inner Mongolia Military Government under Prince De in 1935-36. After July 1937, the latter was enlarged to become the Federated Autonomous Government for Inner Mongolia. A Provisional Government of the Chinese Republic was inaugurated at Beiping in December, with Wang Keming as the nominal head. On 28 March 1938, a Reformed Government of the Republic of China was established in Nanjing, with Liang Hongzhi as Chief of its Executive Council. F.C. Jones, *Japan's New Order in East Asia, 1937-45* (London: Oxford University Press, 1954), 71-74; Chalmers A. Johnson, *Peasant Nationalism and Communist Power* (Stanford: Stanford University Press, 1962), 41-43.

16. Japanese authorities tried unsuccessfully to induce Tang Shaoyi and Wu Peifu to head a unified separatist government during 1938. Richard Storry, *The Double Patriots: A Study of Japanese Nationalism* (London, 1957), 239. The *North China Herald*, 5 October 1938, reported Tang's assassination. Wu's contacts with Japanese agents are best described in The Memorial Committee for Wu Peifu, ed., *Wu Peifu xiansheng ji* (A Record of Mr. Wu Peifu) (Taibei, 1960).

17. *North China Herald*, 28 December 1938; 4 January 1939. *Foreign Relations of the United States*, 1938, Vol. III, *The Far East*, 441 (hereafter, *FRUS*).

18. Wang failed to persuade Governor Long Yun to respond to his call. Wang's biggest disappointment was the reaction of the Guangdong generals, Zhang Fakui and Xue Yue, who were his close military associates. They denounced him when his intentions became known. *North China Herald*, 4 January 1939.

19. See the PPC Manifesto in *Shiliao*, 11-13.

20. Proposals of the Third Session of the First PPC, Group I, in *Guomin canzhenghui* ([Complete Records of Meetings of] the People's Political Council) (Secretariat of the PPC, 1938-1947; hereafter, *GMCZH*).

21. *Shiliao*, 192-193.

22. See n. 3 above. For a detailed account of developments leading to the GMD-CCP agreement, see Warren Kuo, "The CCP Pledge of Allegiance to the Kuomintang," *Issues and Studies* 4, nos. 11 and 12 (1968).

23. Van Slyke, 154-155; Rosinger, 28-30.

24. Ibid, 29-30.

25. The CCP tactic was best explained in a series of lectures delivered by Mao Zedong in May and June of 1938, and later published with the title, "On Protracted War," in *Selected Works of Mao Zedong* (Peking, 1965-67), 2: 113-194. An informative account of the CCP's effort to establish guerrilla bases in North China in 1937-39 is given in Tetsuya Kataoka, *Resistance and Revolution in China: The Communists and the Second United Front* (Berkeley: University of California Press, 1974), chaps. 4, 5.

26. Lyman P. Van Slyke, ed., *The Chinese Communist Movement: A Report of the U.S. War Department, July 1945* (Stanford: Stanford University Press, 1968), 70-72.

27. Kataoka, 220-228. Chen Yongfa made a detailed study of the history of the New Fourth Army in his *Making Revolution: The Communist Movement in Eastern and Central China, 1937-1945* (Berkeley: University of California Press, 1986), chap. 7.

28. For a sketch of Liang's life, see Howard L. Boorman and Richard C. Howard, eds., *Biographical Dictionary of Republican China*, 4 vols. (New York: Columbia University Press, 1968), 2: 357-359.

29. Ibid.

30. *GMCZH*, Fifth Meeting of the Fifth Session, First PPC, 5 April 1940, "Report No. 2 of the Third Standing Committee."

31. *Shiliao*, 231-233, 243.

32. Ibid, 227.

33. *China Handbook*, 67-68.

34. *Shiliao*, 398-410. An abridged English version is found in *China Handbook*, 81-94.

35. *Shiliao*, 410-415. With more independent members joining the LCDPG, a name change was demanded by its Kunming Branch. Hence, in late 1944, it came to be known as the China DL. This merely meant the deletion of two Chinese words, "*Zhengtuan*," and yet it involved political infighting in the LCDPG. Luo Longji, "Cong canjia jiu Zhengxie dao canjia Nanjing hetan de yixie huiyi" (Some Memories from My Participation in the Old Political Consultative Conference to My Participation in the Nanjing Peace Talks), *Wenshi ziliao xuanji* 20 (1986): 193-284.

36. Tang Tsou, *America's Failure in China, 1941-50* (Chicago: University of Chicago Press, 1963), chap. 8.

37. A seventh member, Wang Yunwu, claimed illness and declined to go. *FRUS*, 1945, VII: China, 416-417, 428-429. For an account of this trip by one of the participants, see Huang Yanpei, *Yanan guilai* (Return from Yanan) (Chongqing: Guoxun shudian, 1945).

38. "Democracy vs. One-Party Rule in Kuomintang China: The 'Little Parties' Organize," *Amerasia* 7, no. 3 (1943): 100-101; Zhou Tiandu, ed., *Jiuguo hui* (The National Salvation Association) (Beijing: Renmin, 1981).

39. Zou Taofen, *Taofen wenji* (The Collected Works of [Zou] Taofen) (Hong Kong: Sanlian, 1959), 3: 188-89.

40. *Shiliao*, 62.

41. Zhang Jinglu, ed. and comp., *Zhongguo xiandai chuban shiliao* (Historical Materials on Contemporary Chinese Publications) (Beijing: Zhonghua shuju, 1954-59), 3:497-499.

42. "Democracy vs. One-Party Rule," 104-105; Li Huang, 587-588.

43. "Democracy vs. One-Party Rule," 105-110.

44. *The China Yearbook, 1943* (Chongqing: Council of International Affairs, 1943), Appendix: "The National General Mobilization Act."

45. *China Handbook*, 79-81.

46. Zou, 3:226-237.

47. *Shiliao*, 139.

48. *China Handbook*, 118; Ch'ien, 308.

49. *Shiliao*, 477-478; *GMCZH*, "Record of the Sixteenth Meeting of the First Session, the Fourth PPC."

50. *Shiliao*, 150.

51. Zou, 3:242.

52. *Shiliao*, 166-180; Ch'ien, 308.

53. *Shiliao*, 353-355.

54. Ibid, 351; Ch'ien, 309.

55. *Shiliao*, 518-520.

56. Ibid.

57. Luo, 207-208; Liu Wenhui, "Liu Wenhui fan Jiang tou Gong de zibai" (Liu Wenhui's Confession Concerning His Rebellion Against Chiang [Kai-shek] and His Surrender to the Communists), " *Zhuanji Wenxue*, no. 341 (1990): 61-74; no. 342 (1990): 93-102.

58. *FRUS*, 1945, VII: China, 182-184, "Report of the Vice-Consul at Chengtu" (R.M. Service).

59. The League's liaison with Long Yun was maintained through Luo and Zhang Xiruo. Contacts with Liu Wenhui and other Sichuan generals, such as Pan Wenhua and Deng Xihou, were made mainly through Zhang Lan. Recently published sources reveal that Liu and Pan secretly joined the DL in 1944-1945, and provided considerable financial support to it. See n. 57 above; Qiao Cheng, "Wo canjia Pan Wenhua qiyi jingguo" (My Participation in Pan Wenhua's Revolt), *Zhuanji Wenxue*, no. 342 (1990): 49-52.

7

The Miscellany of China's Political Spectrum, 1945-1950

Peter Ivanov

The end of the Second World War stimulated strong hopes in Chinese society for the nation's movement towards parliamentary democracy. Although during the war the United Front (UF) of the Guomindang (GMD) and the Chinese Communist Party (CCP) had already experienced a considerable rift, which after August 1945 kept growing, a number of circumstances permitted the anticipation of a peaceful outcome of events. The inevitability of the final battle between the two big political parties did not seem that obvious just after the war, though many mainland and some Taiwan publications try their best to prove it so.

The Political Consultative Conference (PCC) was convened in January 1946 to discuss a transition to constitutional rule. Opening the first session, Chiang Kai-shek declared the equality of different political parties (all of them legalized), announced the release of political prisoners, called for general elections, and guaranteed democratic freedoms.[1] His statements gave impetus to a sharp rise in activity of different social groups, which started creating their own political organizations. Their purpose was the speedy and effective incorporation of a new establishment, which later turned out to be an illusion. The period immediately after World War II can be called the second Chinese experiment in multipartyism, the first having occurred during the post-1911 period. The number of parties in China from 1945-1949 was close to one hundred. Usually scholars pay attention to those that became allies of the CCP or the GMD, and whose histories usually had their roots in the 1920s and 1930s. At the same time, the activities of minor parties with special social affiliations (secret societies, peasants, etc.) have remained outside the scope of research. Some of these associations even tried to cooperate with the Communist regime after 1949. This essay is an attempt to trace the tiniest of the tiny in China's political history, 1945-1950.

Political organizations uniting members of secret societies (*huidang*) pursued the goal of adapting the societies' traditional structures and forms of activity to the new realities. One of these parties, the largest among the émigré associations,[2] was the Chinese Hong Men People's Rule Party, established in Shanghai in July-August 1946.[3] Despite the protests of some Hong Men leaders,[4] Situ Meitang and Zhao Yu proclaimed the party's program. Its five basic points demanded an immediate end to the Civil War, creation of a coalition government based on interparty cooperation, depoliticization of the army, introduction of "new politics experimental regions" to implement democratic reform by independent civil servants, and a struggle for national unity and against any outside involvement in civil strife.[5] The party's position was supported by the *Hongsheng* radio station and a journal, *Minzhi zhoukan* (People's Rule Weekly), in Shanghai. The party claimed to represent the interests of three million Chinese émigrés in their motherland. In order to be allocated one hundred places in the National Assembly (NA), part of the leadership met with Chiang Kai-shek to express full support of his policies and deplore the Communist stance. Situ held a special position and tried to keep a certain distance. As early as September 1946, he demanded the speediest establishment of a coalition government. Some weeks later, he proposed to General George C. Marshall and U.S. Ambassador John Leighton Stuart a conference of all political parties, presided over by Chiang, to find a peaceful solution to the crisis. The GMD government was dissatisfied with Situ's excessive activity and decided not to invite to the NA anybody from the party except Situ himself. Indignant, he declined the invitation. Conflict with the authorities was understandable because of certain demands by his party.[6] In addition, his previous activities gave the GMD grounds for irritation.[7]

The situation inside the party was aggravated by the struggle for power between Situ and Zhao, with the latter supported by the Hong Men members in Southeast Asia. Several attacks came from outside. Some forces were against politicization of the Hong Men, i.e., against the Chinese Hong Men People's Rule Party. They gathered around the Hong Men People's Rule and National Reconstruction Society, which emerged in Shanghai in 1946 and was organized by Lin Youmin.[8] There was one more opponent--the Hong Men Revival Association, organized in 1935 and reanimated in Shanghai in 1946 by Zhang Zilian. Zhang thought it wrong for the émigrés to try to intervene in the sphere of influence of the local secret societies. In March 1946, the Association joined the People's

Livelihood and Progress Party, led by GMD General Fan Songfu and based in Xi'an.[9] This new organization strove for the activization of secret societies against the Communists, beginning in the provinces of Shaanxi and Henan. Fan criticized Situ, claiming he was a leftist. He proclaimed his own program of "improvement of the people's lives," which was mostly a combination of the commonplace. In fact, the party preserved the traditional structure of a secret society. In the summer of 1947, with the beginning of the Civil War, the party practically ceased its activities. It was finally suppressed by the authorities, for Chiang Kai-shek thought it inexpedient to nurture political bodies based on secret societies and independent of the GMD.[10]

As the GMD-CCP conflict progressed in 1947, the prospects for a peaceful settlement kept diminishing. Obviously unsuccessful were the attempts of the Democratic League (DL) to act as an independent mediator in negotiations between the rival parties. The position of the DL itself constantly shifted to the left, and many of its demands coincided with those of the Communists. These developments convinced some of the members of the Chinese Hong Men People's Rule Party to create a new coalition of minor parties. The proponents of the coalition supported the government, and that provoked a split.[11] Not willing to be the leader of a party controlled by the GMD, Situ publicly announced his withdrawal in July 1947 and went to Hong Kong.[12]

The League of Middle Parties was founded in Shanghai on 21 June 1947. Its program stressed the necessity of national unity, introduction of a multiparty system, stabilization of the economy, an immediate end to the Civil War, and an end to any outside interference in Chinese internal affairs.[13]

The League was joined by the Chinese Hong Men People's Rule Party and the People's Livelihood and Progress Party, which found it possible to cooperate after the leftists split from the émigré party and the latter promised not to interfere in the sphere of influence of local secret societies. One more member of the League was the Chinese National Liberal Party, founded by Lin Donghai.[14] This party united representatives of the university intelligentsia, students, and some businessmen. It was supported by Sun Fo (Sun Ke). There were branches in Hong Kong and Southeast Asia. Probably this last factor led to the alliance with the Chinese Hong Men People's Rule Party, which had strong émigré connections. Lin's party was the only one in the League not connected to secret societies. It represented the intellectual ferment so necessary for the League's effective inclusion in the process of political struggle.

In addition to the three parties mentioned above, sessions of the new coalition in Nanjing were attended also by observers from the Chinese Harmony Party and the Chinese Democratic Party, which were both connected to secret societies. The Chinese Democratic Party was founded in August 1943 and began legal activities in October 1945.[15] Its leader, Hou Yejun, a journalist from Chongqing, strove for a place in the PCC. To that end, he unsuccessfully tried to unite with the DL. Gradually, the party became dominated by members of the Sichuan secret societies. It claimed a membership of 637,000 in Southwest China and the Yangtze basin. Financial support came from the revenues of two companies, *LianHua* (Unite China) and *JianHua* (Build China). The Party's program mostly followed the main principles of the PCC, but also contained some original proposals on rural and general social reconstruction.[16] It supported the leading role of Chiang Kai-shek and the Three Principles of the People, although it retained a strongly anti-bureaucratic flavor. Its ideas were propagated by the newspaper, *Minzhu daobao* (Democratic Guide).

The Chinese Harmony Party opened its first congress in Guangzhou in August 1946. It was presided over by You Yongchang, the son of Sun Yat-sen's associate, You Lie. You insisted on his party's uniting three million members. The party asked for the allocation of fifty seats at the NA, but only two of its members became deputies. Financing came from the *Zhonghe gongsi* (Harmony Company). The party published the newspapers *Yuandong zhoubao* (Far Eastern Weekly) in Shanghai and *Guomin ribao* (National Daily) in Kuala Lumpur. Some members of the Chinese Harmony Club (*Zhonghe tang*), which served as the basis for the party, did not want to accept You's leadership. Therefore, they established their own headquarters in Hong Kong and elected Li Shaoqi as the new president. The rival factions carried on incessant negotiations in search of compromise.

The League of Middle Parties had liaisons with other ex-secret society parties: the Chinese Self-Strengthening Society, active in Sichuan;[17] the Loyalty and Justice Party; and the Restoration Society. We have information about only the last of these.

The leader of the Restoration Society, Yin Ruizhi, and her husband, General Zhou Yawei, were followers of Qiu Jin (1875-1907), a Revolutionary Alliance member and heroine of the revolution. Like You Yongchang, they hoped to use the Sun Yat-sen connection to strengthen their political position. Initially, the Society supported Chiang Kai-shek, even "receiving guidance" from him. However, having launched its activities during the fall of 1945, it practically disintegrated after a considerable number of its members aligned themselves with the DL and the CCP.

Not a single one of the above-mentioned secret-society parties succeeded in gaining political weight, either in the GMD establishment or in attempts to operate independently. Traditional organizational stereotypes turned out to be insurmountable.[18] The adoption of a new name and the semblance of a political program were obviously insufficient to become a real political party. Considerable disparity of social backgrounds (giving birth to moderate and vague demands, initially concerning rural and urban reconstruction) seems to be among the main reasons for the defeat of these parties, and led to incessant splits and internal strife.

During the war, the GMD bureaucracy managed to create secret mechanisms of social control quite comparable to the potential of secret societies, which had been weakened considerably. That was the principal reason why so many anti-bureaucratic slogans appeared.

As already stressed, the GMD simultaneously tried to limit the independent activity of the secret societies and to use them for its own ends. The CCP also sought cooperation with secret societies. One of the best illustrations of this was the fate of Zhu Xuefan and his group.

Zhu was born in Shanghai in 1905.[19] He was educated at a missionary school, and joined the labor movement at an early age. According to Taiwan sources, he came under the patronage of Du Yuesheng and Lu Jingshi as early as 1928.[20] In his reminiscences published on the mainland, Zhu insists that he met Du for the first time in 1931.[21] It is understandable that he tried to conceal the truth, for GMD historiography tells of his active participation in the struggle against the Communists in Shanghai trade unions from 1928 to 1931.

Gradually, he became leader of one of the most powerful, and obviously gangster-controlled, trade unions of postal workers. In 1935, the Chinese Association of Labor (*Zhongguo laodòng xiehui*; CAL) was organized, and he was elected president. This permitted him to acquire high international status and represent China at international forums of the labor movement. One can judge his relations with Du by the fact that no other close associate of Du's was allowed to have his own organization outside the Constancy Society. Zhu's Society of Determination had more than one thousand members.[22]

There is no information on possible contacts between him and the CCP. However, his subordinate at the CAL was Yi Lirong. In his earlier years, Yi was friendly with Mao Zedong in Changsha, both of them being members of the New People's Study Society and proprietors of a small press, the Cultural Bookstore (*Wenhua shushe*). When the United Front (UF) appeared, Mao appealed in August 1936 to Yi, who had become one of the leaders of the despicable "yellow trade unions," with a proposal for cooperation. In his letter, Mao asked also about the possibility of regular, secret contacts.[23] From that time on, the Communist movement kept growing in Zhu's sphere of influence. The CCP's courting of him became especially intensive after the war.

In May 1945, the GMD itself gave him the impulse to move to the left. The Chinese Workers' Welfare Association (*Zhongguo gongren fuli xiehui*), founded by Chen Lifu, Gu Zhanggang, and Ma Chaojun, was intended to challenge CAL authority. Being a member of the Legislative Yuan and the

PCC, Zhu established closer relations with the CCP and the DL in the second half of 1945. His contacts with Deng Fa in Paris during the Twenty-Seventh World Congress of Trade Unions played a considerable role in this process.[24]

Zhu then took part in a demonstration in Chongqing (the Jiaochangkou Incident). This led to a riot and increased tensions in his relationship with the government. After the headquarters of the CAL moved to Shanghai, its office in Chongqing actually served as a Communist underground liaison center. This was documented by a police raid in August 1946. Authorities used this pretext to take over a cinema, a hospital, a cultural center, and several schools and kindergartens belonging to the CAL in Chongqing.

Under pressure from the GMD and Du, Zhu was compelled to exclude trade unions in CCP-controlled territories from the CAL in September 1946. In November, however, he fled to Hong Kong and launched oppositional activities. He was financed by Zhou Enlai, who transferred money to him as union fees from the "liberated areas."[25] For that reason, the CAL leaders remaining in Shanghai dismissed Zhu from the post of chairman in December. That did not prevent him, however, from running a "CAL office" in Hong Kong. Simultaneously, rumors spread (despite his refutations in the press) about the emergence of a Chinese Labor Party. According to GMD secret-service data, Society of Determination members Wang Jinyi, Tang Xiangjie, and Li Huanying developed a clandestine organization of that name in Chongqing. It had thirteen cells at factories in the city.[26]

Nothing is known about the further activities of the Chinese Labor Party. As for Zhu, he arrived in the liberated areas in February 1948 and joined the Revolutionary Committee of the GMD (hereafter, RG). It is obvious that the Labor Party was a temporary organization aimed at fulfilling the goals of the Communists inside the trade unions he controlled.

A special band of the political spectrum was represented by forces whose political ambitions had been crushed after the defeat of Japan and the demolition of the puppet regimes. Former collaborationists desperately looked for ways to regain lost positions. First among them were some members of the Chinese Youth Party (CYP),[27] who had remained in the occupied territories during the war and had cooperated with the government of Wang Jingwei. Leading figures of this group held high administrative posts in the Wang government; for example, Zhao Yusong was minister of agriculture.

Backed by Zhou Fohai, one of the leading figures of the Wang regime, Zhou Jidao became chairman of this faction of the CYP. After the war, he did his best to prove that during the Japanese occupation he had assisted the patriotic forces. Nevertheless, the traitors were not invited to the Tenth Congress of the CYP. Zhou Jidao then decided to escalate the conflict with the CYP. He founded a "Central Committee" of the CYP and sought cooperation with the DL through negotiations with its vice-chairman, Zhu Yunshan. Unfortunately for Zhou, only individual membership in the DL was permitted. Subsequently, he proposed founding the Chinese Party of the Masses, but lack of funds put an end to his ambitions.[28]

These minor political parties and groups, animated by the awakening of society and activated by the mirage of coming democracy, were extremely impressive. Whatever the deficiencies of the GMD regime, which resorted to strict oppressive measures only in circumstances of extreme danger, its attitude toward different political trends was quite liberal (though, of course, not one of indifference). There was nothing resembling the total control after 1949. This can be illustrated by the attempts of some of the minor parties, previously not allies of the CCP, to join the new regime.

On 1 May 1948, the Central Committee of the CCP called on all the democratic parties (hereafter, DPGs)--that is, those who supported the Communists--to participate in the new UF organization, the Chinese People's Political Consultative Conference (CPPCC). Preparatory work started at CCP and DPG meetings in Harbin on 25 November 1948, and was completed with the opening of the first session of the CPPCC on 21 September 1949. The new leadership was meticulous in selecting the members of the CPPCC, which was to legitimize the regime. Li Weihan, responsible for CCP UF work, reported in June 1949 ("Clarification of the Draft Rules of the Organization's Representation and Quotas in the CPPCC") that participation of forty-five parties, societies, and trade unions had been approved. There were only eleven DPGs among them.[29] It is reasonable to ask about the fate of the numerous other parties that inhabited the political scene before 1949 and had not fled to Taiwan.

It is clear from Lin Boqu's "Report on the Preparation of the CPPCC," made on 22 September, that thirty associations applied for inclusion in the CPPCC list. Some were refused because of "reactionary elements" in their ranks and "black pages" in their history.[30] Thanks to the reminiscences of UF Department official, Yu Gang, there is information on the unsuccessful applicants to the CPPCC.

1. The Revolutionary League of Sunism (RLS). In 1944, two opposition clubs appeared inside the GMD, the Peasants' and Workers' Society and the Society of the Masses. They dissolved in the course of time, but some of their members, such as Xu Wentian, joined the *Sanminzhuyi* Comrades' Association; some, including Deng Haoming, joined representatives of the former Third Party (TP); others, for example Chen Tilu, united with a number of high-ranking military; several, such as Ning Guangkun, joined with oppositional-minded youth; and some founded the Chinese Peasants' and Workers' Socialist Party. The latter began its activities in 1947, when the war between the GMD and the CCP was in full swing. It proclaimed the

goal of overthrowing Chiang Kai-shek's dictatorship and implementing the Three Principles of the People.

In time, a proposal to change the name to the *Sanminzhuyi* Leftist League (*zuoyi lianmeng*) was discussed. Finally, the name RLS was adopted during negotiations for uniting with the RG. In the spring of 1948, the latter insisted on the name change. That the merger never occurred can be explained by the complicated composition of the RLS. It included a considerable number of persons with dubious political reputations, such as a past association with Chiang Kai-shek (Chen Tilu).

The RLS had branches in all the provinces of Southeast China and strong ties with railway engineers and officials. In general, the majority of members were lower- and mid-level bureaucrats, teachers, engineers, and students. Several outer-circle organizations acted on behalf of the RLS: the Chinese Information Agency for Peasants and Workers, the Zhejiang Society for the Promotion of Culture in Rural Areas, the New Masses Society, and others.

The RLS had close relations with civil and military officials in Nanjing and Shanghai, Zhejiang and Jiangsu. For example, Xu Wentian, a former member of the Reorganization Clique, used his historical relationship with Wang Maogong, governor of Jiangsu, to achieve favorable conditions for RLS activities in that province. An understanding was also reached with Chen Yi, governor of Zhejiang, and only his execution put an end to active anti-GMD cooperation. In the course of the Communist southward offensive, the members of the RLS acted in close concert with the CCP and the RG, and influenced the military to betray Chiang Kai-shek. He Yaozu, a former governor of Gansu and later mayor of Chongqing, offered the Communists strategic maps of the provinces of Jiangsu, Zhejiang, and Anhui in February 1949.[31] The RLS hindered the withdrawal of industrial equipment, resources, and medicine from regions abandoned by government troops (the role of the railways here was indispensable).[32]

Some of the RLS people were members of the Legislative Yuan, where they carried out opposition. They demanded a complete halt to fighting and were against the dominance of bureaucratic capital. Sessions of a special seminar on Tuesdays and Fridays (which explains the name, *Erwu zuotanhui* or Tuesday-Friday Forum) were attended by fifty-six deputies. The RLS supported Li Zongren in the vice-presidential election, with the futile hope of relying on him to attain its political goals.[33] It also published the *Zhongguo zhoubao* (China Weekly) in Shanghai, and the *Daxue pinglun* (University Review) in Nanjing, where it became popular among university professors and students, and soon was closed down.[34]

It did not go unnoticed by the authorities. In March 1949, some of its members were arrested. The government was compelled to release Legislative Yuan deputies Xu Wentian and Jin Shaoxian, but Chen Tilu,

Zhang Dasheng, Zhu Datong, Fang Zhinong, and Wang Wenzhong were executed in May. This tragic event resulted in the mass exodus of RLS activists to Hong Kong.

While in the colony, RLS people sharply criticized Li Zongren for not accepting Communist terms at the peace talks. They interviewed GMD figures, as well as liberals, who gathered in Hong Kong, trying to persuade them to support the Communist cause. A declaration of support was compiled by the RLS and published on 13 August 1949, with forty-four signatures, including those of Long Yun, Li Moyan, Huang Shaohong, and Liu Fei. Some refused to sign, including Hu Shi's associate from the "human rights" faction, Chen Shewo.

The problem of the political status of the RLS in the new regime had already emerged in the summer of 1949. Li Weihan proposed to disband it and insisted on gathering all former GMD members in the RG. He also pointed to the "reactionary past" of some members of the RLS (he meant Lu Butong and Chen Tilu, whose executions were probably still a secret). Despite the resistance of Xu Wentian and Han Meicen, the declaration of self-dissolution appeared in Shanghai on 2 August. Inquisitor Li insisted on no references to the CCP position: "You must decide yourselves; we have no special opinion."[35] In compensation, Xu, now a member of the RG, and Deng Haoming, who had returned to the TP (now called the Chinese Peasants' and Workers' Democratic Party), were included in the list of delegates to the CPPCC.

2. The Reform Faction (RF) of the Democratic Socialist Party (DSP). The DSP was the result of a merger of the National Socialist Party (NSP), led by Zhang Junmai, and the Democratic Constitutionalist Party (DCP). The latter held its First Congress in Montreal in November 1945. It grew out of the North American branch of Liang Qichao's Constitutional Party. Wu Xianzi, a man of letters with a solid Confucian background, became its leader. Its program was quite conservative. It had contacts with the Guangdong Hong Men and hoped to use them as a means to penetrate the local political arena. There were ambitious plans involved in the merger with Zhang and the common struggle for the "third way" in China.

The RF appeared after Zhang began to collaborate with the GMD in forming the new government and Constituent NA, and its members were expelled from the DSP on 25 July 1947. Indignant former members of the DCP in the United States convened an extraordinary congress in San Francisco, and on 1 August, they severed relations with the DSP. On 25 August, the RF established itself as a party in Nanjing and elected Wu Xianzi president. By then, he had chosen Hong Kong as a permanent place of residence and was trying to keep away from politics. He insisted on equal remoteness from the two big political parties and supported the idea of creating in Hong Kong a "Political Society for a Democratic, Peaceful, and

United China." Its program was aimed, above all, against any one-party dictatorship.[36]

At the same time, some RF cadres were more and more oriented toward the CCP (Wang Shimin and Sha Yanjie). After they supported, on their own initiative, the CCP declaration of 1 May 1948 (on the new CPPCC), the struggle escalated within the RF between friends of the CCP and those who later were characterized as "agents of American imperialism" and of the "GMD secret service." The result was the expulsion of the main "rightists," Sun Baogang and Luo Jianbai, in August, and the retirement of Wu Xianzi. Sha became chairman. On 22 June 1949, he sent a cable to Mao Zedong, expressing the hope of participating in the CPPCC, but did not receive a positive answer. In spite of protests by the rank and file, the RF was dissolved in September 1949. Sha and Wang Shimin joined the DL and were awarded CPPCC membership.[37]

3. The Chinese Young Labor Party (CYLP). Its leader, An Ruoding, started his political career in 1923 as a founder of the Lone Star Society in Shanghai. He also edited the *Guxing* (Lone Star) magazine, in which the "Three Principles of the People" were appraised. In 1927, he became an active proponent of the theory of "the great chivalrous spirit" (*da xiahun jingshen*). He insisted that self-perfection was the most important prerequisite for class liberation, for the implementation of the ideas of Sun Yat-sen, and for the attainment of the traditional "Grand Unity" (*datong*)."[38] In 1931, he founded the strongly anti-Japanese "Formation-of-the-Spirit Learned Society." Critical of the one-party system, he nevertheless called on the people to unite with the GMD to fight the enemy. He was an advocate of the *baojia* (mutual responsibility) system of social control, and proposed to use the experience of the European fascist states to strengthen discipline and unity.[39] By 1937, he had already served as leader of the National Labor Union for the Construction of the State (*Guomin laodong jianguo tongmeng)*, which was joined by some other associations and in the course of time became the CYLP. The CYLP agreed to cooperate with the GMD in the NA and demanded that Mao Zedong put an end to the Civil War. This fact precluded any possibility of CCP sympathy after 1949. Hence, the party was dissolved on 1 September 1949. An received the post of councilor in the Central People's Government Council, and was included in the CPPCC in 1954.[40]

4. We have already mentioned the Restoration Society. Some of its members gathered in Hangzhou on 26 May 1948. They proclaimed a program of struggle for the rights not only of the national and petty bourgeoisie but of the whole nation, and called for a coalition government. In January 1949, the Society declared its support for the CCP, and some of its members assisted the Communist offensive in the province of Zhejiang. Zhou Yawei applied for membership in the CPPCC. In June, however,

Zhou Enlai pointed out that there had been too small a percentage of "democratic elements" in the party and refused. The Society disappeared, and Zhou Yawei had to wait until 1954 to join the CPPCC.[41]

5. For the Chinese Hong Men People's Rule Party, collective or individual participation in the CPPCC was flatly refused. This was due to its membership in the League of Middle Parties, its contacts with the CC Clique in the GMD, and other reasons (for example, one of the leaders, Zhang Shucheng, had been a delegate to the Sixth Congress of the GMD, and the party was a serious obstacle to Communist influence among émigrés). After it was disbanded, its members were not allowed to join the puppet émigré party, the Chinese Justice Party.[42]

6. The Chinese Peasants' Party. It appeared in Sichuan on the basis of the Chinese Agricultural Society (*Zhongguo nongye hui*) and the Chinese Agricultural Reform Association (*Zhongguo nongye gaijin she*). Its leader, Dong Shijin, was a professor of agriculture and editor of a magazine, *Zhongguo nongmin* (Chinese Peasant), in Chengdu. At first, he hoped to rely on the DL to implement his plans for rural reform. He was even a member of its Central Committee. But then, dissatisfied with its leftist trend, he dropped his membership. The Chinese Peasants' Party convened its first congress in Shanghai in May 1947. Its program called for modernization of agriculture as the true path to democracy and progress. The party had two "outer-circle" associations: the Chinese Agricultural Society and the Sichuan Association in Nanjing, which published a journal, *Shu lian nongchang* (Sichuan Union of Farms). A centrist, Dong refused to participate in the NA. At the same time, he bitterly criticized the agrarian program of the CCP. He demanded that a fair price be paid for confiscated land and rejected the use of political pressure to reduce rent and redistribute land.

Antipathy to the CCP hindered cooperation with the Chinese Peasants' Liberal Party, whose leaders were He Lu and Hu Wenlan, and which grew out of several unions of Sichuan peasants.[43] After the failure of attempts to receive seats in the NA, and as a result of Communist infiltration, the party began intensive cooperation with the CCP (in the movement against taxes, grain exactions, and military service).[44]

Changes of political climate forced Dong to express support for the CCP in January 1949. In April, he began to cooperate with the Communists and the once-despised DL. Nevertheless, his party was forced to dissolve on 25 June. On 12 December, Dong could not refrain from writing a letter to Mao Zedong sharply criticizing atrocities in rural areas. The only result was the increasing pressure that led to his involuntary emigration in April 1950.[45]

7. The Chinese Association for the Promotion of Mass Education (usually known simply as the Mass Education Association). It launched its

activities in 1923. Here we will note only that beginning in the last years of World War II, it acquired special political importance. That was due to its leader, Yan Yangchu (James Y.C. Yen), who was touring the United States, collecting donations and criticizing the Communists. On the verge of the CCP takeover, he escaped to Hong Kong. Some of his associates sought official registration for the Association in the spring of 1950, through the services of Huang Yanpei.[46] The "American connection," however, was too strong a charge. Hence, it ceased to exist, and Zhou Enlai ordered its schools secured under government control. Military authorities in Chongqing took over the property and liquidated the Association on 2 December.

8. There were three small parties with headquarters in Hong Kong that desired cooperation with the CPPCC. We know nothing about them but their names: the People's Democratic Liberal Union, the Chinese People's Liberal Party, and the Democratic Progressive Party.

As can be seen from the history of the minor political parties, the Communists were very particular about keeping files on all opponents and even temporary allies. After the new regime was established, all suspected of partial disloyalty had to pay the price for their light-mindedness. Only those leaders who betrayed their comrades and destroyed their parties were awarded sinecures and attached to this or that DPG.

These fragmentary notes may shed some additional light on the socio-political situation in China from 1945 to 1950, when the different forces of the nation tried to contribute to the cause of democracy and revival. Of course, this process was ambiguous, and narrow personal ambitions intermingled with lofty aspirations for social reconstruction. However, it was a beginning, which, if not for the Civil War and the fatal blows of 1949 and 1957, would have brewed a new society. One may argue that Chinese reality did not permit any but the given outcome. Such a point of view is probably absolutely true. Nevertheless, the feeble undercurrents of social life must not be forgotten. Without them, history is incomplete, simplified, and too burdened with the triumphs of "great forces," leaving no room for the natural pluralism of thought, romanticism, and intrigue.

Notes

1. Chiang Kai-shek, "Jiang Jieshi zai zhengzhi xieshang huiyi shang zhi kaihui yici" (Chiang Kai-shek's Opening Address in the Political Consultative Conference), *Xinhua ribao*, 11 January 1946; cited in *Guogong tanpan wenxian ziliao xuanji, 1945.8-1947.3* (Selected Documentary Materials Concerning the Negotiations Between the Nationalists and the Communists, August 1945-March 1947) (Nanjing, 1980), 39. This section of Chiang's speech is omitted in *Xianzongtong Jiang gong sixiang yanlun zongji*

(The Complete Thought and Speeches of the Late President Chiang [Kai-shek]), (Taibei, 1984), 21: 229.

2. Another of these associations was the Chinese Radical Party. It was created by Zhong Shuren in Hong Kong in February 1947, based on the local Triads, and had the active participation of émigré youths. It stood for moderate reforms, with bourgeois democracy its goal.

3. This party was established by the Hong Men secret society, which was largely active in the Chinese diaspora following the 1911 Revolution. Branches in the U.S. included the *Jinlan gongsuo*, *Daquan she*, *Hongshun tang*, and *Zhigong tang*. The Justice Party emerged from the *Zhigong tang*. Its first congress was held in San Francisco in 1925, with Chen Jingcun and Situ Meitang as the main organizers. Chen Jiongming, a notorious figure in Chinese politics, was elected president of the party and guided its headquarters in Hong Kong, where he resided after his 1925 defeat in Guangdong. Chen formulated a theory of Chinese socialism or "three principles of construction" (for China, Asia and the world). He insisted that the socialization of property, administration, and consumption in China would lead to the emergence of a new and united nation. The peoples of Asia, fecundated by the life-giving forces of Chinese culture, would constitute the axis of world development. The worldwide dissemination of the fruits of the Chinese spirit would inevitably push mankind along the path of peace and progress. Zong Zhiwen and Zhu Xinquan, eds., *Minguo renwu zhuan* (Biographies of Republican Figures) (Beijing: Zhonghua shuju, 1981), 3: 168; Howard L. Boorman and Richard C. Howard, eds., *Biographical Dictionary of Republican China*, 4 vols. (New York: Columbia University Press, 1967), 1:179; Liu Shaotang, ed., *Minguo renwu xiaozhuan* (Biographical Sketches of Republican Figures) (Taibei: *Zhuanji wenxue* chubanshe, 1977), 1:188; Shen Yunlong, "Youguan Chen Jiongming pan Sun de ziliao" (Materials Concerning Chen Jiongming's Rebellion Against Sun [Yat-sen]), *Zhuanji wenxue* 32, no. 4 (1978): 81-82. The Second Congress decided the party would play a leading role in relations with the Hong Men societies (*yi dang zhi tang* or "use the party to control the lodges").

After the death of Chen in 1933, the Hong Kong center was taken over by Chen Yansheng. Following Japanese occupation of the colony, the Justice Party existed only outside China. Subsequently, the Hong Men representatives' congress in New York in March 1945 decided to change the name of the party to the Chinese Hong Men Justice Party. Its representatives travelled to China in hopes of defending the interests of overseas Chinese.

Some sources say that Situ Meitang spoke against changing the name of the party on Chinese soil. However, Zhao Yu, influenced by the GMD's CC Clique, insisted. For this reason, Situ left the constituent congress and was elected chairman in absentia. In short, his prestige was so great that the new organization could not do without him. Situ Binghe, "Situ Meitang yu Meizhou Hong Men Zhigong dang" (Situ Meitang and the Hongmen Justice Party in America), in *Wenshi ziliao xuanji* (Beijing) (Selected Historical and Literary Materials), 38: 241.

4. For many, the goals of the society and the party seemed incompatible. Some of the Hong Men members, dissatisfied with Situ Meitang and Zhao Yu, joined the U.S.-based Democratic Constitutionalist Party, which later merged with Zhang Junmai's National Socialist Party to form the Democratic Socialist Party.

5. Ibid., 246.

6. It also demanded the suppression of bureaucratic corruption, the establishment of local self-government, and limitations on land ownership and private capital. The economic security of overseas Chinese businessmen was specially emphasized. Wang Jueyuan, *Zhongguo dangpai shi* (A History of Chinese Political Parties and Groups) (Taibei, 1983), section on the Chinese Hong Men People's Rule Party.

7. For example, Situ organized a trip around the world for Cai Tingkai, who fled China after the Fujian Incident, and rendered assistance to such oppositionists as Tao Xingzhi, Feng Yuxiang, and Yang Hucheng. In the early 1940s, Situ had contacts with the Communists in Chongqing. He often criticized the state-owned banks for plundering the hard currency sent by overseas Chinese to their relatives in China. Zhang Xinghan, "Situ Meitang yu zuguo kangzhan" (Situ Meitang and the Fatherland's War of Resistance), *Jinan xuebao* (The Jinan Journal) (Guangzhou), no. 1 (1988): 38-44; Chen Changfu, "Situ Meitang yu Zhongguo Zhigong dang" (Situ Meitang and the Chinese Justice Party), *Huasheng bao* (Voice of China) (Beijing), 14 June 1988.

8. This group represented the interests of the leader of the Shanghai harbor gangsters, Yang Hu, who was supposed to use it as a springboard to a political career.

9. In Shanghai, this party was assisted by the Hong Progress Society, led by Yuan Shikai's son, Yuan Hanyun. Only members of secret societies had the right to join General Fan's party. In Shaanxi province, the party was active under the name of the Majesty of China Society. A number of enterprises provided economic support. Cooperation with gang leaders, such as Du Yuesheng, was maintained. Fan kept Chiang Kai-shek informed, but he irritated the GMD by also trying to maintain independence.

In Shanghai, in the autumn of 1946, Dai Li's secret service organized the Chinese Association for the Development of New Social Services, which was to place secret societies under strict official control. With the assistance of Du, many leaders of secret societies in Shanghai and elsewhere were included in the leadership of the association, e.g., Xiang Haiqian (Shanghai), Tian Desheng (Sichuan), Zhang Fang (Henan), and Du Xianwu, Xu Chongzhi, Yang Hu, Fan Shaozeng, Mo Dehui, and others (Northeast China). The association's declaration was published in Shanghai on 18 October. It claimed a membership of 560,000. Xu Liang presided over the executive council. *Haishang wenren Du Yuesheng* (The Shanghai Man of Letters, Du Yuesheng) (Zhengzhou, 1987), 250-51.

The Association was based on numerous societies personally controlled by gang leaders; for example, Du Yuesheng's Constancy Society, with branches in Nanjing, Hangzhou, Beijing, Tianjing, Wuhan, Chongqing, Shenyang, Qingdao, Xi'an, Lanzhou, Chengdu, Kunming, Guilin, Nanning, Fuzhou, Taiwan, and Hong Kong; the Society of Generosity and Justice of Zheng Ziliang (around ten thousand members); the Society for the Revival of China of Yang Hu (also around ten thousand); the Glorious Society of Huang Jinrong, with branches called the Revival Society and the Star Society; and the Society of Benefit of Fan Shaozeng. All these bodies were based on principles of mutual assistance and cooperation in overcoming difficulties. See, for example, the charters of the Constancy Society and the Society of Benefit. Ibid., 249-

51, 367; *Banghui qiguan* (The Spetacular Phenomenon of the Secret Societies) (Beijing, 1989), 310-11.

Apart from the above-mentioned Association, there existed other organizations with the help of which the GMD manipulated secret societies for its own political purposes. For example, the Friends of the Constitution Society and the National Society for Constitutional Government appeared by the end of 1946. Officially, they were guided by deputies of the NA. In reality, all the strings were in the hands of Lu Jingshi, Du Yuesheng's closest associate and an official in the GMD's Central Executive Committee apparatus. Wang Jueyuan, 422, 829, 831.

There was heated discussion concerning Zhang Shizhao's proposal to convert the Constancy Society, in which he was an activist, into a political party. As a result, Du Yuesheng allegedly became the leader of the Chinese Liberal Party (not to be confused with the party of the same name founded in Changsha in 1938), but nothing is known of its activities.

10. Fan Songfu, "Wo suo zhidao de Hong Men shishi" (What I Know About the Hongmen [Secret Society]), in *Wenshi ziliao xuanji* (Beijing), 38:222-27.

11. In May 1947, the proponents of the pro-Communist line, led by Chen Qiyou, convened the Third Congress of the Chinese Justice Party in Hong Kong, thus reviving the old name. It gathered the opposition to the Chinese Hong Men People's Rule Party and deplored the one-party dictatorship of the GMD. It also demanded guarantees of democratic rights, equality of political parties, revision of the constitution, and new elections to the NA. The congress insisted on a reduction of the pressure exerted by state-owned monopolies and bureaucratic capital on private enterprise and protested protectionist taxation, as well as high land rents and interest on loans. Li Jishen was elected the new leader, but he did not publicize it because of his position in the GMD RG.

12. By this time, he had become an ally of the CCP. In August 1947, he wrote a letter of support to Mao Zedong, and in August 1949, he moved to Beijing. Wu Juetian, "Situ Meitang yu Zhongguo Zhigong dang" (Situ Meitang and the Chinese Justice Party), *Wenshi ziliao xuanji* (Beijing), 38:163-65.

13. "There are no democratic states that are not united. There are no democratic parties that try to come to power by force. Unity is the basis of order. Democracy is the necessary form of political process." Wang Jueyuan, addendum.

14. Formerly the Chinese Liberal Party, founded in Changsha in 1938. Inactive during the war, it was revitalized in 1946 in Chongqing, Nanjing, Lanzhou, and Fuzhou. The party supported democratization slogans. In the preamble to its program, the sharpest criticism was aimed at the bureaucracy, which had brought the country to the brink of economic catastrophe. It stood for "political and economic democracy as the foundation of freedom" and demanded the election of 950 additional deputies to the NA, to represent the intelligentsia, émigrés, and national minorities.

15. It was founded at a ball and provided the party with the nickname, the "dancing party."

16. It declared that agrarian reform had to start with the equalization of land rights and the creation of cooperatives and state-owned farms. The gradual elimination of private ownership of land was to culminate in complete state ownership. The goal of the elimination of classes had to be attained through planned production and

distribution, socialization of industry, democratization, and the development of education and culture.

17. During the war years, the province of Sichuan became China's political and economic center. These developments made local secret societies start seeking new methods of fighting back at the government, which was very active in taking over the secret societies' sphere of influence. Therefore, many local societies turned into parties, e.g., the Society for the Promotion of Democracy and Socialism, with Fang Maoshan as chairman; the Chinese Party of Social Construction, Leng Kaitai, chairman (they published *Datong ribao* [Grand Unity Daily] and *Datong huakan* [Grand Unity Pictorial]; and the Chinese Socialist Party, Ye Daoxin, chairman. The Chinese Party of Social Construction and the Chinese Socialist Party had very similar programs, demanding equal land rights, harmonization of labor-capital relations, and the realization of the ideal of Chinese socialism, "Grand Unity" (*datong*). There also were the Social Democratic Party, Shi Xiaoxian, chairman, and the Chinese Party of Peace, Zhang Zhijiang, chairman. The Chinese Party of Grand Unity, which united members of secret societies north of the Yangtse, was also founded in Sichuan, though its headquarters later moved to Shanghai. All of the above-mentioned parties appeared in 1946.

Of course, one can find politicized associations based on secret societies in other regions of China, too, e.g., the General Society of New China in the province of Shaanxi, led by Jiang Panjia; the Association for the Construction of North China, led by Gu Zhen and Jiang Weizhou; and the Blood and Iron Party in the province of Jiangsu, led by Gao You. Wang Jueyuan, 432-37.

18. Sometimes, the word "party" became camouflage for criminal activity. For example, the Chinese Democracy and Freedom League, founded in Kunming in October 1946 by Wang Huisheng, was mostly engaged in smuggling weapons and opium. The Chinese Democratic Radical Party of Shu Hanxin was actually an army of bandits on the borders of the provinces of Shandong, Henan, and Jiangsu.

19. A biographic dictionary published in Taiwan gives the date of Zhu's birth as 1907. *Zhonggong renming lu* (A Record of the Personal Names of Chinese Communists) (Taibei, 1983), 152. A biography of Du Yuesheng, compiled by Zhu's closest associates, says 1904, and a Mainland publication gives 1905. Zhang Jungu, *Du Yuesheng zhuan* (A Biography of Du Yuesheng) (Taibei, 1986), 1: 72-73; *Xinbian Zhongguo tongyi zhanxian dacidian* (The Newly Compiled Dictionary of the United Front in China) (Changchun, 1988), 634.

20. Zhang Jungu, 72.

21. Zhu Xuefan, "Shanghai gongren yundong yu banghui ersanshi" (Two or Three Things Concerning the Shanghai Labor Movement and Secret Societies), *Jiu Shanghai de banghui* (Old Shanghai's Secret Societies) (Shanghai: Renmin chubanshe, 1986), 5.

22. Zhang Jungu, 73.

23. *Mao Zedong shuxin xuanji* (Selected Letters of Mao Zedong) (Beijing, 1983), 47.

24. Mao Zedong and Zhou Enlai personally controlled the "conversion" of Zhu Xuefan. After Deng Fa perished in a catastrophe, Zhu was approached by Deng's successor, Liu Ningyi. In addition, his secretary and close friend, Li Pei (the wife of

writer and social activist Nie Ganpu), was also a Communist agent. *Zhonggong renming lu*, 152; Lu Xiangjian, "Dang de tongyi zhanxian yu Zhongguo laodong xiehui" (The United Front of Political Parties and the Chinese Labor Association), in *Tongzhan gongzuo shiliao* (Historical Materials on United Front Work) (Shanghai, 1986) 5: 121-22.

25. Lu Xiangjian, 123.

26. Wang Jueyuan, 400-401.

27. A group of collaborationists (Ren Yuandao, Xu Busheng, Zhou Gongmao, and Liu Kaizhang) founded the Democratic Liberal Party in Hong Kong in October 1947. Ibid., 424.

28. Ibid., 428-31.

29. *Li Weihan xuanji* (Selected Works of Li Weihan) (Beijing, 1987), 206-11; Wang Jueyuan, 490-91.

30. Yu Gang, "Xin zhengxie choubèi qijian dui yixie zhengzhi paibie he tuanti yaoqiu canjia xin zhengxie de chuli guocheng" (The Process of Dealing with Some Political Factions' and Organizations' Requests to Participate in the Political Consultative [Conference] During Its Preparatory Period), *Wenshi ziliao xuanji* (Beijing), *Zengkan* (Supplementary issue), no. 1 (1985): 1-19.

31. Xu Wentian et al., "Sun Wen zhuyi geming tongmeng gailue" (An Outline of the Revolutionary League of Sunism), *Wenshi ziliao xuanji* (Beijing), *Zengkan*, no. 2 (1987): 100, 103.

32. Ibid., 108-109.

33. Jin Shaoxian, "Wo zai Lifa yuan canyu Sun Wen zhuyi geming tongmeng gongzuo huodong jilue" (A Brief Account of My Legislative-Yuan Participation in the Revolutionary League of Sunism Work and Activities), *Wenshi ziliao xuanji* (Beijing), *Zengkan*, no. 2 (1987): 129.

34. Xu Wentian, 116.

35. Ibid., 124.

36. Wang Jueyuan, 421, 825-27.

37. Gao Han and Wang Dachuan, "Minshe dang de yanbian ji gexin pai de xingcheng" (The Development of the Democratic Socialist Party and the Nature of the Reform Faction), *Wenshi ziliao xuanji* (Tianjin) 22 (1983): 59-70.

38. See *Da xiahun* (Great Chivalry), no. 16 (1932): 9; no. 20: 6.

39. Ibid., no. 40 (1932): 8.

40. Wang Jueyuan, 402-3, 789.

41. Yu Gang, 10-12.

42. As Situ Meitang's secretary recollected, his boss was visited in Beijing in September 1949 by Zhao Li, who asked him to reorganize the party in order to adapt it to the new circumstances. Situ refused. *Huiyi Situ Meitang laoren* (Reminiscences of the Aged Situ Meitang) (Beijing, 1988), 90.

43. In 1946, there were two more parties in China that, in their programs, stressed the rights of peasants: the Chinese Society for the Promotion of the Unity of Peasants and Workers in Sichuan and the Chinese Peasants' Party in Guangdong.

44. *Zhongguo dangpai* (Chinese Political Parties and Groups) (Nanjing, 1948), 341-5.

45. Wang Jueyuan, 394-6, 412-13, 798.

46. Yan Shengdong and Sun Nuchao, "Yan Yangchu yu pingmin jiaoyu" (Yan Yangchu and Mass Education), *Wenshi ziliao xuanji* (Beijing), 95:143-62. Liang Shuming recalled that after Yan's return to China in 1948, Huang tried to persuade him to side with the Communists. Yan decided to stick to his principles, however, and refused. Liang Shuming, *Yiwang tanjiu lu* (Reminiscences) (Beijing, 1987), 124.

8

China's Democratic Parties and the Temptations of Political Power, 1946-1947

Lloyd E. Eastman

After seizing national power in 1927-28, the Guomindang (GMD) lost its revolutionary dedication with astonishing suddenness. Corruption quickly became widespread; factions within the party began struggling against each other for the spoils of office; and many party members became more concerned to maintain themselves in power than to fulfill the promises of the revolution.

Why did men, having once risked life and limb in the revolutionary cause, so quickly become transformed into self-serving bureaucrats? Was there, perhaps, something special in the organization, or in the class character, of the GMD that contributed to its revolutionary failure? A study of the small democratic parties in 1946 and 1947 suggests, to the contrary, that there was something in China's political culture at the time that caused many Chinese--and not just members of the GMD--to be easily corrupted by the temptations of political power.

During the 1940s, foreign observers of the political scene in China viewed the small democratic, or "minor," parties, such as the Democratic Socialist Party (DSP), the Chinese Youth Party (CYP), and the Democratic League (DL), with special hope and affection. In them, it seemed, resided the best chance for the realization in China of liberal values and democratic

This article is reprinted with permission and minor changes, from *Republican China* XVII (November 1991).

government. General George C. Marshall expressed this sentiment in January 1947, on the eve of his departure from China following his long, but vain, endeavor to mediate the GMD-CCP conflict. "The salvation of the situation," he wrote, "would be the assumption of leadership by the liberals in the Government and in the minority parties, a splendid group of men, but who as yet lack the political power to exercise a controlling influence."[1]

An examination of these democratic parties in the process of establishing a coalition government during 1946-47 reveals, however, that few of their members had truly imbibed democratic values. In all probability, therefore, China would not have known democracy, or good government, even if these minor parties had somehow, against all odds, become a major force in Chinese politics.

Following the defeat of Japan in 1945, as the threat of civil war between the Communists and the Nationalists loomed ever more ominously, a coalition government, erected on democratic principles, appeared to be China's chief hope for peace. For a brief moment in January 1946, that goal seemed attainable when representatives of the GMD, the CCP, and the minor parties, together with several social notables, met in the Political Consultative Conference (PCC). There, they agreed upon a draft constitution and a set of procedures to establish a democratic, coalition government.

The agreements of this conference quickly disintegrated, however, in an atmosphere of mutual distrust and enmity. The United States, nonetheless, made it clear to Chiang Kai-shek that future military and civilian aid to the Nationalist Government (NG) was contingent upon democratization of the government. Chiang consequently pressed ahead, during the spring and summer of 1946, with preparations for the establishment of a coalition government. But Zhou Enlai, the Communist liaison to the NG at this time, distrusted Chiang. He was convinced that the projected coalition government would actually be dominated by the GMD and that the proposed constitution would, in fact, formalize Chiang's dictatorship.

Hope for a political resolution of the GMD-CCP conflict persisted, nevertheless, until November 1946. But that month, Chiang, unilaterally and in violation of the procedures set up by the PCC, convened the National Assembly (NA) for the purpose of adopting a constitution. This action polarized the nation's political forces. Zhou Enlai denounced it as a "nation-splitting" maneuver, and declared that the door to further negotiations had been slammed shut.[2] This forced the two most important of the minor parties--the CYP and the DSP--to choose sides and decide, once and for all, whether to lean toward the Communists or toward the Nationalists.

For the CYP, the decision to send representatives to the NA and participate in the projected coalition government was easy. Its leaders were advocates of democratic constitutionalism; in the past, therefore, they had been critical of the GMD. But they were even more strongly, as a matter of principle, opposed to Communism. The CYP had, in fact, withdrawn from the DL in December 1945, because it opposed the growing influence of the CCP upon the League. Because Chiang was now promising the establishment of a democratic, constitutional government, there no longer existed any basis for opposition to him and the NG.

For the DSP, however, the decision was more wrenching. After the withdrawal of the CYP from the DL, the DSP was the largest, and probably the most powerful, single component of the League.[3] But this party was a recent creation, riven with numerous fault lines, which now widened into factional conflicts.

The DSP existed as a result of the merger of two pre-existing parties, the National Socialist Party (NSP) and the Democratic Constitutionalist Party (DCP). In the spring of 1945, the secretary-general of the NSP, Zhang Junmai, had gone to San Francisco as a member of the Chinese delegation to the United Nations Conference on International Organization. While in the United States, he met Li Daming, a leader of the DCP, and the two agreed that their two parties could maximize their chances of promoting democratic government, in competition with both the GMD and the CCP, if they joined forces. This merger was formally approved in a national party congress, held in Shanghai in August 1946.

The NSP, originally formed in 1932, was made up mostly of intellectuals, many of them professors who had studied abroad, who advocated Western-style political democracy and an economic system that combined free enterprise with state ownership and planning. The party was, however, almost the personal creation of its secretary-general. Although Zhang has been described as "almost a saint,"[4] a succession of prominent members of the party--such as Luo Longji, Chen Bosheng, Jiang Yong, Pan Guangdan (Quentin Pan), and Fei Xiaotong had found it impossible to work with him and had sooner or later dropped out of the party.[5] His closest supporters in the party, in fact, were his former students, and he thus frequently felt free to make critical decisions regarding the party without consulting other leaders.

The DCP had been less prominent than the NSP, although it boasted a more venerable history, tracing its ancestry back to the Society to Protect the Emperor of Kang Youwei and Liang Qichao, formed in 1899. Most members of the party were overseas Chinese in North America, although its chairman at this time, Wu Xianzi, was living in Hong Kong.

Relations between the two constituent parts of the new DSP--those from the DCP and those from the NSP--were strained from the very beginning of the merger. The NSP elements resided in China and had been active in Chinese politics throughout the war. They viewed members of the

DCP as upstarts and political opportunists, entering the Chinese political fray now in the hope of obtaining political office--but without contributing to the strength of the new party. DCP elements resented this attitude and claimed that, with their control of influential Chinese-language newspapers in San Francisco, Hawaii, and elsewhere, they brought to the new party a priceless political resource.[6]

The first split within the ranks of the DSP developed, however, not between the DCP and NSP elements, but between factions of the former NSP. At issue was the question of whether or not to participate in the NA and coalition government. Zhang Dongsun--a professor at Yenching University in Beiping, a co-founder of the NSP, and now also serving as secretary-general of the DL--was vehemently opposed to allying in any way with the GMD, unless it adhered to the procedures laid down by the PCC. He was supported, at this time, by several other members of the DSP residing in Beiping, and they were thus known as the "Northern Faction."[7]

Opposing him was a "Southern Faction" in Shanghai, which favored participation in the coalition government. This group coalesced around Zhang Junmai. He had initially also opposed joining the coalition government. But during the summer of 1946, he met several times with Chiang Kai-shek, who was intent on persuading Zhang to lead the DSP into the coalition government. For Chiang, the participation of at least some of the minor parties in the NA and in the coalition government was crucial, if he were to convince the United States that his government was truly being democratized.

He finally won over Zhang by promising that the forthcoming NA would ratify the constitutional draft just as it had been approved by the PCC.[8] One might well ask how he could guarantee the precise outcome of the deliberations of the NA, which was ostensibly to be a free and democratic body. In any event, because Zhang was the chief author of the constitutional draft that had been prepared for the PCC, and Chiang was now promising that the draft would be accepted unchanged, Zhang felt that he could not but support the NA. As a consequence, on his own authority and contrary to prior decisions of the DSP's Organization Committee, he announced that representatives of his party would attend the forthcoming NA.[9]

Zhang Dongsun and the "Northern Faction" were infuriated by Zhang Junmai's action. The decision to participate in the NA violated the policy of the DL, of which the DSP was at this time still a part. The decision, furthermore, had been made without consultation among the party leaders. As a consequence, Zhang Dongsun now severed relations with Zhang Junmai, who had been his close friend and political ally for thirty years.[10]

Soon thereafter, Zhang Junmai angered yet a different segment of his party--in this case, one that favored participation in the new coalition government. Zhang, in agreeing to send representatives to the NA, had also declared that members of his party would not actually assume government office. His view, as he later explained, was that the DSP was still too small and weak, and its members too young and inexperienced, to take on governmental responsibilities. In particular, he thought that the GMD would inevitably dominate the policies of the coalition government, and he did not wish his party to assume responsibility for governmental actions upon which it had no real influence. Some years hence, he said, after his party's members had gained political know-how by serving in the NA, and after the party had recruited men of experience and prestige, the DSP might accept governmental posts.[11]

Just a few months later, however, in the spring of 1947, he again changed his mind. This time, after discussions with Zhang Qun, who was the incoming premier--and, some say, as a result of discussions with his younger brother, the banker and government official Zhang Jia'ao (Chang Kia-ngau)--he announced that the DSP would accept a limited number of government offices after all. He now agreed that members of the DSP would name one member to serve as a minister without portfolio and would accept three seats on the State Council (which was to be the highest policy-forming body of the coalition government). DSP members would not, however, accept ministerial positions with actual administrative responsibilities.[12]

The result of this decision, Zhang later wrote, was that "my party began to split wide open."[13] At a meeting of the party's Standing Committee on 9 April, Sun Baogang expressed his displeasure with Zhang's dictatorial methods, and particularly charged that Zhang was surrounded by a group of *xiaoren* (petty and small-minded men), who misled him. One of Zhang's supporters, Feng Jinbai, thereupon angrily asked Sun who were these *xiaoren*. To this, Sun replied, "You!" With this exchange, the meeting broke up, tempers so inflamed that no further business could be discussed.[14]

Sun Baogang was but one of many who resented Zhang's decisions regarding the scope of the party's participation in the coalition government. Unable to debate the question in party councils, Sun's group took its case to the public, venting its dissatisfaction with Zhang in the nation's newspapers. Zhang's group, in turn, convened a rump session of the party's Organization Committee--twenty-five of the seventy-three members in attendance--to punish the fractious dissidents. Actually, Wu Xianzi, Vice-Chairman of the party, attempted to attend this meeting. He claimed that he carried with him the proxies of twenty-six members of the committee who resided overseas (who were, of course, his followers from the former DCP). Realizing that Wu would control the session if he were permitted to vote these proxies, the Zhang group did not allow him to participate in the meeting.[15]

Thereafter, the rupture in the party widened. Sun and his faction organized a "Reform Committee" of the DSP. Soon, this new committee included not only former members of the DCP, who had favored participation in the coalition government, but also those former members of the NSP, such as Zhang Dongsun, who had opposed naming delegates to the NA.[16] The DSP was, therefore, riven in two.

Zhang Junmai's faction expelled the members of the Reform Committee from the party and, in July, convened a national congress that was attended only by members of their faction. The next month, the "Reformers," representing about three-quarters of the original DSP's membership,[17] convened their own national party congress, and elected Wu Xianzi as the new party chairman. By August 1947, therefore, two separate political parties existed, both claiming the name "DSP."

The events of this squabble within the DSP were, in themselves, of little moment within the great revolutionary drama then being played out on the Chinese stage. But an analysis of the participants' motives in the quarrel provides useful insights into the values of China's so-called "liberals."

Primarily at issue in this party fight was who among the members would receive appointments to the NA and to offices in the coalition government. Not all members of the party, it is true, saw the advent of coalition government as an opportunity to gain office. The principal leaders of the party--notably Zhang Junmai, Wu Xianzi, and Zhang Dongsun--were indifferent to the allure of high position, and their quarrel with each other was largely over who controlled the party and how.[18] Most of the party rank and file, however, coveted public office. For the critics of Zhang Junmai, what was most objectionable about his decision regarding, first, non-participation, and then, only limited participation in the coalition government was that he was cutting them off from that avenue of advancement. That, at least, was the construction that Zhang himself put on their motives. "These young members of my party want to grab ministerial jobs," he told an American consular official, "and because they are unable to get them, they slander me."[19] Xu Fulin, a Zhang supporter, also criticized the members of the Reform Committee, asserting that "Lu So-and-so wants to become a member of the State Council, Wang So-and-so wants to become a governor of a province.... Therefore, they all join hands together."[20] Outsiders, too, viewing the vicious bickering among the DSP members similarly assumed that the fighting was over a division of the spoils to be gained when the party joined the government.[21]

The desire for public office by members of the so-called democratic parties can be seen even more clearly in the experience of the CYP, because the leaders of that party have left behind remarkably candid memoirs of this period. In the coalition government scheduled to be established in April 1947, the CYP was to be allotted the headships of the Ministry of Economic

Affairs and the Ministry of Agriculture and Forestry. Of these, the Ministry of Economic Affairs was a particularly choice plum, because it comprised more than a thousand personnel positions, had a sizable budget, and, through such offices as the Fuel Control Commission and the Cotton-Goods Control Commission, gave promise of lucrative contracts with the business and industrial community.[22] Li Huang, one of the three major leaders in the CYP, was initially designated to head that ministry. As soon as news of his pending appointment leaked out, he was deluged by office-seekers. For two solid days, he recalled, members of his party, as well as relatives, streamed into his home in Chengdu, ostensibly offering their congratulations, but actually seeking jobs. As he prepared to leave Sichuan for Nanjing, he was again surrounded by party members beseeching him to take them with him.[23]

In Nanjing and Shanghai, Li Huang found that party members there were no less ambitious to obtain government posts. Their assumption was that Li would dismiss all the ministry's current employees, so that he could fill the vacancies with members of the CYP. At a meeting of that party's Central Committee, however, Li expressed the opinion that it would be improper to dismiss the experienced personnel in the ministry and replace them with inexperienced party members. Only a small number of CYP members, therefore, would receive appointments in the ministry. "This proposal," recalled Li, "aroused the vociferous opposition of the attending central [committee] members who became quite discourteous to me."[24]

Many of these men had served loyally and selflessly in the CYP for twenty and more years. Yet, as soon as it became evident that the party would participate in the coalition government, they became swept up in what Li Huang called an "opportunistic psychology." Concern for party policy, he added, now took a back seat to concern for administrative appointments.[25]

This desire of party members to obtain government office inevitably led to factional quarrels. Just as the DSP had split when one segment of the party saw that Zhang Junmai's faction would secure the fruits of joining the coalition government, so the CYP now fell apart. "Party comrades whom I had laboured with for many years," Li Huang complained, "seeing that they could now become officials, suddenly changed their customs and contended amongst each other."[26] Chen Qitian, another CYP leader, similarly observed that, as long as the party was out of power and suffering adversity, the most severe problems for the party came from the outside. As soon as the party approached power, however, the party's gravest difficulties were those caused by its own members vying for jobs.[27] Nor was it only a few of the party members who thus fought to obtain office. "The majority of the members of the Chinese Youth Party," Li Huang wrote, "could not escape from the habits and atmosphere of the ... old Chinese gentry, and consequently the party broke up. Although there were still a minority of comrades with self respect ... they were powerless in their environment. This is why the Chinese tragedy was inevitable."[28]

In seeking government office, the hope of these men was not primarily to serve the nation or even their party. Rather, they sought personal glorification and enrichment. "Most of [the Youth Party members] nominated to the National Assembly or as members of the Legislative and Control Yuan," Li wrote, "were not conscious that their duties as the elected was to foster democracy and to protect the legal system. Instead most of them regarded themselves as officials rather than representatives of the people.... Doubtlessly they had fought hard for their positions in order to get closer to power and honour which would dazzle the [members of their] villages. Only a minority of those elected had any understanding and capability of protecting the constitution and supervising the government."[29]

Being motivated by self-interest, members of the democratic parties who obtained administrative posts quickly succumbed to fiscal temptation. John Leighton Stuart, the U.S. Ambassador in China at the time, recalled in his memoirs that "Not unlike our own discredited practise of spoils of office, these minor parties wanted jobs for their members, nor were the new ministers and their subordinates any improvement over the displaced Kuomintang officials."[30] Zuo Shunsheng, the CYP leader who served as the Minister of Agriculture and Forestry, added a qualification to Stuart's observation. Because his own ministry was actually small and poor, Zuo said, corruption was not a large problem there. He agreed with Stuart, however, that in the Ministry of Economic Affairs, "some of our Party members made a bad impression.... It was too easy [in that ministry] to get mixed up with business people who tried to bribe the ministry's staff."[31]

Not all members of the democratic parties were prostituted by the temptations of government office. Yet many were. Li Huang suggested that "the majority" of his party succumbed to political and fiscal temptation. Why?

Chinese, of course, were not alone in being seduced by holding political power or tempted by easy but improper financial gain. Every nation and every people provides more than adequate demonstration of the frailty of human ideals. The particular manifestations of political corruptibility, or the extent thereof, probably differed from place to place and from time to time. In examining the experience of China's democratic parties, we are interested,therefore, in understanding the manifestation in twentieth-century China of a universal phenomenon.

Chinese at the time had a term for it: *Shengguan facai* ("to become an official and grow rich"). The *locus classicus* of this term is probably unknowable; certainly, the concept was a venerable one, extending far back into the dynastic period. In traditional times, every ambitious and able young man aspired to just one goal: to pass the civil-service examinations and thence to become an official. China was distinctive in that this one route to power and prestige was valued above all others. Mercantile wealth, military rank, and certainly athletic prowess, ranked far behind in the scale of socially admired attainments.

But in traditional times, to *shengguan* (become an official) implied to *facai* (grow rich). Why governmental office had come to be viewed as a pathway to wealth is a difficult question. Perhaps it was because the traditional bureaucracies did not sharply distinguish between the public and private finances of the officials. Or perhaps it was because government salaries were usually inadequate to supply even the officials' most modest requirements, and there was, consequently, an institutionalized inducement for the officials to supplement their incomes by means that would today be called corrupt.

Whatever the explanation, many centuries had nourished the view, almost the instinct, that, by attaining government office, one could also obtain the wealth that would redound hugely to the benefit of oneself and one's kin. It is hard for us to comprehend how profoundly that concept was embedded in the minds and values of China's educated classes. Indeed, it was difficult even for an idealistic Chinese like the chairman of the CYP, Zeng Qi. After witnessing the unseemly grasping for office and wealth by members of his party, Zeng rued that "I overestimated the knowledge and morality of the intellectual class, and I failed to anticipate that their knowledge could be so shallow, or their character so base, as this!"[32]

Since even members of the democratic parties, who were often from the nation's intellectual elite, succumbed to the temptations of office as soon as their parties were invited to join the coalition government, it is not surprising that members of other Chinese political parties were possessed of the *shengguan facai* mentality. This, in large part, was why the GMD so quickly lost sight of its revolutionary ideals after seizing power in 1927-28. Since 1949, the CCP has similarly suffered the effects of *shengguan facai*-ism. By 1961, 80 percent of the seventeen million members of the party had joined since the establishment of the People's Republic. Inevitably, many of these new party members, and perhaps many of the old as well, had absorbed the view, however subconsciously, that by becoming an official one gained special rights and privileges. Corruption, back-door-ism, and self-serving bureaucratism have consequently become hallmarks of Communist rule.

Even within the ranks of China's current democratic dissidents--among the publishers of the journal *Zhongguo zhi chun* (China Spring) and the survivors of the Tiananmen massacre who are now in the West--some of the same tendencies toward corruption and self-serving have raised their ugly heads. Indeed, China may never know good government until the *shengguan facai* mentality disappears, or until Chinese devise governmental institutions that can effectively contain this corrosive element in their traditional political culture.

Notes

1. United States Department of State, *United States Relations With China, with Special Reference to the Period 1944-1949* (Washington, D.C.: U.S. Government Printing Office, 1949), 688.

2. Ibid., 683-85.

3. *Dazhong Wanbao*, in *Chinese Press Review* (Shanghai), 20 December 1946, 9 (hereafter, *CPR*).

4. Zuo Shunsheng, "The Reminiscences of Tso Shun-sheng (1893-1969)," as told to Julie Lien-ying How (Chinese Oral History Project, East Asian Institute of Columbia University, 1965), 263.

5. Lu Yian, *Zhongguo minzhu shehui dang fenlie zhi jingguo* (Events in the Split of the Democratic Socialist Party) (n.p., n.d; republished by the Center for Chinese Research Materials, Washington, D.C.), 4.

6. Ibid., 20-21.

7. This Northern Faction did not include all DSP members residing in Beiping, however, and a significant number of them opposed Zhang Dongsun and favored participation in the NA. *Pinglun Bao* (The Critic), no. 5 (7 December 1946):8; *Dazhong Wanbao*, in *CPR* (Shanghai), 20 December 1946, 9.

8. Carsun Chang, *The Third Force in China* (New York: Bookman Associates, 1952), 228; Li Huang, "My Memoirs," trans. Lillian Chu Chin (Chinese Oral History Project, East Asian Institute of Columbia University, 1971), 842.

9. Lu, 3.

10. *Pinglun Bao*, no. 5 (7 December 1946): 8; and ibid., no. 7 (21 December 1946): 19.

11. Chang, 223-24, 231-34.

12. Ibid., 231-32; John F. Melby, *The Mandate of Heaven: Record of a Civil War, China, 1945-49* (Toronto: University of Toronto Press, 1968), 165.

13. Chang, 233.

14. Lu, 5.

15. Ibid., 10.

16. Zhang Dongsun was named a member of the Presidium of the "reformist" DSP, and he served as an adviser to it. Whether or not he actually accepted membership in the party, however, is unclear. See *Shen Bao* (Shanghai Daily), in *CPR* (Shanghai), 16 August 1947, 4-5.

17. *Dagong Bao* (L'Impartial"), in *CPR* (Shanghai), 8 August 1947, 3.

18. Chang, 232; Lu, 4-5.

19. Chang, 233.

20. *Li Bao*, in *CPR* (Shanghai), 7 August 1947, 9.

21. Lu, 4.

22. *Xinwen Tiandi* (News World), in *CPR* (Shanghai), 7 October 1948, 14.

23. Li, 851-55.

24. Ibid., 859.

25. Ibid., 845, 859.

26. Ibid., 860.

27. Chen Qitian, *Jiyuan Huiyilu* (The Memoirs of Chen Qitian) (Taibei: Commercial Press, 1965; rev. ed. 1972), 198.

28. Li, 861.

29. Ibid., 869.

30. John Leighton Stuart, *Fifty Years in China: The Memoirs of John Leighton Stuart, Missionary and Ambassador* (New York: Random House, 1954), 188.

31. Zuo, 265.

32. Chen, 198.

PART FOUR

Opposition Parties and Isms: Anarchism and Anti-Communism

9

The Chinese Anarchist Critique of Bolshevism During the 1920s

Edward S. Krebs

Today, when what is left of the system they set up in the Soviet Union is being reshaped or discarded, parts of the Bolsheviks' legacy remain. One of the major historic effects of the October Revolution outside Russia was its impact on China. This study surveys the Chinese anarchists' response to the introduction of Bolshevism to China. Through their knowledge of the history of anarchism in Europe, Chinese anarchists were predisposed to criticize the Marxist movement from its beginnings in China. Although the recent opposition to Communist systems in the Soviet Union and Europe is centered on disillusionment, rather than ideology, many of the arguments made against those systems today were stated by Chinese anarchists seventy years ago, as they responded to this new movement in Chinese political life. During the period dealt with here, 1919 to 1925, the Chinese anarchists also were impressed with the success of their rivals on the left; thus part of their response was self-criticism of their own shortcomings, which also is addressed below.

Diane Scherer and Peter Zarrow made helpful comments on an earlier version of this study. I am also grateful to Ms. Scherer for generously sharing materials and insights.

Introduction

The background of enmity between Marxists and anarchists can only be suggested here.[1] Both Pierre Proudhon and Mikhail Bakunin had tangled with Karl Marx in the formative periods of the two movements. Disagreements between Bakunin and Marx culminated in the breakup of the First Communist International; the issue was discipline or the autonomy of individual units, depending on one's point of view. In Europe as in China, Marxism's success in guiding revolutionary movements to power has obscured the historical importance of anarchism. These alternative visions of socialist revolution both arose in the 1840s; the two movements defined themselves through their mutual struggle, especially the conflict between Marx and Bakunin. Of the differences separating Marx from Proudhon and Bakunin, it seems fair to observe that the early anarchist leaders sought to begin a revolution with workers and their perceived needs and have them evolve their own organizations, while Marx looked to the gradual development of the proletariat, who would evolve such a level of consciousness as to be able to undertake the historic role he envisioned for them.

By the turn of the century, Peter Kropotkin was recognized as the major theorist of anarchism. His mutual-aid theory and concept of voluntary association were widely accepted by anarchists in Europe. When World War I began, Kropotkin set aside his internationalism to support the Allies, because of deeply rooted anti-German feelings. After the February Revolution, Kropotkin decided to return to Russia, hoping to contribute to the construction of a new society; in the summer of 1917, he went home after an absence of some forty years. But again Kropotkin and other Russian anarchists saw the hope of cooperation with the Marxists turn into enmity. Kropotkin's age and prestige shielded him from the Bolshevik repression of anarchists for their opposition to centralized authority.[2] Comment in the Russian anarchist press (before their journals were repressed) and accounts written by Russian anarchists as emigres years later express the same themes, based on bitter experience, that the Chinese anarchists stated more abstractly in debates with their Marxist rivals.[3]

Both anarchism and Marxism were introduced to China during the first years of the century. However, Marx's formulation that only advanced industrial societies would be properly prepared for proletarian revolution made his theories seem inappropriate. Anarchism was intermixed with "nihilism" and was initially (1903-04) attractive for its use of assassination; early writings also cited rudimentary theory to support this tactic. Then, in 1907, Chinese anarchist groups in Paris and Tokyo began to publish journals that cleared up the earlier confusion about anarchist theory. By this time, a number of Chinese activists were especially attracted to Kropotkin's theories; his mutual-aid concept seemed to fit China's needs.[4] Sun Yat-sen's Revolutionary Alliance made room for this group because of Sun's relationships with Wu Zhihui, Li Shizeng, and Cai Yuanpei, all anarchists and important figures among Chinese sojourning in Europe. Wu and Li were the moving forces behind the Paris anarchist journal, *Xin shiji* (New Era).

The anarchists' principles forbade office-holding, but after 1912, several of them found ways to compromise on this point and served the Republic. After World War I, this first generation of anarchists sponsored the Work-Study Movement, under the auspices of which many Chinese students went to France. With the split between the Guomindang (GMD) and the Chinese Communist Party (CCP) in 1927, Wu and Li cast their lot with Chiang Kai-shek. Their decisions reflected their long association with Sun Yat-sen, as well as their anti-Marxist commitment, but disappointed most younger anarchists, who saw little to attract them to Chiang.[5]

During the first years of the Republic, China's most persistent anarchist was Shi Fu (Liu Sifu),[6] who had been introduced to anarchism through Wu and Li's *Xin Shiji.* Shi Fu had been a member of the Revolutionary Alliance, but his single-minded devotion to anarchism after 1912 led him to attack Sun Yat-sen for the latter's plan to implement "social policies" (*shehui zhengce*), instead of "social revolution" (*shehui geming*). Shi Fu presented his views in *Min sheng* (Voice of the People), the journal he and his associates began publishing in Guangzhou in 1913.[7] He meant to reach the masses, who, when sufficiently awakened to the evils of the capitalist-controlled authoritarian system, would rise up and carry out a "great people's revolution" (*pingmin da geming*), to be triggered by a general strike or similar action.

Shi Fu saw a grand opportunity for anarchism in post-revolutionary Guangdong, but following the unsuccessful "Second Revolution" in 1913, he was forced to leave Guangzhou. He moved to Shanghai, where *Min sheng* appeared weekly through the summer of 1914. His health broke at that point, and he died the following spring. He had drawn attention to issues affecting workers, and his initiatives bore fruit in unions organized in the late 1910s (see below). His insistence on correct theory did much to establish the ideological basis from which the anarchists attacked Bolshevism.

While these early efforts produced a large following and built a sense of common purpose, they did not result in the formation of a political party. Some of the anarchists used the word *dang* (political party) to refer to their movement in the debate with the Marxists, perhaps partly in response to the CCP's growth as a party. Anarchists also used the term *pai* ("group" or "faction") to refer to their movement. But well into the 1920s, some still used the suffix *zhe* (*wuzhengfuzhuyizhe* or "anarchists"), presumably to indicate that they meant to be simply a movement and not a party. These choices in terminology surely affected their sense of how to organize.

By the early 1920s, and certainly after the GMD-CCP alliance was launched, the anarchist movement began to slip in both influence and numbers. The anarchists made almost no use of nationalism, which soon proved to be the most powerful ideological appeal in China. They were repulsed by the idea that "political power grows out of the barrel of a gun." Thus, whatever their shortcomings, they rejected the two keys to popular appeal that both the GMD and the CCP had begun to use so effectively. The anarchists had been linked historically with the GMD and ideologically with the CCP, but by the middle 1920s, they felt acutely what it meant to be a "third party." The link between the anarchists and the Communists was perhaps as important in launching the CCP movement as was the inspiration of the Bolsheviks in Russia; as Arif Dirlik has shown, the anarchists' implantation of radical socialism prepared the way for Marxism in China.[8]

What did "Bolshevism" mean to Chinese intellectuals in the late 1910s? As both Dirlik and Maurice Meisner have demonstrated, Li Dazhao and others who first embraced Bolshevism did not understand much about it initially. Li's article, "The Victory of Bolshevism," published in *Xin qingnian* (New Youth) in November 1918, introduced the term and also connected Lenin with the movement (although in a single reference).[9] Li was attracted to "Bolshevism" because it had worked, much as earlier Chinese activists had been attracted to "anarchism" initially because they associated it with the apparently effective tactic of assassination. Li began to study Marxism in order to understand it better. He did not immediately grasp the connection between Bolshevism and Marxism.[10]

My use of the word "critique" in the title of this study is meant to indicate a focus on the ideas or theoretical points presented by the anarchists, rather than on any political or organizational effort they made to counter their Marxist rivals. The discussions produced some overlap between Marxism and Bolshevism. This mattered less as both sides came to distinguish Marxism as theory and Bolshevism as practice. The anarchists consistently attacked the "dictatorship of the proletariat," a concept of Marx's implemented politically by Lenin. Some of their arguments concerning this and other issues were original and perceptive.

The Initial Response

Huang Lingshuang, one of the most active anarchists during these years, wrote what appears to be the earliest anarchist response to the revolution in Russia. Of Cantonese background, he had come under Shi Fu's influence as a young teenager. A few years later, he was a student at Beijing University and an editor and essayist for such important publications as the anarchists' *Shi she ziyou lu* (Liberal Record of the Realists' Society) and the *Beijing daxue xuesheng zhoukan* (Beijing University Student Weekly). He was active in at least one of Li Dazhao's Marxist study groups.[11] Returning to Guangzhou in 1921, Huang was one of those anarchists who worked with the early Marxist organizations, as the two groups briefly sought to cooperate with each other.

His article, "A Critique of Marxist Theory," addressed not Bolshevism but Marxism, and appeared in *Xin qingnian* in May 1919. He sought to be objective, crediting Marx with achievements in economic theory while criticizing his political-theory implications for the socialist future. He especially praised Marx's work on the labor theory of value and surplus value, and offered the opinion that the materialist conception of history "marked the beginning of a new era in the academic world."[12] In reading *Capital*, however, he noted that Marx sometimes forced conclusions after offering evidence that led in other directions. "Wishful thinking can ruin science," he observed; "I am afraid that Marx cannot free himself from blame."[13]

He found Marx most disagreeable on political theory. For Huang, as for other anarchists, the essential issue was the nature of the state; no matter who held it, state power did "nothing more than establish private authority and protect the organization of a privileged minority."[14] Such a state would control the individual, he noted, in another standard anarchist argument against state authority.

The question of distribution also divided anarchists and Marxists. Marxists wished to reward people on the basis of their work, he wrote, and this would give an advantage to the strong. Anarchists followed the principle of "from each according to his ability, to each according to his *needs* [italics mine]." Only this principle, he observed, could provide an equitable distribution of society's wealth. "This has been a central issue in the struggle between anarchists and Marxists," he concluded.[15]

An exchange of views published in *Fendou xunkan* (Struggle), in early 1920, reflected some refinement in the anarchists' arguments. This short-lived journal was published by the Struggle Society, a group of law students at Beijing University. In keeping with the anarchist practice of setting aside family names, writers identified themselves only with English initials, so most are unrecognizable. One of the editors, "A.D." (probably Yi Jiayue), launched a symposium with "We Oppose Bolshevism," in a February issue.[16]

He lamented the shortage of reliable information on developments in Russia. As the "front door" to Bolshevik Russia was closed, he said, he would proceed by way of a "back door"--Marxism. He divided his critique of Bolshevism into comments on theory and methods. He called Bolshevism "the method for implementing Marxism" and "the most filial of Marx's offspring." Part of his argument on theory made perceptive use of contemporary developments to find flaws in Marx's view of history. While Marx had believed that labor value would continue to decrease and the value of capital to increase, he wrote, the reverse had happened since the end of the war in Europe. A.D. observed that the Russian Revolution had not followed Marx's prediction that socialist revolution would occur first in mature capitalist systems, such as the United States or Germany; "... surprisingly," he noted, " it occurred earlier in Russia during its period of domestic economy."[17]

The Bolsheviks violated important principles, he continued, in establishing a new state, in using authority, and in advocating class war. One of his basic points combined all three of these themes: Russian workers and peasants were deceiving themselves in accepting these features of Bolshevik control as necessary to end capitalist control. In summary, he argued: "Why just bring down the capitalists and not bring down the state as organized by the capitalists?"[18]

Much in his analysis was predictable and naive, and his article provoked several responses. Most original was "Why Oppose the Bolsheviks?" by "A.F."[19] He urged A.D. to distinguish between capital, capitalism, and a capitalist state. His point was that all societies needed capital, or new wealth, which required both labor and capital. China was a good example of a situation in which capital was needed, he wrote: "We try to think of ways to create capital to improve our material life, but we do not agree with capitalism." The Bolsheviks "support the function of capital but do not support capitalism." The Bolshevik state had two characteristics. Besides the usual functions of government, the Bolsheviks "manage matters of production and consumption; so this kind of state can be called a state that manages goods." Second, the Bolsheviks operated a "class state." "A laboring-class state is not a capitalist-class state, and I think a statement like A.D.'s that the Bolsheviks run a capitalist state shows that his analysis is not penetrating."[20]

He next sought to clear up confusion among the concepts of social revolution, class struggle, and class dictatorship. Social revolution was not simply class struggle, he argued, nor did class struggle necessarily achieve social revolution. Referring to the French Revolution as an early example of class struggle, he observed that, despite a great deal of class struggle, revolution still had not produced a social revolution. He admonished A.D. to accept class struggle as a practical requirement, even if he could not accept it in theory. On the question of "class dictatorship," he observed that just as individuals were selfish, a class also might be selfish and rule only in its own interests. In that case, a class dictatorship also would not necessarily achieve social revolution.

He concluded that he was neither an anarchist nor a Bolshevik. He gave three reasons for this, which matched the anarchists' major objections to the Bolshevik approach to ruling Russia. The Bolsheviks were not concerned with the individual, he declared; they abused authority and operated an absolute dictatorship:

> Bolshevism wants to use the authority of the state to interfere with the individual and material things to intervene in the individual spirit, so all publishing and education are in the hands of the state. Thus, how are they not setting aside the individual and causing society to regress?... Our democratic spirit lies in enabling people to determine their own affairs, but the Bolsheviks are precisely the opposite; they are autocratic and dictatorial.[21]

Hence, he shared most anarchists' reasons for opposing Bolshevism. He and the other participants in these first discussions admired much about the Bolsheviks' success, and recognized that certain aspects of Marxist theory, on the basis of which the Bolsheviks had acted, were unavoidable in practical terms, if not logically irrefutable. But their admiration ended where Bolshevik rule decided the issue of freedom versus authority in favor of the latter. Until 1920, discussion was based on theory, supplemented by information that was limited or difficult to confirm. The anarchists had their arguments ready, because they knew the history of the anarchist-Marxist relationship in Europe. The May Fourth student generation had developed great admiration for individualism and democracy, and the anarchists were not prepared to set those principles aside.

The Debate Between Ou Shengbai and Chen Duxiu

The most important single debate over the relative merits of Marxism and anarchism, which involved Ou Shengbai and Chen Duxiu, took place in Guangzhou in early 1921. It was provoked by a lecture Chen gave not long after his arrival in Guangzhou to serve as educational commissioner in the government of Chen Jiongming, following the latter's success in wresting Guangdong from the control of Guangxi warlords in the autumn of 1920.[22]

This political change helped to make Guangzhou a hotbed of radical political activity. It was the scene of intense activity by political parties and movements on the left in the early 1920s, with their efforts focused on labor organization.[23] Some of the first modern labor unions had been organized in Guangzhou before the 1911 Revolution. Because of newly aroused worker consciousness in the wake of the May Fourth Movement, labor activity broadened and twenty-six new unions were organized in Guangdong in 1919.[24]

The period 1920-1922 brought a wave of activity, due to several factors. An economic boom resulted from the growth of Chinese-owned modern industry, launched while the Western powers were preoccupied with World War I. This created a sellers' market for workers, whose wages had not kept pace with inflation. The opportunity for workers to gain through organization stimulated a rising spiral of union growth and strikes, bringing wage increases in the range of 20-30 percent. By 1922, Guangzhou had about eighty labor unions.[25]

Organization gave labor unprecedented political power. This was brought to bear repeatedly in Guangzhou during the 1920s. Labor unions had supported Chen Jiongming in his campaign to dislodge the Guangxi warlords, at which time Chen was allied with Sun Yat-sen. By 1922, Sun was ready to launch his northern expedition, but Chen, like some anarchists, favored federalism. Their split brought another struggle for local control. In 1923, when Sun succeeded in reestablishing himself in Guangzhou, while forming his alliance with the CCP, the labor unions sided with him. From that point on, the alliance with labor remained a keystone of Sun's policy in his southern stronghold.

Formalized at the beginning of 1924, the GMD-CCP alliance brought an even greater emphasis on the political power of labor. There were strains from the beginning between the CCP unions and relatively conservative GMD groups, and between them and the even more conservative merchant community in Guangzhou. As early as 1924, Sun's government encouraged the unions, as they built independent armed militia for use against the merchants and their supporters, and a violent clash between these two forces broke out in October of that year.[26] Renewed anti-imperialist feeling, because of the May Thirtieth Incident in 1925, brought even greater growth to the labor movement. By late 1926, there were some 250 labor organizations in Guangzhou, with a total membership approaching 300,000.[27]

These successes masked the divisions described above, which grew ever more apparent in the succession struggle following Sun's death (March 1925) and culminated in the breakup of the GMD-CCP alliance in the spring of 1927. The abortive attempt to establish a "Canton commune" in December added several thousand more to the number of workers victimized in the tragic conclusion to this period of unfettered growth in the Guangzhou labor movement.[28]

Anarchists and anarchist ideas played a major role in this labor organizing, at least through the early 1920s. Shi Fu had reached out to workers; his associates in Guangzhou helped to organize the Teahouse Union in the summer of 1918 and a barbers' union in early 1919. The Teahouse Union amalgamated some eleven thousand food service workers from forty previously existing guilds, to become the first union in China organized on an industry-wide basis.[29] In 1920, Xie Yingbo, an earlier associate of Shi Fu who ultimately opted to support Sun Yat-sen, adopted an anarchist name--the Mutual Aid Society--for the network of organizations he formed after Chen Jiongming's return. By 1922, Xie's network claimed some 100,000 workers in more than one hundred affiliates.[30] Anarchists also published a number of journals in Guangzhou. Shi Fu's comrades revived *Min sheng* in 1921, and its role in the debate between anarchists and Marxists is suggested below. Another journal launched at this time was *Laodongzhe* (Laborers), which has been regarded as one of the first Marxist labor journals. *Laodongzhe* did indeed advocate "communism," which accounts for its reputation as a Marxist journal, but the communism it propagated was anarchist-communism rather than Marxism.[31] *Min zhong* (People's Bell) became the major anarchist organ in Guangzhou, beginning in mid-1922. Another was *Wuyi yuekan* (May First Monthly). Both played roles as the anarchists continued their critique of Bolshevism.

This survey suggests conditions in Guangzhou at the time of Chen Duxiu's arrival there in late 1920. Chen and other Marxists became active in the revived revolutionary setting in Guangzhou. Anarchists were equally active, and probably more effective, in 1921-22 because of their earlier efforts in the city. Guangzhou provides the best illustrations of the two groups' efforts to work together and the reasons they were unable to cooperate. As of the spring of 1921, the activity of anarchists and Marxists (as well as GMD members) created an atmosphere charged with revolutionary energy. The most fitting way to summarize this setting is to note the symbolism displayed at the May Day celebration in Guangzhou that spring. An estimated 200,000 workers paraded, waving both red and black flags, while at a major intersection hung large portraits of Karl Marx and Peter Kropotkin.[32]

The debate between Chen Duxiu and Ou Shengbai was launched by Chen's lecture at the Law and Political Science School in March 1921. Presented as a general discussion of socialism, his talk included a number of criticisms of anarchism.[33] Ou, who had been a student of Chen's at Beijing University, responded with a letter to Chen, which was published in the Guangzhou journal, *Guangzhou qun bao* (The Guangzhou Masses). Two further exchanges of letters followed, which also appeared in that journal.[34] Ou's part in the debate was reprinted in a special supplement to *Min sheng*, dated 5 April.[35] Initially, the exchange seems to have been published only in Guangzhou, where it represented an early skirmish in the battle for the hearts and minds of the area's intellectuals and workers. It was reprinted in a special issue of *Xin qingnian* in August, through which it gained a much broader circulation.[36]

Most of the debate was quite civil, with differences expressed more in philosophical than ideological or personal terms. Chen and Ou spoke for groups which were attempting to cooperate and might remain allies. At issue were such questions as how they might work together, what kinds of organizations they should create and under what kind of leadership, and what society would be like following the social revolution they both wanted. A philosophical approach was appropriate for other reasons as well. Although this debate concerned two forms of modern socialism, many of the same issues had divided Mencius and Xunzi (Hsun-tzu), in their respective interpretations of Confucian principles, or Daoism and Confucianism. Is human nature good? Can people achieve the common good by working together and releasing the talent and good will basic to human nature? Or do people require strong leadership, authority, and discipline? Such basic questions were at issue, and the debate cast them in terms of modern political philosophies.

Chen and Ou argued over the gamut of issues that divide Marxists and anarchists: individual freedom and the free association that anarchists proposed as the means to organize society and manage production; law and discipline, including the question of how to achieve compliance with the principles of socialism; and education as the conveyor of values and a means to change those who were not prepared to participate in social revolution. In responding to Ou's appeal that special schools be established for recalcitrants, Chen noted that Marxists agreed that education was preferable to law, "but we cannot superstitiously believe that education can do everything" or "that education can replace law." The notion that such a transformation could occur in people's heads was "the fatal flaw of you anarchists," he asserted.[37]

Perhaps it took an anarchist to make a Marxist appear conservative. Chen argued for law and order and showed no reservations or misgivings on the point. Even though law in its present forms had flaws, he argued, national unity and the systems of law that accompanied it were the results of historical process. It was impractical--and naive as well, he implied--to try to replace that binding power of law with voluntary agreements.

The question of free association had direct relevance to the labor-organizing efforts in which the anarchists and Marxists were engaged at Guangzhou. The anarchists maintained that each organization should retain autonomy concerning joint actions with other groups, as in general strikes or support for another union's action. The Marxists sought to build a disciplined united front among workers, primarily for political purposes. They were apprehensive of "syndicalism," the tendency for workers to use their power only for short-term economic gain.[38] Disagreement on this point was crucial in ending the anarchists' willingness to work with the Marxists in Guangzhou.[39] Thus, there was an immediate issue at stake in the debate, even though Chen and Ou agreed, as their exchanges ended, that many of the points they had discussed involved questions of social organization in the distant future.

Not content to let Chen have the last word, Ou prepared another statement, which appeared in *Xue deng* (Study Lamp), a supplement to the Shanghai *Shishi xinbao* (The China Times), in April 1922.[40] He sent this last rejoinder from Lyons, where he had gone on the work-study program. He concluded with remarks that expressed the attitude of many anarchists at that time, and indicated what they regarded as the "fatal flaws" in the Bolshevist approach:

> Although I believe in Kropotkin, I am not like you in making Marx the founder of a faith, making holy books of *Capital* and the *Communist Manifesto*, and making enemies of socialists in other parties.... Marx's method of social organization not only will not liberate workers, it will cause workers to experience the great suffering of national capitalism. However, Marx's materialist view of history and theory of class struggle have a great deal of truth, so we would advocate them in the period of revolution. On social organization, we must choose Kropotkin's great non-nationalist world federation.... I think that in China both the party of Marx and the party of Kropotkin are good, and we ought to combine our strength to bring down the power of the old society, and then later resolve the question of social revolution.... If we think that only one party is able to carry out the revolution, not only will we not succeed, there will certainly be no good result. I do not know what you think?[41]

As his closing query suggested, he was prepared to continue the debate, but Chen did not respond (he had returned to Shanghai in August 1921).[42] The Marxists had begun their own approach to structure and discipline, and during 1923 the CCP and GMD began building the alliance that put the *coup de grace* to further cooperation between anarchists and Marxists.

Chen's transition to Marxism and the task of party organization was the result of his own movement away from the heady atmosphere of the "new culture" which he had done so much to create. For him, action meant the need to abandon new enthusiasms for their own sake and get down to the business of making revolution.[43] In his debate with Ou, he sought to lead his former student and other "new youths" in the direction he himself had decided to take. But Ou and other anarchists, especially those from Guangzhou, were working from a deeper base. They saw the success of labor organization in Guangzhou as the fruits of years of anarchist effort there, and saw no reason to compromise their views.

After Establishment of the GMD-CCP Alliance

Sun Yatsen's GMD began its working cooperation with the Communists in 1923, and formal agreements linking the two parties took effect at the beginning of 1924. Despite this heavy blow to their efforts, the anarchists continued to attack Bolshevism.

In early 1923, a new anarchist journal, *Huzhu yuekan* (Mutual Aid Monthly), attacked the GMD-CCP alliance.[44] It published a list entitled "Our Propaganda Materials over the Past Twenty Years." Zheng Peigang, writing under the pen name "Ke lao," listed more than seventy journals and books published by China's anarchists.[45] Although his statement made no reference to the Marxists' activities, the list seemed intended to show that the anarchists had been working for social revolution much longer than the Marxists.

The first issue of *Huzhu yuekan* carried an article entitled "The Labor Movement," by "An" (Peace or Anarchist), who offered some trenchant observations on the Marxists' approach to labor organization.[46] Both anarchists and Marxists have been active in the labor movement, he noted, and both wanted workers to accept their views. But anarchists wanted workers to organize themselves and assume leadership, while Marxists usually took both organizational and leadership roles:

> Anarchists are opposed to workers' organizations in which a small number of intellectuals appeal to uncomprehending workers to accept their control. And we support workers' organizations based on our principles, with self-consciousness and self-determination, able to struggle for basic things, freely organized, and not receiving someone else's direction and control.

He then described some of the potential problems with a cadre of professional revolutionaries:

> Because Marxism is unable to eliminate government, class, or capitalists, they switch over and arouse people's greed. A kind of low-class politician, careerists of a domineering nature (many such people have sneaked in among Chinese Marxist labor organizers, because there is a salary), all steal into the movement and plan to grab the present controlling class and replace them. And also because they do not pay any attention at all to mankind's innate capacity for mutual aid, they strongly advocate their class struggle.... In the society of the future, they will only "work for the people" to make their living [lit., "eat rice"].[47]

He concluded that the Marxists' "monopolistic" approach to labor organization would ultimately fail. His remarks suggested the beginnings of a party infrastructure that eventually could grow into a bureaucratic monolith. But the anarchists' comments on organization carried a significant irony; for all their emphasis on the need for voluntary organization, few of the anarchists seem to have been adept at organizing people. While their volunteer approach had begun to pay off in the laborers' world at Guangzhou, it was not working in other places in the early 1920s. Yet their understanding of the flaws in Marxist-style organizing was accurate, and An's proved prescient.

The Guangzhou anarchist journal *Wuyi yuekan* carried several discussions of Marxism during 1923. "A An" (Elder [?] Peace or Anarchist A) presented his views in August, in an article entitled, "The Revolution I Believe In."[48] He began by describing the kind of revolution he was opposed to, i.e., a mere political revolution, which was all that had been attempted in Russia. Marx had been right in the *Communist Manifesto*, when he wrote that all classes struggled for political power, he observed. In Russia, the problem was indeed political power, which led

> those who consider themselves extraordinary in a period of brutality to arouse the ignorant masses to do battle for them; and when the struggle is over, they use the educated to devise a set of laws to bind the people, and train police and soldiers to massacre them. Ah! Power, power! People who have died cruel deaths throughout history, and the poor with their existence as beasts of burden, all have received your favor![49]

The kind of revolution he did believe in was social revolution, as outlined in anarchist theory. Anarchists must study and propagandize, he argued, and then at the right opportunity join in what would become a great general strike which "the powerful and the capitalist masters will not have the strength to oppose."[50]

By late 1923, some anarchists were discouraged, as indicated by a member of the Star Society who called himself "W." In an open letter to anarchists in *Xue hui* (Sea of Learning) in December, he expressed his concerns.[51] Our organizations do not have any staying power, he complained; only rarely was there a good one. He believed his comrades did not understand the importance of organizational life or the need for discipline. He also offered the view that anarchist groups should "give attention to their members' lives," suggesting that organizations should provide a livelihood for those who served them, as did the Communists. He concluded with an exhortation and a poem:

> The execution ground is our quiet country home;
> prison is our villa; death is our last hope.
> Because I cannot contain my feelings, I leap with
> joy and shout:

> When things come to this, what can they
> do to us! What can they do to us!
> Fortunately we have this star, a tiny point
> of light
> Leading the traveler, hopeless to death,
> across the desert night!
> With the present destroyed,
> The future shines before us.
> Cast life aside and advance! Walk toward
> the bright and brilliant end of our journey![52]

Much of his analysis had been practical, but the desperate romanticism of his conclusion showed that he was vulnerable to the Communists' charge that anarchists were excessively idealistic.

However, the July 1925 comments of "Kuli" (Bitter Strength) indicate that other anarchists viewed the movement's problems in strictly down-to-earth terms and sought to counter their Marxist rivals in practical ways. In "Problems Facing Us Now," published in *Min zhong*, he acknowledged that the anarchists were plagued by organizational problems that hurt their effectiveness.[53] He sought to blame the problems on shortcomings in propaganda work. He referred to a discussion by Chen Muqin (a Sichuanese anarchist), who had observed that while many groups claimed to publish their journals at regular intervals, they did not. Some groups published upon whim or convenience and lacked a serious commitment. A statement quoted from Chen showed Kuli's agreement that the sort of poem that W had written appeared all too often in anarchist publications:

> The publications of comrades everywhere are long on lofty theoretical talk and short on methods; they have many direct translations that are hard to understand but only a few clear edited versions; they have many poems in new forms that moan and groan even though the writers are not sick, but lack investigations of the workers' lives. To sum up, these publications only meet the interests of the intellectual class and are not suitable for propagandizing the masses.[54]

He proposed that anarchists address their problems by making *Min zhong* a nation-wide organ for discussing theory and broad plans for revolution, and that the new journal, *Minzhong* (The Masses), be used as a propaganda organ specializing in practical issues.[55]

Another discussion by Kuli, "A Draft Program for Anarchist Organizations," published in the September 1925 issue of *Min zhong*, provides further evidence that he was grounded in the practicalities of revolution-making.[56] His comprehensive discussion covered political and economic questions, as well as the workers' and peasants' movements. In a section on "assassination and violence," he stated that these were legitimate methods for those prepared to use them. As for the "mass revolution" (*minzhong geming*), he called on his comrades to participate in the revolutionary movement of workers and peasants. While improving the living conditions of these classes was an ongoing goal, the anarchists should look to a period of revolution when efforts would go beyond general strikes and tax resistance to providing arms, so that the workers and peasants could defeat the militarists and display their own military power. In conclusion, he spoke of cooperation with other parties. He specifically mentioned the "democratic party, socialist party, and Leninist party."[57] Cooperation was possible with any party, he wrote, but anarchists should not permit their own revolutionary goals and methods to be compromised. There were good people in these other parties, and they could join the anarchists as individuals.

Perhaps his approach could muster no more disciplined effort than W's emotional appeal. Still, his concerns were stated in practical terms, and in his second article they were laid out systematically. His determination suggests an important point: although things were not going well for the anarchists by the mid-1920s, their movement still had a core of experienced and devoted revolutionaries. Thus the anarchists were not finished as of 1925, anymore than they were irrelevant after the May Fourth movement.

By 1925, however, the anarchists were not as effectively organized as the CCP or GMD. Their sensitivity to the problem of poor organization shows up often in the writings surveyed here. Moreover, Kuli's second article reveals that the anarchists began to appropriate Communist terminology. Up to 1921, the anarchists spoke of a "plain people's revolution"; by 1925, Kuli looked to a "mass revolution" and a "workers' and peasants' revolution," and even wrote about using armed force. Thus, for some anarchists, the momentum generated by the CCP produced a change in the way in which revolution was conceived and described. Kuli, and presumably others as well, also adjusted by suggesting a more "China-specific" and "class struggle-oriented" approach to revolution, even though they still presented no direct appeal to Chinese nationalism and abhorred "class dictatorship." These adjustments were made as the anarchists sought to counter the successes of their great rival in the struggle for the allegiance of those Chinese who were prepared to accept radical socialism. There was much on which the anarchists could agree with the Marxists; their differences still lay in the questions of how to carry out a socialist revolution and organize the post-revolutionary order.

Concluding Reflections

Many have observed that anarchism has its greatest appeal at times when old orders are crumbling and new beginnings seem possible. At such times, anarchism holds particular appeal for socially conscious intellectuals as a plan for ideal development in society. This observation also applies to those Chinese intellectuals who became anarchists.

The anarchists' early discovery of the possibilities for social revolution gave them the initial leadership in radical thought and political activism. Probably their early success made them somewhat complacent. As conditions changed following the May Fourth period, the anarchists seem simply to have been caught off guard. Then the rapid mobilization of the Communist movement in the early 1920s put them on the defensive.

Much of the appeal of anarchism to Chinese intellectuals in this transitional period lay in its emphasis on moral principles. The breakdown of the old order seemed to them ultimately a moral breakdown. China's anarchists seized the moral high ground and held it. As their comments repeatedly show, they believed that the question of the ends versus the means was vitally important. But while many anarchists during the 1920s acted on the powerful moral impulse of their principles, others did not; the latter could satisfy themselves by sitting down to discuss the truth with their comrades or writing about it in their journals.

The contrast between the anarchists and the Marxists was pointedly revealed in the career of Chen Duxiu. His roles in intellectual life and CCP organization make him a figure of first importance in China's history in this century. Yet, he was disgraced in his lifetime, and even today he does not receive credit for his achievements. Perhaps he realized that one risked such treatment, even as he insisted on the necessity of discipline, in his debate with Ou Shengbai. Revolutions have ways of consuming the people who make them, of course; but the revolution that Chen did so much to launch seemed specifically designed to do that.

The tragic events affecting the labor movement in Guangzhou in 1927 also pointed up the relevance of anarchist principles. The effect of labor organization in Guangzhou during the 1920s was to align workers with rising political parties which had their own ambitions. When the GMD and the CCP ended their alliance, several thousand workers paid in blood. While special conditions in the city's politics contributed to the strength of the workers' organizations, the worker control that the anarchists sought would have provided a less volatile, more enduring basis for these groups. This alternative course to revolution, which now seems attractive, lost in appeal as the anarchist movement waned.

Of alliances that did *not* develop in China's modern history, the possible one between anarchists and Marxists, as of 1921, seems a most tragic case. Had the two movements been able to agree on terms for cooperation, their differences might have been muted, the relationship mellowed over time, and, in the process, China's experience of revolution rendered less violent.[58]

Notes

1. For a discussion of the differences between Marx and these early anarchists, see Paul Thomas, *Karl Marx and the Anarchists* (London: Routledge & Kegan Paul, 1980), chaps. 4, 5. These issues are also outlined in George Woodcock, *Anarchism* (Cleveland: Meridian Books World Publishing Company, 1962), chaps. 5, 6.

2. Woodcock (pp. 218-220) describes Kropotkin's experiences after returning to Russia. For a fuller account of the anarchists' role in the revolutionary period, see Paul Avrich, *The Russian Anarchists* (Princeton: Princeton University Press, 1967), Part II.

3. A good example of such an account is Voline (V. M. Eikhenbaum), *The Unknown Revolution, 1917-1921* (New York: Free Life Editions, 1975). For the journalistic comment by Voline (or Volin) and others, see Avrich, especially chap. 7.

4. In *The Chinese Anarchist Movement* (Berkeley: Center for Chinese Studies, University of California, 1961), Robert A. Scalapino and George T. Yu observed that Chinese intellectuals were particularly attracted to anarchism because of Kropotkin's presentation of mutual aid as an alternative to the Social Darwinist notion of struggle, which put China near the bottom among the nations of the world.

5. Arif Dirlik discusses these decisions and their effects in "The Revolution That Never Was: Anarchism in the Guomindang," *Modern China* 15 (October 1989): 419-462 (especially pp. 419-433). His article concerns the anarchists in the late 1920s. Its publication affected my decision to conclude this study at 1925.

6. His use of "Shi Fu" followed the anarchist practice of dropping surnames.

7. The first two issues of *Min sheng* were published at Guangzhou in the autumn of 1913 under the title *Huiming lu* (Cockcrow Record). Nos. 3 and 4 were published in Macao. Nos. 5-22 were published in Shanghai under Shi Fu's editorship. His associates published nos. 23-29 in Shanghai during the period 1914-1916. It was revived at Guangzhou (nos. 30-33) in 1921; its role at that time is suggested below. Longmen Press in Hong Kong reprinted *Min sheng* in 1972.

8. Demonstrating the role that anarchism played as background to Chinese Marxism has been an important theme in Dirlik's work in recent years. For his comments on this subject, see *The Origins of Chinese Communism* (New York: Oxford University Press, 1989), 3-5, 10-11. Chap. 3 on the Chinese response to the Bolshevik Revolution discusses some of the material presented in this study.

9. Maurice Meisner, *Li Ta-chao and the Origins of Chinese Marxism* (Cambridge: Harvard University Press, 1967), 68-70.

10. Ibid., 71-72.

11. For these publications, see Chow Tse-tsung, *Research Guide to the May Fourth Movement* (Cambridge: Harvard University Press, 1963), items 70, 253 (hereafter, *RG*). On Huang's participation in the study group, see Dirlik, *Origins*, 202.

12. Huang Lingshuang, "Makesi xueshuo de piping" (A Critique of Marxist Theory), in Gao Jun et al., *Wuzhengfuzhuyi zai Zhongguo* (Anarchism in China) (Changsha, 1984), 295-300 (hereafter, *WZZG*).

13. Ibid., 297.

14. Ibid., 298.

15. Ibid., 299.

16. "Women fandui 'Buersaiweike'," in *WZZG*, 355-360. On *Fendou xunkan*, see *RG*, item 252, where "A.D." is identified as Yi Jiayue. Like many other journals, this one did not last long; publication ended in April, and its leaders were subsequently arrested.

17. *WZZG*, 357.

18. Ibid., 358.

19. "Weishenma fandui Buerxueweike," in *WZZG*, 386-393. A.F. seems to reflect the influence of Hu Shi. In his introductory comments, he observed: "I hope we youth will not become followers of such 'isms', but will act as critics of 'isms'." For other responses to A.D.'s article, see *WZZG*, 393-94, 396-98.

20. Ibid., 388.

21. Ibid., 392.

22. As his invitation to Chen suggests, Chen Jiongming sought to advance socialism in the areas he governed. He was especially attracted to anarchism and earlier was associated with Shi Fu in various ways. Winston Hsieh, "The Ideas and Ideals of a Warlord: Ch'en Chiung-ming, 1878-1933," *Harvard Papers on China* 16 (1962): 198-252. One of Chen Jiongming's sons, Leslie H. Chen, is studying his father's career.

23. The major source for the discussion that follows is Ming K. Chan, "Labor and Empire: The Chinese Labor Movement in the Canton Delta, 1895-1927" (Ph.D. diss., Stanford University, 1975), chap. 1. I am also indebted to Diane Scherer, who is preparing a dissertation (University of Michigan) on the anarchist movement in Guangzhou during the 1920s. Her paper, "Organizing Anarchy in Canton: The Chinese Anarcho-Syndicalist Movement," presented at the 1990 Association for Asian Studies meeting, supplements Chan's study.

24. Chan, 44.

25. Ibid., 49. Chan notes the influence of the strike by the Hong Kong Seamen's Union against their British employers, and adds that some one hundred more strikes occurred throughout China during 1922, many of them against foreign-owned enterprises.

26. Ibid., 61-62.

27. Ibid., 55.

28. Ibid., 76-79. Cf. Harold Isaacs, *The Tragedy of the Chinese Revolution* (Stanford: Stanford University Press, 1951; repr., New York: Atheneum, 1966), 291.

29. Chan, 42.

30. Ibid., 50.

31. Diane Scherer has shown that *Laodongzhe* was primarily an anarchist, not Marxist, journal. A reprint edited by Sha Dongxun of the Guangzhou Academy of Social Sciences (Guangzhou: Guangdong renmin chubanshe, 1984) includes interviews and memoirs by Huang Lingshuang, Liang Bingxian, and Shi Xin (a younger brother of Shi Fu), all of whom emphasize that it was anarchist-communism they were propagating in *Laodongzhe*.

32. The estimate of the crowd's size is from *Min sheng*, no. 32 (1921), English section. Even if the number is halved, to allow for the editors' enthusiasm, it would still be 100,000. Zheng Peigang recalled seeing the portraits of Marx and Kropotkin, in his "Zheng Peigang de huiyi" (Reminiscences), in *WZZG*, 521.

33. Dirlik gives the title of Chen's lecture as "The Critique of Socialism." His discussion of the debate follows. Dirlik, *Origins*, 239.

34. *Guangzhou qun bao* began publication in October 1920 as a joint effort of the anarchists and Marxists. Ou was one of the anarchists involved, along with Liang Bingxian and Huang Lingshuang. Disagreements had developed by the spring of 1921, but cooperation continued for a time. Dirlik, *Origins*, 170, 212. This would explain why *Guangzhou qun bao* published the letters of both Ou and Chen. Both sides in the debate have been reprinted in Chen Duxiu, *Chen Duxiu shuxin ji* (Collected Correspondence of Chen Duxiu) (Beijing, 1987) (hereafter, *CSXJ*). Citations are from *CSXJ*, 330-368.

35. This edition of *Min sheng* was a supplement to no. 30. The editors prefaced Ou's material with a statement, "Wuzhengfuzhuyizhe duiyu tonglei yipai de zhenzheng taidu" (The Anarchists' True Attitude toward Different Factions in the Same Group).

36. It is not clear whether Chen's last response appeared immediately in *Guangzhou qun bao*, or whether he prepared it only for the special edition of *Xin qingnian*. His third reply to Ou began with the statement that he had seen Ou's latest offering in *Min sheng*.

37. *CSXJ*, 349.

38. See Scherer, 19-20, for Chen's concern about this point, and pp. 22-23 for an example of "syndicalism."

39. In reminiscences recorded in the 1960s, several of the anarchists recalled a meeting in the spring of 1921 where the issue of discipline was made specific, and they rejected "the dictatorship of the proletariat." *WZZG*, 509, 521, 526. Dirlik shows that the Communists were seeking to ensure organizational loyalty at this time. Willingness to accept "the dictatorship of the proletariat" was more important as an organizational principle than as a theoretical point. Dirlik, *Origins*, chap. 9.

40. On *Xue deng*, see *RG*, item 603. This supplement to the debate is entitled, "Da Chen Duxiu xiansheng de yiwen" (Questions In Reply to Mr. Chen Duxiu), and was reprinted in *WZZG*, 425-445.

41. Ibid., 444.

42. The time of Chen's return to Shanghai is noted in Lee Feigon, *Chen Duxiu: Founder of the Chinese Communist Party* (Princeton: Princeton University Press, 1983), 168.

43. As Dirlik and others have noted, Chen's response to the Bolshevik Revolution differed from Li Dazhao's. When Li decided that the revolution was significant, his response was largely emotional, but by the time Chen was ready to move ahead with party organization, Li was not certain it was time for that. By autumn 1920, the two were in agreement on the need to proceed with organization. Dirlik, *Origins*, 195-96, 209.

44. Both *RG*, item 519, and *WZZG*, 576, say *Huzhu yuekan* was published in Beijing. Another source, however, maintains that the journal was published in Shanghai. Ge Maochun et al., eds., *Wuzhengfuzhuyi sixiang ziliao xuan* (Selected Materials on Anarchist Thought) (Beijing: Beijing daxue chubanshe, 1984), 1080 (hereafter, *ZLX*). This is confirmed in Zheng's reminiscences in *WZZG*, 522. Perhaps the group involved wished to confuse the authorities.

45. "Wuren ershinian lai zhi chuanbopin," in *WZZG*, 456-461. *ZLX* (p. 971) identifies Zheng as "Ke lao." As a disciple, Zheng was so close to Shi Fu that he married one of the latter's sisters. He learned the printing trade while working on *Min sheng*, and produced many anarchist materials in Guangzhou and Shanghai during the 1920s.

46. "Laodong yundong," in *WZZG*, 453-56. *Annaqi* was often used as the transliteration for "anarchy," so this is the likely meaning of the pseudonym.

47. *WZZG*, 455.

48. "Wo suo xinyang de geming," in *WZZG*, 475-478. *Wuyi yuekan* was launched in 1922.

49. Ibid., 477.

50. Ibid., 478. This issue of *Wuyi yuekan* also included two articles in which the problem of the warlords was addressed. *WZZG*, pp. 468-75. One responded to comments that Chen Duxiu had made on the warlord problem. Both anarchists and Communists were painfully aware of warlord dominance. Warlord power was an important factor in the formation of the GMD-CCP alliance, which in turn adversely affected the anarchist movement.

51. *Xue hui* was a supplement to Beijing's *Guofeng ribao* (National Customs Daily) from late 1922 to the middle of 1923, and an important anarchist publication. *RG*, item 600. Thus, W's letter was widely circulated and presumably reflected problems of general concern to anarchists. The letter is reprinted in *WZZG*, 478-80.

52. Ibid., 480.

53. "Women muqian de wenti," in *WZZG*, 480-82. *Min zhong* began publication in Guangzhou in 1922, and was a major anarchist journal through the middle 1920s. Its importance and longevity--it lasted until mid-1927, relocating in Shanghai earlier that year--probably were due to the involvement of the veteran anarchists Liang Bingxian, Huang Lingshuang, and Ou Shengbai. It was probably one of these who wrote as "Kuli." See also *RG*, item 506.

54. *WZZG*, 481. Chen Muqin, also known as "Xiaowo" (Small Ego), organized several anarchist groups and journals in Chongqing and Chengdu, beginning in 1920. *ZLX*, 1010ff. Kuli identified Chen's article as "Annaqi geming zhi taolun" (A Discussion of the Anarchist Revolution), but did not indicate where it had been published.

55. *Minzhong* (The Masses) began publishing in Shanghai in 1925. Several of the people active on *Min zhong* (People's Bell) moved back and forth between Guangzhou and Shanghai fairly often during this period, and this proposal suggested a plan to divide the talent and produce two journals.

56. "Zhongguo wuzhengfu tuan gangling caoan," in *WZZG*, 483-88.

57. Ibid., 487.

58. Dirlik suggests, in the closing paragraphs of *Origins*, that the rethinking of history in progress in China since the late 1970s might result in recognition of the contributions that anarchist principles could make. At the moment, such recognition by the authorities seems unlikely.

10

Zenq Qi and the Frozen Revolution

Marilyn A. Levine

Writing to his son upon the death of his wife, less than a decade before his own demise, the founder of the Chinese Youth Party (CYP), Zeng Qi (1892-1951), lamented that in thirty years of marriage he had spent limited time with his family. There was no home-style felicity, no family, no self, but just striving for the benefit of the nation.[1] Full of bitter self-reproach, the passage also reflects a lifelong concern with personal destiny and national leadership. With some justification, he felt himself part of an incorruptible intellectual elite. Except under the extreme conditions of foreign invasion, neither the Communist Party (CCP) nor the Guomindang (GMD) could entice him into their ranks. In contrast with many Chinese politicians and reformers, who changed their agendas to include new strategies and fluid objectives, he held fast to his original vision of the CYP. It was this inflexible sense of destiny that provides the keenest insight into the true tragedy of Zeng and the CYP. While the ideology of the CYP was coherent and modern, in terms of Chinese revolutionary realpolitik, Zeng and his compatriots could not totally break with their heritage as intellectuals. Instead, they pursued a revolution which was frozen in the ethos of May Fourth youth activism.

This essay will explore a revolution caught between modern politics and the traditional role of the Chinese intellectual class. The first half will discuss the early commitment of Zeng to the revolution of youth. Resisting his own sympathy for the worker-students in France, he founded the CYP in 1923, as a response to the growing power of Communism within the Chinese community there. The second half will analyze the ideological bases of the CYP. Often labeled opportunists or fascists by their competitors, the CYP did in fact have a philosophy which reflected many of the same concerns as the French radical right. This coherent modern ideological platform etches in sharper relief the political incongruities between the desire for modern revolution and the limitations of the traditional intellectual role assumed by Zeng and his cohorts in the CYP.

Zeng Qi and the Formation of the CYP (1923)

Born in Luchang, Sichuan, in 1892, Zeng was part of the transitional generation which enjoyed both Confucian training and the new Western learning. His parents both died before he reached the end of his teenage years. Deciding on an independent course, he often supported himself through journalism.

Attending a Westernized high school in Chengdu, which included among its graduates Wang Guangqi and Li Jieren, he then matriculated at Zhendan (Aurora) University in Shanghai, where he met such lifelong political compatriots as Li Huang and Zuo Shunsheng. Zhendan University was run by French Jesuits, and while he later denounced Western missionaries in China, he obtained a basic grounding in advanced Western learning at the school.[2]

In 1916, he began a period of study overseas, which, with only one interlude, lasted for almost eight years. Like many Chinese high school and college graduates, he decided to study in Japan. Under increasing nationalistic pressure, however, he returned to China in 1918, where he helped to form the Young China Association (YCA). The proliferation of warlords and the threat of foreign imperialism were incentives for youth to organize during the New Culture Movement (NCM). Zeng was henceforth to see the whole future of China invested in his generation of youth:

> Those of the older generation over thirty, with their superficial knowledge of the New Learning, totally exert themselves attaining power on their own behalf (like those returned students who studied in the East and the West). Those of the older generation over fifty, with their corrupt old minds, are vehemently sworn to oppose world trends (like those who want to restore the legacy of the Qing dynasty).... Therefore, our generation of youth has no option but to rise up and make our own plans, to break away from the concept of dependency.[3]

The YCA, informally launched in 1918, was a vibrant part of the NCM. The major figures behind the organization were Zeng, Wang Guangqi, and a nucleus of Sichuan intellectuals, including Li Huang, Chen

Yusheng, and Zhou Taixuan. However, the group was also supported by prominent intellectuals from other regions, such as Li Dazhao (who was a founder).[4]

In an article published in the August 1919 issue of *Shaonian Zhongguo* (Young China), the goals of the YCA were discussed by Wang Guangqi. It was the harbinger of a cultural revolution in Chinese society which had to precede any serious political revolution. There was to be a new way of life for the development of a "Young China." First, "Young China" must be creative and not just imitate the past or the West. Second, "Young China" must exercise its social responsibilities and not just base itself on the family system. Mutual systems of support should be developed within society, with a broadening of relationships (for example, between intellectuals and workers). Third, "Young China" must adopt a scientific approach to all facets of reform, as expressed in the Association's motto: "Our association dedicates itself to Social Services under the guidance of the Scientific Spirit, in order to realize our ideal of creating a Young China."[5]

The YCA served as an important forum for intellectuals in their search for national salvation. With over one hundred members, it published journals in Beijing, Nanjing, and Shanghai. The journals dealt with issues, such as religious intrusion into Chinese education and the feminist movement, and discussed various theories, such as Marxism.

Another important dimension of the NCM was the Work-Study Movement (WSM), which sent over 1,600 Chinese youth to France between 1919 and 1921. The goal was to work in the undermanned French factories, so that the Chinese youth could study in French schools and obtain technical information to modernize their homeland.[6] Zeng was not part of the WSM, but since almost one-third of the YCA members traveled to France, he decided to follow his friends Li Huang and Zhou Taixuan. In fact, the advice of his friends and his desire to pursue overseas studies were included in his rationales for the sojourn in France, and, in contrast to many of the worker-students, he was quite clear that his going was "definitely not to uphold a narrow nationalism."[7]

He stayed in France from 1919 until 1924. He became an ardent journalist, writing under the pseudonym "Yu Gong" for *Xinwen bao* (The News), and contributing articles to *LüOu zhoukan* (Weekly Journal of Students in Europe) and *Shaonian Zhongguo* (Young China). While not a worker-student, he was interested in worker education and was definitely sympathetic to the increasing problems within the WSM. Showing some influence by the work-study scheme, he wrote an article in 1919 entitled, "What Do Today's Workers Need?" He claimed that the capitalists and politicians could oppress the Chinese people because the latter lacked knowledge. If the workers would read after their factory labor was through for the day, it would provide a basis for modernity from which nothing could detract.[8] As the WSM grew beyond manageable proportions during 1920 and 1921, he wrote of the misery of the worker-students and the inequities of the struggles they were enduring.[9]

He did not confine himself to writing about the WSM. Rather, he was concerned with defining an overall strategy for a Chinese cultural renaissance. This need for redefinition of Chinese culture in a modern context meant that he was concerned with exploring European civilization. Along with fellow YCA members Li Huang, Zhou Taixuan, He Luzhi, Li Jieren, Li Sichun, and others, he founded a Paris branch of the YCA, where they discussed issues of national salvation. In 1920, they published a special issue on France in *Shaonian Zhongguo*.[10] Zeng's article on French civilization was the most speculative and analytical in the special issue. One can glimpse the elements of his growing emphasis on national character and nationalist ideology. His characterization of national ideologies included perceptions which were widely held in the Chinese community. The Germans were motivated by the need for power (*shili zhuyi*), the British by the need for profit (*liyi zhuyi*), while the French were infused with the need for freedom, equality, and fraternity (*ziyou, pingdeng, boai zhuyi*). Building on mysticism and nationalism, the Germans had developed the military as a basis for power, while the British developed their patience and legal system in order to gain every advantage. The French, with their high principles and rationality, had developed emotionally and were spontaneous. With the implication of close affinities between French and Chinese culture planted in the reader's mind, Zeng claimed that the most important component of civilization was intellectual thought and that the French were the most intellectual of the Europeans.[11] This superiority arose, he conceded, in part because the geography of France was more advantageous to agriculture, and the struggle with nature therefore did not retard the development of their civilization. As fruits of that civilization, he noted the unique contributions of the *philosophes* and the elegance of the French language.[12]

His articles were widely read and--in addition to his prestige as a prominent member of the YCA, which was viewed as the most elite youth society[13]--he was also seen as an important youth leader, as evidenced by his activities during the Railroad Struggle of 1923. This controversy stemmed from the Lincheng Incident, when Chinese bandits robbed a train, kidnapped twenty-six foreigners, and demanded a huge ransom. Foreign opinion was outraged, and a call arose for foreign administration of Chinese railways.[14]

Upon hearing of the proposal for international control of China's railways, the Chinese in France called a meeting on 3 July.[15] It resulted in protests being directed to foreign consulates, the French newspapers, and their own consulate. During this struggle, twenty-two Chinese organizations formed the United Federation of Chinese Organizations in France (*Zhongguo luFa ge tuanti lianhehui*), and between five and six hundred Chinese attended a meeting on 15 July. YCA member He Luzhi presided over this large gathering. Although the assembly was called to organize a strategy for opposing the railroad consolidation scheme, many used it as a forum to espouse their ideas on national salvation. While Zhou Enlai's (1898-1976) hour-long speech has drawn the most scholarly attention, Zeng's speech was, in fact, more radical. He proposed to: (1) arouse public opinion; (2) stir up mass movements like the May Fourth Movement; (3) overthrow the corrupt government and institute fundamental reforms in order to restore the momentum of the 1911 Revolution that had been halted by rotten government; and (4) initiate an assassination movement. This last point was clearly the most important aspect of his plan. This speech was an important link with the radical-right platform of the CYP and was not inconsistent with radical-right philosophies espoused in Europe at that time.[16]

For Zeng, the railroad affair, which ended in successfully blocking foreign control of Chinese railways, was a first and last moment of organizational cooperation with the Communists, who had formed a European Branch of the Chinese Communist Youth Corps (ECYC) and Party (hereafter collectively referred to as ECCO) the year before. Zeng was elected a secretary of the United Federation, along with Zhou, and the finance committee included He Luzhi, an anti-Communist who served alongside the prominent Communist schoolteacher, Xu Teli. Communists occupied over one-third of the committee posts.[17]

In Zeng's lifetime, 1923 was a turning point. He began the year in illness, restlessly sitting in a sanitorium and outlining schemes in his diary for political activity. It took him an entire year to commit himself to forming the CYP. It was difficult for him to overcome his bias, encouraged by close friends like Wang Guangqi, that to become involved in political parties was a repudiation of the responsibility of the intellectual. However, there were both ideological and personal reasons why he founded the CYP.

First, with his relatively advanced understanding of Western philosophy and culture, he was able to appreciate the diversity of socialist theories. He understood that Lenin's form of Communism was not the only Marxist blueprint. In fact, he and his core of CYP followers--Li Huang, Hu Guowei, and He Luzhi--became devout anti-Communists and regarded the Communist International as an imperialistic arm of the Soviet Union.

Second, he became convinced that nationalism was the ideology to be promoted for the Chinese social revolution. The formation of a political party, led by an enthusiastic nucleus of leaders, was necessary to bring about a fundamental change in Chinese society.

Third, he was particularly dismayed by the increasing success of the ECCO and the growing leadership of Zhou Enlai. In his diary, he claimed that while Zhou, who was then general secretary of the ECYC, used "high-sounding phrases," he nevertheless was full of "a huge amount of empty talk."[18] It was this hostility to Zhou and the ECCO which brings to light the question of personal reasons behind Zeng's decision to form the CYP. It is ironic that one could argue that, in background and temperament, Zhou and Zeng were quite similar. Both were orphaned early, attended Western-oriented educational institutions, and had unfruitful sojourns to Japan; both returned to China for the May Fourth Movement and formed elite youth groups; both went to France *not* as worker-students (neither worked in the factories), but as journalists; both were concerned with practical and strategic issues, as opposed to reflecting on philosophical points; both kept control of their youth group leadership roles *after* they reached France; and both became increasingly popular within the Chinese community in France, as indicated by the railroad struggle. In fact, during the latter, they had to cooperate as co-secretaries of the protest committee. Finally, both had numerous personal contacts in common, such as Zhao Shiyan.

During 1923 and 1924, pressure was brought to bear on Zeng for reconciliation and unification, and several meetings were arranged in cafes between he and Zhou. Sometimes cordial and other times stormy, Zeng would not relent in his anti-Communist stance. Four issues divided the two men. First, as mentioned above, there were significant ideological differences, which should not be underestimated. Second, Zeng favored a regional cohort from Sichuan, while Zhou had broader regional contacts. This may have served as an underlying point of tension for Zeng, to whom issues of regional loyalty were important. Third, Zeng may have felt directly competitive with Zhou, precisely because they had so much in common. It is important not to overlook personal ambition and issues of power. Finally, one might look more deeply at the relationship between Zeng and the only member of the YCA to become a Communist in Europe, Zhao Shiyan (1901-1927). Zhao, a precocious and brilliant young man, was a protege of Zeng's, although almost ten years younger.[19] Zeng and others were not satisfied when Zhao insisted on keeping within the WSM, and offered to pay his college tuition. Not only was this offer refused, but Zhao became increasingly inclined towards Communism, and, in fact, without his organizational abilities, it is conceivable that the ECCO would not have been formed.[20] This organizational activity required a conscious break with Zeng, his former mentor. Li Huang recounted an extraordinary scene in which a weeping Zhao confided his organizational plans to Zeng in 1922.[21] One of the most important steps in Zhao's increasingly radical commitment was a study group organized by Zhang Shenfu, which Zhou also attended. It is not improbable that, from a personal perspective, Zeng felt animosity toward Zhou and the ECCO for this betrayal by his promising protege, in addition to his own antipathy towards Communism. Thus, it was a strong mixture of ideological and personal reasons that drove Zeng to overcome his scruples and follow through with the difficult decision to establish a political party.

The CYP and the Philosophy of the Radical Right

By the end of 1923, Zeng and his friends had created the CYP.[22] Cleansing the nation of internal factionalism, brought on by warlords, and protecting the nation against invasion by outside forces (*neiqu guozei, waikang qiangquan*) were essential goals of the new party. To accomplish them, the CYP formulated a program almost synonymous with the integral nationalism espoused by Maurice Barres. The CYP's platform called for the harmonious unity of all classes in pursuit of economic revitalization, as well as a cultural restoration of China's greatness as a civilization. Social reformation would be brought about by an informed society, which would be exposed to an intensive program of national education.[23]

Consciously defining nationalism with European terms, definitions, and examples, the philosopher of the CYP, Li Huang, explained in October 1924 that modern nationalism could only emerge in conflict with foreign pressures, and cited examples such as the 1870 Franco-Prussian War and the mobilization of nationalist forces brought on by the Alfred Dreyfus affair. Much of the essence of nationalism involved the territorial imperative, as well as the nation's spiritual soul. Thus, he defined "nationalism" as a "specific people, occupying a certain piece of land, protecting certain ownership rights." These rights evolved from the shared cultural legacy, as well as the common territorial borders. Mixing the ideas of Confucian filial piety and late nineteenth-century European nationalism, he asserted that it was the responsibility of the descendants of a nation to preserve it, in light of the sacrifices of earlier generations [24]

From 1923 until 1929, the CYP was a secret party and officially admitted only to being a youth corps. This subterfuge was deemed necessary for self-preservation until the situation in China became mature enough for revolution. However, this did not stop the CYP from aggressively pursuing its political activities.[25] Although Zeng and Li left Paris in September 1924, the political diatribes between the CYP and other groups continued. In addition to attacks and counterattacks in their rival newspapers, several members of the CYP and the ECCO also bought handguns, which they brandished at each other, and several instances of violence occurred at assemblies. Numbering over one hundred members in their first year, the

CYP had some notable successes, especially when the ECCO occupied the Chinese legation in Paris during the May Thirtieth Incident and the CYP provided the French police with the names of the ECCO members involved to be used in expulsion proceedings.[26] This resulted in ECCO leaders such as Ren Zhuoxuan, Lin Wei, Deng Xiaoping, and Fu Zhong leaving France.

One of the most damaging charges in the CYP quest for political power was the accusation by their opponents that they were "fascists." This charge was leveled at them as early as 1924 and not just by Communists. The fascist label, in the Chinese context of the early twenties, connoted warlord linkages, violent methods, and aspirations to dictatorship. As proof of the CYP's fascist leanings, the ECCO asserted that the CYP was cooperating with warlords.[27] Epithets such as "running dogs of the warlords" and mentions of warlord connections peppered many of the ECCO anti-CYP critiques.[28] As late as 1930, the journal *Chiguang* (The Red Light) was still discussing these contacts, accusing the CYP of becoming tools of Wu Peifu.[29]

A more sophisticated critique was offered by the Paris branch of the Chinese Social Democrats, who argued that the ideology of nationalism, especially the territorial nature of the CYP definition (culled from the *Nouvelle Larousse Dictionnaire*), was one whose highest development resulted in militarism and imperialism, hence fascism.[30] The Social Democrats also, however, emphasized the warlord connections of the CYP.[31]

Zeng Qi initially provided fuel for this fascist appellation by praising Mussolini in a poem and declaring his admiration for the way Italian youth had recently revived their state.[32] Although Zeng felt personally maligned by these attacks, which in May 1927 he termed slander,[33] the example of the efficiency and unity of the Italian fascist state was still cited in party propaganda. However, a 1930 CYP manifesto distanced the Party from fascism in declaring that "the Young China Party is not ashamed to profess that in the love of their motherland, nationalism and fascism do stand on common ground, but the nationalist stands for democracy, while the fascist stands for dictatorship."[34] The taint of fascism and the perception of warlord connections were major factors in undermining support for the CYP.

The issue of fascism in China has been discussed in studies of the GMD, such as William Kirby's work on the relations between China and Germany and Lloyd Eastman's, on the Blue Shirts.[35] Authoritarianism and its place within Chinese tradition and Communist centralized control has also been extensively discussed.[36] However, the CYP never attained any semblance of political control of the nation, and it would be speculative to conjecture about its authoritarian proclivities. Nevertheless, the ideological perspective, organizational ethos, and CYP programs were identical with many central points of European radical-right groups and, in particular, French fascism.

First, the reliance upon youth in the spiritual battle against Communist materialism and for the restoration of national greatness were important elements of the CYP philosophy and agenda, as symbolized by its retention of the word "youth" in the Party name. It also was articulated in its platform: "It falls upon our generation of youth to rise up in a flesh-and-blood struggle with the dark forces,..."[37] The platform further stated that the Chinese people only needed the spirit of youth, the will, the confidence, and a national consciousness to overcome the warlords and deal with foreign imperialism. According to Zeev Sternhell, these orientations were also prevalent in French fascism:

> This dimension of fascism was of great importance. All the revolutionaries--the pure fascists, such as Drieu and Brasillach, who described themselves as such, and fascists like Maulnier, Jouvenel, and Deat, who shrank from the appellation--were agreed on this point: fascism was a revolt against materialism, a revolt of the spirit, the will, the instincts; it was a revolt of youth.[38]

An important rationale of this spiritual, as opposed to materialist, revolution was a regeneration of Chinese culture. It is an interesting contrast that when the ECCO formed their youth branch in mid-1922, they held three days of meetings, with intense argument and genuine debate, whereas the founding meeting of the CYP affirmed a prediscussed platform and structure and was celebrated with traditional Chinese opera songs and classical recitation. Not unnaturally, many of the nationalist writings included arguments from traditional Chinese philosophers. Likewise, according to George L. Mosse, European fascists equated the spiritual nature of the fascist revolution with a cultural resurgence.[39] For the CYP, the cultural restoration meant a strengthening of national social bonds. A common heritage meant a common destiny.

Second, the ideas of nationalism, economic autonomy, and class harmony, as opposed to class struggle, were distinct features of the fascist agenda. One of Zeng's seminal articles, published in October 1924, was entitled, "A Discussion of Central Ideas and Leadership," in which he claimed that a specific political agenda, based on the ideology of nationalism, could unify the country. Guided by new leaders, in particular youth, China could both adopt Western ideas and make significant contributions to the culture of the world, if it were to adopt a centralized nationalism and leadership. A purifying revolution could recapture the greatness of Chinese traditions, and because it included the modern ideology of nationalism, both social and economic inequalities could also be rectified for all classes.[40] As Chen Qitian wrote in 1930, the CYP "does not advocate individualism, clan ideology, tribal ideology, or class ideology but nationalism." The nationalism of the CYP was to enter all levels of society.[41]

The unifying power of nationalism as the fundamental of modern ideology, the emphasis on creating a structure of national economic autonomy, the opposition to a revolution by the proletariat counterpoised by belief in the concept of class harmony and national unity, and the need for a central leadership all were elements espoused by the "Prince of Youth," Maurice Barres, and later fascist ideologues, such as Georges Valois and Marcel Deat.[42]

Third, resolute anti-Communism also was a strong feature of both CYP and French fascists. As Soucy remarks, "Indeed, French fascist writings sometimes leave the impression that all else was secondary to one primary goal: to mobilize France against communism at home and abroad."[43] The CYP targeted the Communists as the worst enemies of the modern national revolution. Certainly, their most vehement activities and perhaps most efficacious historical legacy was their active fight in the European arena against the ECCO. As mentioned above, they contributed directly to the expulsions of 1925.

Fourth, the CYP tactical program, such as the advocacy of mass mobilization, the control of public opinion, and the use of violence all reflected methods also espoused by fascist ideologues. That violence was seen as a necessity of the times can be seen from contemporary CYP writings, as well as memoirs. For example, Hu Guowei, who was in charge of CYP "training" in the use of weapons, asserted that target practice was necessary to deal with Communists and for guerrilla training when they returned to China.[44] In a passionate public letter written during the furor of the May Thirtieth Incident, Deng Xiaoqing, a CYP member, argued for the necessity of military organization to fight against foreign encroachment.[45]

Fifth, the ethos of the group and the sense of personal loyalties outweighing ideological loyalties was a strong component of the CYP. This loyalty was exemplified by the uncontested leadership of the Party by Zeng until his death in 1951. This was closest to the *espirt de corps* of the French fascists, who were also similar in their advocacy of an elite group, rather than the German and Italian emphasis on one leader. The CYP was adamantly opposed to dictatorship and would have agreed with the sentiments of Drieu La Rochelle: "There is an appalling weakness in men who give themselves to another man. When there is a dictator, there is no longer an elite; it means that the elite is no longer doing its duty."[46] Zeng would have further argued that dictatorship preempts democracy.

However, within the Chinese context, elite meant intellectual leadership by the "central leaders" Zeng advocated head the revolution.

Lastly, two contrasting features in the outlooks of the CYP and the European fascists should be noted. First, the CYP lacked a racial basis of discrimination against foreigners. Their denunciation of foreign encroachment into China had a basis in reality and was not the political tactic of finding a scapegoat. Second, there is little evidence to indicate that they were anti-parliamentarian or anti-democratic, a feature of most fascist groups. However, given their traditional stance of personal and group loyalty, it is not clear whether Zeng would have appreciated Western-style pluralism.

Although they never had the opportunity to obtain governmental control, the ideological platform of the CYP stood for a clear alternative in Chinese politics during the Republican period. In a broader context, their philosophy--which emphasized nationalism, the purity of youth, strong anti-Communism, a nucleus of leaders to preside over a cultural renaissance, and a program of economic autonomy--put them in the mainstream of world politics.

Zeng Qi and the Responsibility of the Intellectual

The case of Zeng and the CYP is important because it raises the generic question of cultural transference in the realm of politics. On the one hand, the CYP political ideology was in tune with the world trend of an upsurge in radical-right politics. In this regard, Zeng was not close to the opportunism of Jacques Doriot--who changed from an avid Communist leader to the organizer of a fascist party--but rather to the integral nationalism of Maurice Barres. On the other hand, the Western concept of the political party was particularly difficult for Chinese intellectuals to adopt as a career role. It was pedagogy, not politics, that was the traditional role of the Chinese leadership. The realms of morality and education were above the narrow confines of political ambition and were seen by many Chinese intellectuals as the key to true change. Although Zeng and the CYP advocated a modern political ideology and formed a modern political party, they could not totally break with the traditions of the Chinese intellectual heritage. This is important, because it limited their practical involvement in revolutionary tactics.

The campaigns against the ECCO by the CYP were effective, to some degree, in diminishing the positive response to the ECCO among young Chinese intellectuals. They provided a real ideological alternative and an active, feisty political leadership. Yet, the CYP was in many ways a feeble shadow in the cataclysmic Chinese political environment. With the escalation of violence, foreign invasion, and civil war, there was no opportunity for a revolution based on a nationalist ideology which sought to harmonize classes and promote economic autonomy and national education. Events moved too quickly to allow consolidation of power in the hands of an intellectual leadership. Ironically, in terms of the Chinese generational revolt during the early 1920s, the CYP contained some of the most astute and well-informed patriots. The paradox was that by aspiring to a cultural restoration, the CYP *de facto* exemplified the political restraints of the traditional intellectual role, which precluded any chance to obtain power to implement their modern reformation of the Chinese state. Because their ideological horizons were rooted in the past, they became frozen in time. While they were walking to the revolution, the revolution ran right by them.

Notes

1. Zeng Qi, *Zeng Muhan xiansheng yizhu* (The Posthumous Works of Mr. Zeng Qi), in *Jindai Zhongguo shiliao congkan* (Collected Materials on Modern Chinese History), ed. Shen Yunlong, vol. 68 (Taibei: Wenhai chubanshe, n.d.), *Jiaxun* (Family Lessons), 287 (hereafter, *Yizhu*). He was not only a prolific journalist, but also an ardent diarist. See vol. 94 in the same series: *Zeng Muhan xiansheng riji xuan* (Selections From Mr. Zeng Qi's Diary) (hereafter, *Riji xuan*). The July 1976 issue of *Zhuanji wenxue* (Biographical Literature) contains several articles commemorating him.

2. Ruth Hayhoe, "Towards the Forging of a Chinese University Ethos: Zhendan and Fudan, 1903-1919," *China Quarterly*, no. 94 (1983): 323-341.

3. Zeng Qi, "Xuehui wenti zatan" (A Random Discussion of the Association's Problems), *Shaonian Zhongguo* 3, no. 8 (1922): 76-80.

4. Zhou Taixuan, "Guanyu canjia faqi Shaonian Zhongguo Xuehui de huiyi" (Recollections of Participating in the Founding of the Young China Association), in Zhang Yunhou, Yan Xuyi, Hong Qingxiang, and Wang Yunkai, comps., *Wusi shiqi de shetuan* (The Organizations of the May Fourth Period), 4 vols. (Beijing: Sanlian, 1979), 1:536-49.

5. Wang Guangqi, "Shaonian Zhongguo zhi chuangzao" (The Creation of the Young China [Association]) *Shaonian Zhongguo* 1, no. 2 (1919): 1-7. As if to emphasize his seriousness, Wang concludes with an English-language quotation.

6. For a review of materials on the WSM, see Marilyn A. Levine, "ECCO Studies: Overview of an Emerging Field," *Republican China* 13 (April 1988): 4-23. There are several other essays on ECCO in this special issue. For another recent article on the WSM, see Paul Bailey, "The Chinese Work-Study Movement in France," *China Quarterly*, no. 115 (1988): 441-461. A catalogue of holdings at the Archives Nationales has been prepared by Genevieve Barman and Nicole Dulioust, *Etudiants-ouvriers chinois en France, 1920-1940* (Chinese Student-Workers in France, 1920-1940) (Paris: Editions de l'Ecole des Hautes Etudes en Sciences Sociales, 1981). There also are several useful Chinese compendia: Qinghua daxue zhonggong dangshi jiaoyu shi

(Qinghua University Faculty Research Unit on the History of the Chinese Communist Party), comp, *Fu Fa qingong jianxue yundong shiliao* (Historical Materials on the Travel-to-France Work-Study Movement), 3 vols. (Beijing: Beijing chubanshe, 1979) (hereafter, *FFSL*); Zhang Yunhou, Yan Xuyi, and Li Junchen, comps., *Liu Fa qingong jianxue yundong* (The Work-Study Movement in France), 2 vols. (Shanghai: Shanghai renmin chubanshe, 1980, 1985); and Chen Sanjing, comp., *Qingong jianxue yundong* (The Work-Study Movement) (Taibei: Zhengzhong shuju, 1981).

7. Zeng Qi, "Liubie Shaonian Zhongguo Xuehui tongren zhehui fu Fa de yuanyin" (A Farewell Explanation on Going to France for Compatriots of the Young China Association), *Shaonian Zhongguo* 1, no. 3 (1919): 50-51.

8. Yu Gong [Zeng Qi], "Jinri gongren suo xuyao de shi shemma?" (What Do Today's Workers Need?), *LüOu zhoukan* 4 (6 December 1919): 1.

9. This series of articles, published originally in *Xinwen bao*, are reproduced in *FFSL*, vol. 1. Interestingly, although sympathetic to the WSM, these articles are published in small print in appendices.

10. This special issue, published in October 1920, included an array of interviews, articles, and translations. Li Huang wrote overviews of French social studies and literature, as well as a report on an interview with the artist, Charles Albert. He Luzhi penned a short biography of Jean Jaures and translated a story by Guy de Maupassant. Zhou Taixuan gave a lengthy survey of French literature and translated poetry. Li Jieren's article on the Louvre included descriptions of the various *salles* and pictures of art objects. Duan Zibian explored the work of the French mathematician, Gaston Darboux, and Hua Lin reviewed the fine arts. There was an article by Hu Zhu on living in Montargis with a French family, while Li Sichun also described scenes from Montargis, in his reflections on French civilization.

11. Zeng Qi, "Falanxi wenming tedian de yibian" (A Discussion of the Special Features of French Civilization), *Shaonian Zhongguo* 2, no. 4 (1920): 65-66.

12. Ibid., 67-70.

13. Writing to Mao Zedong on 13 August 1920, the New People's Study Society leader, Cai Hesen, mentioned that he had spoken to members of many of the other Chinese organizations in France. He linked a discussion with Zeng Qi with a characterization of "the more elite youth" [*gaoming yidian qingnian*], and reported: "I spoke in depth with Zeng Muhan about this intention [of creating a Communist Party in France], and we were both very moved. I dare predict it will not be long before this exerts an influence on the members of the Young China Association,... It seems as if a Chinese Communist Party will be established in this place under a new, fresh banner." *Cai Hesen wenji* (The Collected Writings of Cai Hesen) (Beijing: Renmin chubanshe, 1980), 52.

14. *FFSL*, 2:789-92.

15. Zeng Qi, "LüFa Huaren fandui liechiang gongguan Zhongguo tielu jishi" (An Account of the Spirited Opposition of the Chinese in France to the Public Consolidation of Chinese Railroads), *Shaonian Zhongguo* 4, no. 8 (1923), in *FFSL*, 2:759-773.

16. Ibid., 766-67.

17. Ibid., 771.

18. 5 July 1923 entry in Zeng, *Riji xuan*, 55.

19. It is probable that Zeng was one of those who introduced Zhao to the YCA. This is difficult to prove, because Zhao's entry was not announced in either *Shaonian Zhongguo* or *Shaonian shijie* (World of Youth). Zhao was one of the youngest members of the Association, but had proved his mettle by serving as the May Fourth Movement representative from his high school and concurrently publishing three newspapers during 1919.

20. Zheng Chaolin, interview by author, Shanghai, 25 October 1985; Sheng Cheng, interviews by author, Beijing, 12 and 18 October 1985. See also the numerous memoirs of Zhao in *Zhongguo shehui kexueyuan xiandaishi yanjiushi* (Institute of Modern History, Chinese Academy of Social Sciences), comp., *Yida qianhou* (Before and After the Founding of the CCP), vol. 2 (Beijing: Renmin chubanshe, 1980).

21. Li Huang, "Xuedun shi huiyilu" (Memoirs of the *Xuedun* Chamber), *Zhuanji wenxue* 17 (July 1970): 9-10.

22. For a partial history of the CYP, see Chan Lau Kit-ching, *The Chinese Youth Party, 1923-1945*, Centre for Asian Studies Occasional Papers and Monographs no. 9 (Hong Kong: University of Hong Kong, 1972). Two useful memoirs by CYP members are Hu Guowei, *Bali xinying* (Impressions of Paris), 2nd ed. (Taibei: Puti chubanshe, 1970) and Li Huang, *Xuedun shi huiyilu*, which was published in serial form in *Zhuanji wenxue* in 1970 and in book form by the same publishers in 1978.

23. For several CYP platforms and memoirs, see *Zhongguo qingnian dang dangshi ziliao* (Materials on the History of the Chinese Youth Party) (Taibei: Minzhu qiaoshe, 1955). The CYP proposals parallel much of Barres' final political platform. Robert Soucy, in his insightful study of Barres, details several political programs of this important French fascist. See his *Fascism in France: The Case of Maurice Barres* (Berkeley: University of California Press, 1972).

24. Li Huang, "Shi Guojiazhuyi" (An Explanation of Nationalism), in *Guojiazhuyi lunwen ji* (Collected Writings on Nationalism), comp. Shen Yunlong (Taibei: Wenhai Chunban she, n.d.), 971: 1.

25. See "Zhongguo qingnian dang gongkai dangming zhuanhao" (Special Issue Making Public the Name of the Chinese Youth Party), *Xiansheng zhoubao* (The Pioneer Weekly) (Paris), no. 311. In reality, this secrecy did not deceive anyone, and although it was often referred to as the Nationalist Clique--or more often, by its opponents, with epithets like "running dogs"--one finds numerous references to it as the CYP.

26. Nora Wang, "Da Chen Lu le mouvement du 30 mai 1925 a paris" (Down with Da Lu: The May Thirtieth Movement in Paris), *Approches asie*, Nouvelle Serie 2, no. 7 (1983): 1-33; Wang Yongxiang and Kong Fanfeng, "Zhonggong lüOu zhibu fandui Guojiazhuyi pai de douzheng" (The Struggle of the Chinese Communists in Europe Against the Nationalist Clique), *Zhongguo xiandaishi fuyin baokan ziliao* (Reprinted Press Materials for Contemporary Chinese History), no. 3 (March 1982): 11-18.

27. Scholars in both the Republic of China and Hong Kong are beginning to conclude that the CYP was supported by warlords. For example, Chen Zhengmang, who is writing a history of the party, has found proof that Zeng Qi and Li Huang were directly linked with Zhang Zuolin and that fellow CYP members had connections with other warlords. Interview by author, Taibei, 10 July 1990.

28. Several of these ECCO articles, including some of the earliest writings of Deng Xiaoping, have been published in *FFSL*. For example, see Wu Hao [Zhou Enlai], "Shihua de fangan" (Anti-Truth), *Chiguang* 3 (May 1924): 265-66; Xi Xian [Deng Xiaoping], "Qing kan 'xiansheng' zhoubao zhi disipi zaoyao de xinwen" (Please See the Fourth Bunch of Lies about the News in the "Pioneer" Weekly), *Chiguang* 3 (January 1925): 273-74.

29. Zhao Ming, "Guojiazhuyizhe guqin xuejiao 'geming'" (The Touted "Revolution" of the Nationalists), *Chiguang* 55 (1930): 15-16. It should be noted that the CYP was also criticized by the GMD Right for their warlord connections throughout the decade.

30. Bi Yinglin, "'Ou' pian buying zuo er youtuo neng buzuo de wenzhang" (An Essay of "Criticism" Which Should not be Written, But Which Must be Written), *Fendou* (Struggle), no. 30 (1926): 8-16.

31. See, for example, "Guojiazhuyizhe zitao meiqu" (The Lack of Interest in the Self-Analysis of the Nationalist [Clique]), *Fendou*, no. 37 (1926): 4-5; "Jizhang (!?) sanzhi de shili" (The Power of Several Essays!?), *Fendou*, no. 30 (1926): 16.

32. See the original declaration of the CYP (n. 25 above), as well as that in *Xingshi zhoubao* (The Awakened Lion Weekly) 1, no. 1 (1924): 1-2. Numerous articles on nationalism by CYP members praised the unification of Germany and often linked the example of the Young Italians with that of the Young Turks (see, e.g., n. 24). In 1983, the Central Party Section of the CYP in Taiwan published a two-volume reprint edition of *Xingshi zhoubao*.

33. Zeng Qi, "Gongchandang pumie guojiazhuyizhe zhi zelue" (The Plot by the Chinese Communist Party to Destroy the Nationalists), in Zeng, *Yizhu*, 90-91.

34. "The Nationalist Movement and the Young China Party," 10 October 1930, English-language pamphlet, in the Archives Nationales Section d'Outre-Mer, Service de Liaison avec des Originaires des Territores de la France Outre-Mer, Carton V, Dossier 43.

35. See William C. Kirby, *Germany and Republican China* (Stanford: Stanford University Press, 1984), particularly chap. 6: "Frugality, Fascism, and 'New Life'." Lloyd Eastman's article, "The Rise and Fall of the 'Blue Shirts': A Review Article," *Republican China* 13 (November 1987): 25-48, poses a salient question on the difference between fascist ideology and action when he asks "whether a group employing fascist methods for their 'mobilizing and control capabilities' was any less fascistic because it advocated the Three People's Principles than if it advocated the racism of *Das Volk* or the imperial principle of *kokutai*."

36. See, for example, the assertions in Ping-ti Ho, "Salient Aspects of China's Heritage," in *China in Crisis: China's Heritage and the Communist Political System*, eds. Ping-ti Ho and Tang Tsou (Chicago: University of Chicago Press, 1968): 1:1-37.

37. "Zhongguo qingnian dang jiandang xuanyan" (The Founding Manifesto of the Chinese Youth Party), in Zeng, *Yizhu*, 51-52.

38. Zeev Sternhell, *Neither Right nor Left: Fascist Ideology in France*, trans. David Maisel (Berkeley: University of California Press, 1986), 248. Most other studies of fascism in Europe also point to youth; for example, the importance of a youth cohort in the rise of Hitler is explored by Peter Loewenberg, "The Psychohistorical Origins of the Nazi Youth Cohort," in his *Decoding the Past: The Psychohistorical Approach* (New

York: Alfred A. Knopf, 1983), 240-83. A general study of the crisis of youth brought on by twentieth-century modernity is Robert Wohl, *The Generation of 1914* (Cambridge: Harvard University Press, 1979).

39. George L. Mosse, "Introduction: The Genesis of Fascism," *Journal of Contemporary History*, no. 1 (1966): 19-20.

40. Zeng Qi, "Lun zhongxin sixiang yu zhongxin renwu" (A Discussion of Central Thought and Central Leadership), in Zeng, *Yizhu*, 62-73.

41. Chen Qitian, "Chuangzao zhong de Zhongguo qingnian dang" (The Chinese Youth Party in the Process of Creation), *Xiansheng zhoubao*, no. 318 (1930): 1.

42. Soucy, chap. 7; Sternhell, chaps. 1, 5.

43. Robert J. Soucy, "The Nature of Fascism in France," *Journal of Contemporary History* 1, no. 1 (1966): 35.

44. Hu Guowei, 24-25.

45. Teng Hiao-King, "Lettre a M. Li Hoang," *La Chine*, 11-12, in Archives du Ministere des Affaires Etrangeres, Asie Serie E Chine 492. There is a fascinating passage where Deng quotes the eloquent German nationalist Johann Gottlieb Fichte (1762-1814) on the necessity for discipline and order.

46. Soucy, "The Nature of Fascism in France," 47.

11

The Alternative of Loyal Opposition: The Chinese Youth Party and Chinese Democracy, 1937-1949

Edmund S.K. Fung

For more than a decade before the fall of the Nationalists in 1949, there was an opposition that consistently rejected the idea of one-party rule and advocated the establishment of a multiparty system, but cooperated with the Guomindang (GMD) to bring about political reform. I call it "loyal opposition," a term which describes the Chinese Youth Party (CYP), a minor political party, yet the largest after the GMD and the Chinese Communist Party (CCP) in the 1930s and 1940s (a claim made on the basis of its membership and its representation on the People's Political Council [PPC], at the Political Consultative Conference [PCC], and in the reorganized National Government [NG] of 1947).[1] The CYP opposed the GMD dictatorship, as well as communism, and demanded an immediate end to political tutelage and a beginning of constitutional rule. Standing for nationalism and democracy, it spurned a violent revolution that could result in another form of dictatorship.

Loyal opposition was distinguished from other types of opposition to the GMD leadership--such as warlord revolts, intraparty strife, student and

---

This article is reprinted, with minor changes, from *Modern China* 17 (April 1991): 260-89, by permission of Sage Publications, Inc., which holds the copyright.

intellectual dissent, and the revolutionary challenge of the CCP--in that it provided a framework for cooperation with the ruling party. For the CYP, it opened up the possibility of changing the political system by working within it. It was an alternative to class war and armed struggle when Chinese life was steeped in violence and revolution and the minor parties were unable to compete for power with the two major parties. It was both organized and unorganized: organized in the sense that political action was taken, and unorganized in that it did not seek either to replace the government in the short or medium term or challenge the right of the GMD to exercise political authority, provided there was a real role for the minor parties in the political processes. Because of its limited political clout, the CYP itself is not a very important subject for scholarly pursuit. But it raises broader issues about democracy in China. These include: What was the CYP's conception of democracy? What did democracy in China entail? Was democracy suitable, practicable, and a viable alternative to party dictatorship? If so, where and how should it all start? And finally, why did it fail? Not only are these questions of historical interest, they could be asked about China today.

The political thought of the CYP is remarkably interesting. It represented a minority view in that it departed, in important respects, from the dominant tradition of Chinese democratic thought. Although not all that the CYP expounded was brilliant, as a body of ideas the political views of this minor party reflected an important trend of thought in modern China--that, since the 1920s, there had been a movement, however ineffectual it may have been, among a significant section of the intelligentsia for political pluralism, for a competitive party system, and for the guarantee and protection of the same basic rights and freedoms that radical democracy activists in the late 1970s and throughout the 1980s would demand of the Communist government. Long before the present generation of advocates of democracy sought to challenge the CCP dictatorship without seeking to overthrow the Party or the government, the leaders of the CYP challenged the GMD dictatorship within the framework of loyal opposition. In short, the democractic movement in Republican China is relevant to the democracy movement in China today.

This essay explores the idea and practice of loyal opposition during the period 1937-1949, focusing on the CYP's conception of democracy and the ways in which it attempted to achieve constitutional reform. It is argued that the CYP's was the voice of liberal democracy, aired during a time of foreign aggression and civil strife--a time when many Chinese intellectuals favored benevolent dictatorship or enlightened despotism as a solution to China's ills--and expressed in the face of a political culture that had always been authoritarian. For the CYP, democracy was both good and practicable in China, and deserved to be given a second chance, despite the failure of the early Republic. It was both an end in itself and a means of achieving good government and preventing violent revolution. Finally, this essay seeks to explain the CYP's failure to achieve its objectives, as well as the larger failure of democracy in Nationalist China.

The Background to CYP-GMD Cooperation

The CYP was formed in December 1923 in Paris by a group of patriotic Chinese students who had been members of Beijing's Young China Association (YCA; founded in 1918) and who did not wish to be associated with either the GMD or the CCP, which were in the process of forming a united front (UF).[2] From the outset, it was staunchly anti-communist and attacked the GMD leadership for cooperating with the fledgling CCP. It saw itself as a third force (TF) aimed at "internally eliminating the national robber [meaning the Communists] and externally resisting the foreign powers" (*neiqu guozei waikang qiangquan*), as well as achieving China's freedom and national independence and building a nation for the well-being of all its people.[3]

Early in 1924, its founders, Zeng Qi and Li Huang, returned to China to set up a headquarters in Shanghai, where they launched a magazine entitled *Xingshi zhoubao (The Awakened Lion Weekly)*, which would carry articles on nationalism, education, national construction, and the like. Subsequently, a number of patriotic youth organizations were formed in various provinces and cities.[4] In the summer of 1926, the party held its First National Congress in Shanghai, with thirty delegates from various branches. A seven-man Central Executive Committee (CEC), headed by Zeng, was also set up.[5] Until 1929, however, the CYP remained an underground organization with its Youth Corps acting as a front.

The CYP leadership consisted of half a dozen or more scholars and educationalists; none were eminent figures in the history of modern China. They made a living by teaching at universities or as writers and editors, and came together in academic and educational circles. Their writings show that they were aware of the need to mobilize popular support and tackle the socioeconomic problems facing the masses. In practice, they were incapable of addressing those problems, and recruited members largely from the educated class--professors, scholars, writers, journalists, university and college students, engineers, accountants, bankers, industrialists, and public servants. There were also army officers and military students,[6] but not enough to produce an organized militancy that might have turned it into a power-broker. The numbers of peasants and workers in the organization were infinitesimal, too, reflecting weak links with the masses. Nor were there many merchants and businessmen--evidence of a failure to tap the classes and social groups that might entertain liberal, democratic ideas.

The CYP opposed communism, not only because it was perceived to be an international movement directed by Moscow, but also because it was undemocratic in its insistence on one-party rule and the dictatorship of the proletariat. It was further argued that China was predominantly an agrarian society in which there were no capitalists as a class, and therefore lacked the conditions necessary for a socialist revolution. What China needed was not communism but economic growth through class cooperation.[7] Like the GMD, the CYP feared unbridled capitalism, the evils of which it sought to avoid by nationalizing important aspects of China's economy and regulating capital.[8]

The CYP regarded itself as a more committed champion of Chinese nationalism than the GMD. Party leader Zeng defined nationalism in the context of a China confronted with the overriding problem of national survival and security. For him, nationalism meant patriotism; love for and devotion to the nation; a shared spirit on the part of the people, especially when oppressed; and a movement to resist foreign encroachments. It meant also national independence and freedom and the building of a modern nation-state.[9] This strong emphasis on nationalism resulted in the party sometimes being known as the Nationalist Faction.

Marilyn Levine has suggested that CYP leaders manifested some "fascist" traits in their ideological perspective, organizational ethos, and party programs, because of their emphasis on nationalism, anti-communism, mass mobilization, and personal loyalties, as well as their contacts with warlords. Yet, she concedes that they "lacked a racial basis of discrimination against foreigners" and that "there is little evidence to indicate that they were anti-parliamentarian or anti-democratic, a genuine feature of most fascist groups."[10] There may have been admiration for the achievements of Germany and Italy and some early flirtation with fascist ideas at a time of competing ideologies, but the CYP leadership never abandoned its commitment to parliamentary democracy. It was this commitment that provided the theoretical underpinning of the Chinese Youth movement.

The Nationalists' rise to power in 1928 and the inauguration of a period of political tutelage presented the CYP with the options of either disbanding and joining the ruling party on the common grounds of nationalism and anti-communism or facing Nationalist repression. The first option, actually offered by Chiang Kai-shek, was rejected because of the GMD's insistence on one-party rule.[11] The CYP leadership saw no difference between the GMD's promises of constitutional government and those made by the Qing dynasty almost twenty years before. Unless one-party rule was abandoned, it warned, the GMD would soon become degenerate (*fuhua*) and misrule would follow, thereby giving rise to popular discontent.[12] The GMD's response was to outlaw the CYP, sending Zeng and others fleeing to provinces controlled by warlord forces opposed to Chiang.

This hostile relationship persisted until the Manchurian crisis in late 1931, when the CYP declared itself ready to support the government, provided the latter decided to fight the Japanese. But the issue of one-party rule remained unresolved. In December, Zeng wrote an article stating his party's position on Japanese aggression. Echoing the sentiments of patriotic students, he urged resistance and national unity. But he added that the prerequisite to national unity was the dismantling of the single-party system. While one-party rule might be a necessary expedient under some circumstances, even if China needed a period of political tutelage, he argued, the Nationalists' monopoly on power must still be justified on the basis of their achievements since coming to power. What were their achievements? To him, the Nanjing government's record was a bad one. Internally, there was nothing to be proud of. Taxes were multifarious and exorbitant, and civil wars incessant. Externally, the much-publicized movement for the abrogation of the unequal treaties had been lackluster. The recovery of tariff autonomy was more apparent than real, while the vexed question of extraterritoriality remained unsettled. The armed clash with Soviet Russia in 1929 was a disaster, and there had been troubles with Japan long before the Manchurian crisis. His point was that one-party rule had been of little benefit to China and must therefore be brought to an end. Its termination, he went on, would help to unite the people behind the government at a time of national crisis. Since the people had lost faith in the government, the ruling party alone would be unable to mobilize popular support for its war effort, and this was precisely where other parties and organizations could make significant contributions to the state. He, however, excluded the Communists from any UF that might be formed at once, and was adamant that the CCP was seeking to promote the interests of international communism rather than those of China.[13]

He further argued that single-party systems should have a capacity for political liberalization. In particular, he drew attention to Mustafa Kemal Ataturk's rule in modern Turkey and its achievements. Although Kemal had been authoritarian at the beginning, he later attempted to establish a Western parliamentary system, and yet he did not lose control of the government because an opposition had been institutionalized.[14] Zeng saw no reason why the Nationalists should not follow the Turkish model by encouraging a responsible opposition that would impose efficiency and accountability on the government.[15] His high regard for Kemal reflected his party's admiration for the Young Turks movement, which had been instrumental in making modern Turkey such a success, and which apparently was a source of inspiration for the Chinese Youth movement.[16] If the sick man of the Near East could transform himself into a strong man, why could not the sick man of the Far East do the same?

He was not arguing for benevolent dictatorship. What he was advocating was an immediate change to multiparty rule in China, for he believed in the possibility of an authoritarian regime reforming itself. Was there a Chinese Kemal? Could Chiang Kai-shek be the one? He did not raise such questions in his article. But he considered a multiparty system to be feasible in China, if only the Nationalist leadership gave it a chance. Moreover, the fact that China was in the midst of a national crisis made it all the more important that the interests of the ruling party be subordinated to those of the state. His idea was that the interests of the state would be better served by a democratic system in which the CYP would be the opposition party, without wishing in the short or medium term to replace the government.[17] He acknowledged the weakness of his party vis-a-vis the GMD.

But the GMD, like the CCP today, desired "multiparty cooperation" under its leadership, not a multiparty system. That became apparent when the government organized a National Crisis Conference (*Guonan huiyi*) in 1932 and invited non-GMD elements, including seven CYP leaders, to attend (but no Communists). Many expected the conference to be the precursor of a wartime national defense government, in which political participation would be broadened. Unfortunately, it proved to be a farce, because the agenda was restricted to Japanese aggression without any reference to domestic issues.[18] Plainly, the GMD did not entertain the idea of power-sharing. As a result, the CYP boycotted the conference. Subsequently, it organized a volunteer corps and, cooperating with some regional troops, took up arms against Japan sporadically in North and Northeast China.[19]

It was not until after the Xi'an incident of December 1936 and the outbreak of full-scale war with Japan in the following year that "multiparty cooperation" became a real possibility. At the Lushan Conference (July 1937)--to which the CCP, the minor parties, and a number of prominent civil leaders with no political affiliations were invited--the idea of cooperation was canvassed.[20] For the GMD, cooperation meant multiparty support for the government's war effort, which would restore a semblance of national unity and thereby win the support of the middle-of-the-road intellectuals and perhaps foreign aid also. But Chiang Kai-shek did not spell out a role for the minor parties when he invited them to nominate representatives to serve on the PPC, scheduled for 1938. In formulating a cooperative framework, Chiang had no intention of encouraging them to become opposition parties; even their legal status was yet to be recognized. His aim was merely to seek their advice on major policies and to appoint a token number of their delegates to investigative committees of the PPC.

For the minor parties, cooperation meant some sort of informal recognition of their party status, which might later lead to formal recognition. It meant also a temporary respite from Nationalist repression. As far as the CYP was concerned, its anti-communist and anti-government manifestations ceased, but it continued to press for constitutional change during the War of Resistance.[21] In an exchange of letters with Chiang and Wang Jingwei, CYP representative Zuo Shunsheng made a point of relating the government's declared policy of wartime national reconstruction to constitionalism, stating that the guarantee of such basic freedoms as speech, publication, assembly, and association should form the basis of constitutional rule in the years to come.[22] Indeed, cooperation was regarded as a first step toward multiparty rule.[23]

The CYP's Conceptions of Loyal Opposition and Democracy

It was during the wartime period that the CYP developed its ideas on democracy and conceptualized loyal opposition in those terms. The term opposition was used in an English sense--that is, the opposition party stands opposed to the ruling party and the government of the day, and sees itself as an alternative government ready and anxious to take over administration. The original idea, which dated back to eighteenth-century England in the aftermath of the Glorious Revolution of 1688 and the doctrine of Locke, was that two political parties competed for office openly, peacefully, and in accordance with the law of the land, so that a change of government could occur without resorting to violence. The idea, of course, had since been adapted in a number of Western democracies, with very different party systems from that of England. Nevertheless, for the CYP, the important thing was peaceful competition for power in a parliamentary system where the political rights of opposition parties were guaranteed by the constitution.

The CYP's idea of loyal opposition could best be understood in the context of its conception of democracy, which was inspired by Anglo-American thought. Zeng admired Kemal, but his wartime heroes were Winston Churchill and Franklin Roosevelt, "the models of Western democracy."[24] While Zeng had written a great deal on nationalism, it was left to his party colleague, Chen Qitian, to expound the idea and practice of democracy and constitutional government.

Chen, a long-serving member of the party's CEC, was an educationalist and one-time editor of Shanghai's China Books Company (*Zhonghua shuju*). A prolific writer, he had published several books on nationalism, political philosophy, and Chinese education, as well as a treatise on anti-communism and opposition to Soviet Russia. In 1938, he was a delegate to the PPC and became a member of its Association for the Promotion of Consitutionalism, in which capacity he devoted a great deal of time and attention to the subject of democracy and constitutionalism, reflecting his personal views as well as those of his party.

He seems to have been profoundly influenced by the writings of British philosopher Bertrand Russell and political scientist Harold J. Laski. Democracy, he learnt, is premised on the sovereignty of the people; it is a form of representative government of the people, by the people, and for the people. The term "people" refers to all citizens of the state. A democratic government is not the privilege of any single class, and as such it is opposed to party or class dictatorship, just as it is opposed to absolute monarchism, theocracy, warlordism, and plutocracy. Nor does it maintain itself with brute force. Democracy, as he understood it, assumes unity between people and government, a complementary relationship in which the people can freely criticize the government without being hostile to it. If the government is unpopular, it can be replaced through the electoral processes, without resorting to violence. In a democratic state, there is no need for repression or a reign of terror. Democracy, therefore, is superior to all other forms of government in that it makes for relative peace, harmony, and stability--all of which China badly needed.[25]

But, as Russell wrote, democracy demands a readiness for compromise, which in turn "requires practice, respect for the law, and the habit of believing that opinions other than one's own may not be a proof of wickedness. What is even more necessary, there must not be a state of acute fear."[26] Given these conditions, democracy is capable of being the most stable form of government. Chen agreed with Russell that although democracy does not insure good government, it prevents certain evils and is a safeguard against civil war.[27] He further accepted the argument that democracy is capable of coping with national crises, because it maintains the channels of communication between ruler and ruled.[28]

An institutionalized opposition is the first and ultimate criterion of a democratic state. In his view, opposition was necessary even in times of revolution.[29] Here, the influence of Laski is noticeable. As Laski wrote:

> In general, revolutions fail because those who make them deny freedom to their opponents. Losing criticism, they do not know the limits within which they can safely operate; they lose their power because they are not told when they are abusing it. I can think of no revolutionary period in history when a government has gained by stifling the opinion of men who did not see eye to eye with it; and I suggest that the revolutionary insistence that persuasion is futile finds little creative evidence in its support.[30]

For the CYP, the functions of the opposition were twofold: to be a "loyal friend" who "criticizes, exhorts, and persuades," and to be an alternative government. Opposition is necessary in the interests of good government. Yet, it ought to be fair, responsible, and constructive, and not just for the opoosition's sake, or else the quality of the democratic dialogue would diminish. The relationship between government and opposition need not be adversarial. Rather, Chen stressed, it should be one of "coexistence," "coprosperity," and "mutual supervision."[31] The idea of "coexistence" is to enable the opposition to function properly, thereby obviating the need for revolutionary violence--again an echo of Russell.[32] The idea of "coprosperity" is to ensure that both government and opposition are in a healthy position to perform to the best of their abilities. He no doubt shared the Western view that where an opposition is rendered ineffective by the government, rather than by division within itself, the *raison d'etre* for its existence is lost. He also agreed with Russell that democracy, if it is to succeed and endure, "demands a tolerant spirit, not too much hate, and not too much love of violence."[33] Finally, the idea of "mutual supervision" is to provide the mechanisms for checks and balances, for insuring fair play and maintaining a high standard of public debate. It follows that the government of the day would benefit from public opinion and opposition criticism. Given this kind of relationship between government and opposition, there would be no need for revolutionary violence.[34]

The idea of "criticism, exhortation, and persuasion" was different from the tradition of remonstrance, in which loyal and presumably unselfish scholar-officials in imperial times gave honest advice to the emperor. Whereas the ancient tradition involved no mobilization of public opinion either inside or outside the bureaucracy, the CYP idea of loyal opposition was a modern one that rested on the notion of popular supervision of government through representative institutions and *minyi jiguan* (organizations representing public opinion or articulating their views of public opinion). Here, the thought of the CYP reflected an important trend in modern China's democratic movement--that is, the demand for two basic rights essential to authentic democracy, namely, free elections and an independent press. There could be no representative institutions if free elections were not held, nor could *minyi jiguan* exist or operate if there were no free press. It was political participation (with influence) and free speech that would make popular supervision of government possible. The CYP rejected the argument that the ruling party and the government alone were capable of supervising themselves and correcting their own mistakes. It differentiated between public opinion (*minyi*) and government opinion (*guanyi*); it was the former that would insure good government.[35] Many decades later, Chinese democracy activists would make similar demands, and Deng Xiaoping would argue that the mistakes of the party were always corrected by the Party itself, not by any other force.[36]

Chinese democrats, past and present, radical and conservative, have invariably asked why China was (and still is) behind many other countries, and have insisted that the answer lies in the absence of a stable democratic government. The questions the CYP leadership asked were phrased differently, but essentially were the same: Why did China fail to compete with other nations? Why had China suffered repeated defeats and humiliations at the hands of the foreign powers? Lamenting that China's weaknesses had invited foreign aggression, the CYP attributed the political roots of China's backwardness to the fact that Chinese politics had always been the politics of private self-interests, the privileged few, autocracy, hypocrisy, and corrupt officialdom. Only with a new sort of politics emphasizing the public interest, popular and open government, and the rule of law could China's problems be remedied.[37]

The emphasis on the rule of law (*fazhi*) is especially remarkable; it is essential to any democracy yet contrasts sharply with the Confucian tradition of rule by man (*renzhi*). Confucianism presupposes that the emperor was duty-bound to be virtuous and benevolent and that the ministers of state ruled in his name accordingly. In reality, of course, *renzhi* had often been a source of conflict and corruption, precisely because of the lack of an institutionalized legal base. In Chen's view, what China needed was an independent judiciary, a legal system that protected individual freedoms and under which every citizen was equal. He did not dismiss the idea of *renzhi* outright, but he gave it a new meaning, arguing that it must entail majority rule and that benevolent rule was possible only in a democracy. Without a modern legal framework, *renzhi* was reduced to rule by a privileged few. While appreciating social harmony, which Confucianism stressed, he did not think that order alone should be used to maintain the status quo. Order in a democracy is not static. It is positive and active, offering equal opportunity and room for political pluralism; it is maintained not by coercion, but by public opinion and an independent judiciary; and it is a means to progress, not an end in itself.[38]

Traditional *renzhi*, with its emphasis on personal relationships (*guanxi*), was a feature of Nationalist rule--and is of Communist rule today. Personal ties, not institutionalized systems, determined what could or could not be done in government. Despite a series of legal and judicial reforms, the party and the military were still practically above the law. There was no separation of party and government, the military was highly politicized, and a system of checks and balances did not exist. All of this gave rise to inefficiency, corruption, and repression. In addressing these problems, Chen sought remedies in a democratic system that maintained a separation of powers, the independence of the government from the party, and the depoliticization of the military. He advocated a new *renzhi* that would be integrated with *fazhi* in a constitutional government.

He did not think that Western democratic thought ran contrary to the traditional Chinese concepts of unity, balance, and cooperation. He illustrated this by articulating his ideas on the individual's relationship to state and society. He accepted the intrinsic worth of the free individual. But, drawing on the Chinese philosophy of the "golden mean," he advocated a balance between state powers and personal freedoms, in order that a relationship of cooperation, of rights and obligations, could be forged.[39] The individual is the citizen of the state, free and equal before the law, but one must also have regard for the public good and display a sense of responsibility and fair play. Because people are part of society, they should be at one with it in a harmonious way, as in Confucian society. Hence, while they should be free to do whatever they like within the limits of the law, liberty is not absolute and the exercise of their civil and political rights need not be at the expense of, or contrary to, the public good. If this sounds like J. S. Mill, whose *On Liberty* Chen had read, it was probably the influence of Laski, who maintained that the state imposes certain rules and codes of behavior upon all its citizens because that, broadly speaking, is essential to liberty, since it makes for peace.[40] And the CYP, while supporting a strong state that could hold the country together, rejected the idea of an authoritarian state, both in principle and practice.

The central principle of the liberal creed is individualism. Individualism is a good thing when it raises the value of the individual and releases energies for personal development. It is a bad thing, however, when it expresses itself in extreme selfishness. Indeed, some CYP leaders feared that the nihilistic individualism of the romantics, with its emphasis on rights rather than public duties and obligations, would pose a new threat to Chinese society. When they uttered the words "Down with individualism," they represented a common concern among intellectuals of all political persuasions about the evils of "excessive individualism." But they did not deny individual consciousness or the contribution such consciousness made to the liberation of thought.[41] They recognized those strands in Western democratic theory which posit a fundamental conflict between the interests of the individual and those of the state.

How then is one to resolve the conflict? Liberals would argue that this could be done through a process of reasoning and reconciliation. Thus, for Chen, the answer lay in social cooperation, based on the belief that private and collective interests could be reconciled and mutually beneficial, made possible by a democratic system of government. "Neither sheer selfish individualism nor sheer autocratic corporatism is good for democracy," he wrote. "This is because the ideal of democracy lies in mediation between the individual and the state, between liberty and order, and between equality and organization."[42] Such an assumption was shared by some contemporary

Western thinkers. Russell, for one, opined: "Where democracy does not exist, the government mentality is that of masters towards dependents; but where there is democracy it is that of equal cooperation."[43]

It was this very sense of balance, of social cooperation, that enabled CYP leaders to reconcile Western thought with what they regarded as the best of Chinese culture. On the one hand, they called for an end to traditional clanism and local particularism and advocated an independence of mind, a positive attitude toward life, a sense of progress, and a determination to succeed in life.[44] On the other, they upheld the traditional values of *li* (propriety), *yi* (righteousness), *lian* (honesty), and *qi* (sense of shame),[45] values not necessarily incompatible with the basic requirements of democracy. They were not torn intellectually between Western and Chinese thought. They did not advocate wholesale Westernization, nor did they call for a return to Confucianism, despite their interest in preserving some traditional values, for they realized that there was no place for "mainstream Confucianism" in a modern society. They saw no dichotomy between East and West, between old and new; they felt that the important thing was to absorb and preserve what was good and to reject what was bad.[46] Chen, in particular, maintained that such Confucian values as public morality and care for the people were merely high-sounding principles that had proved incapable of realization in an autocratic state and that, on the contrary, these would have a better chance of success under a democratic system of government.[47]

His idea of democracy was optimistic, if not idealistic: democracy, once established, would safeguard against civil war, cope with national crises, effect good and open government that combines *fazhi* with *renzhi*, maintain social cooperation, and produce a synthesis of modern liberal thought and traditional Chinese values. It would also arouse a socio-national consciousness that transcended class, racial, religious, occupational, and party boundaries, and would ensure competition on the one hand and cooperation on the other, all toward a common goal.[48] Further, democracy, in his view, would produce what Thomas Metzger calls *xianren zhengfu* (government by intellectually and morally superior persons, or governmental actions identical with those of such superior persons), which is dedicated to the promotion of the public good. Metzger draws attention to the concepts of a "moral community" and of a society free of selfishness in the Confucian tradition, which continued to influence the thoughts of twentieth-century Chinese liberals and democrats, who believed that such a society could be achieved through the unification of individual freedom with the will of the state.[49] Through his emphasis on social cooperation and interparty coprosperity and mutual supervision, Chen synthesized his idea of democracy with that of a moral rule which would bridge the gap between ruler and ruled, as well as between superior and subordinate. To apply Metzger's concept of the "moral community," it becomes clear that Chen did not follow the Millsian vision of democracy based on competition between parties and interest groups in morally neutral political procedures while legally pursuing selfish ends.[50] Thus, Chen wrote:

> The politics of democracy is the politics of morality; it should not be unscrupulous. . . . Political parties which apply morality will win popular sympathy as well as maintain solidarity within themselves. Such a principle might seem pedantic to the selfish elements. But for the state and the people, even for the future of the parties themselves, it is necessary to establish party morality. If a political party does not concern itself with morality, it will become an intriguing and self-serving cabal (*pengdang*) incapable of assuming the important duty of national salvation.[51]

For him, then, democratic government was the real "rule of virtue" (*dezhi*); authoritarianism in whatever form was immoral. The *dezhi* in the Confucian tradition was unreal because Confucian statecraft was the privilege of rulers who manipulated the concepts of *renyi* (benevolence and righteousness) and *tianming* (the mandate of heaven) to further their own ends.[52]

Yet, while Chen was part of Metzger's "moral community," his concept of democracy differed significantly, in some respects, from such "mainstream" liberal thought as had been advocated by Liang Qichao.[53] Chen did not assume, as Liang had, the original goodness of human nature and the natural harmony of the social order--one of the tenets of Confucianism. Rather, like Adam Smith, he appreciated that individuals pursue selfish ends and consequently come into conflict with the state from time to time. To reconcile their differences, he suggested a mediative process, not arbitrary action by the state. Democracy could give rise to conflict and disorder, but these could be contained by democracy itself.

Second, whereas Liang had found it necessary to balance democratic processes with powerful rulership in order to prevent people from pursuing their private ends at the expense of the public good, Chen's emphasis on social cooperation did not give the state the automatic right to suppress democracy and the basic rights of the individual in the name of unity and order. Unlike some of his contemporaries, such as Jiang Tingfu, Qian Duansheng (Ch'ien Tuan-sheng), and Ding Wenjiang,[54] Chen had no faith in benevolent dictatorship or enlightened despotism. Instead, like Hu Shi, he insisted that the state should guarantee and protect people's basic rights intrinsic to them as human beings. The rule of law, not autocratic government however enlightened it may be, is the best means of preventing the individual from abusing liberty to the detriment of the state.

Third, whereas Liang had feared that Chinese society was still too backward to allow the people to hold real power, the CYP advocated an immediate beginning of democratic government. To be sure, democratization would be a long process. But the important thing was to make a start so that people could learn about democracy by practicing it, just as one learns to swim by actually swimming. (Hu Shi, it may be noted, also held the view that "the only way to have democracy is to have democracy."[55]) Only in this way could a democratic tradition be established. The CYP leadership took the Russellian view that civic consciousness could be produced, not by political tutelage, but by a liberal education that tames the power of the state and gives a sense of the value of social cooperation.[56]

In short, the CYP's version of democracy was closer to the Western version than was the dominant tradition of Chinese democratic thought, which revolves around a philosophy of politics as a realm of harmony rather than conflict between the individual and the state, of the precedence of the public interest over private ends, and of the power of the state over the rights of the citizens.[57] On the other hand, CYP intellectuals shared with other liberals and democrats of their time and later decades the belief that democracy has functional benefits. Democracy prevents party dictatorship. It legitimates both government and opposition. It regulates conflict in a peaceful manner and thus diminishes the chances of violent upheavals. Finally, it allows political participation with influence, as well as popular supervision and control of government. However, CYP leaders paid little attention to the political instability that democracy is capable of causing. Nor did they appreciate that in a changing society, such as China in the 1930s, a multiparty system would be a weak party system, owing to the absence of a social base and the low levels of mobilization and political participation.

No doubt the CYP failed to see the need for radical change in existing social relationships. But the Communists' accusations that it represented the interests of the landlords and the bourgeoisie and acted as "the accomplice of the Chiang Kai-shek regime" are misleading.[58] In fact, the CYP did not represent the interests of any particular class. Its bases of support were narrow, resting as they did on an intelligentsia in which political cleavages existed. It was driven to a position of loyal opposition not by a desire to curry favor with the government, but by a conviction that a competitive system that involved the mobilization of public opinion was good for China and that it would work on the principles of coexistence, coprosperity, and mutual supervision. Loyal opposition, then, was a means of working toward such a system.

Assuming that democracy was desirable for China, was it practicable, especially in times of war?

The Practicality of Democracy in Wartime China

Writing in 1938, Russell opined that in a country like China, where the bulk of the population was illiterate and without political experience, it was difficult for democracy to succeed. Democracy, he noted, had been attempted in China after 1911, but it proved to be a "fiasco from the start." When the Chinese Republic was proclaimed and a parliamentary constitution decreed, the public was apathetic, and the regime quickly came under the control of the warlords.[59] As for democracy during wartime, many would have argued that there was no "acute and immediate need" for China to pursue it and that even in advanced democracies like Great Britain and the United States there was, during the two world wars, "a conspicuous shrinkage of democratic practices."[60]

The CYP took a different view. While acknowledging the lack of a democratic tradition in China, Chen Qitian contended that significant changes had taken place since 1911, which could form the basis of such a tradition. First, the demise of absolute monarchism was permanent. Although the Republic was more nominal than real, it was significant as a symbol of democracy in the name of which there could be no return to monarchism, as the abortive attempts of Yuan Shikai and Zhang Xun had demonstrated. And the GMD itself was committed to democracy as a political ideal, at least on paper. Second, the trend toward constitutionalism had been set, and the idea of democracy had been advocated in China by Sun Yat-sen and others for several decades. (Chen ignored the differences between Sun's idea of democracy and his own and the fact that Sun was not a consistent democrat.) As for the problem of mass illiteracy and political inexperience, Chen did not argue, as Hu Shi did, that democracy was "kindergarten government," the least sophisticated form of political life.[61] But he was confident that people could be trained in the exercise of their political rights through a liberal education without the Nationalist doctrine of tutelage.[62]

Chen further argued that wars were not necessarily barriers to constitutional reform, pointing out that such reform had been achieved in England during times of civil war and by Americans in their War of Independence. Even in China, he went on, the 1912 Provisional Constitution of the Chinese Republic was the result of civil war. Taking a cue from Zeng Qi, he contended that if the War of Resistance was to succeed, the support of the Chinese people was absolutely essential. What better way to obtain their support and thereby unite them in a common cause than by offering them constitutional government? In his view, in times of crisis people could survive only on hopes, and such hopes as were held out by constitutionalism would be the most gratifying. In other words, constitutional rule would provide the rallying point. To be sure, the government needed more powers to prosecute the war. But such extraordinary powers should be given only to a coalition government that replaced one-party rule. Finally, he argued that the demands of prosecuting the war were no justification for the denial of free speech and other civil rights.[63]

His position was based on his party's political platform, which advocated, *inter alia*, the freedoms of person, speech, the press, assembly, and association; representative institutions and constitutional government by general elections; the equality of all races and respect for their religions, languages, customs, and habits; and a bicameral parliament, as well as a responsible cabinet with a ceremonial president as head of state. On provincial self-rule, the CYP advocated a policy of decentralization that would raise the status of the provinces and provide a satisfactory framework for their relationships with the center.[64]

It was hoped that these policies--or at least some of them--could be adopted through cooperation with the government in the PPC. The Council, established at the outset of the war and comprising representatives from the ruling party, the CCP, the minor parties, and a few "independents," held its inaugural meeting in Hankou in July 1938. Many expected it to be a sort of "wartime parliament."[65] Despite its limited powers, it provided the only forum for public debate on the important national issues of the day, and oppositionists pinned high hopes on it as a constitutional convention presaging a new political dispensation for China. At its first session, the CYP put forward a proposal for the establishment of consultative assemblies (*canzhenghui*) at the provincial, district, and municipal levels before the end of the year, with the exception of the war zones and Japanese-occupied areas. It suggested that two-thirds of the members of the assembly be elected by geographical areas and the remainder on a professional/vocational basis and that the representatives serve terms of three years. Later, at the third session held in Chongqing in February 1939, it further proposed that district assemblies be formed within six months.[66] Both proposals were approved by the Council and favorably considered by the government.[67] Following this, at the fourth session in September 1939, the CYP took the lead in submitting a proposal for the termination of political tutelage and the beginning of constitutional rule. It called for the formation of a committee for the purpose of drafting a new constitution, and proposed that pending the opening of the National Assembly (NA), the Executive Yuan should be responsible to the Council, while the provincial and district administrations should be responsible to the newly formed provisional assemblies. Finally, it demanded the early promulgation of a constitution and official recognition of all the minor parties.[68] In all this, the CYP enjoyed the support of the other minor parties, which desired the formation of a responsible wartime multiparty cabinet, pending the opening of a properly elected NA.[69]

Like the late-Qing reformers and constitutionalists before them, the minor parties regarded consultative assemblies at the provincial, district, and municipal levels as a necessary first step toward constitutional rule and a means of promoting local self-government as an essential part of the democratic process. Sun Yat-sen had decreed that constitutional government must await the completion of provincial self-rule, a process that could take many years. To the CYP, the process would be too long. Instead, it advocated immediate and coordinated action in both directions: "Local self-government is the foundation for central constitutionalism," wrote Chen Qitian. "Central constitutionalism is the model for local self-government. Without local self-government, it is difficult to establish constitutionalism at the center. And without central constitutionalism, it is equally difficult to complete [the process of] local self-government. This is their relationship."[70]

The CYP also considered that local self-government would be easier to launch in the cities by virtue of the higher literacy rate and economic capabilities of the urban population, as well as a better transport infrastructure. From the cities, it would spread to the countryside. An immediate start could be made in every capital city and all other cities and townships at the *xian* level that had populations in excess of 100,000 each. Village communities below the *xian* level would have to wait until the conditions were right, notably a higher literacy rate and an improved system of transport and communications.[71]

The difficulty of putting democratic ideas into practice was not ignored. But the CYP was not arguing for quick, let alone instant, democracy. In fact, Chen proposed a three-stage development. The first stage was that of "unwritten constitutionalism," in which democracy would be practiced in some places pending the adoption and proclamation of a constitution; it was to spread to other places progressively. A second stage, that of "written constitutionalism," would be reached after the war when a constitution was adopted and promulgated and when the country was ready for more democracy. There would be a third stage when democracy was to be further expanded, improved, and a democratic tradition established.[72]

Clearly, democracy in China would be a long-term development. The big question was where and how it should all start. Rejecting Russell's pessimistic view, Chen was impatient with the long wait that would be necessary if democracy was to be predicated upon a significant rise in the population's literacy rate. Instead, he argued, people who had received a primary education--about 20 percent of the Chinese population--could be the starting point. They should be given the right to "participate in constitutional rule," meaning, presumably, the right to vote and to be elected to office. And, as access to education was expanded, more and more people would enjoy the same right.[73]

However, neither the domestic situation nor the international scene was favorable to the constitutional movement. Between 1940 and 1943, the PPC became less interested in the movement, partly because of the threat of renewed civil war following the New Fourth Army Incident of 4 January 1941 and the unfavorable attitude of the government leaders toward constitutional change, and partly because of the outbreak of the Pacific War and other external developments.[74] Contrary to the expectations of the minor parties, the Council did not evolve into a wartime parliament; it was dominated by GMD forces after the Third Council in October 1942.[75]

As the GMD-CCP differences intensified, the minor parties made a series of attempts to mediate through the League of Chinese Democratic Political Groups, (formed in 1941, and renamed the Democratic League [DL] in 1944)--a loose organization consisting of elements from the CYP, the National Socialist Party, the Third Party, the Rural Reconstruction Association, the Vocational Education Society, and the National Salvation Association.[76] All these efforts were unsuccessful, which reflected the chasm that separated the two major parties. This spelled the end of a TF in Republican politics.

Immediately after the Japanese surrender, the most important tasks for China were to prevent a renewal of civil war, achieve peaceful unification, and work out a program of national reconstruction. At the PCC held in January 1946, the CYP urged an immediate cessation of civil hostilities, the dispatch of multiparty observation teams to the troubled areas, the nationalization of all the armies in the country, and the separation of civil and military authorities.[77] It supported the idea of a coalition government and put forward a program of political liberalization along the following lines: (1) replacing the wartime National Defense Committee with a new multiparty Central Political Council; (2) completely reorganizing the Executive Yuan and other government bodies with a view to attracting talent from all quarters; and (3) increasing the membership of the PPC to five hundred, especially the number of "independents," and empowering it to instruct the government to implement any proposals that had been approved by the new Central Political Council.[78] It was hoped that the PPC would be transformed into a parliament or replaced by a properly elected NA.

While the government made some concessions, it insisted on nominating half of the members of the State Council, which replaced the wartime Defense Committee. The position of the CYP on the question of membership and representation was not immediately clear. The Communists, it might be noted, proposed a three-thirds system--that is, one-third to consist of GMD members, one-third members of all other parties, and one-third "independents."[79] The government pledged itself to a reorganization of the Executive Yuan so that "talent from all quarters" could be recruited into it. But when the NA began sitting on 15 November 1946, it was boycotted by the CCP and the pro-communist DL, from which the CYP had withdrawn earlier.[80] On 25 December, the Constitution of the Republic of China was adopted and promulgated, thus officially ending the period of political tutelage. But it was too late to give the GMD the prestige and credibility it desired.

In the government reorganization following the 1947 elections, a number of non-GMD members gained office. In the new State Council, there were eighteen Nationalists, four CYP members, four Democratic Socialists (DSP), and five "independents." Further, the CYP held thirteen seats in the Legislative Yuan and five seats in the Control Yuan. In the Executive Yuan, two CYP members--Zuo Shunsheng and Chen Qitian--were appointed minister for agriculture and forestry and minister for industry and commerce, respectively, while the DSP held two portfolios. Wang Yunwu, an "independent," became deputy head of the Executive Yuan.[81] The CYP and the DSP were coopted into the government, but cooptation fell far short of the goal of a multiparty system. As Li Huang recalled, the GMD never consulted the minor parties in the government on important financial and military matters.[82] Cooptation only served to diminish the autonomy of the opposition parties.

Conclusion: Failure of the CYP and Democracy in Republican China

If one assumes that democratic and liberal thought was important in Republican China, two questions must be addressed. Why did parties like the CYP remain small and weak? And why did democracy fail in China?

Let us take the second question first. Democracy failed in China during the 1930s and 1940s for a variety of reasons. For a start, it was never given a chance by the Nationalist authorities: political tutelage was not terminated until the end of 1946. Second, China was in chaos and revolution, torn by civil war and invaded by an imperialist power. Chinese political life was steeped in violence; the political process was dominated by force. Democracy requires peace and order; it lives on reasoned public debate. Third, China did not have--and still does not have--a liberal tradition; liberal ideas were never sufficiently articulated nor sufficiently popularized to make a profound impact on Chinese thinking. As Chen Qitian lamented, many of his fellow intellectuals had difficulties with the idea of democracy, while the masses, accustomed to an authoritarian state, had absolutely no understanding of it.[83] Then again, as Hu Shi had argued, democratic values could not flourish in the absence of democratic processes of government.[84]

Neither the GMD nor the CCP were noted for their political tolerance; both believed in party dictatorship. Fourth, democracy offered no real solutions to China's most pressing socioeconomic problems; by their failure to communicate with the masses, the liberals and democrats only succeeded in encouraging a continuation of authoritarian rule in China. In the absence of economic modernization and of a largely urbanized society with a sizable middle class, the prospects for democracy were extremely slim. Furthermore, events in Europe, unlike developments in the Eastern bloc in the late 1980s, were anything but conducive to democracy movements. And finally, it failed because changes in China have always taken a long time--two decades is too brief by Chinese standards.

Now the first question can be answered in perspective. The minor parties such as the CYP remained small and weak because they could not compete with the GMD and the CCP: they had no access to China's political, military, economic, or social resources, nor did they enjoy any foreign backing. They failed because in Chinese political life there was no room for a TF that advocated a non-violent means of conflict resolution; in the end, they were forced to choose between the government and the CCP. They failed because their leaders, such as those of the CYP, were political amateurs who revealed a lack of confidence, as well as a certain timidity and a degree of the intellectual's superciliousness,[85] and who could not communicate with the masses, let alone answer their basic needs. The CYP represented only a section of an intelligentsia that was politically and ideologically divided--the dominant state idea remained authoritarian. It lacked a popular base of support, to which must be added a lack of leadership, a problem confronting all minor parties.

In the final analysis, though the CYP had failed to achieve its objectives--loyal opposition proved to be anything but a viable alternative to revolution and one-party rule--the kind of democracy it advocated both as an end and a means is significant. CYP democracy, though inspired by Anglo-American thought, showed a remarkable continuity with the Confucian tradition in its insistence on the politics of morality, on *dezhi*, the rule of virtue. CYP intellectuals were part of the "moral community" of which Metzger speaks, whose political ideal was a *xianren zhengfu* dedicated to the promotion of the public good in a society free of selfishness. But more striking is their departure from the dominant tradition of Chinese liberal thought in some important respects. Their recognition of the fundamental conflict between individual and state, and their insistence on the rule of law, separation of powers, social cooperation, mediation between private and public interests, and the sanctity of civil liberties, personal freedoms, and human rights, distinguished them not only from the authoritarian ideologies of the Nationalists and the Communists but also from the ideas of Liang Qichao and other like-minded intellectuals who had no problem with enlightened despotism and benevolent dictatorship as far as China was concerned. They rejected all the grounds on which party dictatorship maintained itself, and argued for a beginning to democratic rule. Though not every one had truly imbibed democratic values and though some may have been motivated by the desire for office,[86] as a party they were not "thoroughly medieval" in their mentality, as Qian Duansheng argued.[87]

CYP intellectuals were not alone in advocating a liberal alternative in China. Frederic Spar's essay in this volume on Luo Longji in the 1930s shows that there were other Chinese intellectuals of the minor parties who advocated liberal democracy, engaged in politics, and unwaveringly placed the individual, not the state, at the center of their considerations.[88]

Finally, the CYP's was the pluralist conception of democracy, which reflected a continuing movement against party dictatorship. But in their optimistic view of democracy, CYP intellectuals had underestimated the traditional Chinese concern, indeed obsession, with order. All this is relevant to the contemporary democracy movement culminating in the Tiananmen incident of 1989. The CYP argument that a competitive party system and a free press are necessary to allow popular supervision and control of the rulers are likely to be made more often by China's democracy activists in the years to come. In the meantime, fears of chaos and instability that might befall the country if Western-style democracy were instituted remain very strong among China's leaders and intellectuals.

Notes

1. By the end of 1948, the membership of the CYP was around 300,000. Chen Qitian, *Jiyuan huiyilu* (The Memoirs of Chen Qitian), enl. 2nd ed.(Taibei: Shangwu yinshuguan, 1972), 306 (hereafter, *Huiyilu*). When the PPC assembled in Hankou in July 1938, seven of the councillors were from the CYP, with the same number from the CCP and the National Socialist Party [editor's note: The NSP had eleven seats]. Shen Yunlong, *Minguo shishi yu renwu luncong* (Collected Essays on Republican History and Figures) (Taibei: Zhuanji wenxue chubanshe, 1981), 378. In the postwar PCC, there were five representatives from the CYP, only two fewer than from the CCP. Ch'ien Tuan-sheng, *The Government and Politics of China, 1912-1949* (Stanford: Stanford University Press, 1950), 376. And in the reorganized government of 1947, the CYP held more seats than the Democratic Socialists. Chen, *Huiyilu*, 224-225.

2. On the formation of the CYP in Paris, see Chan Lau Kit-ching, *The Chinese Youth Party, 1923-1945*, Centre for Asian Studies Occasional Papers and Monographs No. 9 (Hong Kong: University of Hong Kong, 1972), 1-19.

3. Zeng Qi, *Zeng Muhan xiansheng riji xuan* (Selections from the Diary of Mr. Zeng Qi) (Taibei: Wenhai chubanshe, n.d.), 76-77 (hereafter, *Riji xuan*); Li Huang, *Xuedun shi huiyilu* (Memoirs from the Xuedun Chamber) (Taibei: *Zhuanji wenxue* chubanshe, 1973), 96-97 (hereafter, *Huiyilu*).

4. Chen, *Huiyilu*, 144-147, 264.

5. Li Yibin, ed., *Zhongguo qingnian dang* (The Chinese Youth Party) (Beijing: Zhongguo kexue chubanshe, 1982), 126-36.

6. Yu Yuntang and Yao Chuankeng, *Zhongguo dangdai zhengdang lun* (On Contemporary Chinese Political Parties) (Guangzhou: Zongheng wenhua shiye gongsi, 1948), 79; Chen, *Huiyilu*, 264.

7. Zeng Qi, *Zeng Muhan xiansheng yizhu* (The Posthumous Works of Mr. Zeng Qi) (Taibei: Wenhai chubanshe, n.d.), 80-82 (hereafter, *Yichu*); Chen, *Huiyilu*, 284; Li Yibin, 149-159.

8. Liu Xia, *Shiba nian lai zhi Zhongguo qingnian dang* (The Chinese Youth Party During the Past Eighteen Years) (Chengdu: Guoyun shudian, 1941), 21-22.

9. Zeng, *Yizhu*, 177-180.

10. Supra, 231-35.

11. Li Huang, *Xuedun shi zhenglun xuanji* (Selected Political Commentaries from the Xuedun Chamber) (Taibei: *Zhuanji wenxue* chubanshe, 1975), 125 (hereafter, *Zhenglun xuanji*).

12. See the letter from the Youth Corps to the GMD, in Li Yibin, 216-217.

13. Zeng, *Yizhu*, 97-100.

14. In 1924, Kemal encouraged the formation of an opposition party, the Progressive Republican Party, which was dissolved a year later as a result of a serious revolt in Southeast Anatolia led by the Kurds. In 1930, after effecting a series of reforms in his government, Kemal helped set up a new opposition party (the Free Republican Party) to give the National Assembly, the government, the people, and, not least of all, his own Republican People's Party the stimulus necessary for them to work more efficiently for the common good. Kemal was a sincere believer in free debates in the National Assembly; his party preserved the appearance of a parliamentary party, hence the capacity for political liberalization, and he experimented with a multiparty system. Stanford J. Shaw and Ezel Kural Shaw, *History of the Ottoman Empire and Modern Turkey*, Vol. 2: *Reform, Revolution, and Republic: The Rise of Modern Turkey, 1808-1975* (Cambridge: Cambridge University Press, 1977), 373-396.

15. Zeng, *Yizhu*, 100-101.

16. See the declaration of *Xingshi zhoubao* in its inaugural edition and the manifesto of the CYP on the occasion of its emergence from underground as a political party. Li Yibin, 108-109, 221.

17. Zeng, *Yizhu*, 100-101.

18. Urged by the CYP to end political tutelage before the conference, Wang Jingwei, president of the Executive Yuan, was quoted as saying that the GMD had won power by revolutionary means over many years and that anyone wishing to abolish political tutelage immediately would have to start a new revolution. Liu, 49; Zeng, *Yizhu*, 114.

19. *Zhongguo qingnian dang Guangdong sheng dangbu* (Guangdong Provincial Branch of the Chinese Youth Party), ed., *Zhongguo qingnian dang shilue ji zhenggang* (Brief History and Platform of the Chinese Youth Party) (Guangzhou: Zhongguo qingnian dang, Guangdong sheng dangbu, 1947), 8-9 (hereafter, *Shilue ji zhenggang*); Li Huang, *Huiyilu*, 176-198.

20. Liu, 49-50; Zuo Hongyu, *Kangzhan jianguo zhong zhi Zhongguo qingnian dang* (The Chinese Youth Party During the War of Resistance and National Reconstruction) (Chengdu: Guoyun shudian, 1939), 10-12.

21. *Shilue ji zhenggang*, 5.

22. Zuo Hongyu, 13-14; Liu, 50.

23. *Zhongguo qingnian dang jiandang wushi zhounian jinian tekan* (A Special Publication Commemorating the Fiftieth Anniversary of the Founding of the Chinese Youth Party) (Taibei: Zhongguo qingnian dang, zhongyang dangbu, 1973), 20.

24. Zeng, *Yizhu*, 120-126.

25. Chen Qitian, *Minzhu xianzheng lun* (On Constitutional Democracy) (Taibei: Shangwu yinshuguan, 1966), 34-36 (hereafter, *Minzhu*).

26. Bertrand Russell, *Power: A New Social Analysis* (London: Allen and Unwin, 1938), 131-132.

27. Ibid., 129, 187; Chen, *Minzhu*, 215.

28. Ibid., 36.

29. Ibid., 102.

30. Harold J. Laski, *Liberty in the Modern State* (Harmondsworth: Penguin Books, 1930), 113-114.

31. Chen, *Minzhu*, 53-54, 102-103, 168.

32. Russell, 130-131.

33. Ibid., 200.

34. Chen, *Minzhu*, 53, 102.

35. Ibid., 116-117, 138-139.

36. Andrew J. Nathan, *Chinese Democracy: The Individual and the State in Twentieth-Century China* (London: I.B. Tauris and Co., 1986), 36-37.

37. Chen, *Minzhu*, 111-120.

38. Ibid., 47-51.

39. Ibid., 44-46.

40. Laski, 159.

41. Liu, 26-27; Hu Guowei, *Zhongguo qingnian dang jianshi* (A Short History of the Chinese Youth Party) (Taibei: Puti chubanshe, 1967), 20-21.

42. Chen, *Minzhu*, 16-17.

43. Russell, 202-203.

44. Hu, 19-21.

45. Zeng, *Riji xuan*, 43, 48.

46. Liu, 32-33; Hu, 25.

47. Chen, *Minzhu*, 82-83.

48. Ibid., 81.

49. Thomas A. Metzger, "Oppositional Politics and the Problem of Secularization in Modern China," Paper presented at the Conference on "Oppositional Politics in Twentieth-Century China," Washington and Lee University, 20-22 September 1990, 8.

50. Ibid., 12-13.

51. Chen, *Minzhu*, 108.

52. Ibid., 77-78.

53. I have drawn on Nathan (pp. 51, 57-58) for Liang's ideas about the individual and the state in modern China.

54. For the ideas of Jiang, Qian, and Ding in this regard, see Jerome B. Grieder, *Hu Shih and the Chinese Renaissance: Liberalism in the Chinese Revolution, 1917-1937* (Cambridge: Harvard University Press, 1970), 259-260, 265-266.

55. Ibid., 336.

56. Chen, *Minzhu*, 219-223; Russell, 207.

57. Nathan, iv.

58. Li Yibin, 1-2.

59. Russell, 28, 128.

60. Dison Hsueh-feng Poe, "Comments on Lawrence N. Shyu, 'China's "Wartime Parliament": the People's Political Council, 1938-1945,'" in *Nationalist China During the Sino-Japanese War, 1937-1945*, ed. Paul K.T. Sih (New York: Exposition Press, 1977), 315.

61. Grieder, 261.

62. Chen, *Minzhu*, 111-113, 216.

63. Ibid., 147-149.

64. *Shilue ji zhenggang*, 17-20.

65. For a scholarly treatment of the PPC, see Shyu (n. 60).

66. Zuo Hongyu, 31-32, 62.

67. Guomin canzhenghui shiliao bianzan weiyuanhui, comp., *Guomin canzhenghui shiliao* (Historical Materials on the People's Political Council) (Taibei: Guomin canzhenghui zai Tai lijie canzhengyuan lianyihui, 1962), 91.

68. Chongqing shi zhengxie wenshi ziliao yanjiu weiyuanhui, ed., *Guomin canzhenghui jishu* (A Record of the People's Political Council) (Chongqing: Chongqing chubanshe, 1985), 581-582, 584-585.

69. Shyu, 298-299.

70. Chen, *Minzhu*, 154.

71. Ibid., 155.

72. Ibid., 152-153.

73. Ibid., 153-154.

74. Shyu, 301.

75. Ibid., 288.

76. Zuo Shunsheng, *Jin sanshi nian jianwen zaji* (Miscellaneous Notes on What I Have Seen and Heard during the Past Thirty Years) (Taibei: Zhonghua yilin wenwu chubanshe, 1976), 79-93; Luo Longji, "Cong canjia jiu zhengxie dao canjia Nanjing hetan de yixie huiyi" (Some Recollections of [My Participation in Politics] from the Old Political Consultative Conference through the Nanjing Peace Talks), in *Zhongguo ge minzhu dangpai* (China's Various Democratic Political Parties and Groups), ed. Yu Gang (Beijing: Zhongguo wenshi chubanshe, 1987), 121-123.

77. Li Yibin, 297-304; Chen, *Huiyilu*, 201-203.

78. Ibid., 201-03; Li Yibin, 297-304; Zeng, *Yizhu*, 220-221.

79. Carsun Chang, *The Third Force in China* (New York: Bookman Associates, 1952), 148.

80. Jiang Ping, *Zhongguo minzhu dangpai shi* (A History of China's Democratic Political Parties and Groups) (Wuchang: Hankou daxue chubanshe, 1987), 304-308; Qiu Qianmu, *Zhongguo minzhu dangpai* (China's Democratic Political Parties and Groups) (Hangzhou: Zhejiang jiaoyu chubanshe, 1987), 183-195.

81. Chen, *Huiyilu*, 224-225; Wang Yunwu, *Xiulu lun guoshi* (Comments on National Affairs) (Taibei: Shangwu yinshuguan, 1965), 222-223.

82. Li Huang, *Zhenglun xuanji*, 126.

83. Chen, *Huiyilu*, 198-199.

84. Grieder, 336.

85. When Zeng Qi first suggested forming a political party to Li Huang and Yu Jiaju early in 1923, Li was silent, as he was anxious to finish his Master's degree at the University of Paris, and Yu responded that a good leader was difficult to find and that, instead of getting involved in party politics, he would rather work for the good of the country in a manner transcending party lines. Eventually, both Li and Yu joined the party. Li Huang, *Huiyilu*, 97; Yu Jiaju, *Huiyilu* (A Memoir) (Shanghai: Zhonghua shuju, 1948), 48-49. Chen Qitian admitted being afraid of party politics and was pessimistic about the prospects for political reform under Nationalist rule. Chen, *Huiyilu*, 46, 158, 199. Zuo Shunsheng, too, treated politics as no more than "a casual pastime." Zuo Shunsheng, "Ji Zeng Muhan" (Memories of Zeng Qi), in Zuo Shunsheng, *Zhongguo xiandai mingren yishi* (Interesting Stories of Prominent Contemporary Chinese) (Hong Kong: Ziyou chubanshe, 1954), 101. Li Huang described himself and his colleagues with self-mockery as "merely scholars attempting to save the nation (*shusheng jiuguo*)." Li Huang, *Huiyilu*, 112-115.

86. When the CYP was coopted into the reorganized government in 1947, there was a jockeying for positions among some party members. The original list of members to serve in the government, drawn up by the party's Standing Committee, had to be revised by the CEC on the demand of some members. Chen Qitian, who first became minister of finance and later minister of industry and commerce, recalled that many of his party colleagues asked him for jobs in his ministry, regardless of their expertise. On one occasion, a party veteran, probably drunk at the time, threatened to kill himself if he were not appointed a deputy minister of sorts. Chen, *Huiyilu*, 224-225, 227, 230-232; Zeng, *Riji xuan*, 117-118. Chen's portfolio was originally intended for Li Huang, but because of "some internal personnel problems," Li felt compelled to give it up to Chen. Zuo Shunsheng, *Jin sanshi nian*, 110-111.

87. Ch'ien, 353.

88. See supra, Chap. 2.

PART FIVE

Opposition Parties in the People's Republic of China, the Republic of China (Taiwan), and Elsewhere After 1949

12

The Third Force in Hong Kong and North America During the 1950s

Yang Tianshi

Translated by Young-tsu Wong

In 1952, a secret organization named the Fighting League for Chinese Freedom and Democracy (FL) appeared in Hong Kong. Its founders included Zhang Fakui, a former Guomindang (GMD) general; Zhang Junmai, chairman of the Chinese Democratic Socialist Party; Gu Mengyu, a former Beida professor and key figure of the GMD Reorganization Clique; Tong Guanxian, ex-president of the Legislative Yuan of the GMD government; Zhang Guotao, an ex-communist leader; Li Weichen, a liberal intellectual; and others. The total membership was approximately two hundred to three hundred persons scattered throughout Hong Kong, North America, Japan, Australia, India, and the Chinese mainland. They called themselves the Third Force (TF). Theirs was a secret organization that opposed the Soviet Union, the Chinese Communist Party (CCP), and the Chiang Kai-shek regime on Taiwan.

The key documents of the FL were the "Proclamation of the Fighting League" by Zhang Junmai, the "Outline of the League's Organization during the Preparation Period" by Tong Guanxian and Li Weichen, the "General

---

This essay is based on the Zhang Fakui Oral History Memoir and papers in the Rare Book and Manuscript Library at Columbia University.

Rules of the League," and the "General Rules for a League Member's Life Style" by Zhang Guotao.

The Proclamation was the most important of these. It was a declaration of the League's political objectives and expressed its political viewpoints and social ideals. First, it attacked the Soviet Union under Stalin's rule, which was described as a "new slavery system" (*Xin nuyu zhidu*) installed in all Communist countries. It then promoted five basic principles: (1) Freedom is the most fundamental of all human objectives--freedom of individual lives and of personality development; (2) pluralism allows progress of human thought and culture, while control of culture and thought can only freeze human creativity; (3) democracy has become the main political trend of mankind, so no form of dictatorship has any existential value; (4) private property is a part of human civilization and should be allowed, together with a policy to bridge the gap between rich and poor; (5) the responsibilities of a government are to reconcile the people's interests and protect their well-being, on the one hand, and maintain national interests and friendly international relations, on the other.

On the basis of these five principles, the Proclamation condemned the CCP, which forced the Chinese people to worship a Marxism distorted by Stalin, arbitrarily divided Chinese society into opposing classes, wantonly destroyed Chinese cultural tradition, and single-mindedly executed a pro-Soviet, "lean-to-one-side" policy. Along this line, all aspects of CCP beliefs and policies, whether political, economic, diplomatic, or cultural, were criticized and condemned. In short, the intention of overthrowing one-party dictatorial rule was made amply clear. In current political terminology, the FL can be called the ancestor of "bourgeois liberalism."

The FL was first organized with American support. According to Zhang Fakui's reminiscences, while he was in Hong Kong in 1950 the former president of Lingnan University, Dr. James McClure Henry (1880-1958), came to see him and inquire about anti-communist guerrilla activities on the mainland. Henry said that many Americans and Chinese believed Zhang could unify the Chinese in South China. Henry also expressed his distaste for Chiang Kai-shek's political oppression.

Zhang then expressed his hope of rallying dedicated and prominent Chinese to form a new secret organization and political force. For members of this organization, Zhang suggested Gu Mengyu, Tong Guanxian, Zhang Guotao, Li Huang, Li Weichen, and Wu Xianzi. Henry added Zhang Junmai and Xu Chongzhi. Shortly afterward, Zhang Fakui and Xu Chongzhi met Henry again, and the latter promised that he would see certain persons after returning to Washington and would write back about the results.

Several months later, an American came to Hong Kong with Henry's letter. He insisted that he was not a representative of the U.S. government, but rather of the American people. He introduced Zhang Fakui and Xu to two Americans, one of whom had worked with General Claire Chennault at Kunming Air Base during World War II. They asked Zhang and Xu who represented the democratic force in Hong Kong, what they should do, and how the American people could help. Zhang and Xu then presented a proposal. The two Americans said they had to ask the American people for approval, in order to obtain financial aid. Before long, the FL began activities with American financial assistance.

The League had an eleven-member executive committee, of which Wu Xianzi, Zhang Fakui, and Gu Mengyu were standing committee members. Later, Wu was dismissed because he visited Taiwan, and was replaced with Zhang Junmai. The standing committee supervised several departments, namely, organization, finance, politics, military, and propaganda. The secretary-general was Cheng Siyuan. After Cheng returned to mainland China, Li Weichen assumed the post. Zhang Junmai, then in India, claimed to know General George C. Marshall, and hoped that the American general would help the FL.

After having discussed it with the two Americans, Zhang Fakui decided to send Zhang Junmai to America. In March 1952, Zhang Junmai arrived in Hong Kong from India. He spent two weeks talking to Zhang Fakui and others before going to the U.S. via Japan. From then on, Zhang Junmai was the League's representative in America, and he registered it with the U.S. Department of Justice.

The League's headquarters were in Hong Kong. In May 1952, Gu Mengyu went to Japan in the hope of moving the headquarters there, but it did not materialize. The key elements of the League were intellectuals, mostly teachers and a few students, as well as workers and businessmen. Their basic units were "small groups" (*xiaozu*). In Hong Kong alone, there were more than ninety small groups.

The League's activities by and large focused on culture and propaganda. It possessed four publications: *Duli luntan* (The Independent Forum), edited by Gu Mengyu; *Zaisheng* (The National Renaissance), edited by Zhang Junmai; *Zhongguo zhi sheng* (The Voice of China), edited by Zhang Guotao and, after September 1952, by Li Weichen; and *Huaqiao tongxun* (Overseas Chinese Newsletter), whose editor is unknown. In addition, the League assisted a number of newspapers and edited a series of books.

Another important activity was making contacts with overseas Chinese. The League sent its agents to Australia, India, and other places in order to extend its influence among overseas Chinese. It also attempted to unite other anti-Communist forces in Asia, with Vietnam as the base. In a letter to Zhang Junmai dated 23 September 1954, Zhang Fakui wrote that "it would be a great opportunity for us if Ngo Dinh Diem should agree with us," and "since you are well acquainted with Diem, you can surely encourage him to fight against the Communists and thus help our task of defeating them and restoring our own country." Zhang Fakui also contacted the South Korean envoy in Vietnam in support of the "Chinese, Korean, and Vietnamese Military Alliance." For Zhang Fakui, if they could develop this three-country military alliance into a free-Asia alliance, echoing the free world, it would be easy to check the Soviets' aggressive ambitions and weaken the Chinese Communist regime. As for the League's claim that it sent agents to mainland China to carry out underground activities, there is no confirmation.

From the very outset, the League suffered from endless conflicts. First, there were conflicting opinions. Zhang Junmai formally proclaimed the founding of the League in America on 10 October 1952. Gu Mengyu, however, considered it premature. This set the stage for antagonism between the two leaders. There was also controversy over the attitude toward Taiwan. Wu Xianzi was expelled for going to Taiwan; however, quite a few members of the League went to Taiwan to attend the National Assembly without being punished. Gu Mengyu once commented that, however unsatisfactory the Chiang regime was, it remained the symbol of free China, and thus should be encouraged and supported in its fight against the Communists. Zhang Junmai and others bitterly opposed the idea, however.

Another difficulty was finances. American aid amounted to a mere $20,000 per month. In 1953, due to financial difficulty, the League reduced the budget of the *Zhongguo zhi sheng*. As a result, its editor, Zhang Guotao, angrily withdrew from the League.

The League was opposed by both the mainland and Taiwan. New China had greatly elevated its international standing since the Geneva Conference of 1954, and thus weakened the League's popularity. Zhang Junmai wrote on 15 July 1954 that "after Zhou [Enlai]'s attendance at the Geneva Conference, we could no longer obtain overseas Chinese support even if I personally visited India, Indonesia, and Malaysia." And Taiwan, he continued, remained extremely hostile to the League. The letter vividly conveyed the political difficulty the League confronted at the time.

Last, but not least, the U.S. government lost its enthusiasm for the League. In a letter dated 23 February 1955, Zhang Junmai wrote that the U.S. government was more interested in aiding Taiwan. "Even though many of my colleagues wish me to get something [from the U.S. government], I have nothing to report this day." As a result, many League members also lost their enthusiasm.

Gu Mengyu persistently suspected that there were spies in the League. In a letter of 31 October 1953 to Zhang Fakui, Gu demanded a reorganization of the League. Again, on the first day of 1954, he wrote to Zhang Fakui and Tong Guanxian to complain of the "unsatisfactory performance of the League" in the past and demand a reorganization in order to eliminate "spies," "sabotaging elements," "self-publicists," and "reckless activists." On 31 January, he further demanded that Zhang cease all activities, pending reorganization. In March, Zhang sent Tong to Japan to talk with Gu on the matter of reorganization. In addition to proposing a seven-point plan, Gu wanted to change the League's name to the League for Chinese Freedom and Democracy.

Zhang Junmai accepted Gu's plan of reorganization but rejected changing the name. "Once the flag has been raised," he said, "we shall never retreat." Zhang Fakui also expressed doubt about changing the name. In August, Zhang Fakui and others gathered in Hong Kong and decided on a "fundamental reorganization," but preserved the original name. The meeting also authorized the formation of a reorganization committee.

In September, Gu Mengyu withdrew from the League. Shortly afterward, Zhang Junmai followed suit and withdrew the League's registration with the U.S. Department of Justice. At this point, the FL came to an end.

The FL was not the only TF organization in Hong Kong and North America during the 1950s. Others included The Association of Comrades for the Restoration of the GMD, headed by Li Zongren; the Democratic Constitutionalist Party, headed by Li Daming; the Hong Men Zhigong Dang, headed by Tan Hu; the Freedom Front, headed by Xie Chengping; and the Chinese Democratic League, headed by Chen Zhongfu. All these organizations formed the League of Free China Democratic Political Groups in 1954.

13

Minor Parties in Taiwan

John F. Copper

Introduction

As of the end of July 1990, Taiwan had fifty-two minor parties (see the appendix for a list).[1] In fact, all of the Republic of China's political parties may be classified as minor parties, with the exception of the Guomindang (GMD) and the Democratic Progressive Party (DPP), based on their memberships and their performances in the last national election.[2] Taiwan has traditionally had minor parties, although they did not challenge the GMD's one-party system before the 1980s. They did not constitute a real opposition, nor did they seem to have any hope of growing. New political parties began to emerge in 1986, when President Chiang Ching-kuo suggested that martial law be terminated and the ban on the formation of new political parties lifted. They proliferated following the end of martial law in July 1987.

It is now easy to found a political party in Taiwan, and, as a result, many new parties have formed in the last few years. This will probably continue to be the case until some legal restraints are applied. There is considerable doubt, however, whether these new parties (except for a very few, if any) will exert any appreciable influence in an election or in Taiwan politics generally.

The presence of a large number of political parties, on the other hand, has led many observers to call Taiwan's political-party system a multiparty one. Others, however, argue--based on the miserable performance of all parties except the GMD and the DPP in the national election in October 1989--that Taiwan has a two-party system.

The author will assess the formation of the new minor parties before and after martial law, the system in which they have been established and now operate, their performance in the 1989 election, and some other aspects of minor-party politics. Lastly, some scenarios regarding the future of minor parties will be presented.

Minor Parties Before and After Martial Law

Taiwan had two minor "opposition" parties in the 1940s that originated on the mainland: the Chinese Youth Party (CYP) and the Chinese Democratic Socialist Party (DSP). At various times, observers thought these parties might gain in strength and become true opposition parties. This, however, has not happened.

The CYP, founded in 1923, is the oldest. In April 1947, the CYP joined a coalition with the GMD, winning 237 seats in the National Assembly (NA) and fourteen in the Legislative Yuan (LY). In addition, four party members were commissioners in the National Political Council. After the government moved to Taiwan in 1949, the CYP left the government (or, more accurately, its close association with the GMD) and tried to become a true opposition party. It recruited locally born Taiwanese and tried to win some local elections.[3] In 1960, two of its members joined the abortive effort to found the China Democratic Party, which was strongly anti-GMD.[4]

Since 1960, however, the CYP has been allied with the GMD to the extent that it is often called a satellite party. It has received financial help from the GMD and generally adheres to the latter's line on domestic and foreign affairs--taking a somewhat stronger line on environmental issues, privatization, veterans' benefits, and the reunification of China.

The CYP has been represented in the NA, LY, and the Control Yuan (CY).[5] Its membership is estimated at twenty thousand--making it by far the largest minor party. However, it has failed, in the wake of the end of martial law and the growth of opposition politics and a multiparty system, to attract more support from the electorate or from those active in politics in Taiwan. Since 1949, it has not received more than 1 percent of the total vote in a national election.[6] In the 1989 national election, the CYP lost the two seats it held in the LY, as well as its single seat in the Provincial Assembly (PA).[7]

The DSP was formed in 1946 in Shanghai and fled with the GMD and the Nationalist Government to Taiwan in 1949. At that time, it was a coalition partner with the GMD. It failed to gain even a semblance of opposition status after that. It also suffered from the lack of an independent platform and voter support, and from factionalism. It has had a small representation in all three elective bodies--the NA, the LY, and the CY.[8] But after the 1989 election, it had virtually no representation, and lost the only seat it had in the PA. Its membership is estimated at six thousand, and is not increasing.[9]

In April 1986, after President Chiang Ching-kuo instructed members of the GMD's Central Standing Committee to examine lifting martial law and legalizing new political parties, the die was cast to get rid of the one-party system in Taiwan, wherein the CYP and DSP served as token opposition. Before President Chiang's order became legislation, however, an opposition known as *dangwai* ("outside the [GMD] party"), which had participated as a meaningful opposition in national elections since 1980, formed the DPP in September. The DPP participated in the December national election as a "fully accredited" party in the minds of most voters and observers.[10] In the 1989 election, it "won" a startling victory, with gains in every election contest, and has since come to be regarded by many as *the* opposition. In fact, it is viewed as the second major party in a two-party system.[11]

Meanwhile, after the LY officially ended martial law, a spate of new parties appeared. By March 1989, Taiwan had twenty-one more, for a total of twenty-five. Twenty-three of these could be classified as minor parties.[12]

There were several reasons for the new parties. First, it was very questionable at this time whether the DPP would succeed in becoming a sufficiently strong opposition party to challenge the GMD. It was plagued by factionalism and recruitment was not going very well, certainly not up to the predictions of DPP leaders. Moreover, it was having difficulties soliciting funds. Finally, the DPP did not perform as well in the 1986 national election as the party had predicted.[13]

A second reason was that the independence issue, with the DPP advocating Taiwan independence, aroused considerable controversy and opposition. A number of the minor parties that formed at this time did so in reaction to the independence issue; in other words, they opposed the separation or fragmentation of China.[14]

Third, many political activists perceived that the GMD had moved to the left in response to foreign pressure, DPP prodding, and in an effort to win the vote of the silent majority in the center and take options away from the DPP by advocating "socialist" issues. Thus, most of the new parties that appeared at this time were right-of-center parties in terms of issues and ideology (athough most of the parties were not ideological as such).[15]

Fourth, there was a perception by those interested in forming a party that neither the GMD nor the DPP represented groups that needed to be heard. This was true of the GMD because it had taken many voting blocs for granted. It was the case for the DPP because of its dependence on the protest vote that represented extreme views and interests, leaving behind large groups of voters.

Finally, election laws in Taiwan were such that it was easy to form and maintain the status of a party. There were no real restraints on party formation; one could form a party simply by filing. Demonstrated voter support in an election, a meaningful membership, a budget, or some activities were not required. The Civic Organizations Law, passed in early 1989, further clarified the status of parties and retained the easy qualifications for party status. It required that the party founder be twenty years of age and that the party have thirty members--certainly nothing that would impede the formation of more parties or force already existing minor parties out of business.[16]

The Chinese Freedom Party, which formed in July 1987, was an activist party like the DPP, except that it generally pushed positions diametrically opposed to the latter. Some said its policy was to attract media attention away from the DPP and to engage in pro-government demonstrations that the GMD was unwilling to stage.[17]

A few months later, in November 1987, the Labor Party (LP) registered with the Ministry of the Interior. It was established by a former DPP leader, who stated that neither the GMD nor the DPP represented labor. With a large labor force in Taiwan that was not well organized by unions nor strongly linked to any party, an opportunity to claim to represent labor existed. There were several intense labor disputes at the time which further aided the LP's cause.[18]

Other parties of various stripes formed during this time. A socialist advocacy party formed. Another supported Confucius and Mencius. A third called for world salvation. A Buddhist party was founded. And there were many more....[19]

However, all of these minor parties--even the LP--failed to perform in the December 1989 national election. The DPP did well. The GMD, though it experienced serious internal problems and suffered from poor campaign strategy and later admitted "defeat," still had a large majority of the popular votes and won most of the seats. It thus appeared that Taiwan was headed toward a two-party system, and one in which minor parties would play little, if any, role.[20] It even seemed that the GMD and the DPP had conspired against the other parties. The new election law, written in 1989 prior to the election, discriminated against "frivolous parties" in some important ways.[21]

Nevertheless, this did not deter even more new parties from forming. In fact, it seemed to encourage more to announce. The reasons seemed to remain much the same, although it is clear that most of the new parties forming after 1989 were right-of-center parties, and thus were reacting to the DPP election "victory" and its advocacy of independence, media-attracting antics, and its penchant for stirring up controversy.

Minor Parties' Approaches and Strategies

The minor parties that have formed in Taiwan since the lifting of martial law, both before and after the 1989 national election, have tended to be more ideological than their Western counterparts, notwithstanding the fact that ideological candidates have not fared well in election contests since 1980. The reason is that it is not their major objective to campaign in an election and win seats in an elective body of government; rather, a cause or historical mission is the goal of most of the minor parties.[22]

This reflects the fact that most of Taiwan's new minor parties were formed by intellectuals or unsuccessful politicians (or both) and leaders who have not served in office or who are out of office. Most may be called disgruntled. Also, many minor party leaders are not serious about politics in the normal sense of the word. They seek to oppose the DPP and the GMD, express patriotism, make headlines, solicit money, or use the party name to start a business or consolidate an existing commercial enterprise.[23]

Most of the new minor parties have been national, not local, and reflect causes and issues that affect most of the nation's population. Thus, they are generally not parties that advocate decentralization of political power nor "states rights" in the American sense. Nor do they represent religious groups or faiths, or focus on regional or local political issues. Hence, the new parties cannot be said to cause national disintegration; rather the opposite, since most oppose Taiwan independence or localism of any sort.[24]

Because of the nature of Taiwan's electoral system--especially the multiple-member electoral district in LY elections, and something less than that in county magistrate and other county office elections--minor party candidates (when they have entered election competition seriously) have aimed at LY seats or something below the county level. In short, they seek to win offices where they can maintain their less than middle-of-the-road status and do not need to appeal to the electorate in general or a broad segment of it.[25]

The LP and the Workers Party (WP), two of Taiwan's most successful minor parties, are an exception to the rules of appealing to a special class, as well as many of the other generalities made above. Thus, elaboration is necessary to describe the goals of these two parties.

The LP, as noted earlier, was established in late 1987, a few months after the end of martial law. Its founders were socialist intellectuals and labor activists. Its head, Wang Yixiong, was a DPP LY member and labor lawyer. The LP's manifesto stated the hope that the party could become the vehicle and spokesman for Taiwan's labor force of over seven million. It supported trade unionism, and hoped to become a major political force like labor parties in Japan and a number of European countries. It was clearly the perception of LP leaders that both the GMD and DPP failed to represent workers and appealed to business interests too much; it was therefore possible to attract worker organizations into their party.[26]

The WP was formed in March 1989, after breaking with the LP. Its leadership was also made up of left-wing socialists, intellectuals, and labor activists. It broke with the LP over issues (it considered the LP too pragmatic) and personalities.

Both the LP and the WP lost in the 1989 national election. The LP ran a female candidate who had been a stripper. She undressed publicly during the campaign, promised an "open" campaign, and challenged her opponent (also female) to a debate in English and a comparison of nipples. Some observers felt this discredited the LP in the minds of workers and the public.[27] The LP Chairman lost in his election bid, as did other candidates, and the same was true for candidates of the WP.

There is a host of reasons for their election failures. Most important, the DPP came to be perceived as *the* opposition party and got nearly all of the anti-GMD, anti-government, and protest votes. Few votes were cast for any of the minor parties to promote democracy or protest current policies or conditions.[28] Both parties also suffered from GMD and DPP efforts to win labor support. The two leading parties were quite effective in attracting worker support. The LP and the WP also lacked grass-roots organization and financial strength.

Both parties, on the other hand, have sufficient membership to make them more serious contenders than the other minor parties. The LP has an estimated five thousand members, while the WP has more than three thousand. This compares to one thousand or fewer members of the other minor parties, excluding the two older minor parties, the CYP and the DSP.[29]

The remaining minor parties also failed in the 1989 election, or so it appeared when the ballots were counted. But the "two-party" election and the failure of minor parties did not discourage the latter from staying on or new ones from forming. The primary reason, to repeat a point made above, was that they did not seek to do well in this or any future election. Rather, they had other goals.

In the spring of 1990, ten to twelve of the minor parties came out in support of Lin Yanggang and Jiang Weiguo for president and vice-president, in opposition to President Li Denghui. Most of these parties were right-of-center groups made up more of Mainland Chinese (those moving to Taiwan after World War II) than locally born Taiwanese. Some also ran candidates at this time, though their efforts generally were not serious.

Since then, there has been little activity among the minor parties. They remain exactly that: minor, or perhaps even insignificant, parties.

Problems and Prospects for the Minor Parties

Taiwan's older minor parties (the CYP and the DSP), while they have large memberships and are better organized than most of the other minor parties, seem to have little hope of substantial growth or prospects for attracting voter support and thus succeeding at the polls. They seem destined to be viewed as adjuncts to the GMD and thus can offer little in terms of "another voice." Consequently, it is likely that they will decline in importance in the future and have little effect on Taiwan's political future.[30]

The future might be different if the GMD experiences a serious problem with factionalism or splits in an irreparable fashion. One faction may see sufficient utility in making an alliance with one or both of the older minor parties. Clearly, such an alliance would not present serious difficulties for either side. Such a coalition could include some of the other right-wing parties.

One or both of the labor parties appear to have better prospects of gaining membership and winning seats in an election.[31] Their success depends on a number of factors. One is the success or failure of the GMD and DPP to represent labor in Taiwan. If the GMD and the DPP fail to attract labor support, or damage each other seriously with the labor vote, the LP, the WP, or both will benefit. These two parties will likewise gain by building better ties with Taiwan's labor unions. To a large extent, their future will be determined by the course labor organization takes in the future regarding ties with political parties and the unionization process. This is clearly yet to be decided.

Both of the minor parties representing, or trying to represent, labor did poorly in the 1989 election. Yet, at least in the opinion of this writer, this may not be particularly meaningful. Taiwan's political system, in terms of electoral politics, is changing rapidly, and one election does not seal the fate of a party movement or candidate. The DPP has been counted out at times. Some are quite pessimistic about the DPP at present.[32]

The two minor parties representing labor may join or cooperate. This would give them added strength. They may abandon their socialist ideology; this would no doubt help their prospects at the polls. Socialism does not have much appeal in Taiwan; it is seen as promoting laziness, poor quality production, and as damaging to the national interest. Taiwan must maintain quality control and competitiveness to compete internationally. Yet, Taiwan's workers seem destined to organize much more than at present, and this probably means ties with parties or even forming their own party.

One cannot be sanguine about the future of any of the other minor parties. They are too small. They are not seen as serious. They have not performed credibly in any election. Thus, they have in no way proven themselves.

On the other hand, Taiwan's political system--at least in the sense of allowing new parties to form easily and survive--means that in the immediate future it will have a multitude of political parties. If legislation is passed requiring political parties to win a certain percentage of the vote in an election or gain a certain membership within a set time, then the minor parties--at least most of them--will die. GMD-DPP efforts to kill the minor parties could certainly be successful through legislation that discriminates against them. In addition, a change in the voter-district system could also have this effect. A single-member district system would be disastrous to the minor parties, especially if they were required to win a certain proportion of the vote to participate in future elections.

Yet, there are many reasons for thinking this will not happen. The DPP benefitted from the fact that forming a political party was easy. It is still having difficulties recruiting. There is a possibility it will split and thus become vulnerable to minimum-voter-support laws. Thus, it seems unlikely that the DPP will support such legislation at present. The public also views destructive laws aimed at the small political parties as undemocratic. For now at least, there is public support for allowing parties to form easily and keep their present status without legal discrimination.[33]

The minor parties would improve their status and their ability to influence political decisions in Taiwan if they were to form coalitions. However, it seems unlikely, and perhaps virtually impossible, for a large number to join together. On the other hand, it seems quite feasible for a few to join forces. In fact, they have already done this effectively in one or two cases.[34] Coalition politics among the minor parties seems to have potential.

A weakening of the GMD's strength and decline of its prestige would also help the minor parties, assuming that the DPP does not commensurably benefit from the GMD's problems. Inasmuch as the GMD occupies a wide band on the political spectrum, it is vulnerable from both right and left, though it is somewhat more vulnerable from the right, since the DPP is seen as a left-of-center party. This is why most of the minor parties are rightist parties. If the GMD alienates conservatives, as has been evidenced in the last several years by efforts to preempt the DPP's campaign issues, a number of the minor parties may benefit. Clearly, the GMD has been moving to the center or left politically.[35]

If the GMD splits, the minor parties will have an even better chance. One or several could immediately become competitive if this happened, especially if they could take over some of the GMD's bases of support and sources of financial power. However, the more likely possibility is that they will form a coalition with one of the GMD factions if and when the GMD loses strength or suffers from a factional split. A DPP split would also be beneficial to the minor parties, particularly those on the left of the political spectrum. They could claim to be important in building a meaningful opposition to the GMD in the wake of a DPP "failure." They could align with a DPP faction or form a coalition. If the DPP failed to gain in strength, they could attain the status of opposition party among a group of such parties, as is the case with Japan's opposition.

The evolution of some important election issues in Taiwan could also benefit the minor parties. If the Taiwan independence issue becomes heated and divides the GMD and the DPP, or they are not effective in dealing with it or try to become too moderate on the issue, it may allow some minor parties an opportunity to rise in popularity. This seems particularly true if the GMD alters its views on this issue. Many of the minor parties, it should be noted, are "unification" parties.[36]

The environment is another issue that may benefit minor parties. Both the GMD and the DPP, to some degree, lack credibility on this issue. The GMD has allowed the problem to get worse "on its shift." The DPP has offered few serious ideas, and its leaders, many now in office in the counties, do not seem to be acting on the problem. The DPP has some links with the Greenpeace movement, but this may not last. If this does not work, it will allow a minor party to make this link or an environmental party to develop.[37] Another possibility would be for the movement to become unpopular, thereby hurting the DPP and allowing an environmental party to develop at some future date and/or locally.

There are also some groups in Taiwan that may need party representation in the future, for example, the farmers.[38] In addition, businessmen and government officials may seek more direct representation and thus decide to form a new party or support an existing minor party.

Thus, the possibilities for the minor parties, while not good, are not bad either. The minor parties seem destined to be around for the time being. However, conditions must change for them to play a significant political role in Taiwan.

APPENDIX: POLITICAL PARTIES IN TAIWAN

Party Name	Chairmen
China All-People's Party	Ye Yong
China Constitutional Democracy Party	Chen Shou
China Datong Democratic Party	Chen Hengsheng
China Datong Socialist Party	Ma Shouxuan
China Democracy Justice Party	Zhang Dacheng
China Democratic Party	Shen Chaoqiang
China Democratic Reform Party	Gao Zhaoxiong
China Democratic Reunification Party	Wen Zhongxia
China Heroic Patriotic Party	Zhao Guoliang
China Human Rights Promotion Party	Han Weifu
China Iron Guardian Party	Fei Jiliang
China Justice and Peace Party	Zheng Xianglin
China Justice-Upholding Party	Liu Haiyang
China Liberal Democratic Party	Zhang Maolin
China Loyalty and Justice Party	Huang Zhen
China National Security Party	Mo Qifu
China Neo-Socialist Party	Chen Jianfu
China Peace Party	Zhang Wenyang
China People Protection Party	Zhuang Chendong
China People's Party	Wang Zhongchuan
China People's Politics Party	Lu Zhenjiu
China People's Wealth Party	Yu Jinying
China Restoration Party	Wang Chongsan
China Reunification Party	He Maosong
China Revival Party	Li Xiguang
China Rule-By-People Party	Xiao Bolong
China Self-Strengthening Party	Chen Xinfu
China Taiwan Aborigines' Democratic Party	Wu Wenming
China United Party	Xiao Linxiang
China Unity Party	Wu Zhiyi
China Veterans Reunification Party	Zhang Zhenghuang
Chinese All-People's Wealth Even-Distribution Party	Yin Liyan
Chinese Republican Party	Wang Yingchun
Chinese Righteous-Tradition Party	Feng Yue
Chinese Youth Party	Xu Zhenfeng
Datong Party	Jiang Lianxing
Democratic Action Party	Wang Minglong
Democratic Liberal Party	He Weikang
Democratic Self-Reliant Party	Zheng Cunlin
Democratic Socialist Party	Yang Wenzhang
Farmer's Party	Zhang Mingxian
Public Party	Lei Yuqi

Reunification and Democracy Party	Che Hong
Virtuous Public Party	Diao Ping
Young China Democratic Party	Hong Binglu
Young China Party	Chen Hanzhen
Young Chinese Party	Lao Yongqing

Notes

1. This figure was provided in August 1990 by the Election Commission in Taibei. The Appendix is based on this data.

2. Membership data alone may provide a different picture, as will be noted below.

3. *Republic of China Yearbook, 1989* (Taibei: Kwang Hwa Publishing Company, 1989), 194-95.

4. Hung-mao Tien, *The Great Transition: Political and Social Change in the Republic of China* (Stanford: Hoover Institution Press, 1989), 92.

5. Ibid.

6. Ibid.

7. John F. Copper, *Taiwan's Recent Elections: Fulfilling the Democratic Promise* (Baltimore: University of Maryland School of Law, 1990), 78.

8. *Republic of China Yearbook*, 195.

9. Copper, *Taiwan's Recent Elections*, 78.

10. Ibid., 45-59.

11. For further details, see John F. Copper, "The Evolution of Political Parties in Taiwan," *Asian Affairs*, 16, no. 1 (1989): 3-21.

12. *Republic of China Yearbook*, 197.

13. Copper, *Taiwan's Recent Elections*, 61-62.

14. One can realize this simply by looking at the names of the minor parties listed in the appendix.

15. Probably 80 percent of the minor parties are right-of-center, an opinion shared by a number of observers in Taiwan.

16. *Dongyuan zhanluan shiqi renmin tuanti fa* (Law on Civic Organizations During the Period of Mobilization) (Taibei: Ministry of Domestic Affairs, 1989).

17. For further details, see Copper, "The Evolution of Political Parties in Taiwan," 16-17.

18. Ibid.

19. Ibid.

20. For further details, see Copper, *Taiwan's Recent Elections*, 78. For a more general discussion, see ibid., 93-95, 97-98.

21. Ibid. The new election law may be found in the appendix of this work.

22. For further details, see Ya-li Lu, "Party Politics in the Republic of China on Taiwan," in King-yu Chiang, ed., *Political and Social Change in Taiwan and Mainland China* (Taibei: Institute of International Relations, 1989).

23. Ibid.

24. Ibid.

25. This was especially evident in the 1989 national election.

26. Tien, 102-03.

27. At the time, there was some speculation that the GMD surreptitiously helped finance this candidate to embarass the LP.

28. Ibid.

29. Estimates of party strength are based on conversations, during July and August 1990, with a number of observers of party politics in Taiwan. The author assumes that published figures on party membership are not accurate.

30. This opinion is shared by most political observers in Taiwan. In fact, the author has not heard a serious voice to the contrary.

31. Again, this opinion is shared by many experts in Taiwan.

32. This was noticeably true in Taiwan in July and August 1990. DPP leaders expressed concerns over financial problems and recruiting at this time.

33. The author asked a number of experts, including both scholars and officials, about this, but there was no consensus about where Taiwan was heading. However, most did not expect any immediate change.

34. Six minor parties jointly sponsored a candidate in the 1989 election, though this did not get very far. *Duli Wanbao* (Independence Evening News), 3 May 1989, 3.

35. Some observers opine that this is the reason most of the minor parties are right-of-center parties.

36. This is apparent from the names of many of the minor parties.

37. This is the opinion of several observers in Taiwan, as stated to the author in July 1990.

38. At present, the farmers are represented by a minor party.

14

A Half Century Later

James D. Seymour

Following the Communists' takeover of China in 1949, the non-Communist parties seemed to lose their souls. Appearances, however, may have been deceiving. Certainly the groups' behavior during the democracy movement of 1989 provided a few surprises.

These organizations were now called "democratic parties and groups" (*minzhu dangpai*; DPGs)--the term "democratic" intended to suggest tolerance on the part of China's leaders. The 1949-1985 history of these restructured remnants of pre-1949 liberal parties has been told elsewhere.[1] In a word, they became satellites of the Chinese Communist Party (CCP), which in the early 1950s reorganized and perpetuated them for its own purposes. Often they were run by people who were Communists with dual party membership.[2] The minor "parties" (the latter term a misnomer) were seen not only as having propaganda value, but also as potential links with overseas Chinese, and--most important--being in a position to contribute to China's modernization. Comprised of intellectuals and professionals, it was believed that these parties could help promote China's economic development. At any rate, they were seen more as assets than liabilities. With the

---

This is an updated abridgement of a paper which appeared in the spring 1991 issue of *China Information* (Leiden University), and is reprinted with permission and minor changes. Many of the original source citations which appeared in the journal have been dropped here. An earlier version was presented at the Columbia University Seminar on Modern China on 14 March 1991. The author is grateful for comments made by participants at this and the Washington and Lee University meetings, as well as to many DPG informants who must go unnamed.

exception of two brief periods, they gave the outward appearance of being loyal followers of the CCP. The first exceptional period was the famous 1956-57 "hundred flowers" thaw, when DPG members lashed out at the CCP. Three decades later, at the height of the Zhao Ziyang reforms, the parties once again became self-assertive. This essay tells the story of the latter and subsequent developments.

Beginning in the mid-1980s, there was some sentiment in China for a genuine multiparty system. After the democracy movement of late 1986, the CCP moved to check this and other liberal trends, particularly on college campuses, and for the next few years there was heavy propaganda concerning the need to avoid "Western-style democracy." Still, the idea continued to be advocated, most vocally by Chinese students abroad. In response to the demand for a multiparty system, the moderates in the CCP took a number of steps, including the re-coöptation of the democratic parties. At the beginning of 1989, just a few months before the demonstrations that rocked China and brought down his administration, CCP Secretary-General Zhao Ziyang declared that building the multiparty system was the year's "principal task." We will never know exactly what this regime would have looked like, but it can be assumed that it would have represented some kind of compromise between the open-system ideas of the more radical reformers and the hard line of the conservatives. One obvious point of compromise would have been to allow the relatively innocuous democratic parties (which in 1990 still had only 337,000 members[3]) greater autonomy and clout. In the event, the reformers were purged, and the hardliners saw no need to make any compromises at all.

Various Chinese leaders had quite different levels of interest in "united front (UF)" sectors such as the DPGs. Deng Xiaoping and Jiang Zemin paid little attention to them. Mao Zedong, on the other hand, used to take such UF organs very seriously. The front, after all, had been a key part of the strategy which brought him to power. In the 1950s, the "democratic personages" were rewarded in many ways, including public office (see Appendix B). Although such people suffered during the Cultural Revolution, Mao often provided them protection. It is perhaps ironic that in this narrow regard Hu Yaobang and Zhao Ziyang were closer to Mao than to Deng and Jiang.

Hu had a great appreciation of the DPGs. Perhaps in part out of his own desperation to expand his inadequate political base, from 1977 until 1986 he assiduously cultivated relations with them. He promoted the rehabilitation of many of their members and encouraged the parties to grow. In 1986, Democratic League (DL) luminary Fei Xiaotong accompanied him on a much-publicized trip to Europe. Fei was quoted at the time as saying, "The democrats are in the limelight now." (The term "democrats" in such a context refers to DPG figures and also to people of similar standing and outlook who belong to no party.) Later, he said: "The fact that I was able to join the visiting delegation in itself shows the position members of the democratic parties now hold."[4] As a result of Hu's ouster in 1987, which was unrelated to his support for the DPGs, the latter lost an important patron.

Still, Hu's successor appeared to share his views on this subject. "Our previous achievements," Zhao Ziyang declared, "were inseparable from the cooperation of the democratic parties."[5] With Deng Xiaoping's approval, Zhao allowed the plan to expand the role of the parties to proceed. In January 1989, an ad hoc group was formed to prepare a plan for increased DPG participation in government. This group, comprised of CCP, government, and DPG representatives, worked for several months and, by May, had drafted its proposal. Although the text is not available, it apparently stated that the DPGs should participate in organs of state power, be consulted on the choice of state leaders, and participate in the formulation of state principles, policies, laws, and decrees. It anticipated more non-Communists becoming involved in government and judicial work.[6] By this time, however, the general political situation had gotten out of hand, and the whole matter was shelved.

Nonetheless, the DPGs themselves had not been standing still. During the Zhao years (1987 and 1988), most of the bylaws were rewritten, primarily to reflect the emerging CCP line on the role of the parties.[7] To some extent, the changes had to do with the peculiarities of each group, such as the decision to permit the Revolutionary Committee of the Guomindang (RG) and Taiwan Autonomy League (TAL) to recruit from broader categories of people with Taiwan connections.[8] Indeed, many of the changes in the DPGs had to do with current events in Taiwan. The new policies toward the parties were in part a guarded response to the toleration of opposition parties in Taiwan and elsewhere in the hitherto Leninist world.[9] The CCP did not want to be obviously outdone by the GMD, but at the same time it did not want to go as far as the GMD in legitimizing an opposition. Furthermore, China's official policy was to encourage contact between the DPGs and Taiwan's parties (with the exception of parties which favor Taiwan independence). Indeed, many DPG people were genuinely interested in reaching out to Taiwan, and perhaps even serving as an alternative to the CCP in this process.[10] Although this was not quite the thinking of the Communists, the latter did try to facilitate DPG-Taiwan links by such measures as giving the DPGs younger heads--closer in age to the leaders of the parties on Taiwan. But all this tended to call attention to Taiwan's democratization. It put ideas in the heads of some DPG people, and fears in the minds of the Communists.

These fears were not unfounded. Most people in the parties would have preferred to do more than echo the CCP line. In 1990, a moderate DPG member told me that "99 percent" of the members of the DPGs would like their parties to enjoy much greater independence from the CCP. Around 1988, DPG people began talking as though such hopes were close to realization. As a China Association for the Promotion of Democracy (APD) figure opined at a press conference, "Each democratic party, according to its special characteristics, is determining its own political aims and its organizational lines." (That this was wishful thinking is suggested by the fact that the sentence was dropped from the published transcript.[11]) Some even wanted all the parties to combine or confederate, at least for purposes of conducting activities in the National People's Congress (NPC).

The most audacious DPG during this period was the Zhigong Dang (ZGD).[12] In part a cover for the Hong Men secret society, by operating as a "party" this sprawling organization legitimized the Hong Men's existence. In September 1988, at the ZGD's eighth congress, the mood favored explicit independence from the favored CCP. After two days of discussion, Chairman Huang Dingchen seemed to agree, and announced that they would attempt to remove from the bylaws the clause requiring the ZGD to operate under the leadership of the CCP. Furthermore, the organization took steps to achieve financial independence. Whereas the other DPGs were utterly dependent on the Ministry of Finance, the ZGD, many of whose members are returned overseas Chinese, could easily dispense with its subsidy from the CCP. Thus, it decided to cut its financial ties with the latter. As one spokesman explained, real political independence required financial independence. "Times have changed. What the CCP did to the democratic parties in the past has proven to be very wrong. They really need us now, so all parties should operate on an equal basis." He acknowledged that other DPGs could not yet survive without government funds, but, for its part, the ZGD intended to "run our own business."[13]

Although the ZGD was a special case, the DPGs in general were obviously ripe for change. They were seriously afflicted with intergenerational conflicts. In 1988, the average age of members in the largest group, the DL, was under 50, which means that most had little or no recollection of the prerevolutionary period. But despite a few leadership changes (discussed below), a majority of the people at the top levels were elderly. A DL vice-chairman acknowledged: "As is the case elsewhere in society, we have a generation gap, with the older and younger members not always seeing eye to eye."[14] Indeed, while the leaders generally remained loyal to the CCP, they were losing control of their restless, independent-minded memberships.

The shifting mood of the parties was exemplified by a forum held by the DL, in March 1988, on the subject of improving China's legal system. The theme was that the feudal practice of "rule of man" (i.e., arbitrary government; *renzhi*) must end. What is now eye-catching about the forum was the roster of participants, which included such supporters of the 1989 democracy movement as "comrades" Yu Haocheng (who would later spend over a year in jail for his indiscretions) and Yan Jiaqi (now exiled). These and others used the DL forum to point out how serious was the problem of absence of the rule of law (*fazhi*). The transcript, which was published in the DL's magazine, was a scathing indictment of the Communists.[15] Even though many of the participants were not DPG members, it is no wonder that many CCP members harbored doubts about these organizations.

During this period, some significant leadership changes were taking place in these groups, both locally and nationally. At least a few of the newcomers had ideas redolent of those of the Hundred Flowers "rightists." For example, whereas DPGs normally disclaim any intention to rule in rotation or succeed the CCP, Deng Weizhi, who was elected APD vice-chairman in 1988, began urging that the DPGs be allowed to act like real parties, even selecting their own platforms and candidates. He said that they were enjoying greater popularity precisely because of declining confidence in the CCP. "Many intellectuals and political analysts now see the DPGs as the only hope. . . . Everyone realizes that you can no longer demand that everyone have the same dream. Trying to restrict the government to one party is harmful, and indeed is becoming impossible." Deng almost seemed to taunt the Communists: "Just because you are the biggest party today does not mean you will always be!" He noted, however, that before the DPGs could realize their potential, legal measures would have to be enacted to guarantee their autonomy. "Too many of our laws are about control, control, control. They should *protect* us, not control us." He was not optimistic that things would change soon, but insisted that the sooner they did, the sooner Zhao Ziyang's reforms could be realized.[16]

Although people like Deng were getting a bit ahead of events, in the permissive atmosphere of late 1988 the DPGs did appear to be making some subtle, yet unmistakable, changes along the lines he advocated. For one thing, at the lower levels they were becoming more democratic internally, with elections in which there were more candidates than positions to be filled. (However, in elections at the municipal and provincial level and above, there was no choice.) At the same time, the parties began to operate in a more autonomous manner.

CCP Policies in Flux

Despite the tone of some of the rhetoric, these developments did not constitute a rebellion against the CCP. Rather, the DPGs were being given a green light by the Party. The Communists were actually encouraging the DPGs to "replace the old with the new." In 1987, the CCP even indicated that the DPGs would be allowed political freedom, legal equality, and organizational independence, though there was little clarification. A 1988

Renmin ribao (People's Daily) article, entitled "Uphold and Gradually Perfect the Multiparty System under CCP Leadership," explained that although the DPGs were to follow the political leadership of the CCP,

> multiparty cooperation is political cooperation and CCP leadership is political leadership. Political leadership is different from organizational leadership, which generally finds expression in the relationship between the higher authorities and the lower levels. In China, the relationship between various political parties, including the CCP, is obviously not a relationship between the higher and lower organizations. Political parties participate in this cooperation on equal terms, and no party is entitled to issue orders to another party.[17]

Such was the CCP (i.e., Zhao) line of the moment, which also called for expanding the DPG's "supervisory" role. This meant having the various groups keep close watch on government agencies by means of their own reporting systems. It did not mean allowing the DPGs to contend for power, something that even Zhao opposed as "not conforming with Chinese realities."[18] The acceleration of political reform "is not intended to change the system, but to further bring out its superiority."

Throughout this period, the DPGs remained accountable to the CCP's United Front Department (UFD). Thus, the Party man responsible for implementing that line was Yan Mingfu, who had been UFD director since 1986. Although the Soviet-educated Yan was on good terms with Party conservatives, and sometimes sounded like one of them, he was in fact a (cautious) reformer and relatively popular with the DPG rank and file. Immediately after his appointment as UFD head, he called upon DPG people to express their opinions and criticisms without reservations. The parties should "develop a political network and major channels that are in touch with, and reflect the opinions and desires of, the great mass of people."[19] Although he advocated "a high degree of democracy," he cautioned against "mechanically transplanting the model of the West."[20] In other words, there would be no real opposition parties. Yan spelled out the policy of "developing and perfecting the multiparty-cooperation system under the leadership of the CCP" by noting that it was to apply to four areas: the NPC, the Chinese People's Political Consultative Conference (CPPCC), government at all levels, and relations with the CCP.[21] We shall discuss these one by one.

Relations Between the DPGs and the CCP

Although the DPGs were "locked into the establishment," many Communists remained suspicious of them. In response, in 1988 the UFD was instructed to analyze whether the DPGs could be trusted to follow the

CCP during the next decade or two. The UFD reported back that they could.[22] Thus fortified, Zhao Ziyang made a point of cultivating "democrats," especially those in the DPGs (though to a lesser extent than Hu Yaobang had). Beginning in 1988, he brought DPG figures to CCP headquarters at Zhongnanhai to air their views. Many had sharp words on the economy, the environment, lawless cadres, and the education system. At the end of one session, Zhao promised: "You will not find that you have said all this in vain." He strongly hinted that he needed DPG help in overcoming resistance to his reforms on the part of conservatives in the Party.

CCP reformers were especially in need of help outside of Beijing. Local officials were instructed to hold meetings modeled after the ones at Zhongnanhai. CCP members were urged to "respect the authority" of such people and "encourage them to exercise supervision and make criticisms and suggestions."[23] It is difficult to know what to make of press reports of the encounters that took place. At a March 1989 meeting of the Sichuan CCP committee, one DL leader delivered a stinging indictment of the Party's neglect of education, after which, according to the *Renmin ribao*, the Party representative "smiled and nodded, accepting this criticism."[24]

The DPGs in Government Administration

During the first few years of the Communist regime, and even as late as 1957, almost half of all members of the central government's commissions were DPG people. Thereafter, DPG members did not hold many conspicuous government positions. They did not have ministerial rank until early 1988, when the China National Construction Association (NCA) member Feng Tiyun was appointed vice-minister of the newly established Ministry of Supervision.[25]

At this time, Deng Xiaoping issued instructions on the need to enhance the status of the DPGs in the government. It fell to Yan Mingfu to effect these changes. Yan expressed the hope that "leading cadres at all levels of government would raise their understanding of the multiparty cooperation system under the leadership of the CCP and strive to do this work well."[26] To facilitate matters, he even suggested amending the 1982 state constitution. That instrument barely mentions the DPGs; the preamble merely makes reference to the historic role of the UF "composed of democratic parties" and others. In 1988-89, there was sentiment among rank-and-file DPG people to have the constitution explicitly assert the parties' right to exert more influence on the political process. Some DPG leaders said that this was unnecessary, and it is not known just what sort of amendment Yan himself had in mind. A writer in *Renmin ribao* suggested that any changes follow suggestions by Zhao Ziyang concerning the expansion of DPG rights to participate in the administration of state affairs, an increase in the number of DPG members in government, and the enhancement of the parties' "supervisory" role.

"Supervision" did not mean giving anyone orders. As the vice-chairman of the Liaoning People's Congress explained in 1987: "The political consultative conferences [PCCs] and the democratic parties and groups offer criticisms and advice on the work of the government. This is their supervision. It is not that they have a right to perform any governmental function. Supervision has no legal binding force."[27] Supervision was now supposed to take place at all levels and not merely be focused on the central authorities (who could more easily cope with it). New mechanisms were established through which the "supervision" could take place--such as the above-mentioned Ministry of Supervision, which was supposed to ferret out corruption. DPGs were also urged to set up centers to monitor errant CCP and government people, and many were established. But there was much skepticism from both communist and non-communist members of the NPC. It was noted that Communists were often people of very low quality, who failed to appreciate democratic methods and did not even understand matters of policy. "They only listen to words of praise, and will not heed opinions that differ from their own."[28] One person complained of the perfunctory way that "supervision" was instituted. Apparently, word would come down from above that there was to be "supervision" from the DPGs, so a meeting would be quickly called. "If there is a session tomorrow, we are notified today. The materials are issued at the last minute; then, when the meeting is convened, we are asked to give our opinions. This approach easily leads to political consultation and democratic supervision being no more than going through the motions." The speaker urged that supervision be systematized, with the assignment of specific duties to the standing committees of people's congresses and PCCs at every level.

"Supervision" did not usually entail people holding administrative posts. At the height of the Zhao reforms, the DPGs did come close to having quite a few of their people in major government positions. In the midst of considerable wrangling over the division of the spoils, candidates were nominated by the parties, apparently approved by the CCP Organization Department, and may even have been nominated by the State Council. In March 1989, word leaked that twelve senior government posts, or a third of the total, might go to "democrats"--one state councillorship, three full ministerial positions, and eight vice-ministerships. If the experiment went well, it was promised, there would be more such appointments.

But aside from Feng Tiyun, only a few new appointments were made; notable were aeronautics engineer Li Peiyao as vice-minister of labor and Hong Bazeng as vice-minister of agriculture, both having had ties with the

GMD. The choices strongly suggest that the appointments were intended to send a signal to the authorities in Taiwan. However, even though the two are members of the RG and the September Third Study Society (*Jiusan*), respectively, a Hong Kong source asserts that both are long-time CCP members who joined the DPGs on Party instructions.[29] Certainly, Zhao Ziyang was being very careful with these appointments. Any obstreperousness on the part of DPG administrators would outrage CCP conservatives and force the whole experiment to be called off. Still, such appointments (which also took place in the intermediate levels of the bureaucracy[30]) were not meaningless.

But no sooner did word of the "cabinet appointments" begin to circulate than things began to stall. Yan Mingfu claimed that more time would be required to make necessary changes in the law. With the ouster of the reformers soon thereafter, further plans were shelved.

National People's Congress

Forty-five percent of the delegates to the first NPC (1954) belonged to the DPGs. After that, the percentage was much smaller, though in 1990 they enjoyed six vice-chairmanships of the standing committee. Enhancing the role of the NPC, and permitting parties to function therein, was potentially one of the most far-reaching reforms entertained by Zhao Ziyang. The only organized group within the NPC was the CCP. Everyone else was only allowed to "represent the voters," meaning that DL congressmen, for example, were not allowed to organize themselves and promote legislation. Before the 1989 crackdown, "democrats" in the NPC were actively engaged in such undertakings as opposing, on environmental grounds, the Communists' pet Three Gorges project for the Yangtze River. Some of the DPGs even sought to form party blocs in the Congress. Yan Mingfu worked to rein them in, reiterating that there could be no "advocating multiparty politics." In the end, even the limited unhobbling of the DPGs that Zhao and Yan were promoting was overruled by others in the CCP. As of 1990, there were only 540 "democrats" in the 2,967-member NPC, which at any rate was too large and unwieldy to exercise effective power over the CCP.

Chinese People's Political Consultative Conference

If the DPGs had any forums at which to expound their views, they were the 2,931 PCCs at the various levels, which altogether had 410,000 members. The apex of these conferences was the 2,081-member CPPCC, 701 of whose members were DPG people (all 1991 figures.) The term "Chinese People" (not to mention "consultative") is somewhat misleading. The population of China is overwhelmingly comprised of workers (including farmers), whereas only about 7 percent of the members of the CPPCC represented them.[31] The remaining conferees were usually intellectuals and could hardly speak for China. Still, the CPPCC probably reflected at least *urban* public opinion better than any other central political organ. And, after all, conferees were often intelligent, independent-minded people.

Nonetheless, the CPPCC has often been characterized by such apt derisive phrases as "flower vase" and "second-class rubber stamp." In 1988, there was a movement to change this situation. The Seventh CPPCC was probably the liveliest one China had seen. Altogether, 1,540 motions were submitted, of which 81.5 percent were "handled" by the appropriate committees or commissions.[32] Whatever the disposition of these motions, conferees were active as never before in speaking up for the interests of the groups they represented, and the proceedings were fully reported in the media. It is not clear that the DPGs were functioning collectively *as parties* (though this was beginning to happen in local PCCs), and the process does not appear to have been really democratic or to have had much impact. However, the reformers seemed willing to go further. Thus, "Provisional Regulations of the CPPCC National Committee Concerning Political Consultation and Democratic Supervision" were drawn up and published in newspapers around the country.[33] According to these, there were to be "unimpeded channels for participating in and commenting on political affairs." The regulations were quite generous and explicit concerning the manner in which DPG people could criticize the authorities and the subjects that were fair game. These included "how the Constitution and state laws and decrees are implemented. . . , how state organs and their staffs perform their duties," and so forth. "The democratic rights of CPPCC members shall be well protected. It should be possible to air fully views of all types."

But conferees were in for considerable disillusionment, even during the heady months of the Beijing Spring. In March 1989, "some conferees noted that in most cases they simply aired views on political affairs, rather than getting directly involved in political operations, or that they often had to endorse the government without being able to voice alternative opinions. The government usually makes important decisions without fully consulting with the CPPCC, any consultations actually being perfunctory." Thus, members of the TAL, for example, complained that the PRC's policies toward Taiwan were made without consulting them. A RG Central Committee member found that most proposals received stereotypic responses ("under consideration") and only 28 percent of them were taken seriously.[34]

There has long been a widespread awareness in the CPPCC that a prerequisite to empowering its constituent groups would be to allow the latter to have their own news media. A 1988 poll revealed that 63 percent of CPPCC delegates came down strongly on the side of a more open press.[35] DPG people, even at the upper levels, were particularly outspoken on the need for greater freedom of information and ideas. One DPG luminary stated cautiously that inasmuch as "the truth is on our side, so long as we clearly reason things out with the masses we will earn the support of the masses. Do not fear attacks of hostile elements. Let the public judge opposing points of view. Trust their consciousness." Another who urged more openness in the press said: "It is better for people to hear something through official channels than as hearsay. That way, the people will be more apt to rally around the government. When news is reported in a timely and objective way, the media enjoy more respect. To do otherwise only creates additional listeners for Voice of America."[36]

Most of the organizations do have their own organs, such as the RG's semi-weekly journal *Tuanjie Bao* (Unity), the DL's monthly *Qunyan* (Voice of the Masses), and the *Jiusan*'s monthly *Jiusan zhongyang shexun* (*Jiusan* Central Bulletin). During the winter of 1988-89, there were indications that the DPGs would be allowed to publish their own newspapers. That did not happen, but the parties continued to press for a more open news media.

From all this, we can see that the mood of the DPGs was changing and they were becoming more self-assertive. However, society at large was moving even faster than they were.

Tiananmen and Its Aftermath

How did the DPGs behave during the spring of 1989? Although they were overshadowed by more militant organizations, and it is difficult to know how the DPG branches around the country were responding, the DPGs as a whole appear to have risen to the occasion. Indeed, during the demonstrations, the national organs refused to cooperate with the government (though a few local branches apparently did). Before the massacre, they barely gave lip-service support to Li Peng. Some DPG contingents, sporting their own party logos, marched in solidarity with the Beijing citizenry. Outside of the capital, there was also vocal support for the Tiananmen demonstrators. For example, shortly before the declaration of martial law, DPG spokespersons at Tianjin University declared that the student movement "has won strong response and support from the people throughout the country."[37] Even after the declaration of martial law, criticism of the demonstrators, if any, was muted. In the words of "some democratic party figures" in Shenyang: "The extremely small number of [miscreants] should be distinguished from the overwhelming majority. The patriotic zeal of young students should be protected, and the work of the Party and government should be improved."[38] In other words, the dissidents were not wrong when it came to the merits of the issues.

During the month of May, various DPGs issued a series of "urgent appeals" in connection with the student-led demonstrations. For example, the chairman of the ZGD's CC declared that the students' demands were entirely reasonable and in line with the ostensible CCP position. But he did urge the students to return to the classroom and abandon their hunger strike. Likewise, his RG counterpart appealed to the CCP CC to meet with DPG leaders and also to conduct a dialogue with the students. Even the DL's Fei Xiaotong, who rarely wavered from the CCP line, signed a petition urging that such a dialogue be held and the authorities refrain from using force against the Tiananmen demonstrators. Beijing radio repeatedly broadcast such appeals, indicating their (for the moment) "mainstream" nature.

It would be an understatement to say that after the massacre the tone of published pronouncements changed. First, the DPGs all sent delegations to pay their respects to the wounded soldiers. ("Your action shows that the People's Liberation Army is an army composed of our sons and brothers. We will never forget your merit."[39]) In late June, it was declared that the DPGs supported the crackdown. Obviously, this did not reflect the sentiment of the rank and file. Later, it was admitted that there had been disloyalty among DPG people (indeed, some arrests were reported[40]), and the *Renmin ribao* emphasized the need to keep "dissidents" out of the organizations. Attention was first directed to leadership organs. It was declared that everyone must "adhere to the principle of paying attention to both ability and political integrity, and give prominence to political stand and to ideological and moral quality."[41] Then the system for recruiting new members was tightened. In addition to fulfilling all the previous requirements, a person could now join a DPG only with the approval of the CCP secretary in his or her unit. There had not been such a requirement until this rule was quietly introduced in 1990.

Were one to judge by media accounts, DPG organs around the country were trying to outdo everyone in their support of Zhongnanhai. This required taking an unambiguous position regarding the "counterrevolutionary rebellion." Elements in the RG (probably the most conservative of the parties) seem to have prided themselves on their role in taking "a clear-cut stand during the turmoil."[42] Likewise, the *Jiusan* in Shandong pointed (not too convincingly) to the "great efforts" it and the other parties had made to safeguard stability, and promised to continue. It was admitted that there was more "stabilizing" to do, but the *Jiusan* promised to "try every possible means to convert negative factors into positive ones."[43] A Liaoning DL spokesman declared: "We shall deliver a powerful counterblow to those hostile international forces who hope in vain to effect peaceful evolution toward Western-style political pluralism."[44] None of this can be taken as reflecting the views of most DPG members.

By the end of 1989, with the DPGs thus cowed, the CCP was ready to formalize new arrangements. The CC held a plenary session, during which it called for "enhancing" the role of the DPGs in the NPC. Work resumed on the policy statement that had been set aside in May, and on 30 December, amid much fanfare, the CCP issued its twenty-four point "Proposals of the CCP Central Committee on Persisting in and Improving the System of Multiparty Cooperation and Political Consultation under the Leadership of the Chinese Communist Party." Said to have been pursuant to Deng Xiaoping's instructions, one suspects that it was a far cry from whatever draft had existed the previous spring. Although there was still talk of DPG participation in "state power," it is clear that the power now rested not with the state but with the CCP. No longer was "supervision" by the DPGs meaningful; rather, it was "of great importance for strengthening and improving the CCP's leadership." The "Proposals" continued:

> In practicing multiparty cooperation in our country, it is imperative to uphold the leadership of the Communist Party and the four cardinal principles. This is the political foundation on which the CCP cooperates with the various democratic parties. The leadership the CCP exercises over the democratic parties is political leadership, i.e. leadership in political principle, political orientation, and major principles and policies.[45]

Thus, CCP committees at all levels were told to strengthen and improve their leadership over the democratic parties.

Nor were things going well in the CCP's UFD. The UFD had been the Zhao administration's channel not only to the DPGs, but also to the democratic activists. Now, Yan Mingfu was purged,[46] accused by Jiang Zemin of having made "major rightist political mistakes" and being "politically immature."[47] Many cadres in the department found themselves in trouble for having been too closely involved with the "counterrevolutionary rebels," i.e., for carrying out Zhao's policies.

Those policies, of course, now lay in shambles. As far as CCP-DPG relations were concerned, the idea of even limited autonomy was dead. DPG leaders advised members that "political consultation" now meant that "the democratic parties can endorse and accept the general and specific policies proposed by the CCP."[48] Typically, the media reported that the CCP CC's decisions were unanimously supported by the various provincial DPGs. Any contributions the latter made pertained to non-sensitive problems. Thus, the DPGs reverted to their role of aiding China's *economic* modernization (running technical schools, consulting with enterprises, etc.[49]) and dissociating themselves from the question of *political* modernization. Any criticism had to be confined to safe subjects, such as environmentalism, poverty, illiteracy, and local protectionism.[50] But the parties were not to broaden their constituencies.

The regime made an attempt to give all this a theoretical gloss and justify it in terms of traditional CCP thinking.[51] Two months after the crackdown, the public was asked to read Deng Xiaoping's April 1957 report on the CCP's need to be "supervised" by the DPGs.[52] (Members must have found it chilling to recall how soon after delivering that report Deng had become a leading persecutor of "rightists.") At the end of 1989, Deng's updated views on the subject were made known. He declared that although the DPGs should be transformed from "flower vases" into "parties that participate in politics," the CCP would not repeat the mistakes of their Eastern European colleagues and permit these, or any other groups, to become opposition parties.

The plan to increase DPG presence in government administration also faltered. In June 1990, Jiang Zemin had to admit that "the number of true slots for non-CCP cadres has decreased, not increased," a situation which he said needed correcting.[53] Amid much praise in the media, there were frequent reports that DL head Fei Xiaotong would be elevated to state vice-president. However, this was finally denied by the secretary-general of the League, who seemed to imply that while the Communists would consult with others when they wanted to, they would not soon be offering high positions to DPG people.

Thus, the DPGs were relegated to their old role as support groups for the CCP, although they continued to have a more conspicuous presence in government than in previous years. This was especially true locally. Still, the emphasis seemed to be on these people lending their professional skills to the government. "Supervision" and "consultation" now took a back seat to "cooperation." As a provincial APD head explained the current line, "Of the three . . . , cooperation is fundamental, and the other two should be centered on cooperation."[54]

In both the central and local governments, DPG-member administrators held their government positions as individuals, not as representatives of their parties. This meant that they need not fear discipline from that particular source. On the other hand, they could not count on their DPG for support. Thus, any impact they might have had doubtless stemmed more from *guanxi* (personal connections) than anything else. Indeed, local officials were urged to promote personally such relationships with DPG people. "Responsible persons of the Party committees at various levels must keep in contact with responsible persons of the DPGs so that they can become close friends and benefit from each other politically and ideologically."[55] But there appeared to be few such friendships.

Certainly, at the national level, Jiang Zemin made it clear that he wanted to hear only "correct opinions" from the DPGs.[56] His main emphasis was on "unity." Instead of giving the DPGs free rein, "We [Communists] should help the DPGs improve themselves."[57] Any government posts earmarked for DPG people were not filled by nominees of the parties; the CCP made the decision. Sometimes increasing DPG representation in government was simply a matter of having a government functionary join a DPG. Even in the CPPCC the picture was bleak.[58] Indeed, word went out to DPG participants that they should avoid making harsh criticisms at CPPCC meetings, in the interest of "harmony and stability."[59] As a reward for conferees' contrition, psychological and financial perquisites were improved, but the Conference was once again a flower vase, and the "unreliable" were forced to resign.

One is struck by how many people misjudged the situation in China in the spring of 1989. As far as the democratic parties were concerned, they mistook CCP offers of enhanced window-dressing status for a genuine liberalization. As it turned out, the real banner of the democratic parties could be carried only by exiled DPG members, who attempted to organize and promote what they considered to be the proper DPG agenda.[60] As for the moderates in the CCP, they thought that minor political reforms were possible and the conservatives' power was waning. The history of other communist countries indicates that once political reforms begin, it is very difficult to stop halfway. At any rate, the conservatives, who were simply biding their time, were of no mind to permit anything except purely economic reforms. Accurately perceiving the situation was Deng Xiaoping, who realized that brutal repression, and nothing else, could sustain the power of the CCP.

The Outlook for the Democratic Parties

One can envisage a scenario in which the DPGs might play a real role in China's political future. A clue came during the spring of 1989, when dissident workers tried to reach out to other sectors for support. Best known is the story of their strained relations with the students of Tiananmen. Less well-known is that the unofficial Beijing Autonomous Workers' Federation tried to legalize the organization by linking up with the democratic parties. They made no progress, though some DPG members were sympathetic. The episode suggests that if Hu-Zhao-type reforms were ever implemented, with the DPGs and no other political parties given autonomy, many socioeconomic groups might gravitate toward them, if only as a cover to legitimize their activities (as the Hong Men succeeded in doing in the case of the Zhigong Dang).

However, it is at least as likely that the DPGs have little future. This assessment is based on a number of considerations.

Their analogues in Taiwan, the old-line minor parties,[61] proved irrelevant in the limited democratization of the early 1990s. True, Taiwanese political culture is in many ways un-Chinese and anathema to Leninism, and we need to look farther afield. As I have explained elsewhere, the DPGs also had close analogues in Eastern Europe.[62] The European "DPGs" usually proved as irrelevant to political modernization as they did in Taiwan. The main exceptions were Poland and East Germany. In the latter, the minor parties were in a position to negotiate between the communists and the real democrats. In 1989, before joining the new coalition government with the communists, several minor parties were able to extract a price: they insisted that a constitutional convention be held, with all political forces represented, and that the leading role of the communists be eliminated from the state constitution.

Developments in China raise doubts as to whether anything along the East German line could occur. Given the unpopularity of people like Li Peng, if the DPGs had had any influence at all, they should have been able to tip the balance in favor of keeping their patron, Zhao Ziyang, in office. They made some unsuccessful efforts to do so in May 1989. They failed in part because, except for their links with the CCP, they were isolated organizations with little following.

This brings us to the subject of how the general public can be expected to view the DPGs. One of the most difficult aspects of these groups to understand is what other people think of them. Out of different considerations, neither serious intellectuals, serious democrats, nor serious communists appear to hold them in very high regard. On the other hand, they are not totally without esteem. After all, these people are usually accomplished professionals. Indeed, standards are such that it is more difficult to join a DPG than the CCP. One never hears it said of a DPG, as is officially admitted in the case of the CCP, that "decadent elements and unqualified members" are a problem.[63] By virtue of one's DPG membership, one has also demonstrated a certain ability to manipulate the system in order to advance, which many will appreciate if not admire. Finally, these organizations have the trappings of respectability. Often, the municipal DPG headquarters is one of the finest buildings in town. In Kunming, the joint CPPCC-DPG headquarters is said to be "the most luxurious public building in the city, complete with western-style executive suites. In interviews, a sense of self-importance is obvious among leaders of the city's democratic parties."[64]

In the face of such conflicting impressions, what did the average Chinese actually think of these "democrats"? These groups were sometimes referred to as "tail parties" or "son parties." Such terms are moderately pejorative. However, the unpublished survey of Shi Tianjian reveals that most people were neutral in their attitudes toward the DPGs, primarily from lack of knowledge. Hardly anyone deemed the DPGs inimical to their own or the public's interests. But respondents who were able to say anything intelligent about them were somewhat negative. Those who seemed to know the most about them held them in the least esteem. The negative responses generally had to do with "opportunism" *(jihuizhuyi)*. Interestingly, the Communists were much more apt to perceive DPG people in this light than were ordinary citizens, but only one in ten Communists made such a judgment. Indeed, what is striking is the fact that the DPGs register so low on the consciousness of the Chinese people. Not only were three-quarters of the respondents unable to make informed comments about them, neither were a majority of CCP members. That is surprising in view of the repeated campaigns to persuade Party members to take the DPGs seriously.[65]

But the future of the DPGs does not hinge on what the public thinks of them. It depends in the short run on how useful they are to the ruling party, and, in the longer run, on the extent to which they service their narrow constituencies. DL head Fei Xiaotong has frankly promoted his organization as an interest group. Indeed, until a few years ago, a DPG was the only such organization an intellectual could join. This explains why they attracted so many respectable names; such people had few other places to go. Some, of course, could join the writers' union, and some even joined the CCP. But the prestige of the latter has long been lower than the largely corruption-free DPGs, and one cannot join the writers' union unless one is a "writer," in the eyes of the Communists. Intellectuals thirsted for other options. In the late 1980s, opportunities presented themselves. Suddenly, China abounded in professional associations and similar organizations, as well as chambers of commerce, philanthropic organizations, and learned societies. As interest groups, the DPGs did not appear to be more effective than the others.

Thus, most people hesitate to attach their fates to these organizations, especially in light of their disreputable leaders. *Renmin ribao's* boast that the DPGs owe their very existences to the Communists has an ironic ring of truth;[66] in the long run, the DPGs may find that debt unbearable. Still, there are so many enlightened people in their ranks and in exile that we should not write them off completely.

Appendix A —The Democratic Parties and Groups

Abbreviated name	English Name	Chinese Name	Primary Constituency	Size	Previous Incarnation or Historic Name
APD/Minjin	China Association for the Promotion of Democracy	Zhongguo minzhu cujin hui	schoolteachers	48,000 (1991)	Related to Sanminzhuyi Promotion Association
DL/Minmeng	China Democratic League	Zhongguo minzhu tongmeng	intellectuals	99,000 (1990)	National Salavation Association; League of Chinese Democratic Political Groups
Jiusan	September Third Study Society	Jiusan xueshe	higher intellectuals	45,000+ (1991)	Democratic Scientific Forum
NCA/Minjian	China Democratic National Construction Association	Zhongguo minzhu jianguo hui	business people	50,000 (1991)	Vocational Education Group
PW/Nonggong	Chinese Peasants' and Workers' Democratic Party	Zhongguo nonggong minzhu dang	health professionals	46,000 (1991)	Third Party
RG/Minge	Revolutionary Guomindang	Guomindang geming weiyuanhui	former GMD members and their offspring	40,000 (1991)	Sanminzhuyi Comrades Association; Sanminzhuyi Promotion Association
ZGD	Zhigong Dang	Zhigong dang	"returned overseas Chinese"	10,000+ (1991)	See note 12.

Appendix B — Pre-1949 Middle Party Personages and Their Post-1949 Positions[67]

NAME	PARTY	DATE	PROVINCE OF ORIGIN	MAIN OFFICE HELD AFTER 1949
Chu Tunan	DL	1899-	Yunnan	Chairman, Southwest Culture & Education Commission
He Xiangning	RG	1878-1972	Guangdong	Chairman, Overseas Chinese Committee
Hu Yuzhi	DL	1896-1986	Zhejiang	Director, Press & Publications Administration; Vice-Minister of Culture
Huang Shaohong	RG	1895-1966	Guangxi	NPC Standing Committee (SC)
Huang Yanpei	NCA	1878-1965	Jiangsu	Vice-Premier; Minister of Light Industry
Jiang Guangnai	RG	1887-1967	Guangdong	Minister of Textile Industry
Li Jishen	RG	1886-1959	Guangxi	PRC Vice-President
Liang Xi	Jiusan	1883-1956	Zhejiang	Minister of Forestry
Luo Longji	DL	1896-1965	Jiangxi	Minister of Forest Industry
Ma Xulun	APD/DL	1884-1970	Zhejiang	Minister of Education and Higher Education
Peng Zemin	DL/PW	1877-1956	Guangdong	Vice-Chairman, Political Science & Law Commission
Shao Lizi	RG	1882-1967	Zhejiang	NPC SC; Vice-President, Academy of Socialism Studies
Shen Junru	DL	1875-1963	Zhejiang	President of Supreme Court
Shi Liang	DL	1900-1985	Jiangsu	Minister of Justice
Tan Pingshan	RG	1886-1956	Guangdong	Vice-Chairman, Supervision Commission
Wang Kunlun	RG	1902-1985	Jiangsu	Vice-Mayor of Beijing
Zhang Lan	DL	1872-1955	Sichuan	PRC Vice-President
Zhang Bojun	PW/DL	1895-1969	Anhui	Minister of Communications
Zhang Naiqi	NCA	1896-1977	Zhejiang	Minister of Grain
Zhu Xuefan	DL	1905-	Shanghai	Minister of Posts and Telecommunications

Notes

1. James D. Seymour, *China's Satellite Parties* (Armonk, New York: M. E. Sharpe, Inc., 1987). There is also useful information in the more recent *Zhongguo dangpai shetuan cidian* (Dictionary of Chinese Political Parties, Groups, and Mass Organizations), ed. Wang Jin and Yang Jianghua (Beijing: CCP Historical Materials Press, 1989).

2. During the spring of 1989, a key demand of the DPG rank and file was that Communists resign from the groups' leadership positions. Sometimes it was a question of the chairpersons, but more often it was the secretaries-general who appeared to have the real power. Indeed, the fact that no one could accuse China's DPGs of being opposition parties is due in large measure to the semi-clandestine role of Communists therein. Although until the 1980s there was little evidence of people having dual CCP-DPG membership, almost half of the elites of these groups also belonged to the CCP. In one survey, of 472 CPPCC members who returned "valid questionnaires," eighty belonged to a DPG, and thirty-five (44 percent) had dual party membership. If one were to assume that non-Communists are more apt to reply than Communists, then the percentage would be higher. Zhou Jiezhai, "CPPCC Wants a Freer and More Open Press," *Xinwen zhanxian* (News Front), August 1988, 7-8; trans. in JPRS CAR-88-079, 1. (Although this is an interesting survey, the results may have been distorted by the fact that only 16 percent of CPPCC members returned "valid questionnaires.") The DPG which seems to have the greatest incidence of CCP members in top positions is the *Jiusan*. He Zhenming, *Zhengming* (Contend), 1 March 1990, 36f; JPRS CAR-90-090, 12). Its head, Zhou Peiyuan, was said to be a CCP member. Qian Jiaju, "Family and National Events in 80 Years of My Life," *Mingbao yuekan*, March 1989, 92-97; JPRS CAR-89-047, 24.

Figures for dual membership for an entire DPG are only available for the NCA, in which just under 3 percent are also in the CCP. Beijing TV, press conference remarks of Wan Guoquan, FBIS CHI-89-056, 30.

3. Figure from Lu Niu, "Jiang Zemin Airs His Views on United Front Work for the First Time Since Taking Office as General Secretary," *Mingbao*, 12 June 1990, 52; U.S. Foreign Broadcast Information Service (FBIS), CHI-90-116, 7f. The figure includes all eight DPGs. In 1949, it is claimed, the parties had only ten thousand members. Yan Mingfu, quoted by Beijing radio, 7 April 1989; FBIS CHI-89-069, 21.

4. *Renmin zhengxie bao* (CPPCC News), 8 July 1986; translated in *Inside China Mainland*, September 1986, 25.

5. Li Shangzhi, "Nonparty Personages Put Forward Suggestions on State Management to CPC Central Leaders," *Liaowang* (Observer) (overseas ed.), 24 October 1988, 3-5; FBIS CHI-88-214, 29.

6. Zhang Mu, "The CCP Says that the 'Two Cold Wars have Started'; the Issue of 'Inviting Other Parties to Join the Cabinet' Will be Discussed After the National People's Congress Session," *Jingbao* (Mirror), April 1990, 42-46; FBIS CHI-90-082, 17.

7. On the APD's new bylaws, see *Renmin ribao*, 29 November 1988, 4; FBIS CHI-88-234, 30. On the Chinese Peasants' and Workers' Democratic Party's (hereafter, PW) bylaws, see Beijing Radio, 10 November 1988; FBIS CHI-88-220, 25f.

8. New China News Agency (hereafter, NCNA), 20 November 1988; FBIS CHI-88-225, 30.

9. The true analogues of the DPGs are not Taiwan's Democratic Progressive Party, but rather the tiny Chinese Youth and Democratic Socialist parties, which have been satellites of the GMD since the late 1940s. The PRC, however, appears to regard all parties on Taiwan as "democratic parties."

10. See Ya Yi, "Guo Gong liang dang bu zai longduan da du...." (No more monopoly for the GMD and CCP....), *Shibao zhoukan* (Times Weekly), 21 July 1990.

11. Press conference of DPG leaders, broadcast live by Beijing Radio, 8 April 1988, and transcript subsequently published by NCNA; *Inside China Mainland*, June 1988, 24.

12. In my *Satellite Parties*, the Zhigong Dang was not considered one of the DPGs. Originally known as the Hong Men (red sect), its origins can be traced to the late Ming Dynasty, and it is said to have been involved with the Taipings in the mid-nineteenth century. It is claimed that Sun Yat-sen turned it into its modern form--a political party of people who are, or have connections with, overseas Chinese. The official PRC government version is that the Zhigong Dang was founded in San Francisco in 1925. Indeed, led by the notorious Situ Meitang, the group did have a substantial presence in the United States, where it was known as the Hong Men Zhigong Tang (a tong, meaning society or gang). By the late 1940s, the term "*Tang*" became "*Dang*" (party), and the "Hong Men" part of the name was officially dropped. The 1947 congress of the renamed organization was held in Hong Kong. The following year, pro-Communist vice-chairman (later, chairman) Chen Qiyou joined with other leaders of the middle parties in signing a letter in support of the Communists. For more information, see Zhang Junmin, *Zhongguo minzhu dangpai shi* (A History of China's Democratic Parties and Groups) (Beijing: Huaxia Press, 1989).

13. Remarks by Qinan University Professor Pan Yadun in *Hongkong Standard*, 9 December 1988, 6; FBIS CHI-88-237, 23ff. In a February 1989 interview with *Zhongguo Tongxun She* (China News Service), Pan appeared to soften his demands somewhat. FBIS, CHI-89-030, 23.

14. Qian Weichang, DL vice-chairman, at a press conference of DPG leaders, broadcast live by Beijing Radio, 8 April 1988, with transcript subsequently published by NCNA; *Inside China Mainland*, June 1988, 25.

15. *Qunyan* (Voice of the Masses), 7 May 1988, 3-9; JPRS CAR-88-056, 31.

16. *South China Morning Post*, 1 December 1988, 13; FBIS CHI-88-231, 16.

17. Sun Qimeng, "Uphold and Gradually Perfect the Multiparty Cooperative System under CCP Leadership," *Renmin ribao*, 7 November 1988, 4; FBIS CHI-88-218, 24.

18. NCNA, 30 January 1989; FBIS CHI-89-019, 29.

19. Quoted in *Inside China Mainland*, April 1989, 30.

20. Paraphrase from NCNA, 21 March 1989; FBIS CHI-89-055, 36.

21. Beijing Radio, 7 April 1989; FBIS CHI-89-067, 26.

22. Ceng Bin, "Party Struggles Exposed by Senior Statesmen Themselves," *Jingbao*, 10 August 1989; FBIS CHI-89-153, 14f. For more on the united front, see Yuan Lizhou, *Tongzhan zhishi yu zhengce* (United Front: Information and Policy) (Harbin: Harbin Industrial University Press, 1985).

23. Governor Shao Qihui, report to the Heilongjiang Provincial People's Congress, 8 March 1990, *Heilongjiang ribao*, 9 March 1990, 1-4; FBIS CHI-90-090, 101.

24. *Renmin ribao*, 13 March 1989, 5; FBIS CHI-89-055, 74. The individual was Zhang Haoruo, who, in addition to being vice-secretary of the provincial CCP, was also governor.

25. For Feng Tiyun's description of his job, see *China Daily*, 3 April 1991, 4; FBIS, CHI-91-066, 33f.

26. Paraphrase on Beijing Radio, 7 April 1989; FBIS CHI-89-067, 26.

27. Remarks by Gu Jingxin, quoted in *Qunyan*, no. 6 (1987): 3-8; trans. in *Inside Mainland China*, November 1987, 20.

28. Fu Shiying (a professor at Harbin Medical School), quoted in *Qunyan*, no. 6 (1987): 3-8; trans. in *Inside Mainland China*, November 1987, 20.

29. Zhou Daozheng, "'Blue Princes' Are in Demand in Mainland China's Political Arena," *Chaoliu* (Tides), 15 February 1990, 31-34; JPRS CAR-90-040, 28.

30. In 1991, it was reported that 1,168 "democrats" occupied posts above the county level, up 49 percent from the previous year. *China Daily*, 8 February 1991, 1; NCNA, 28 March 1991; FBIS CHI-91-060, 22.

31. Anita Chan, "The Challenge to the Social Fabric," *The Pacific Review*, April 1989, 129.

32. By comparison, in 1991 there were 1,915 proposals. Of these, 99.5 percent were "handled," which probably means that, in the wake of the crackdown, hardly anyone introduced motions which would raise the ire of the Communists. NCNA, 30 March 1991; FBIS CHI-91-062, 25f.

33. These were adopted on 27 January 1989. The text was published in *Xinhua ribao* (Nanjing), 28 January 1989, 4; FBIS CHI-89-025, 8f. They appeared in *Renmin ribao* the same day (p. 4).

34. NCNA, 21 March 1989; FBIS, 22 March 1989, 28.

35. Zhou Jiezhai, 7-8.

36. Ibid., 7-8. Although the speakers were not identified, they were both described as "leaders" of DPGs.

37. Tianjin Radio, 17 May 1989; FBIS CHI-89-107, 120.

38. *Liaoning Ribao,* 1 June 1989, 1; FBIS CHI-89-132, 58.

39. *Renmin ribao,* 18 June 1989, 1; FBIS CHI-89-119, 26.

40. Ren Yiju, "Beijingren yanqian de liusi" (June Fourth Before Beijingers' Eyes), *Zhongguo zhi chun* (China Spring), August 1990, 10.

41. *Renmin ribao*, 23 October 1989, 4; FBIS CHI-89-209, 21 (with reference to the PW).

42. Jilin radio, 9 March 1990; FBIS CHI-90-050, 46. See also, Beijing radio, 18 February 1990; FBIS CHI-90-040, 17.

43. Report of the Second Congress of the Shandong *Jiusan* Society, Jinan, 5 March 1990. Jinan radio, 5 March 1990; FBIS CHI-90-052, 33.

44. Gao Qingzhou, quoted in *Liaoning ribao,* 14 February 1990, 2; JPRS CAR-90-027, 70.

45. Text published by NCNA, 7 February 1990; FBIS CHI-90-26, 7-11. Compare this with the earlier *Renmin ribao* statement quoted on p.294. The document also calls for bimonthly meetings between CCP and DPG leaders at all levels and for important documents to be "relayed" to the DPGs.

46. At first, Yan was stripped of his post only as secretary of the CCP Secretariat and not the directorship of the UFD, though as a practical matter he ceased to function in that capacity. A Hongkong periodical reported that he was replaced by Ding Guangen in mid-1990. Qiu Zhen, "Ding Guangen Takes Charge of the UFD," *Zhengming*, 1 August 1990, 13; FBIS, CHI-90-152, 17.

47. *South China Morning Post,* 7 March 1990; FBIS CHI-90-045, 35.

48. PW head Lu Jiaxi, quoted by NCNA, 26 March 1990; FBIS CHI-90-062, 21.

49. Data concerning DPG educational programs and consulting services is contained in Sun Yong, "Chinese Democratic Parties Play an Increasing Important Role," NCNA, 4 April 1991; FBIS, CHI-91-066, 25 f.

50. See, for example, Wang Baowang et al., "We Must Remove Local Protectionism," *Qunyan*, 7 February 1991, 22f.; FBIS, CHI-91-057, 55-57.

51. A long treatise on the subject is Liu Xiaoping and Xu Shuang, "China's Socialist Political Party System," *Guangming ribao* (Guangming Daily), 1 June 1990, 3; FBIS CHI-90-120, 19-23.

52. Deng Xiaoping, "The Communist Party Must Accept Supervision," *Deng Xiaoping wenxuan* (Selected Works of Deng Xiaoping). See *Zhongguo xinwen she* (China News Service), 20 August 1989; FBIS CHI-89-160, 16-18.

53. Zou Aiguo, report on Jiang's 14 June speech, NCNA, 14 June 1990; FBIS CHI-90-117, 25.

54. Liu Guoyu, quoted in *Liaoning ribao,* 14 February 1990, 2; JPRS CAR-90-027, 70.

55. Quoted in *Renmin ribao,* 14 May 1990, 5; FBIS CHI-90-110, 30.

56. Sun Benyao, "CCP Leaders Hold Talks with Other Parties," Beijing radio, 31 December 1989; FBIS CHI-89-250, 29.

57. Beijing Radio, 14 June 1990; FBIS CHI-90-116, 6.

58. See, for example, Qian Jiaju, "Zhengxie jiujing qi shema zuoyong?" (What Use is the CPPCC After All?), *Zhongguo zhoubao* (China Weekly), 2 June 1990, 86f.; Qian Jiaju, "Minzhu kongqi yuyi xibo" (The Democratic Climate Becoming Increasingly Rarified), *Zhongguo zhoubao*, 25 May 1990, 66f. On Qian's background as a "democratic personage," see his "Zhi wu bu yan re da huo" (The Self-inflicted Troubles of One Who Spoke Out), *Zhongguo zhoubao*, 12 May 1990, 38f. The CCP took a dim view of Qian's writings, and in 1991 he was among those dismissed from their DL posts. See NCNA, 20 March 1991; FBIS, CHI-91-055, 12.

59. *Hongkong Standard*, 30 March 1990, 11; FBIS CHI-90-062, 34ff.

60. In 1991, a Chinese Democratic Parties' Overseas Center was established in New York. It plans to publish a monthly magazine called *Shidai baogao* (The Times), which would circulate among members in China. For an exiled DPG member's optimistic view of the possibilities for transforming and empowering the parties, see Ya Yi, "Zhongguo minzhu dangpai gaizao lun" (On Reforming China's Democratic Parties and Groups), *Tansuo* (Explorations) (New York), August 1990, 59-63.

61. Supra, n. 9.

62. Seymour, *China's Satellite Parties*, chap. 1.

63. Chengdu Radio, 12 December 1988; FBIS CHI-88-294, 57.

64. Chan, 130. Elsewhere, the facilities of the DPGs are often dilapidated. Lu Yue, "CCP Losing Legitimacy," *Jingbao,* 10 April 1989, 28-32; JPRS CAR-89-086, 9.

65. The two most common answers were misguided, such as that the DPGs are for famous people. Although it is not false to say that the DPGs have famous people, this is a poor way to describe them and hardly more true for the DPGs than for other national organizations. Furthermore, the emptiness of the response is revealed by how few people could answer the question, "Can you name any leading figures in the DPGs?" Only 13 percent could, compared with 36 percent who could name a Taiwan leader.

The people outside of Beijing (where all of Shi's respondents lived) undoubtedly have an even poorer understanding of the DPGs. One NCA member in Anshan complained in a letter to a newspaper that he was sometimes viewed as a "turncoat." He wondered if he would ever be able to join the CCP. "I run into all sorts of strange notions. Chief among them are the accusations that the party I joined 'belongs to the Guomindang', that it is 'absolutely distinct from and incompatible with the CCP', that because of my NCA membership I am unqualified to be shop manager." The paper replied that all of this was wrong, and that if he met the other qualifications, he would be welcomed as a member of the CCP. *Gongchandang yuan* (Communist Party Member), no. 54 (1987), 48; translated in *Inside Mainland China*, November 1987, 23.

66. "Without the Leadership of the Communist Party,... Today There Would Be No Workers' and Peasants' Party." *Renmin ribao*, 23 October 1989, 4; FBIS, CHI-89-209, 21.

67. Information from Zhou Daozheng, 29-31 (supra, n. 29).

15

Historical Perspectives on Chinese Democracy: The Overseas Democracy Movement Today

Andrew J. Nathan

A reporter called recently and asked for my comments on a story she was writing: "Why has the overseas democracy movement failed?"

The question startled me. I am not sure that the democracy movement *has* failed. At the same time, since I was reading the essays for this volume when she called, the question set me thinking about the lessons of the past for Chinese democrats today. In some ways, the two experiences are parallel, and the democrats of today may learn something, both about the problems they face and the goals they are aiming at, by looking at the experiences and ideas of Chinese democrats earlier in this century.

Survey of the Overseas Democracy Movement and Its Problems

Today's overseas democracy movement (ODM) is a congeries of individuals and organizations who have been trying to promote Chinese democracy from locations outside of China since the crackdown in June 1989.

The two largest groups are called the Federation and the Alliance. The Federation for a Democratic China (abbreviated as *Minzhen*; FDC) has its headquarters in Paris and is headed by Yan Jiaqi, a former advisor to Zhao Ziyang and ex-head of the Institute of Political Science at the Chinese Academy of Social Sciences. Its other most active member is the general secretary, Wan Runnan, the former head of the Stone electronics group in Beijing and fund-raiser for FDC. The latter publishes a magazine, *Minzhu Zhongguo* (Democratic China), whose editors are Su Xiaokang and Yuan Zhiming, well-known writers in China. In September 1990, the FDC convened its second annual convention in San Francisco. At that time, the word was that Yan hoped Fang Lizhi would succeed him as chairman, but that Fang had decided to stay out of political activism and concentrate on his professional scholarship and human-rights activities.

While the FDC is a relatively new group, set up in 1989 by people who fled China after the crackdown, the second organization, the Chinese Alliance for Democracy (abbreviated as *Minlian*; CAD), goes back to 1982. It was founded by people who left China in the aftermath of the less violent crackdown on the Democracy Wall movement of 1978-81, and is still headed mostly by people of this type. It is located in New York and publishes a magazine, *Zhongguo zhi chun* (China Spring). CAD is headed by Hu Ping, who became known by contesting an election at Beijing University in 1980 on a "freedom-of-speech" platform. He later came to Harvard University for graduate study in political theory. In 1988, he quit school to head CAD.[1]

These two groups can be described as movement-organizations, seeking to mount broad-based pressure for change through publicity, theoretical work, and lobbying.

There is also a political party within the ODM called the Chinese Liberal-Democratic Party (LDP).[2] It was recently founded in Columbus, Ohio, mostly by Chinese students and a handful of long-time activists. The LDP seeks to use whatever means necessary to replace the Chinese Communist Party (CCP) in power. This implies the possible use of force, but nobody outside the organization has any idea how such force might be brought to bear, from an American base, on the situation inside China.

Besides these three directly political organizations, the ODM consists of a number of think tanks and organizations of a more academic or intellectual cast. There may be two or three score such organizations, but the more important are:

1. The China Information Center in Boston, a lobbying and information organization.
2. The Center for Research on Contemporary China (*Dangdai Zhongguo yanjiu zhongxin*), a think tank seeking to draft new policies for China's future under a revived reform leadership. It has an office in New York and is headed by Chen Yizi, the former director of the major Zhao Ziyang think tank in Beijing, the

Economic System Restructuring Institute (*Jingji tizhi gaige yanjiusuo* or *Tigaisuo*).

3. The Future of China Society (*Weilai Zhongguo xueshe*), a research and discussion forum headed by Guan Weiyan and Su Shaozhi, well-known pro-reform academics from China. This society focuses on broad theoretical issues, such as the nature of capitalism and socialism.
4. Human Rights in China (*Zhongguo renquan*), a human-rights information and lobbying group located in the offices of Human Rights Watch in New York, which concentrates on publicizing Chinese human-rights abuses and educational work within the Chinese community on the concept of human rights.
5. The interest group of the Chinese students in America, called the Independent Federation of Chinese Students and Scholars (*QuanMei xuesheng xuezhe zizhi lianhehui*; IFCSS), which has emerged as a strong lobby on immigration and other policy issues affecting Chinese students and scholars in the U.S.
6. A democracy movement newspaper, the *Xinwen ziyou daobao* (News Freedom Herald), is published in Chinese in California, and aimed at the overseas student and scholar audience.
7. The Foundation for Human Rights and Democracy in China (*Zhongguo renquan minzhu jijin hui)*, which serves as an umbrella group assisting other groups to raise money.

The ODM is not as crisply divided as this list of organizations suggests. The leaders comprise a small community and almost all of them know one another. Personal relations (*guanxi*) are sometimes better across the organizational boundaries than they are within them. The organizations have some overlapping memberships, and people are brought together by many activities, such as seminars, meetings, and publications. FDC and CAD have some joint activities, such as a newsletter. Some of the most prominent overseas democrats carry out their activities mostly on an individual basis, particularly well-known writers and theorists like Liu Binyan, Su Shaozhi, and Ruan Ming. In short, the ODM is more of a network or circle than a group of organizations.

The total size of the ODM is difficult to estimate. It finds its main base of support among the estimated fifty to seventy thousand Chinese students and scholars in this country, though some Taiwan, Hong Kong, and U.S. residents also participate, and the major organizations also have branches in Europe, Japan, Australia, and elsewhere. None of the groups publish membership figures. Many Chinese are afraid to affiliate openly, because they fear the anger of the regime in China or disagree with one or another aspect of the platforms of the ODM organizations. Nonetheless, I believe that the vast majority of mainland students and scholars morally support the movement as a whole, read the movement's publications, and share many of the viewpoints expressed there. Certainly, it is striking that there is no organized or articulate opposition to the democracy movement among them. No one has organized or spoken up to support the regime.[3]

Despite this, it is easy to understand what observers have in mind when they say that the ODM has failed. In the spring of 1989, we saw a large part of the Chinese people rise against the regime. After the military crackdown, the democratic activists made dramatic underground escapes from China and reconstituted themselves as a movement overseas. Chinese diplomats, sports figures, and others announced their defections from the regime or the party. The activists and their Western supporters anticipated that millions of dollars would be donated by sympathetic individuals and foundations in the West. The exiles appeared constantly in the news. They were lionized as symbols of the people's heroism. They were showered with book contracts and lecture invitations, and had to get agents. (Books by Liu Binyan, Li Lu, Shen Tong, and by the organization Human Rights in China are out or coming out in English; others are in preparation. Works by Su Shaozhi, Chen Yizi, and others have come out in Chinese.) They lobbied Congress over the Pelosi Bill (protecting the status of Chinese students and scholars in the U.S.) and most-favored-nation trading privileges. I recall one Senator quizzing a State Department official who testified before his committee: "Mr. Undersecretary, what am I to tell my Chinese students?"

This potent image has been deflated. The regime is still in power and even gives the impression of consolidating itself. (I think this impression is misleading and that the regime is internally split and unstable, but that is a subject for another essay.) The democrats' publications do not seem to circulate much inside China. The exiles claim there is an organized underground, and *Zhongguo zhi chun* has long claimed a network of secret cells inside the country. But I doubt that this underground is very strong or that the overseas democrats have good connections to it.

There are occasional reports of what seem to be terrorist bombings and arrests of political dissidents. The official *Xinhua* News Agency announced in January the arrest of an alleged GMD-CAD "agent" in Yunnan.[4] The *Xinwen ziyou daobao* recently published news of an underground organization back home called the "Revolutionary Committee of the Chinese Communist Party."[5] But these are small-scale events in such a large country. The regime's physical control still seems secure. The democrats' boldest and most expensive project was the French-financed "Goddess of Democracy" broadcasting ship, which was supposed to transmit to the mainland from international waters. Before it could take up a position off the South China coast, however, it ran afoul of international law, which the ship's sponsors should have researched more carefully in the first place. No government in the region, even Taiwan's, offered support, and the project sputtered to an ignominious end in the port of Kaohsiung.

The regime has mounted a fairly effective propaganda campaign against the exiles. Although the fact that they have taken the trouble to do this suggests that the democrats have some prestige at home, the campaign has played effectively on some of the movement's weaknesses. Its most important theme is that the exiles have made themselves irrelevant by leaving the field of political battle. Now that many of the arrested democratic activists have been released and some of Zhao Ziyang's liberal allies have returned to work, the impression grows that anyone who fled the country, lives off foreigners, and cultivates what is called "anti-China" sentiment abroad is not a good Chinese and will not have a place, even in a future reformist China. On a recent trip to China, I got the impression that intellectuals regard the exiled democrats with a certain human sympathy, but as no longer players in Chinese politics. Hard for an American to understand, I even encountered the feeling that Fang Lizhi had lost face by taking refuge in the U.S. Embassy: he should have confronted the regime unprotected and taken his punishment like a Sakharov--or perhaps, more to the point, like a good Confucian censor. The Hong Kong press reported that one reason the Chinese authorities decided to let Fang go is that they view him as a "dead tiger," in terms of his influence at home.

In the West, most of the exiles abandoned France, which was the country most enthusiastic about receiving them, and gravitated to the U.S., which they view as a more important country and whose language most of them have studied, even if only a little. But significant money from U.S. foundations and philanthropists did not materialize, except for some forty fellowships for leading exile intellectuals that have been provided by two U.S.-based foundations associated with major Taiwan newspapers, the *Zhongguo shibao* (China Times) and the *Lianhe bao* (United Daily News), and smaller, short-term programs of support from the Luce Foundation and the Institute for International Education (IIE), both strongly aimed at academic, rather than political, refugees. In the American media, the vogue of the Chinese democrats has been replaced by other fads, until new dramatic events bring China back to the headlines. The exiles' books have come out into the void that most books published in America enter: a short blip, and then, if you are lucky, course adoption.

In the Chinese-language press in the U.S., publicity about heroic exiles gave way to publicity about the alleged peccadilloes of the student leader Wuer Kaixi and about personality conflicts and power struggles among other democratic leaders. It has been widely reported that the chairman of the FDC, Yan Jiaqi, dislikes the general secretary, Wan Runnan, and that both have trouble getting along with Chen Yizi. A power struggle among them was expected at the Second Congress over the question of who would succeed Yan as chairman. Yan did not want to be chairman, but the newspapers say he also did not want Wan to serve either. This struggle may split the organization. In CAD, the founding chairman, Wang Bingzhang, was expelled from the organization for alleged financial improprieties and sued in state court for misappropriated funds. Wang later launched, through a third party, an accusation that three of the leading CAD cadres are actually CCP spies. The three held a news conference and wrote a series of articles to rebut this. Meanwhile, the organization has been in serious financial trouble, leading the current chairman, Hu Ping, to offer his resignation. Wang Bingzhang tried to join the newly established LDP, but a substantial number of members opposed this because of long-standing questions about his sexual and financial morality, as well as his political style. When he did join, four hundred members of the LDP quit, effectively gutting it. There are similar personality conflicts and splits within most of the ODM organizations.

Comparisons of the ODM to the Pre-1949 Democratic Movement

I am sure these stories remind readers of the essays in this volume of many events in the pre-1949 democratic movement. If the ODM *is* a failure, it is a failure in many of the same ways and for many of the same reasons that the pre-1949 democracy movement was a failure.

The most eye-catching parallel is *factionalism*. As the Chinese saying goes, "One Chinese, an opinion; two Chinese, an organization; three Chinese, factions." This seems to be one of the enduring principles of Chinese politics, whether at the national level or within small organizations. But I resist the idea, implied by Lloyd Eastman's essay, that this is the way Chinese culture is. I think if we probe into further parallels in the situation of these two groups of democrats, we can better understand some of the causes of factionalism, as well as some of the limits placed on any democratizing movement under the circumstances of Chinese politics in this century.

Several of the essays in this volume suggest that factionalism in the pre-1949 Chinese democratic movement was not usually the result of serious doctrinal disagreements (Ivanov, Eastman, Jeans, Seymour). The same is true of the ODM. The only really important doctrinal split is between the LDP, which wishes to use all possible means to overthrow the Communist regime, and the other organizations, which all favor the use of strictly peaceful methods and claim that they do not seek to overthrow the CCP, but only to obtain the right to compete with it for power in a pluralistic China.[6] (Of course, Deng Xiaoping would claim that advocating pluralism amounts to attempting to overthrow the CCP, since to him CCP rule is by definition monocratic. Within the logic of his Four Basic Principles, he would be right.) The LDP is only a small part of the democratic movement; just as in the pre-1949 movement, the mainstream today is occupied by those who favor what we would call "liberal" and peaceful values.

At a more latent level, there is also a split between those in the ODM who are in essence, if not organizationally, still Communists and those who are not. On the one side are those who believe that as China democratizes, it will continue to need the leadership of a reformist CCP. They favor top-down reform under a revived Zhao-type leadership. This group includes people like Chen Yizi and perhaps Su Shaozhi and even Liu Binyan--it is not always easy to tell. The second group argues that the answer for China is to institute economic and political pluralism right away. Both lines of argument should be familiar, from the thirties and forties, to the readers of this volume. One side parallels the earlier liberals who felt that China was not ready for democracy and needed strong authoritarian rule to steer it in that direction; the other side repeats the arguments of those in the past who argued that only by practicing democracy could the Chinese learn democracy. Also present in the earlier period were the arguments one hears today about whether democracy should be postponed in order to permit economic development or whether prompt democratization would actually assist the forces of development. I call this a latent issue because, until the democrats come closer to holding power, it is a theoretical, rather than practical, issue, and it does not seem to affect strongly the factional line-ups within the ODM.

Second, ideology is not a major factor, but factionalism does seem to be related to a second commonality between the democrats of today and those of the past, *funding* problems. For the pre-People's Republic of China (PRC) period, Eastman attributes the factional phenomenon to the scramble for office, while Ivanov suggests that factionalism occurred because some of the politicians were not really interested in political outcomes but in the social status that came from organizational position. Insufficient funds seem to promote, rather than inhibit, factionalism, because it leads to a consolidation of organizations, a reduction in the number of staff and leadership positions, and hence a scramble for these scarce posts. We can speculate that fuller funding would give an organization more power to stay together.

This is the phenomenon the Chinese refer to as "mountain-topism," or "every tiger in his own mountain." The same problem certainly exists in the ODM today. So far as I know, the exile organizations subsist mostly on funding from Taiwan. I do not know specifically which party or government organ in Taiwan provides this money, although most reports identify it as the GMD's Overseas Work Committee.[7] The financial backers seem to feel that there are too many organizations with too many chiefs and have tried to promote consolidation. Under this pressure, the main emigre organizations (not including the LDP) held meetings in Washington, Florida, and Berlin, to try to unify. One of these meetings issued a statement of common purposes. However, no organizational amalgamation followed.

Third, at a still deeper level, the lack of funding reflects the lack of a supportive *civil society* to provide the democratic groups with money, a constituency, and a power base. This problem is flagged for the pre-PRC period by several of the essays in this volume. In the last half of the eighties, some observers noted the sprouts of a regrowth of civil society in China, e.g., some semi-controlled journals, the individual entrepreneurs (*getihu*), etc.[8] These forces played a major role in supporting the Democracy Movement of the spring of 1989. Yet, at the present juncture, the state retains the capacity to crush civil society, so that even if the democrats were back in China, they would have virtually no power base with which to work. Support from Western society, even if it were fuller than it is, would be no substitute.

All the problems mentioned so far relate to a fourth characteristic of the two democracy movements, social and political *marginality*. The sense of marginality is obvious among the exiles today. Each of these people faces pressing and painful personal decisions: should he or she settle down here, apply for political asylum, study English, and give up his career at home and prepare for a life in this country, probably in a lower-status job than at home? Or should he or she plan for only a short-term stay in the West and devote his energies to preparing for the return to China? Also, should they place some limits on their criticisms of the regime at home and keep some personal lines open to friends in the regime, in order to remain acceptable if the reformist faction returns to power in China? Or should they take full advantage of the freedom of speech here to promote a full-fledged alternative to the regime's way of thinking?

Each exiled democrat has to make these decisions for him or herself, depending on his age, family situation, linguistic abilities, political background, and estimate of the way the situation will go in China. Some have the sinking feeling that having left China, they can never really go back. Whoever ends up in power there will not want them, viewing them as out of touch and tainted by their past defection. According to this feeling--of course, no one knows whether it will turn out to be true--those who took a turn in jail this past year have a better chance of coming out on top in China in the end.

Although the dilemmas of the exiles are in some ways special, the democrats of the 1930s and 1940s also felt--and actually were--nearly as marginal, even though they were living in China. At bottom for both groups, the marginality consists not in residing for part of one's life abroad or in espousing what are seen as Western values and ways of life. Rather, the marginality is political and it is chosen. It comes from the very act of being a liberal in a non-liberal political system. Because the liberals perceive authoritarian, coercive politics as illegitimate, they refuse to play by those rules of the game. But until there is a new game, this puts them outside the arena.

It takes a Mao Zedong, who becomes a professional politician and makes violent revolution, to challenge the regime of a Chiang Kai-shek. It is precisely a Mao whom the liberals of both the pre-1949 period and today did not wish to be. This is not only because they do not want to give up comfortable ways of life as intellectuals or that they do not know how to load a gun. More fundamentally, it is their commitment to democratic values that forbids them from taking non-democratic roads to power. In this sense, their marginality is self-willed and, given the nature of politics in China in this century, it is intrinsic to the stance of being a Chinese liberal. If I understand her, this is what Marilyn Levine refers to as "the frozen revolution" in her essay in this volume, although her subject is not a liberal but a conservative. It is also what Edward Krebs describes as the stance of the Chinese anarchists.

Given this situation, a final point of commonality between the situations of democrats yesterday and today lies in what might be called the *tactical temptations of powerlessness*. I would like to focus on two.

One is the temptation to try to influence the regime from within. By serving as an advisor to or member of the regime, one gives up the chance to challenge the system publicly in return for the opportunity to influence its evolution from within.[9] This was the choice by Lawrence Shyu's participants in the People's Political Council and the minor party leaders following 1949. A similar path has been followed by many of today's leading democrats. For example, Yan Jiaqi wrote a pseudonymous article for Democracy Wall, while pursuing a career that brought him a high post as a member of Zhao Ziyang's political-reform brain trust. Chen Yizi served as a reform advisor to the regime for ten years, planning first to promote reform in the countryside that would eventually lead to democratization of the political system.[10] I can think of several other people who followed the same pattern, but since they are now in jail or under surveillance after being released from jail, it is better not to mention their names.

We learn from the essays on the pre-1949 period that this decision often went along with an intellectual rationale which endorsed an authoritarian interlude, on the grounds that social revolution is a prerequisite for political reform. This viewpoint reminds us of the theory of "neo-authoritarianism" espoused in 1988-1989 by some of Zhao Ziyang's supporters, who identified democracy as the goal of reform but called for postponing its realization until economic reform could be completed.

Is this tactical temptation inevitably a mistake? The debate still rages among historians about whether the GMD really had democratic potentialities in the 1940s and whether the Communists really meant to institute a long period of "New Democracy" in the early 1950s. Similarly, with regard to the 1980s, analysts differ about whether the reformers in the CCP were really willing to move the system toward full democracy. From the experiences of these three groups of democrats, one might conclude that "taking the inside route" is always a mistake, because trying to democratize a dictatorship from within is, in the Chinese phrase, "like deliberating with the tiger about taking his skin." Others will argue the gamble was worth taking. We can be sure there are democrats in China who are still taking this risk today.

A second tactical temptation of powerlessness is what might be called the flight from politics to cultural reform. An example from among the figures dealt with in this volume is Zeng Qi (Levine). In essence, this is a decision to try to reform the system by working from the cultural and social environment inwards towards the political regime. It is often based on a theoretical rationale that real democracy will not be possible until the people are wealthier and better educated, and feudal, authoritarian ideas are eliminated from the culture. With the exception of the LDP, the exiled democrats today are essentially caught in the same trap. They see no way to exert leverage on the politics of the authoritarian regime, within the self-imposed limits of their liberal methods, so they turn to the project of intellectual and cultural reconstruction. This project, unfortunately, is infinitely complex and frustrating, and never seems to lead anywhere. Often the first target of cultural reconstruction becomes one's own colleagues within the democratic movement, which leads to time-wasting internecine polemics and infighting. Meanwhile, the political realm is abandoned to the professional politicians, i.e., those with a vested interest in the system who are less likely to change it.

In short, despite a few romantic claims to the contrary, the exiled democrats are not the Sun Yat-sens of the late twentieth century. The 1911 Revolution was a middle-level officers' coup against a rotten and weak regime. Since the Revolutionary Alliance had infiltrated the officer corps, when the regime toppled the officers called in Sun Yat-sen to take power. Nothing like a middle-level officers' coup is likely to happen in China today.[11] And if it did happen, the military would not call upon the ODM to take power, because the latter has not infiltrated the military. Hence, the parallel with Sun Yat-sen, which is sometimes offered, is a fallacious one. It is not one that most of the democrats themselves encourage: in Yan Jiaqi's terms, they are waiting for "an Eastern European-type change" to take place in China, after which they expect to be called back to resume their part in politics. The parallel with the liberals of the thirties and forties, although not a perfect one, is more appropriate than the Sun Yat-sen comparison for understanding what the ODM is and evaluating what it fairly should be expected to accomplish.

Achievements and Evaluation, with Pre-1949 Parallels

If the participants in the ODM are not trying to be Sun Yat-sens, then it is wrong to say they have failed because they do not seem set to accomplish what Sun did. If we evaluate them as liberals, then despite all their problems, they have achieved some important things, perhaps more than were accomplished by their predecessors of earlier decades.

First, the very existence of the ODM is important. It stands as a sign that the Chinese system, which for the moment gives an outward appearance of solidity, has in fact lost the support of an important stratum of its best people, including many who were for a time part of the regime. It reminds the world that China is not an exception to the human yearning for freedom. Our perception of China would be quite different if this movement, whatever its problems, did not exist. The pre-1949 liberal movement had a similar significance and that is why it remains worth studying today.

Second, especially in the months after Tiananmen, some organizations within the ODM channeled important information to human-rights groups like Amnesty and Asia Watch, and thus helped to promote the worldwide campaign against human-rights abuses in China. This function continues, although there has recently been less information to report. This is not the place to discuss in detail whether the international human-rights movement has an impact on China, but I think there is good evidence it does. It is not going to, and does not try to, overthrow the Chinese regime, but it does help persuade that government to moderate its human-rights abuses. I would argue that the ODM has accomplished more in this regard than the earlier liberal movements, partly because the world is smaller today and the Chinese government more responsive to foreign pressure, and partly because the movement, by being located overseas, has much better contacts with the outside world.

Third, the ODM has become a rather sophisticated political lobby, adept at using the mass media, Congressional testimony and lobbying, and executive-branch contacts to shape legislation and get government help in specific cases. This lobbying technique was pioneered by the CAD in the case of the arrest of Yang Wei in 1986.[12] In the discussion of the Pelosi Bill, the IFCSS was particularly effective. This has affected U.S. China policy and, through that, has had an effect on the Chinese government.

Here again I think the achievements of the ODM go beyond those of their predecessors. Some of the earlier generation of liberals had excellent contacts in the U.S., but their political-lobbying efforts were not highly developed.

And fourth, in my view, the most important function of the ODM is the least visible. I refer to fundamental intellectual work to solve the many problems which are confronted by those who would build a workable democratic creed and practice for China. In this work, the ODM is the direct successor of the earlier democratic thinkers and needs to address many of the same questions. Should democracy entail a stress on Western-style individualism, which is not well grounded in Chinese tradition or society? If not, is it possible to base real democracy on a set of values which stresses the interests of the collective over the individual? Are there certain Western constitutional patterns that a democratic China should adopt, such as separation of powers, judicial review, multiparty democracy, and relatively unrestricted freedoms of speech and organization? Or would these patterns, transplanted to China, produce chaos and stalemate? Is China too backward to move immediately to full-scale democracy?

These are not matters of political engineering. As Thomas Metzger has demonstrated, these issues are linked to deep philosophical questions to which Chinese culture has so far given different answers from those of the mainstream liberal culture in the West. To use Metzger's term, democracy in the West is based on "three pluralisms," and all of these are considered of questionable value in Chinese civilization.[13] Thus, the democrats continue to face an agonizing issue which Chinese political thinkers have been confronting for a century: can a workable version of democracy be built on the foundations of the existing culture or do democrats have to try to reconstruct these cultural orientations as well, obviously a very difficult job?

A Useable Past?

So far as I know, few if any of the major democratic activists have looked into the lives and works of the people studied in this volume for answers to such questions. Of course, they have heard of them, and some may have read their works in school. But generally the Chinese democrats look to Western and liberal-Marxist "gurus," rather than to the modern Chinese past, for ideas. The figures we have been studying have undergone much the same neglect within China as they have among Western historians of China. As we are reclaiming them here, it is interesting to ask whether these figures constitute, for the exiled democrats, a "useable past." Do these older figures, who in some sense traveled the same hard road in an earlier time, have something to teach the democrats of today? Did they solve any of the problems that now have to be addressed, in theory if not in practice? The essays in this volume are not necessarily constructed with the aim of answering this question. But there do emerge some points that might be worth pondering by today's democrats.

First, the very existence of these precursors helps dispel the notion that the Chinese tradition is monolithic and liberal or democratic ideas are merely Western and irrelevant to China. Although obviously never achieving mainstream influence, these earlier figures form part of what can be perceived as a liberal tradition within, not external to, the Chinese past. One can point to liberal democracy as a goal that has been around for a long time. A historical pedigree is important for any Chinese movement, and the ODM should make good use of this one.

Second, some articles in this volume show that there have been exceptions to the generalization that the Chinese notion of democracy is not a pluralistic or individualistic one. Fredric Spar argues that Luo Longji placed individual rights and freedoms at the center of his political philosophy. If so, Luo's thought deserves study by the democrats of today to see what elements of his thinking may be useful in their project to construct a workable Chinese theory of democracy. Other thinkers reviewed in this volume, like Zhang Junmai, also used the language of natural rights. Today's democrats need to probe more deeply into their predecessors' thought to discover on what philosophical bases they placed these concepts (a task not performed by the essays in this collection).

Third, another potentially useful theme, which emerges from the articles, is that of "constitutional government," stressed by the Chinese Youth Party (Edmund S.K. Fung). There is a long history of constitutions and debate over constitutions in twentieth-century China. Although not explored in this volume, this history contains learned and perceptive debates over most of the constitutional issues that any future democratic China will have to solve, e.g., federalism, separation of powers, judicial review, positive and negative rights, legal status of rights, the status of property rights, the limits of state intervention in the economy, and so on. The slogan "return to the constitution" (*huigui xianfa*) has long been used as a rallying cry by liberals under GMD rule, both before 1949 and more recently in Taiwan. Since today's mainland Chinese constitution contains many good democratic provisions, the call to put it into effect might be a useful practical tactic for the democratic movement today. The study of history can provide guidelines about the pros and cons of such a tactic.

Overall, however, my sense is that the democrats of the pre-1949 period left most of the hard problems of Chinese democracy yet to be solved (in this I seem to agree with Metzger). For the most part, they did not manage to get beyond the mainstream Chinese conception of democracy, which, as shown in several of the volume essays, is one that sees political participation mostly as a form of communication, views democracy as a process of seeking a consensus on the objectively best policy, and shies away from acknowledging that democracy involves clashing interests, the mobilization of power, and conflict. In short, these earlier democrats did not succeed in squaring the circle between their democratic values of openness and pluralistic participation and their Chinese values of conflict avoidance, consensus, and the assertion of higher community interests. I have no doubt that this problem can be solved in a specifically Chinese way and that the resulting Chinese democratic system will be different in many ways from any Western system, especially the American system.[14] But most of the conceptual work required for this remains to be done.

To do this arduous intellectual work, the tragedy of exile can be turned, to some extent, to advantage. This is an enforced time out from busy careers and established personal networks in China, which gathers together intellectuals from many different circles who did not know one another within China, and joins senior intellectuals with Chinese graduate students. The formal and informal constraints of political censorship, within which people are used to operating at home, are lifted. Western models of democracy, with all their flaws, lie open for realistic inspection, not merely theoretical study. The resources of Western universities are available for probing into the historical roots of democratic theory. In the long run, much will be gained from the debates we see in the pages of *Zhongguo zhi chun*, *Minzhu Zhongguo*, and *Xinwen ziyou daobao* over strategy and tactics; from the workshops and seminars which some of the ODM organizations are arranging on the historical lessons of socialism or the design of a human-rights system for China; and from the time spent in writing theoretical works evaluating the socialist experience in Eastern Europe and China or the roots of the Cultural Revolution. I believe that those who do this work will have a major impact on the future direction of Chinese intellectual life and political culture, even if they do not return to China. Those who do go back will carry the fruits of the overseas discussions into the Chinese political arena.

Thus, the major measure of the ODM's success will be whether they do good intellectual work during the time history allots them. It is too early to reach a judgment on this question. So far, much energy that could have been used in serious intellectual work has been devoted to factional struggle, yet our own experience as intellectuals teaches us that all good intellectual work is surrounded by much wasted motion. The ODM has good personnel for intellectual tasks and has established some good frameworks for it. The opportunity is there, and it will be up to the democrats to make the best of it.

Notes

1. For descriptions of Yan Jiaqi and Hu Ping, see Andrew J. Nathan, *China's Crisis: Dilemmas of Reform and Prospects for Democracy* (New York: Columbia University Press, 1990), chap. 1.

2. The formation of a party called the Chinese Democratic Party was announced earlier, but it was stillborn.

3. I am not counting some fake-looking letters of support for the regime that appeared in the *Renmin ribao* (People's Daily).

4. "KMT [GMD] Agent's Arrest in Yunnan Reported," Beijing *Xinhua* Domestic Service, 13 January 1990; trans. in FBIS-CHI-90-010, 16 January 1990, 45.

5. *Xinwen ziyou daobao*, 20 July 1990, 1.

6. On the rationale for using peaceful methods, see Nathan, *China's Crisis*, chap. 10.

7. See, e.g., Susan V. Lawrence, "A Chinese Marriage of Convenience," *U.S. News and World Report*, 30 April 1990, 34.

8. Nathan, *China's Crisis*, 12, 120-26.

9. This possibility is mentioned in Andrew J. Nathan, *Chinese Democracy* (New York: Alfred A. Knopf, 1985), 43.

10. Chen Yizi, *Zhongguo: shinian gaige yu bajiu minyun--Beijing liusi tusha de beihou* (China: Ten Years of Reform and the 1989 Popular Movement--The Background of the June Fourth Massacre) (Taibei: Lianjing chuban shiye gongsi, 1990), chap. 1.

11. See Nathan, *China's Crisis*, chap. 11.

12. Ibid., chap. 5.

13. Thomas A. Metzger, "Opposition Politics and the Problem of Secularization in Modern China," Paper presented at the Conference on "Oppositional Politics in Twentieth-Century China," Washington and Lee University, Lexington, Virginia, 20-22 September 1990.

14. See Nathan, *China's Crisis*, chap. 11.

PART SIX

Oppositional Politics in Twentieth-Century China

16

An Overview

John Israel

Why study opposition politics? Why should we be so interested in digging half-forgotten men and all-but-inconsequential movements out of the dustbin of history? It may well be that as intellectuals, presumably full of great ideas and high principles, yet without influence in the halls of power, we cannot help being intrigued by our Chinese counterparts.

I am not arguing that any of us are driven solely, or even principally, by subjective and egocentric considerations. We understandably find it worthwhile to examine causes that fail but nonetheless inspire us by their challenge to unbridled authority. We find oppositional individuals and groups inherently fascinating. Yet, we are seldom able to justify our interest solely in terms of the intrinsic importance of our subjects. Rather, we seek to derive from them insights into broader issues, such as liberalism, democracy, and the Chinese political tradition.

In looking at opposition politics as lost causes, our thoughts turn to that controversial and influential article by Ramon H. Myers and Thomas A. Metzger that cautioned us against interpreting history in terms of the "winners," i.e., those who happen to have triumphed at a certain stage in the struggle for national power. Myers and Metzger directed our attention to the "losers" on Taiwan, as against the "winners" on the Mainland.[1] In this volume, however, opposition forces of various stripes are counterpoised against the Guomindang (GMD) and the Chinese Communist Party (CCP), both of whom emerged as "winners" at different stages in an ongoing process.

How important are opposition politics in twentieth-century China? Important enough, it would seem, to make the enterprise a perilous one, important enough, at times, to help shape the forces of public opinion, but never important enough to determine the overall direction in which Chinese politics were headed--surely never important enough to refute the hard reality of twentieth-century Chinese politics, articulated but not invented by Mao Zedong: "Political power grows out of the barrel of a gun."

What are we talking about when we discuss opposition politics? As Parks Coble's study of the National Salvation Association (NSA) reminds us, we are not speaking of political parties alone, and as we see in Thomas Curran's portrayal of Huang Yanpei, we are sometimes not even talking about groups. In some cases, we are not even dealing with individuals who conceive of themselves as part of a political opposition. We might, in fact, be talking about "alternative politics," except that we are not including in our purview mass movements of students, workers, peasants, women, etc. It is striking how few of the figures and groups studied in the essays in this volume had any concept of mass movements. Only a few, such as Deng Yanda, had any notions of where to turn for mass support.

Among the many contradictory elements we find in these articles is the disproportionate relationship between the strength of oppositionists--which was seldom impressive--and the strenuous efforts taken by the authorities to crush these ineffectual forces. Why?

Only on rare occasion was an organization, such as the NSA in the mid-1930s and the Democratic League in the 1940s, in a position to help mold public opinion on crucial issues. None of our opposition groups had a realistic chance of overthrowing established authority. So long as China was governed by parties that considered any deviation from political orthodoxy as "counterrevolutionary," the net of suppression could be--and was--broadly cast. When a figure such as Zhang Junmai was guilty, in addition, of consorting with anti-GMD politicians, such as Liang Qichao, and warlords, such as Sun Chuanfang, as well as of running a school independent of Party control, his fate was sealed.

We could, doubtless, find particularistic reasons for each of the many cases of official intolerance discussed in the essays in this volume. Given the overall weakness of opposition political forces and the persistence of political paranoia, however, we are driven to search for some explanation that goes beyond a case-by-case approach. Logically enough, we focus upon Chinese tradition, in which moral virtue and political power are inseparable and legitimate opposition inconceivable. How much of this is unique to China? A closer examination of other countries would reveal comparable cases on a more or less global scale. As a point of departure, we need look no further than the reports of Amnesty International.

Intolerance on the part of the powerful for even the feeblest voices of dissent is but one dimension of our subject that invites comparative study. Surely China is not the only country where there is no legitimate role for a political opposition, where political associations rely upon personal networks, where they are ridden by cliquism and factionalism, and where they usually fail. As we extend our search from China to other lands, we will need to look for non-culturally specific explanatory schemes.

For the time being, few of us are intrepid enough to place the suppression of harmless opposition in a universal framework of political analysis. Peter Ivanov, however, has at least suggested a theory of history to give coherence to our preoccupation with the backwaters of history. Writing in a Tolstoian vein, he reminds us that "the feeble undercurrents of social life must not be forgotten," because "without them, the history is incomplete, simplified, and too burdened with the triumphs of 'great forces', leaving no space for the natural pluralism of thought, romanticism, and intrigue."

One place where political and ideological pluralism has virtually exploded in the last few years is Taiwan. There, the theoretical perspective is to be found less on the outside, in a comparative or world context, than on the inside, where we may test generalizations in an area that is culturally Chinese but where some of the patterns of opposition politics that we have seen on the Mainland over the past ninety years do not hold. Whatever the cultural constants on Taiwan, we find much that is new in social and political structure. The political focus has been shifting, at least to some extent, from an entrenched political establishment backed by military power to an open, competitive process based upon the ballot box. Here, both the ideological climate and the legal framework now encourage a process very different from anything we have seen on the Mainland. Opposition parties no longer have to worry about positioning themselves between two armed camps or ingratiating themselves with those in power. Rather, dozens of tiny groups find the forum of electoral politics a bully pulpit for positions not articulated by the governing GMD and its significant, if less than equal rival, the DPP.

It is not difficult, however, to find continuities between the histories of opposition politics on Taiwan and the pre-1949 Mainland, as well as parallels with the post-1949 Mainland situation. In Taiwan (1960), as on the Mainland (1957), some of the legal minor parties tried to coalesce into effective opposition forces and were crushed. Subsequent opposition on the Mainland has centered outside of the old-line minor parties, as with various movements from Democracy Wall to Tiananmen Square. On Taiwan, as on the pre-1949 Mainland, we now find opposition leaders using the rubric of political organizations to play out the roles of intellectual gadflies and moral critics.

Having reached the level of audibility after a decade of reforms, the democratic political groups on the Mainland have been unable to articulate even a last hurrah, but have been stifled in the post-June Fourth crackdown. This has occurred at the same time that Taiwan's pre-1949 loyal non-opposition parties have been swept into oblivion by the vital new forces of the post-Chiang Ching-kuo era. James Seymour's conclusion that "the DPGs have little future" applies to their Taiwan counterparts as well, albeit for very different reasons.

Among the most perplexing questions about opposition politicians and political forces is how political were they? Curran refers to Huang Yanpei's aversion to politics and avoidance of power, common features of many of the people and organizations the essays examine. Another author writes of the Chinese intellectuals' preference for moralistic pedagogy over practical politics. Luo Longji was a notable exception to this rule. His reward was to be anathematized as a "politician" by his fellow liberal intellectuals, who lacked, in Fredric Spar's words, "a deeper appreciation ... for the value of the kind of political engagement Luo ... espoused." Even fewer were able to mobilize the rural masses. Fewer still had either the interest or the ability to rally military support. Deng Yanda, who did, was executed. If we speak of China's democratic political parties, we are likely to find, as Seymour notes, that they were neither democratic nor parties. Perhaps they were not even political, if we insist on restricting the term to those who seek power. They were, however, profoundly political, if we understand the term to encompass those who seek influence. And, as Thomas Metzger has reminded us, seeking influence--unselfishly, of course--was one form of political behavior that Chinese tradition clearly legitimated.[2]

Chinese tradition may also help us to understand opposition politicians' egregious failure to rally the military. We discover here the tenacity of the traditional literati preference for *wen* over *wu*--a proclivity reinforced by a nearly universal reaction against the legacy of the warlords, none of whom was embarrassed to admit that a strong military arm was a necessity of life in China. Twentieth-century intellectuals proudly went forth to battle unarmed, without even *yi cun tie*--one inch of iron. Yet, they did so without the philosophical and organizational tradition of pacifist struggle that made Mahatma Gandhi and Martin Luther King such effective leaders. Persecuted, proscribed, beaten, murdered, they were unable to translate moral authority into political power. Even their martyrdoms, as in the case of Deng Yanda and Wen Yiduo, were reinterpreted and coopted into the sanitized history of the Leninist state, making their historic significance as ambiguous as their ends were tragic.

One of the virtues of being a minor party or opposition politician should be that it is easy to remain principled. After all, with no hope whatsoever for power, what has one left but principles? To be sure, many of the individuals and organizations we have been looking at were highly principled. What is remarkable, however, is how easy it is to be corrupt at the same time one is politically ineffectual. In the quest for power or influence, no matter how quixotic, opposition politicians had to make compromises. The more ambitious the effort, the greater the compromise. Of course, the GMD and the CCP were also from time to time aided, compromised, and betrayed by foreign aid. The question in all cases would seem to be whether the individuals, organizations, and China itself gained more than they lost from outside support.

Succumbing to foreign agendas, however, was by no means the most serious form of corruption among opposition politicians. Far more debilitating was the kind of corruption portrayed by Lloyd Eastman, i.e., the corruption of office-seekers who cast their lot with the GMD or the CCP to gain ministerial portfolios. More subtle, and perhaps more insidious, was the intellectual corruption that came with self-delusion, such as Huang Yanpei's faith, until the late 1940s, in the good will of the GMD. It might not be unfair, to be sure, to distinguish between those who *shengguan*-ed and *facai*-ed (became officials and became wealthy) under a corrupt and discredited GMD in 1947 and those who risked their lives when they threw in their lot with the Communists prior to the final stage of the Civil War. Nonetheless, in the course of the political process, we do find how easy it is for finely-honed intellects to lose their critical faculties.

Nationalism is a least common denominator of most popular movements, but by no means all of them. It is striking how little most of our oppositionists gained from their espousal of nationalism. Since nationalism ultimately requires a strong central government, something that none of the opposition leaders and groups came close to providing, their nationalistic efforts--whether for war against Japan or national unity under new leadership--ultimately redounded to the advantage of the major parties.

Almost inevitably, the study of opposition groups suggests an antithetical relationship with the GMD and the CCP. Similarities, however, should not be overlooked. For example, networks, cliques, and factions based upon patron-client relations, personal loyalty, family connections, places of origin, old school ties, etc., characterize both types of organizations. Another common characteristic, less noted, is the paucity of women in political life.

One similarity, so obvious that it is easy to overlook, is that the "successful" parties--the GMD and CCP--also started as tiny bands of opposition politicians and intellectuals. Hence, even a study of the undercurrents and backwaters eventually redirects our attention to the mainstream. The history of the CCP makes it patently clear that at least one tiny group of intellectual dissidents ultimately rose to the top in the struggle for power. When we look at problems endemic to other opposition groups--their failure to build a broader base of social support, their lack of interest in developing a military capacity, their ineptitude in organization, etc.--we might well consider the CCP as a model for everything they were not.

If, however, the question we ask in regard to oppositional forces is, "What are the lessons of failure?", returning to the GMD and CCP we might well ask, "What price success?" We might even question the "success" of these two parties, if we measure it in terms of meeting China's needs with efficient and humane leadership. One reason that opposition politics is riddled with failure is because so much of modern Chinese history is a history of failure.

If the history of oppositional politics in twentieth-century China is indeed one of failure, we naturally want to know why. Some of the answers become apparent if we ask a rather different question: What were the commonalities among opposition groups?

1. All operated within a political culture shaped by traditions that offered little support for the concept of a legitimate and loyal opposition.
2. Opposition political philosophies were poorly conceived, contradictory, inadequate for China's needs, or irrelevant in China's environment. Our essayists have pointed to various weaknesses, many of them inherent in Chinese liberalism. What is the problem with Chinese liberals and Chinese liberalism? How "liberal" are our oppositional leaders and organizations? Have would-be liberals and democrats unwittingly absorbed traditional modes of thought or conduct antithetical to their basic principles? Did liberalism fail because it was historically out of place or because it was hopelessly compromised? Or did it never fail because it was never tried? Though answers to these questions may vary from author to author and case to case, our contributors seem to agree that the political impact of liberalism in twentieth-century China has not been impressive.
3. Liberalism in China, of course, has been filtered through the cultural predisposition of modern Chinese intellectuals. Marilyn Levine suggests a cultural inability to grasp the fundamental concept of a political party, a tendency to think in terms of pedagogy, not politics; morality and education, not partisan struggle.
4. Given these tendencies, it is not surprising that opposition political groups revolved around intellectuals, both as leaders and constituents. In fact, in the essays in this volume, we have examined a virtual honor roll of China's most astute, sophisticated, best-informed patriots--a cluster of the best and the brightest who, in addition to wit and intelligence, shared a singular characteristic--failure. The whole always seems to be less than the sum of its parts.

5. A number of our authors have shown how opposition politicians relied on patron-client relations and other particularistic connections. These features are, of course, common throughout Chinese social and political life, but the minor parties and groups have been so weak organizationally, financially, and in other respects that they could not overcome this handicap.
6. Not the least of their weaknesses was military. Unarmed and unprepared to defend themselves, they were easily crushed by *force majeure.*

Finally, I think it only fitting to note that we are looking at an ongoing pageant. At the moment, oppositional politics is all but dead on the Mainland and of uncertain significance on Taiwan. None of the individuals and groups we have examined established a clear legacy for the future. As Andrew Nathan has demonstrated, the present-day democracy movement ignores its Chinese predecessors, preferring to seek inspiration from foreign exemplars. And yet, in light of the Chinese genius for drawing creatively from various aspects of the past, it would be quite premature to write off as inconsequential not only the individual figures and forces we have been examining but also the ideas they embodied.

Given the twists and turns that the historical process is bound to have in store for us, the heritage of oppositional politics in twentieth-century China, either in discrete parts or in its totality, may have unpredictable consequences in years to come. Just as neither of those great oppositional politicians, George Washington and Robert E. Lee, could have anticipated the configurations of the twentieth-century world, it may be fitting for us to conclude on a note of humility in the face of an uncertain future.

Notes

1. Ramon H. Myers and Thomas A. Metzger, "Sinological Shadows: The State of Modern China Studies in the United States," *The Washington Quarterly*, Spring 1980, 87-114.

2. Thomas A. Metzger, "Oppositional Politics and the Problem of Secularization in Modern China," Paper presented at the Conference on "Oppositional Politics in Twentieth-Century China," Washington and Lee University, Lexington, Virginia, 20-22 September 1990.

List of Political Parties and Groups

All-China National Salvation Association League (see National Salvation Association)	Quanguo gejie guolian hehui
Anarchists	Wuzhengfuzhuyizhe
Association for the Construction of North China	Huabei jianshe xiehui
Association for the Promotion of Democracy	Zhongguo minzhu cujin hui
Association of Comrades for the Restoration of the Chinese Guomindang	Zhongguo guomindang fuxing tongzhi hui
Association of Comrades for Unity and National Reconstruction	Tongyi jianguo tongzhi hui
Association to Save the Nation from Extinction	Jiuwang xuehui
Blood and Iron Party	Tiexue dang
China Democratic League	Zhongguo minzhu da tongmeng
China Democratic National Construction Association	Zhongguo minzhu jianguo hui
Chinese Alliance for Democracy	Zhongguo minzhu lianmeng

This list includes all parties and groups mentioned in the text of the essays (except John Copper's). For further details on parties in the Republic of China (Taiwan) and the PRC, see the appendices to John Copper's and James Seymour's essays.

Chinese Association for the Development of New Social Services	Zhongguo xin shehui shiye jianshe xiehui
Chinese Association for the Promotion of Mass Education	Zhonghua pingmin jiaoyu cujin hui
Chinese Communist Party	Zhongguo gongchandang
Chinese Democracy and Freedom League	Zhongguo minzhu ziyou da tongmeng
Chinese Democratic Party	Zhongguo minzhu dang
Chinese Democratic Radical Party	Zhongguo minzhu jijin dang
Chinese Harmony Club	Zhongguo zhonghe tang
Chinese Harmony Party	Zhongguo zhonghe dang
Chinese Hong Men Justice Party	Zhongguo Hong Men zhigong dang
Chinese Hong Men People's Rule Party	Zhongguo Hong Men minzhi dang
Chinese Justice Party	See Zhigong Dang
Chinese Labor Party	Zhongguo laogong dang
Chinese Liberal-Democratic Party	Zhongguo ziyou minzhu dang
Chinese Liberal Party	Zhongguo ziyou dang
Chinese National Liberal Party	Zhongguo guomin ziyou dang
Chinese Party of Grand Unity	Zhongguo datong dang

Chinese Party of Peace	Zhongguo heping dang
Chinese Party of Social Construction	Zhonghua shehui jianshe dang
Chinese Party of the Masses	Zhongguo dazhong dang
Chinese Peasants' and Workers' Democratic Party	Zhongguo nonggong minzhu dang
Chinese Peasants' and Workers' Socialist Party	Zhongguo nonggong shehui dang
Chinese Peasants' Liberal Party	Zhongguo nongmin ziyou dang
Chinese Peasants' Party	Zhongguo nongmin dang
Chinese People's Liberal Party	Zhongguo renmin ziyou dang
Chinese Radical Party	Zhongguo jijin dang
Chinese Revolutionary Party	Zhonghua geming dang
Chinese Self-Strengthening Society	Zhongguo ziqiang she
Chinese Socialist Party	Zhonghua shehui dang
Chinese Society for the Promotion of the Unity of Peasants and Workers	Zhongguo nonggong lianhe cujin hui
Chinese Young Labor Party	Zhongguo shaonian laodong dang
Chinese Youth Party	Zhongguo qingnian dang
Constancy Society	Heng she

Constitution Research Society	Xianfa yanjiu hui (see Research Clique)
Democratic Constitutionalist Party	Zhongguo minzhu xianzheng dang
Democratic League	(See China Democratic League)
Democratic Liberal Party	Minzhu ziyou dang
Democratic Progressive Party	Minzhu jinbu dang
Democratic Socialist Party	Zhongguo minzhu shehui dang
Federation for a Democratic China	Minzhu Zhongguo zhenxian
Fighting League for Chinese Freedom and Democracy	Zhongguo ziyou minzhu zhandou tongmeng
Formation-of-the-Spirit Learned Society	Zhuhun xueshe
Freedom Front	Ziyou zhenxian
Friends of the Constitution Society	Xianyou she
General Society of New China	Xin Zhongguo zongshe
Glorious Society	Rong she
Hong Men People's Rule and National Reconstruction Society	Hong Men minzhi jianguo hui
Hong Men Revival Association	Hong xing xiehui
Hong Men Zhigong Dang	See Zhigong Dang
Hong Progress Society	Hong jin she

Jiusan Society	See September Third Study Society
Justice Party	See Zhigong Dang
League of Chinese Democratic Political Groups	Zhongguo minzhu zhengtuan da tongmen
League of Free China Democratic Political Groups	Ziyou Zhongguo minzhu zhengtuan tongmeng
League of Middle Parties	Zhongjian dang lianmeng
Lone Star Society	Guxing she
Loyalty and Justice Party	Zhongyi dang
Mass Education Association	See Chinese Association for the Promotion of Mass Education
National Salvation Association	Jiuguo hui
National Socialist Party	Zhongguo guojia shehui dang
National Society for Constitutional Government	Guomin xianzheng she
Nationalist Clique (Faction)	Guojiazhuyi pai (see Chinese Youth Party)
Nationalist Party	Zhongguo guomindang
New Masses Society	Xinqun she
New People's Study Society	Xinmin xuehui
Origin Society	Ben she
Peasants' and Workers' Society	Nonggong she

People's Democratic Liberal Union	Renmin minzhu ziyou lianmeng
People's Livelihood and Progress Party	Minsheng gongjin dang
Political Society for a Democratic, Peaceful, and United China	Zhongguo minzhu heping tongyi zhengtuan
Progressive Party	Jinbu dang
Provisional Action Committee of the Guomindang (The Third Party)	Zhongguo guomindang linshi xingdong weiyuanhui
Reform Committee of the Democratic Socialist Party (See Reform Faction of the DSP)	Minzhu shehui dang gexin weiyuanhui
Reform Faction of the Democratic Socialist Party	Minzhu shehui dang gexin pai
Research Clique	Yanjiu xi
Restoration Society	Guangfu hui
Revolutionary Alliance	Zhongguo tongmeng hui
Revolutionary Committee of the Guomintang	Guomindang geming weiyuanhui
Revolutionary League of Sunism	Sun Wen zhuyi geming tongmeng
Rural Reconstruction Group	Xiangcun jianshe pai
Sanminzhuyi Comrades Association	Sanminzhuyi tongzhi lianhehui
September Third Study Society	Jiusan xueshe

Society for the Promotion of Democracy and Socialism	Minzhu shehui xiejin hui
Society for the Revival of China	Xin Zhong she
Society of Benefit	Yi she
Society of Determination	Yi she
Society of Generosity and Justice	Xieyi she
Society of the Masses	Dazhong she
Taiwan Autonomy League	See Taiwan Democratic Self-Government League
Taiwan Democratic Self-Government League	Taiwan minzhu zizhi tongmeng
Third Party	Disan dang
Tongmenghui	See Revolutionary Alliance
Vocational Education Society	Zhonghua zhiye jiaoyu she
Young China Association	Shaonian Zhongguo xuehui
Zhigong Dang	Zhongguo Zhigong dang

Abbreviations Used in the Text

ACUNR	Association of Comrades for Unity and National Reconstruction
APC	Association for the Promotion of Constitutionalism
APD	China Association for the Promotion of Democracy
CAD	Chinese Alliance for Democracy
CAL	Chinese Association of Labor
CCP	Chinese Communist Party
CEC	Central Executive Committee
CPPCC	Chinese People's Political Consultative Conference
CY	Control Yuan
CYLP	Chinese Young Labor Party
CYP	Chinese Youth Party
DCP	Democratic Constitutionalist Party
DL	China Democratic League
DPGs	Democratic Parties and Groups
DPP	Democratic Progressive Party
DSP	Chinese Democratic Socialist Party
ECCO	European Branch of the Chinese Communist Youth Corps and Party
ECYC	European Branch of the Chinese Communist Youth Corps
FDC	Federation for a Democratic China
FL	Fighting League for Chinese Freedom and Democracy
GMD	Guomindang (Kuomintang, Nationalist Party)
IFCSS	Independent Federation of Chinese Students and Scholars
LCDPG	League of Chinese Democratic Political Groups
LDP	Chinese Liberal-Democratic Party
LP	Labor Party
LY	Legislative Yuan
MPGs	Minority Parties and Groups
NA	National Assembly
NCA	China Democratic National Construction Association
NCM	New Culture Movement
NG	National Government (GMD)
NPC	National People's Congress
NRA	National Revolutionary Army
NSA	National Salvation Association
NSP	National Socialist Party of China
ODM	Overseas Democracy Movement

PAC	Provisional Action Committee of the GMD ("Third Party")
PCC	Political Consultative Conference
PPC	People's Political Council
PRC	People's Republic of China
PW	Chinese Peasants' and Workers' Democratic Party
RF	Reform Faction of the DSP
RG	Revolutionary Committee of the GMD
RLS	Revolutionary League of Sunism
RRG	Rural Reconstruction Group
TAL	Taiwan Autonomy League
TF	Third Force
TP	Third Party (See PAC)
UF	United Front
UFD	United Front Department
VES	Vocational Education Society
WMA	Whampoa Military Academy
WP	Workers' Party
WSM	Work-Study Movement
YCA	Young China Association
ZGD	Zhigong Dang

About the Contributors

Parks M. Coble is a professor of history at the University of Nebraska, Lincoln. His latest publication is *Facing Japan: Chinese Politics and Japanese Imperialism, 1931-1937* (1991).

John F. Copper is the Stanley J. Buckman Distinguished Professor of International Studies at Rhodes College, Memphis, Tennessee. He is the author of thirteen books on China, Taiwan, and Asian affairs, of which the latest is *China Diplomacy: The Washington-Taipei-Beijing Triangle* (1992).

Thomas D. Curran is a professor of history at Sacred Heart University, Fairfield, Connecticut.

Lloyd E. Eastman teaches history at the University of Illinois, Champaign-Urbana. His most recent works include *Family, Fields, and Ancestors: Constancy and Change in China's Social and Economic History, 1550-1949* (1988) and *The Abortive Revolution: China Under Nationalist Rule, 1927-1937* (rev. ed., 1990).

Edmund S.K. Fung is an associate professor (reader) of modern Chinese history and Dean of the Division of Asian and International Studies at Griffith University, Australia. He is author of *The Military Dimension of the Chinese Revolution* (1980) and *The Diplomacy of Imperial Retreat* (1991), and coauthor of *From Fear to Friendship* (1985).

John Israel, professor of history at the University of Virginia, is author of *Lianda: A Chinese University in War and Peace* (Harvard East Asian Monograph, forthcoming).

Peter Ivanov is chairman of the China Modern History Research Section, Institute of Oriental Studies, Moscow, as well as Russian bibliographic correspondent for *Republican China*.

Roger B. Jeans, professor of history, Washington and Lee University, is working on a book about Zhang Junmai (Carsun Chang).

Edward S. Krebs is an independent scholar and sometime teacher at institutions in the Atlanta, Georgia area. He is working on a book-length manuscript on Shi Fu.

Marilyn A. Levine, associate professor of history at Lewis-Clark State College, is the author of *The Found Generation: Chinese Communism in Europe During the Twenties* (University of Washington Press, forthcoming), and has published numerous articles on Chinese political movements in France during the 1920s.

Andrew J. Nathan, professor of political science at Columbia University, is the author of *Chinese Democracy* (1985) and *China's Crisis* (1990).

J. Kenneth Olenik is a professor of history at Montclair State College in New Jersey.

James D. Seymour is a senior research scholar at Columbia University's East Asian Institute. Among his books is *China's Satellite Parties* (1987).

Lawrence N. Shyu is a professor of East Asian history at the University of New Brunswick, Canada. His latest work is *The Chinese Immigrant Experience in Atlantic Canada*.

Frederic J. Spar is a partner with Kekst and Company, a corporation communications consulting firm in New York City.

Yang Tianshi, professor at the Institute of Modern History, Chinese Academy of Social Sciences, Beijing, is the author of several books and numerous articles on the history of Republican China, as well as Chinese culture.

Index

About the Book and Editor

Studies of the political history of twentieth-century China traditionally have been skewed toward a two-dimensional view of the major combatants: the Chinese Communist Party and the Guomindang. Although their struggle undeniably has been the main story, it is neither the only nor the complete story. During the Republican period (1912–1949), many educated Chinese rejected both one-party dictatorships, and some boldly founded or supported alternative movements.

In this volume, the contributors turn their attention to these neglected parties, groups, and figures, making full use of new materials to provide the first English-language book to study these groups systematically. Tracing the post-1949 fates of some of these opposition movements in Taiwan and the PRC, the book also explores the contemporary heirs of the oppositionists of the Republican period, the democratic activists in the Overseas Democracy Movement that mushroomed after the June 1989 massacre in China. The book concludes with an insightful assessment of the parallels between opposition figures of Republican China and those in exile today.

Roger B. Jeans, professor of Chinese and Japanese history, has taught at Washington and Lee University in Lexington, Virginia, since 1974. His research, reflected in numerous articles and conference papers, has focused on Zhang Junmai (Carsun Chang) and his political parties. In progress is a book tentatively entitled, *Third Force: Zhang Junmai (Carsun Chang) and Opposition Politics in China, 1919–1937*.

Jeans received his Ph.D. in Chinese history from George Washington University. He has studied, researched, and travelled in East Asia. In the early 1970s, he attended the Inter-University Program for Chinese Language Studies in Taiwan, and in the early 1980s he carried out research in the People's Republic of China.

Jeans has served as chairman of Washington and Lee's East Asian Studies Program. He is a past editor of *Republican China*, former president of the Southeast Conference of the Association of Asian Studies, and current chairman of the AAS's Council of Conferences.